MONOTHEISM, HERESY, AND THE BIBLE

Monotheism, Heresy, and the Bible

Essays on Biblical Unitarianism

DALE TUGGY

NASHVILLE

Monotheism, Heresy, and the Bible: Essays on Biblical Unitarianism

Theophilus Press
P.O. Box 1036
Nashville, TN 37188
www.theophilus-press.com

Tuggy, Dale (1970–)

xi + 427 pp.

ISBN 978-1-7375783-2-1

CONTENTS

Introduction

Most of the chapters here originated as conference talks, Sunday school presentations, or blog posts, some dating as far back as 2008. My academic publishing has been slowed by my commitment to speak to broader audiences through my *trinities* blog (2006–) and *Trinities Podcast* (2013–). Often I would develop ideas sufficient for a good presentation or a series of blog posts but I would not follow through on developing them enough for a journal article, book chapter, or book, getting distracted by other duties. In 2019 I realized that I had more than enough of such material to shape into a book of related chapters on biblical monotheism and heresy. "I'll just make a few revisions," I thought. "How hard can it be?" What I found was that, in some cases, after five—or seventeen—more years, I had *a lot* more to say!

These chapters are among the fruits of my first college degree, the Bachelor of Arts degree in philosophy that I earned in 1993 from Biola University. Back then a slogan in the evangelical academic world was "integration," meaning a refusal to compartmentalize one's religious beliefs from one's academic subject(s). I was taught logic and philosophy by a series of wise, faithful, humble, and godly men, starting with the late Dr. Delbert Hanson. I eventually came to see that there is no conflict between working hard at these subjects and having an authentic spiritual life, a living relationship with God through Christ.

"Philosophy" is often villainized in Christian circles, but it is just another field of human study, like biology or history, and it can be done well or poorly. It can be turned into a weapon to attack the gospel, or it can be used in its service. Having become interested in apologetics while still a high school student, I knew that analytic and argumentative skills could be employed to remove mental barriers that prevent some people from following Christ. And as a college student I could see my Christian philosophy professors using philosophical tools in such ways. Eventually I realized that they could also be helpful for finding one's way through clashing theologies and christologies.

After Biola I was blessed to study under a series of non-Christian but highly capable, serious, and helpful philosophers, first at the Claremont Graduate University (MA, 1995), then at Brown University (PhD, 2000). I was then blessed with a tenure-track job teaching philosophy at SUNY Fredonia, a position I held for about eighteen years, until I switched careers. There I taught courses in the history of philosophy, philosophy of religion, logic, critical thinking, metaphysics, and religious studies. Just as I started that job, I attempted to get to the bottom of all this confusing Trinity stuff—which led me to switch to a unitarian understanding of God and Jesus based on a better understanding of Scripture.

As I did this, I continually saw the relevance of careful thinking about statements of numerical identity or sameness, such as "Abram is Abraham," or "Yahweh is God"—a topic I first learned about in a metaphysics class at Biola with Dr. J. P. Moreland and which I'd returned to while teaching logic classes at Brown and SUNY Fredonia. This work has paid off in chapters 3, 7, and 8–11. My experience in formulating and evaluating arguments and explanations is utilized in chapters 2, 3, 6, and 10. My interests in history, biblical studies, and theology are evident in chapters 1, 4, 5, 6, and 9. I have worked hard to make this material widely accessible, at least to the determined high school graduate, but I have not dumbed anything down.

Chapter 1 is what I wish someone had told the younger me about the words "God" and "Lord" in the Bible. There's a widespread misconception that only God is called "God" in the Bible, so if Jesus is ever called "God," this shows that he is God. Sometimes the same reasoning is used with the term "Lord." But some basic critical thinking with attention to a Greek lexicon clarifies much of this and even reveals a severe problem for trinitarians who think that if any passage in the New Testament uses the word "God" for Jesus, this somehow supports a trinitarian theology. I also explain some other ambiguous words that are postbiblical, such as "Trinity" and "essence," and make a few suggestions for avoiding ambiguity in our discourse about God and his Son.

Chapter 2 examines common apologists' arguments that the Bible rather obviously implies "the doctrine of the Trinity," finding that they come up *far* short. I interact with the short lists of claims that since B. B. Warfield theologians and apologists have put forward as expressing the essence of the doctrine. I argue that simple deductions from scriptural statements won't do.

Instead, what has to be undertaken is a systematic comparison of explanations. That is the only way one might, theoretically, show that the Bible—or more specifically the New Testament—is trinitarian.

Chapter 3 explains how any trinitarian theology is logically inconsistent with clear New Testament teaching. The trinitarian often supposes that she can agree with the unitarian Christian that in the New Testament the Father and God are one and the same. Some trinitarians, not caring about the incoherence of their views, do embrace that proposition, but it conflicts with the core trinitarian thesis that the one God and the triune God (the Trinity) are one and the same. Here, postbiblical theories should give way to New Testament facts.

Chapter 4 challenges the widespread Protestant practice of merely assuming or groundlessly asserting that postbiblical doctrines like the Trinity and the Incarnation are essential doctrines. I discuss the idea of heresy in the New Testament, traditional catholic heresiology, and how the Roman Catholic approach to heresy differs from some Protestant ones. I then suggest a better, more scriptural and Protestant way of approaching the dropping of H-bombs—that is, declaring a doctrine a "heresy" or a teacher a "heretic."

In Chapter 5, following the example of the Christian philosopher John Locke, I examine the book of Acts to identify what its author Luke considers essential to the gospel—specifically, what a person must believe to be saved. Locke was right: The core message is simple and so is accessible to ordinary people, just as God intended the new covenant through Jesus to be.

Chapter 6 surveys four different approaches to dealing with apparent contradictions in Christian theology. In mainstream Christianity it has long been popular for layperson and theologian alike to sweep a lot of apparent contradictions under the "mystery" rug, resulting in a large, unseemly bulge. This is often viewed as the only humble and reasonable way of proceeding, but I explain why careful, Bible-motivated reforming seems better.

Chapter 7 discusses today's Islamic challenges to trinitarianism and explains how one can be a monotheistic "trinitarian" by rolling back one's theology to ancient, pre-trinitarian models like those of Tertullian and Origen. Muslims have never been and will never be impressed by traditional mystery appeals. But they can recognize that theirs is not the only consistently monotheistic theology, as unitarian Christian theologies are as consistently monotheistic as any Islamic theology.

Chapter 8 is a crash course in modern logic and critical thinking about claims about qualitative and numerical sameness. It is an antidote to a lot of currently fashionable sloppy talk in evangelical apologetics, theology, and biblical studies about "identifying Jesus with God"—whether that means mentally associating Jesus together with God, or rather collapsing the two together, believing them to be numerically one. It shines a light on traditional "only God" arguments, such as "Only God can forgive sins. Jesus can forgive sins. Therefore, Jesus is God." While logically valid, such arguments come at a terribly high price, one no Christian should be willing to pay. Along the way I explain the basic line of thought behind recent relative-identity Trinity theories, and why it is wrongheaded. I also rebut the common mistake of thinking that, for some reason, clear thinking about numerical identity is irrelevant to the task of theology, and I explain how formal logic is topic-neutral. In this chapter I don't shy away from some technicalities and some basic principles of metaphysics. It is the product of roughly three decades of thinking through these topics in a general way, not only in the context of clarifying the New Testament picture of God and his Son, the Lord Jesus Christ.

Chapter 9 applies the principles discussed in chapter 8 to several disputed passages about God and Jesus in the New Testament. Does Jesus claim to be God himself in John 10? Does the favorite text of unitarian Christians (John 17:1–3) really favor their views over those of trinitarian theologians? Can God, by being incarnate, come to be under a god? Does the scriptural Jesus have the divine identity? Does the New Testament teach that God came to us in and as Christ? Does Paul alter Jewish theology by "including Jesus in the Shema"?

Chapter 10 is about what I call "the fulfillment fallacy," an exegetical error that has infected a broad swathe of recent evangelical scholarship. This newfangled mistake starts with a correct observation that a New Testament author applies some Old Testament passage to Jesus, asserting or suggesting that something in Jesus's life fulfills that ancient text. Observing that the older text was originally about Yahweh, some recent interpreters conclude that the New Testament author is thereby insinuating that Jesus is Yahweh himself, or perhaps a divine Person in Yahweh. I show why this is a clear exegetical fallacy and try to explain why this mistake has arisen so late in time.

Chapter 11 develops an objection to relative-identity Trinity theories based on the clear New Testament teaching that Jesus, like you and me, has a god over him: the Father. This, I argue, rules out their being the same god, since just conceptually, no god can be the god over himself. Such Trinity theories clash with a clear New Testament teaching *even if* the relative-identity approach to understanding statements of numerical sameness is correct.

A thread that runs through these chapters is that New Testament teachings about God and his Messiah stand on their own two feet; they make sense on their own, not requiring help from catholic "fathers" like Athanasius, Gregory of Nazianzus, or Augustine, or from the so-called "ecumenical" councils from 325 to 787. Plain old careful reading and clear thinking, guided by our God-given common sense, undermine prestigious traditional speculations, revealing an intelligible, believable, and preachable faith that is suited both to the scholar and to the day laborer.

I pray that this book is helpful to the ongoing cause of biblical reformation. Every day, around the world, scales are falling from believers' eyes as they reexamine Scripture without distorting catholic assumptions about Trinity and Incarnation. These essays are directed to the more educated sort who are not going to easily let go of the catholic traditions into which they have been indoctrinated, and who are able and determined to mount clever defenses of traditional catholic commitments, so as to hold on to prestigious, longstanding speculations—or at least to something close enough. I was, until around the age of thirty, one of these determined dead enders. I am trying to serve them with serious, sustained, clear, informed, and persuasive exegesis and arguments that will help them to untie the mental knots they have inherited, until they can gladly worship the Father as God himself and honor our Lord Jesus Christ as his unique Son, now raised, exalted, active in the church, and preparing to return to rule the world under his and our god.

I wish to thank Thomas Gaston for helpful comments on a draft, Joseph Jedwab for comments on and correspondence regarding chapter 11, and C. S. Lakin for her expert editing and other critical feedback. My thanks also to my patient wife, Candise Tuggy, and to the brothers and sisters at Kingdom Gospel Church for their prayers and support as I was writing this book. Finally, I'm grateful for the support of the Unitarian Christian Alliance as I finished this book in 2025–26. It has been a great privilege to work with its volunteer board of directors: Leah Anderson, Mark Cain, Kegan Chandler, Brandon Duke, and Sean Finnegan. I dedicate this book to them. I must add that the opinions here expressed are solely my own and not those of the Unitarian Christian Alliance or its board.

Dale Tuggy
White House, Tennessee
May 14, 2026

CHAPTER 1

Biblical Words for God and for His Son

1.1 GOD, "GOD," AND AMBIGUITIES[1]

This chapter explores two related subjects: God in the Bible and the word "God" in the Bible, especially in the New Testament. We will stick mostly to facts that must be acknowledged by any informed Bible reader, whatever her theological commitments.

We're all familiar with ambiguous common nouns. For example, if I say, "I went for a walk by a bank," do I mean that I walked by a riverbank or a financial bank? Context usually clarifies which of the possible meanings is being employed. Titles too can be ambiguous. If someone says, "The Boss is singing 'Born to Run,'" do they mean Bruce Springsteen or the boss of the local auto repair shop who moonlights in a bar band? They might mean either one, depending on the context.

Even proper names can be ambiguous. Suppose we obtain a leaked transcript of a phone conversation between Bill Cosby and Bill Clinton.

> "Bill, I've been meaning to ask you something for a long time."
>
> "Go ahead, Bill—I'm an open book."
>
> "Bill, how have you managed to stay married for so long? What's your secret?"
>
> "Well, Bill, I'll tell you—whenever I do something that enrages my wife—which is pretty often—I just tell her I'm sorry and buy her an expensive present."
>
> "Seriously? That works?"
>
> "Yes, Bill, it's true. It has worked for me all these years."

[1] This chapter evolved from Sunday school teachings given on three consecutive Sundays in March of 2018 at Higher Ground Church in White House, Tennessee, later presented as episodes of the *Trinities Podcast* ("Podcast 224"; "Podcast 225"; "Podcast 226").

Who is giving marital advice to whom? And which wife is so easily persuaded to forgive—Hillary Clinton or Camille Cosby? We typically think of proper names as labels unique to exactly one individual, but they, like common nouns and titles, may be ambiguous as to who they are referencing.

Complete sentences can also have widely varying meanings. If someone says, "The man is coming to get you," this could be one hippie warning another that the police are coming, or it could be a friend letting you know that your father is on his way to pick you up from school. The phrases "the man" and "coming to get you" are ambiguous, making the whole sentence ambiguous.

Relevant contextual information is the cure for ambiguity. Often this simply involves knowing where it was said, when it was said, how it was said, to whom it was said, what else was said, and so on. When dealing with a written source, a lot of this clarifying contextual information comes from the surrounding text: the rest of the sentence, the paragraph, the chapter, the whole book, the author's other works, or even other works in that genre and/or written in that same time and locale.

1.2 "GOD" IN THE OLD TESTAMENT

The Old Testament writings apply *many* titles and names to God; we won't delve into this wealth of referring terms here.[2] The most common word translated as "God" in these books is the Hebrew word *elohim*. This word is plural in its form.[3] Yet in that form it can have either a plural or singular meaning, depending on the context. English has a few words like this, such as "pants." Its form is plural (note the "s" at the end), but its meaning can be either singular ("She is wearing new pants") or plural ("The whole team is wearing matching pants"). A sentence in biblical Hebrew, such as "All the people worshipped *elohim*," can be translated "All the people worshipped God," or "All the people worshipped the gods." In isolation the sentence is ambiguous, but the context determines which translation is correct. The biblical authors usually remove the ambiguity by using either singular or plural words in the surrounding text. In the sentence "*Elohim* is watching you to see if you honor him," notice the singular verb "is" and the singular pronoun "him"; thus, we know in that instance *Elohim* means "God." Conversely, if we read, "*Elohim* are watching you to see if you honor them," we know that this person is talking

[2] For a brief survey see Goldingay, *Israel's Gospel*, 241–44.

[3] The word *elohim* is the plural form of the noun *eloah* ("God" or "god").

about the gods, presumably the alleged deities of some ancient pagan pantheon. While the authors of the Old Testament recognize no pantheon, they did believe that God works with his own divine council, not unlike a human king or emperor with his advisors and courtiers.[4] These too are called "gods" or "deities" (*elohim*).[5]

That the plural form *elohim* can be used with a singular or a plural meaning is a quirk of biblical Hebrew. We shouldn't get mystical with these unusual words and claim that this is God's way of hinting that God is both singular and plural, as some trinitarians have imagined.[6]

1.3 PUNCTUATION, MONOTHEISM, AND MONOTHEOSISM

Some ambiguities are due to the less developed writing technologies of ancient times. The oldest Greek New Testament manuscripts are written in all capital letters with no spaces between the words and, generally speaking, without punctuation marks (accents, commas, semicolons, periods, question marks, exclamation marks, or quotation marks). This may shock a present-day reader. But notice that you can read and understand a sentence written in this style:

> FORGODSOLOVEDTHEWORLDTHATHEGAVEHISONLYSONSO THATEVERYONEWHOBELIEVESINHIMMAYNOTPERISHBUTHA VEETERNALLIFE

Writing this way was quick and conserved writing materials. We have some reason to believe that ancient readers most often read texts out loud, which seems to facilitate reading passages done in this unadorned style.

In contrast, today's Bibles feature spaces, capital and lowercase letters, the full array of standard punctuation marks, and various other formatting conventions, such as offsetting or italicizing scriptural quotations and chapter and verse numbers. In general, these were added by the translators and/or the

---

[4] Walton, *Old Testament Theology*, 38–43; Heiser, *Unseen Realm*.

[5] "The First Testament uses the word *elohim* more broadly than English uses the word *god*. It covers subordinate heavenly beings as well as the incomparable God" (Goldingay, *Israel's Gospel*, 342).

[6] This is part of a broader phenomenon in ancient Hebrew that has been called "the plural of majesty." I would call it "magnification by pluralization." As Dustin Smith explains, this is the practice of pluralizing words having to do with honored or important persons or things, and in ancient Hebrew this is done not just for God but also important humans and even for some nonhuman animals. This device is also found in several other ancient languages (Smith, *Plural*).

scholars who prepared the critical editions of the Hebrew and Greek texts used for the translation. Sometimes these reflect important and even controversial choices about interpretation. Today's Bible reader needs to remember that all these elements in modern Bibles are later additions, and that some of them reflect interpretive choices. Any translator will tell you that translation unavoidably involves some degree of interpretation.

Thankfully, modern languages rarely employ the old all-caps, spaceless, punctuation-free form, as lowercase letters, spaces, and punctuation marks are significant advances in avoiding ambiguities. If you write "I like cooking my family and my pets," you may receive a visit from your local police. But if you write "I like cooking, my family, and my pets," all is well. And "My son is a genius" means something very different from "My son is a 'genius.'"

Let's turn now to more theologically significant ambiguities. You are likely familiar with the term "monotheism," the thesis that there is exactly one god.[7] This is a prominent teaching in both the Old and New Testaments. Yet monotheism is often confused with what I call "monotheosism."[8] *Theos* is the Greek word meaning "god" or "God." Monotheosism is the belief that there is only one who can truly be described or properly be addressed using the word "god." In the Bible monotheism is strongly asserted, but monotheosism is assumed to be false. That is, the biblical authors agree there is only one god (God, Yahweh, a.k.a. God the Father), but they assume the falsity of this claim: Only God can be called "god" or "God."

Isaiah writes, "Thus says Yahweh, Israel's king, Yahweh Sabaoth, his redeemer: I am the first and I am the last; there is no God except me" (Isa. 44:6, NJB).[9] Note the first-person pronoun and the first-person singular verb: "I am."[10] The one speaking through the prophet is declaring his own uniqueness, that he has no god-peers. Similarly, we read in the New Testament that there is "one who alone is God," namely, the Father (John 5:44–45)[11], and that "there is one

---

[7] Much scholarly confusion has resulted from the ambiguity of the term "god" when it comes to the view that there is exactly one god, on which see Tuggy, "On Counting Gods."

[8] As far as I know I coined this unlovely term.

[9] Most English translations capitalize the word "god" when it refers to Yahweh, but "god" is a common noun here, not a name or title, so the lowercase form makes more sense.

[10] Unitarian Christians have long observed that the scriptural uses of pronouns and verbs in reference to God strongly support the view that the authors viewed God as a single someone (Worcester, *Bible News*, 28–39.).

[11] Unless otherwise noted, quotations from the Bible are from the New Revised Standard Version, Updated Edition (NRSVUE).

God, and there is one mediator between God and men, the man Christ Jesus" (1 Tim. 2:5, ESV). In my view *all* of the Bible's authors presuppose and sometimes assert what we can call biblical monotheism, that God/Yahweh/the Father is the only god.

Admittedly, many modern scholars have held that true monotheism is only seen in the later biblical books, having been preceded by polytheism or a murky in-between position called "henotheism." And recently some have declared the term "monotheism" problematic since it is of early modern origin. But these claims are wrongheaded, resulting from confusion about what monotheism does and doesn't assert.[12]

While it is beyond dispute that at least *some* Old Testament authors and all New Testament authors are monotheists, the same cannot be said of monotheosism. Although it is concealed by many translations, the great prophet Moses is referred to as "a god" (Hebrew: *elohim*) by no less than God himself: "And the LORD said unto Moses, 'See, I have made thee a god to Pharaoh' " (Exod. 7:1, KJV).[13] This is a literal translation of the Hebrew text. Many other translations read something like "I have made you like God to Pharaoh" (NIV) or "like a god."[14] The idea is that Moses would be *like* a (or the) god in Pharaoh's eyes because of the miraculous events that were to ensue. The word "god" (*elohim*) is being applied to a man—if you like, a "mere" man.[15]

Paul gives us a rather shocking example of the word "god" being used for someone other than God:

> And even if our gospel is veiled, it is veiled to those who are perishing. In their case the god of this world has blinded the minds of the unbelievers, to keep them from seeing clearly the light of the gospel of the glory of Christ, who is the image of God (2 Cor. 4:3–4).

---

[12] See my "On Counting Gods." Briefly, monotheism asserts that the number of gods is exactly one, but it is neutral about the number of mere deities and does not by definition require only one deity. The biblical authors assume the reality of many mere deities, but they are committed to there being exactly one god.

[13] In the Septuagint *elohim* here is rendered as *theon*, the singular, accusative case of *theos*.

[14] See the various translators' decisions at https://www.biblehub.com/Exod./7-1.htm.

[15] For another case of *elohim* probably being applied to a man, see Ps. 45:6; in the ancient Septuagint translation this human king is addressed as *theos*, which is probably applied to Christ in Heb. 1:8. See section 1.4.5 below on the translation choices for both Ps. 45:6 and Heb. 1:8.

Paul seems to be referring to Satan as the "god of this world."[16] He is surely not claiming Satan is the one God or a being of the same type as God. Rather, he's calling Satan a mighty being, godlike in the sense that he, for the time being, has a kingdom and a certain amount of power and control over what happens in this realm. Thus, he can call Satan the "god of this world."[17]

My favorite example of this phenomenon, *theos* used for beings other than God, is from the Lord Jesus himself in John's Gospel. Right before this passage, Jesus claimed that he and the Father "are one."

> The Jews took up stones again to stone him. Jesus replied, "I have shown you many good works from the Father. For which of these are you going to stone me?" The Jews answered, "It is not for a good work that we are going to stone you, but for blasphemy, because you, though only a human being, are making yourself God." (John 10:31–34)

This last phrase could also be translated as "making yourself a god."[18] Either way, it would be blasphemy to claim to be either God himself or *a* god (and, therefore, God's peer).

Some readers suppose that Jesus's Jewish opponents must have understood correctly that Jesus was claiming to be God. But in the Gospel of John, "the Jews" (mainly Jesus's opponents among the Jewish leadership) are continually misunderstanding him.[19] For example, when Jesus says you have to be "born again" or "born from above," Nicodemus questions how it is possible for one to go back inside his mother's womb (John 3:3–4). When Jesus says he's the bread that comes down from heaven and that one must eat him to have eternal life, "the Jews" think this is cannibalism (6:51–52). In this book they are the bad guys, the spiritually blind,[20] who, as Paul would say, can't perceive the work of God's spirit among them.[21] Thus it's misguided to rely on their reactions to Jesus

---

[16] Not all interpreters hold that Satan is referred to in this passage, and some unitarian Christians, such as Christadelphians, deny that Scripture teaches Satan to be a real personal being. But I do not have the space to engage with these views here.

[17] In my preferred terminology: Satan is being thought of as a mere deity who is not also a god ("On Counting Gods," 190–94), which is compatible with having been created by the only god. If God created all other things, then he must have created any other deities that exist.

[18] In my view the "making yourself a god" translation is more likely. See section 9.1.

[19] Carter, *John*, 114–16.

[20] *John*, 67–73.

[21] "Those who are unspiritual do not receive the gifts of God's Spirit, for they are foolishness to them, and they are unable to understand them because they are spiritually discerned" (1 Cor. 2:14).

and stop reading at 10:33 ("making yourself God"), concluding that this is the author's point. Rather, the fuller context reveals the author's actual point. Reading on, we see Jesus offering a sophisticated argument in response to the accusation that he's making himself out to be God or a god.

> Jesus answered, "Is it not written in your law, 'I said, you are gods'? [Ps. 82:6] If those to whom the word of God came were called 'gods'—and the scripture cannot be annulled—can you say that the one whom the Father has sanctified and sent into the world is blaspheming because I said, 'I am God's Son?'"
> (John 10:34–36)

Notice that Jesus corrects their misunderstanding. They said he was making himself God (or a god); he replies that he was claiming to be God's *Son*. He then makes an "all the more so" argument that *by his opponents' own standards*, his claim to be God's Son isn't blasphemy. In their view, certain people who are not as great as the Messiah are, without blasphemy, called "gods" in Psalm 82:6.[22] But if these people are called "gods," and Jesus, being God's Messiah, is greater, then it can't be blasphemous for him to claim the lesser title "Son of God." This is a brilliant and devastating argument; their accusation of blasphemy stands refuted by their own views.

A case can be made that this passage was originally understood to be about unseen beings rather than humans. These are called *elohim*, which can mean deities, mighty beings, or angels; notice that "gods" here is expounded as "sons of the Most High" (Ps. 82:6). Here God is addressing and cursing some of these "gods," saying in effect that they are going to die like mortal humans (82:7).

Jesus's argument works on either interpretation. If these "gods" are humans, God's own Son (the Messiah) is greater than any ancient human religious leader. And even if angels in the divine council are in view, the New Testament makes clear that the angels will also worship the exalted Messiah;[23] even at this point in his career Jesus is destined to be greater than any angel will ever be.[24]

---

[22] "The exact identity of these 'gods' (*elohim*) was . . . an issue for early Jewish interpreters . . . who variously took them to be angels, judges, Melchizedek, or Israel at Sinai. This last interpretation is found in the Jewish midrashic tradition and may well be reflected in John's description of those who are called 'gods' as 'those to whom the word of God came' (10:35). These Israelites were 'gods' because at Sinai they received the word of the one who alone is God" (Thompson, *John*, 235).

[23] "Let all God's angels worship him" (Heb. 1:6).

[24] Compare with John 1:15 (REV), "John testified about him and called out, saying, 'This was the one about whom I said, "He who comes after me has surpassed me because he was

1.4 JESUS AS THEOS IN THE NEW TESTAMENT

Is Jesus called "god" or "God" in the New Testament? Despite considerable complications, nearly all New Testament scholars agree that he is referred to as "god" or "God" at least once. But as we've seen, the word "god" is ambiguous, and can refer to beings other than God.

Evangelical New Testament scholar Murray Harris authored an influential monograph on *theos* being applied to Jesus in the New Testament. He observes that "On no reading of the data could the claim be allowed that the early Christians regularly called Jesus *theos* ["God" or "a god"] or *ho theos* [God, literally "*the* god"].[25] This makes sense, since monotheists typically reserve the title "God" *mostly* for the only god, God. Recall that in the original biblical Greek texts there were no lowercase letters. When referring to God, instead of using a capital "G," the New Testament authors often added the word "the" (*ho*) in front of the word *theos*. Thus "God" was often written in Greek as "*the* god" (*ho theos*). The "anarthrous" *theos* (lacking the definite article *ho*) *could* mean "a god" (New Testament Greek lacks any equivalent of our English indefinite article "a"). But where the one true god is in view, usually *theos* (without the *ho*) also means "God" and is so translated. While some authors, notably, Philo[26] and Origen,[27] make a big deal out of the *theos*/*ho theos* distinction, insisting that the latter should be used for God alone while the former befits a host of other lesser beings, generally in the New Testament both are used for the one true god, a.k.a. "the Father."[28]

Harris examines sixteen New Testament passages where it has been argued that Jesus is called *theos* or *ho theos*. He concludes that three instances are certain, three are very probable, and one is probable,[29] so in his judgment there are seven New Testament passages where some form of *theos* at least probably refers to Jesus. But every one of these passages is problematic because of interpretive difficulties, textual uncertainty, or translation problems (or some mix of these). Let's briefly survey the instances he rates as certain, very probable, or probable.

---

superior to me."'" In defense of this translation, see the REV translators' comments on this verse and Burnap, *Expository*, 56.

[25] Harris, *Jesus as God*, 281.

[26] Philo, *On Dreams*, 385 (1.229–30).

[27] Origen, *Commentary on John*, 98–102 (2.12–31).

[28] *Jesus as God*, 36–38.

[29] *Jesus as God*, 272. Certain: John 1:1, 20:28; Rom. 9.5. Very probable: Titus 2:13, Heb. 1:8, 2 Pet. 1:1. Probable: John 1:18. We shall see that Harris is *far* too certain about his "certain" texts.

1.4.1 JOHN 1:1

"In the beginning was the Word, and the Word was with God, and the Word was God." The last instance of *theos* here lacks the definite article "the"; some translators and interpreters have inferred that instead of "the Word was God" it should be "the Word was a god"[30] (that is, a different and lesser god than the "God" mentioned before). This is how the ancient Logos theologians understood it c. 150–381.[31] But as we've seen, *theos* without the article typically means "God" in the New Testament (*not* "a god"), and so it is even in this passage (verses 6, 12–13, 18).[32] Also, the two occurrences of *theos* here are separated in the Greek by a single word (*kai*, "and"), and it would be poor style to use forms of *theos* with different referents *nearly* back to back. Despite the historical popularity of this reading, we should hesitate to conclude either that two gods or two beings each called "god" are being mentioned in this monotheistic book.

Many or most scholars now hold that the point of leaving out "the" in the last occurrence of *theos* is so that the reader will understand "the Word" to be the subject of that clause[33]—it's saying about the Word that it or he is *theos*, not that *theos* is the Word. That makes sense, as the subject matter of the whole sentence is this Word. Still, what does it mean to say about this Word that it or he is "God" or "god"?

Many recent scholars suggest that the absence of the article is meant to signify that *theos* is a predication of the Word, a description of the Word as divine. These scholars would translate that last part as "what God was the Word was" (REB) or even the trinitarian-theology-motivated "the Word was fully God" (NET). It seems to me that some of these are reasoning as follows:[34]

---

[30] The Jehovah's Witnesses' New World Translation.

[31] Eusebius, *Ecclesiastical*, 193–98 (1.20.1–22), 225–30 (2.6–7), 243–44 (2.14.1–7); Justin Martyr, *Dialogue with Trypho*, 76–77 (50), 82–88 (55–56), 191–95 (127–29); Justin Martyr, *First Apology*, 69 (63); Justin Martyr, *Second Apology*, 77–78 (6); Novatian, *Trinity*, trans. DeSimone, 78–81 (21), 104–11 (30–31); Origen, *Commentary on John*, 98–103 (2.12–35); Origen, *Against Celsus*, 296 (5.39), 377 (6.61), 382 (6.68), 451–57 (8.1–6); *Refutation*, 749–51 (10.33.1–3), 753 (10.33.6–8); Tertullian, *Hermogenes*, 487 (18); Tertullian, *Against Praxeas*, trans. Evans, 138–40 (8), 145–48 (12–13), 153–70 (16–25). For an overview of the ways Logos theologians thought God to surpass the Logos, see my "Podcast 381."

[32] Silva, *New International* 2, 444.

[33] In the Greek the last clause is *theos ein ho logos*, literally "god was the word," but even though *theos* comes first, it is not the subject of the sentence. Translators agree that the subject is *ho logos*.

[34] See Wallace, *Greek Grammar*, 266–69.

1. The second occurrence of *theos* in John 1:1 is to be understood either as definite ("the Word was God"), as indefinite ("the Word was a god"), or as qualitative ("the Word was divine").
2. If that *theos* were definite, then the author would be asserting the numerical identity of God (that is, the Father) and the Word.[35]
3. For this author the Word and the Son of God are numerically one.
4. Thus, if the author were asserting the numerical identity of God (the Father) and the Word, he would also be asserting the numerical identity of the Father with the Son.
5. This author does not identify the Son with the Father.
6. Therefore, the meaning of *theos* here is not definite. (2–5)
7. If that *theos* were indefinite, the author would be a polytheist.
8. This author is not a polytheist but is rather a monotheist.
9. Therefore, that *theos* is not indefinite. (7–8)
10. Therefore, the second *theos* in John 1:1 is qualitative; the meaning of John 1:1c is "the Word was divine." (1, 6, 9)

First, let's grant for the sake of argument that this reasoning is sound, so it establishes its conclusion 10. If the Word is supposed to be the prehuman Jesus in this verse, and now we're told that the Word/Jesus is "divine," what follows for Christology?

Not much! The biblical unitarian Christian can say that Jesus is divine, as "divine" often means something that is importantly related to God. The church is "divine," as it belongs to God. The Scriptures are divine since God inspired them. Certainly, the man Jesus is "divine" in that he is God's unique human Son and Messiah. His calling and commission were divine (from God); so was the power of the spirit that worked in him. His character, his mighty actions, and his teachings are all "divine" (that is to say, both God-like and received from God).[36] The trinitarian interpreter may pound the table and insist that the "divinity" here must be full, Nicene-Creed-compliant divinity—in other words, having the whole divine nature or essence.[37] But mere assertion is not argument. I'm not aware of any way to argue, assuming a qualitative interpretation of *theos* in John 1:1c, that the quality or qualities in view must be essential.[38]

---

[35] That is, that the Father and the Word are the same thing. This fundamental concept of numerical identity is explained more in sections 3.2 and 8.3–4.

[36] Ripley, *Divinity of Jesus*.

[37] Wallace, *Greek Grammar*, 269.

[38] The suggestion is that *theos* in this instance, in effect, has the meaning of the adjective

Moreover, it's too much to grant the soundness of the above argument. It's fundamentally a trilemma; there are three options, and two are ruled out. Therefore, the third option is true. The argument is valid, but in my view premises 2, 3, and 7 are false.

Let's start with 7. Just because this author thinks that something other than the Father can be called *theos*, it doesn't follow that he thinks this other is a *theos* in the same sense the Father is, resulting in two *theoi* (gods). The ancient Logos theologians who read the *theos* in John 1:1c as indefinite were arguably monotheists, indeed, unitarian monotheists for whom the only *true* god is the Father.[39] These same ancient theologians, as well as the ones scholars since the nineteenth century have called the "Modalistic Monarchians," also denied 3.[40]

Premise 3 is an assumption that nearly all modern interpreters bring to this text, that the Word mentioned here is the same person as the man Jesus. But that long-unquestioned assumption should be questioned. Why think that the Word is supposed to be Jesus before he was a man—indeed, before there were any human beings? The text does not say this and arguably makes better sense without that dubious idea.[41] The glaring absence of any other passage in the rest of John's Gospel where Jesus is called the *logos* is telling. The author very well might have called Jesus "God's Word" or "The Word of God," since in this book Jesus is the greatest recipient of and disseminator of God's word, so much so that he is our best guide to how God is. "Whoever has seen me has seen the Father" (John 14:9).

Moreover, this author heaps various other surprising titles onto the man Jesus, such as "the light of the world," "the bread of life," "the resurrection and the life," "the good shepherd," and "the true vine" (8:12, 6:35, 11:25, 10:11, 15:1). Why not also "the Word of God," as in Revelation 19:13? A plausible explanation is that he does not want the reader to take his personification of God's word in John 1:1–14 literally.

Quite apart from concerns about 3 and 7, it's enough to undermine this argument to point out that premise 2 is false; it is a *non sequitur*—in other

---

theios (divine). This can possibly refer to the divine nature but can also mean *things importantly associated with* a god or gods (Danker, BDAG, 395).

[39] Section 7.4.

[40] On the Modalistic Monarchians, see Artemi, "Logos"; Heine, "Christology of Callistus." On the Dynamic Monarchians see Gaston, *Dynamic Monarchianism*.

[41] It is dubious because it is unclear whether a divine spirit or Person that would have existed whether or not humans were ever created could possibly become a human being. See my "Podcast 235."

words, the "then" part doesn't follow from the "if" part. If the *theos* there is to be understood as referring to God, it doesn't follow from that that the "is" there is an "is" of numerical identity. What could "the Word was God" mean if not "the Word and God were one and the same" ("the Word was numerically identical with God")?

To answer this, we need to think about how this passage would have struck the original recipients. "The Word" (*ho logos*) here is plausibly God's word or wisdom by which God made all things, which ultimately came down, so to speak, to dwell in the man Jesus (1:14).[42] A Jew in that time would have been familiar with Old Testament passages such as, "By the word of the LORD the heavens were made" (Ps. 33:6) or the famous personification of God's wisdom as a helper alongside him at creation (Prov. 8:22–36). And he, rightly, would not have taken that "word" or that "wisdom" to be literal agents, intelligent beings, since it is a clear teaching of the Old Testament that God (that is, the Father) created on his own, without the help of any other.[43] We can see the author here exploiting this fact to communicate that the man Jesus is the very embodiment of God's word/wisdom.[44] If someone asks who this word is, by whom God created, or who this wisdom is who helped God in creating, one is missing the point. Being personifications of, respectively, an action of God and an attribute of God, they're not anyone—neither is numerically identical with any *real* someone. They're not even individual things (entities, realities); they are mere ways God is. He is all there is to "them." Let's call a way a thing is, such as an event involving it or a property of it, *a mode of* that thing. We can truly say that each "is" God, but that is a modal "is," not an "is" of identity.[45]

If a reader of Proverbs 8 were getting off-track, we might say to her, by way of correction, "Wisdom *is* God," meaning that "she" is nothing more than a way God is, in other words, "Wisdom is *a mode of* God." Here, our author has just

---

[42] Boyarin, "Logos"; Gaston, *Dynamic Monarchianism*, 216–19; Tuggy, "John 1"; Smith, *Wisdom Christology*, ch. 3.

[43] "I am the LORD who made all things, who alone stretched out the heavens, who by myself spread out the earth" (Isa. 44:24b). See also Isa. 45:12; Ps. 33:6, 148:5; Gen. 1.

[44] In Jewish literature written between Proverbs and this Gospel, the characters of Wisdom and Word are sometimes merged. For references see my "John 1."

[45] Given that the statement is true, any statement of the form "[Some mode of God] is God" *can't* be an assertion of numerical identity since if one thing *just is* another (if "they" are really one and the same thing) then they can't differ. But they do differ, as the first thing is a mere mode of a thing, while the second, God, is not a mere mode of anything but is a real entity in his own right.

personified God's word by which he made all things as being "with" or "toward" him, which suggests a face-to-face, I-Thou relationship.[46] And he's about to continue this personification, to keep using this literary character of God's Word (vv. 3–13).

But before he does that, he is warning us that "the Word *is* [a mere mode of] God." So when "he" becomes a human being (v. 14), this is not a mysterious transformation of some eternal divine Person but is instead like the several "incarnations" or "embodiments" that the readers would have been familiar with from wisdom literature like Proverbs, Sirach, and Baruch.[47] God's word by which he made all things "became" (was well-expressed by) the man Jesus.

It has been observed that the Greek verb *eimi* (to be, exist) "corresponds closely with [the] Eng. *to be* and has a broad range of usage."[48] Certainly we English speakers understand the modal "is." Suppose a White House official gossiped to you that a recent cabinet meeting "was ruined by Grumpy Trump." You might suppose that she's referring to one of Trump's cabinet officials, perhaps calling him "Grumpy Trump" because he resembles Trump and is often grumpy. But then she could correct your misunderstanding by saying, "No, Grumpy Trump *is* Trump"—that is, "Grumpy Trump" is simply Trump being grumpy or acting grumpily. We all understand what "Grumpy Trump *is* Trump" means in this context, and that it would be true, given how the gossiper is using the phrase "Grumpy Trump." It is easy to mistake that sentence for an assertion of numerical identity, not only because of its grammatical form *a is b* but also because of the similarity between assertions of identity and modal assertions.

Suppose someone is reading the story of Abraham in Genesis for the first time and thinks that Abram is one person and Abraham another. We'll correct her, saying that in this story "Abram *is* [identical with] Abraham." What may at first appear to be two characters is really just one going by two names. We have, as it were, taken hold of this thing and that thing and collapsed them together into one thing. What we had overcounted we're now only counting once. That is a common function of identity statements—the reduction of the number of

[46] Silva, *New International 4*, 145. Here the author expects his reader to remember Prov. 8:27–30, which portrays Lady Wisdom as being present with God in the way one person is present with another.

[47] They would have read about God's Wisdom coming down as the Torah (Sir. 24:23), God's Knowledge coming down as "the book of the commandments of God" (Bar. 3:35–4:1), and God's Law having been embodied in Moses (Philo, *Moses I*, 474 [sec. 162]). For other ancient references see Smith, "Incarnation."

[48] Silva, *New International 2*, 106.

purported things (realities, entities). A statement of numerical identity assumes that the "two" things referred to are "both" real, but here we've just referred to a single thing in two different ways, such as by using two different names or titles.

A modal assertion can also simplify matters by reducing the number of entities involved—but it does so in a particular way. Instead of collapsing together seemingly two things, it denies that one of them is truly an independent entity or thing at all. What appears to be a second thing is, rather, just a *mode*—a way in which the first thing exists or behaves. In our example, the supposed second "reality" (a person) is nothing more than an action, event, or quality of the first. It's not that Trump and "Grumpy Trump" are seemingly two entities that are actually identical—that would grant too much reality to "Grumpy Trump." Rather, "he" is not another man at all but simply a way that Trump is—the event *Trump-being-grumpy*. The only entity here is Trump.

There's a crucial difference between the "is" of identity and the modal "is." The former does, but the latter does not, express a symmetrical relation. If it is true that *a* just is *b* ($a = b$) it must also be true that *b* just is *a* ($b = a$). But if "*a* is *b*" means that *a* is a mode of *b*, it must be false that *b* is a mode of *a*.

So far, I've not been able to find any other ancient example of this modal use of some form of "to be." There are plenty of literary scenarios where this sort of character reduction would be appropriate. The pagan crowd in Acts 14, having seen a man healed, concludes that Paul and Barnabas must really be the Greek deities Hermes and Zeus—that is, modes (specifically, appearances) of them (Acts 14:8–18). Our apostles protest that they are mortal human beings, and therefore not manifestations of deities (14:15). But imagine this dialogue in the pagan crowd.

> "Hail, Hermes!"
> "What are you talking about? That's *Paul*."
> "Didn't you see him heal that man? 'Paul' *is* Hermes!"

In other words, what you think is a normal man named "Paul" is *really* Hermes moving among us in the guise of a man. Of course, this pagan would be saying a falsehood using the modal "is."

For a true statement, consider this famous incident in Genesis.

> Jacob was left alone [at night], and a man wrestled with him until daybreak. When the man saw that he did not prevail against Jacob, he struck him on the hip socket, and Jacob's hip was put out of joint as he wrestled with him. Then he said, "Let me go, for the day is breaking." But Jacob said, "I will not let you go, unless you bless me." So he said to him, "What is your name?" And he said,

> "Jacob." Then the man said, "You shall no longer be called Jacob, but Israel, for you have striven with God and with humans and have prevailed." Then Jacob asked him, "Please tell me your name." But he said, "Why is it that you ask my name?" And there he blessed him. So Jacob called the place Peniel, saying, "For I have seen God face to face, yet my life is preserved." (Gen. 32:24–30)

A reader, knowing that the unique god of the Old Testament is not a man (Num. 23:19) may wonder why nothing more is said of this "man" (Hebrew: *enosh*), the wrestler.

But the meaning here, as in some other theophany passages, seems to be: *apparent* man. Plausibly, that man *is* [a mode of, specifically an appearance of] God. Why doesn't the author say this? He doesn't need to. In the account, Jacob has concluded that he's just wrestled with God—that is, with an appearance of God in human form. The only *real* man in this wrestling match is Jacob.[49]

What makes John 1:1–18 different from incidents like these is it's not a straightforward historical narrative. The standard devices one would use to convey that "the Word" is not a literal someone in addition to God but only a mode of God are not available, such as "the Word" doing something and then a character says it was *God* who did that. Instead the author interrupts his personifications of the Word to tell us that the Word *is* [a mode of] God, hence not a literal someone in addition to God.

Since the Socinians in the early modern era, some unitarian Christians have thought that John 1 isn't about the Genesis creation but rather the beginning of the gospel era. The Gospel of Mark and John's first letter begin with the word "beginning" (Greek: *arche*), statements that seem to be of this latter variety (Mark 1:1, 1 John 1:1). And John does use *arche* in this way (6:64, 15:27). Some readers, therefore, conclude that John 1 similarly refers to the beginning of Jesus's public ministry, and so the passage throughout is about the man Jesus.[50]

But I am inclined to think, like most readers, that the "beginning" referred to is the time of the original creation described in Genesis 1. I see a historical

---

[49] I think the text is compatible with the idea that the "man" is really an angel through whom God is acting, although it doesn't address the issue of the "mechanics" of God's acting here.

[50] See the notes on this passage in the British unitarian New Testament in An Improved Version, 5th edition, where this interpretation is urged, although an interpretation like the wisdom Christology one just described is explained too (Belsham, *New Testament*, 184–88). Or similarly: Simpson, *Explanation of John*. For a recent defense, see Perry, *John 1:1–18*. My friend Bill Schlegel has argued for this sort of interpretation in a number of episodes of his *One God Report* podcast, such as "Podcast 66."

progression in what follows: it moves from the time of creation (1–3) to God's Word being the light of all people (4–5, 10), to the Word's revelation in Scripture, enabling a covenant relationship with God (11–13). This is all brushed aside by a reading that focuses solely on Jesus's earthly ministry. Another problem I have with this sort of interpretation is that I can find no evidence of any ancient Christians reading the prologue to John in this way. While such evidence may have been lost, as things stand, this lack of evidence counts against this interpretation.

Much more could be said here, and this is only a very brief survey of the issues surrounding this complex passage. In my view, the only way to understand it will be by seeing what it is doing in the whole chapter and in the entire book, by careful attention to everything else we have from this author's hand, and by considering how the first recipients of this book could have been expected to understand it. Contrary to a common assumption, it is *far* from obvious that Jesus (and not only the Word) is referred to as "God" here.[51] Even if he is, we read later in the book that Jesus got his message from God, and that *theos* can be applied to humans to whom the word of God came.[52] In this way the author rules out the simplistic argument that Jesus is fully divine since he's called *theos*.

1.4.2 JOHN 20:28

"Thomas said to him, 'My Lord and my God!'" There are no disputes about the text or the translation of this passage. At first glance it seems that Thomas is calling Jesus his god as well as his lord. The grammatical construction would lead us to think that probably the "lord" and the "god" are supposed to be the same person. And it *is* possible that a disciple of Jesus is calling Jesus his "god" since we've seen beings other than God can be called "god" according to Jesus himself in this same book.

But there's a more contextual way to understand Thomas's statement. We can see him as making a double confession, like the confession we see at the end of this famous Pauline passage:

> Hence, as to the eating of food offered to idols, we know that "no idol in the world really exists" and that "there is no God but one." Indeed, even though there may be so-called gods in heaven or on earth—as in fact there are many

[51] For a look at the interpretive options for this verse at around the year 200, see my "Podcast 291."

[52] John 7:16–17, 8:26, 10:34–36, 14:10.

> gods and many lords—yet for us there is one God, the Father, from whom are all things and for whom we exist, and one Lord, Jesus Christ, through whom are all things and through whom we exist. (1 Cor. 8:4–6. Compare Eph. 4:4–6)

Paul seems to be exploiting a distinction familiar to a pagan-majority culture. In most cultures that assume a traditional pantheon, not all the deities are equal. Some are higher, both literally (spatially) and metaphysically (that is, greater), and as such are less accessible to us. Others (some of which may be the deified souls of humans) are more accessible and serve as intermediaries to give us access to the higher sort. Sometimes the former are called "gods" and the latter "lords." Paul acknowledges that the pagans believe in many gods (high deities) and lords (lower deities), but for Christians there is one God—the highest and unique deity, the Father—and one Lord, the man Jesus, who has been exalted to a unique, godlike position under God (1 Cor. 15:20–28).[53] The famous episode in John 20:28 can be taken as a similar double confession. But is it plausible that the author expected the reader to interpret Thomas's statement as an acknowledgment of Jesus as the unique Lord *and* of the unique God who has been working in that man? I shall argue that it is plausible.

A clear theme of this Gospel is that God is "in" Jesus and Jesus is "in" God. Thus, immediately after correcting his critics (he's claiming to be God's Son, not God himself—10:36), Jesus adds,

> "If I am not doing the works of my Father, then do not believe me. But if I do them, even though you do not believe me, believe the works, so that you may know and understand that the Father is in me and I am in the Father."
> (John 10:37–38)

What does "in" mean here? Is it some sort of metaphysical mixing or intermingling, such as the later idea of *perichoresis* is imagined to be?[54] No, in context, the point is clear: Jesus is doing God's works, meaning that God is acting through him and he is cooperating with God. It's an "in" of action.[55]

---

[53] On Paul's view that Jesus is a man, see Rom. 5. On the distinction between higher and lower deities and Paul's use of this distinction, see Mede, *Works*, 540–42 and the ancient sources cited in Danker, BDAG, 512b. See also section 9.5.

[54] This speculative dead end is due mainly to John of Damascus (d. c. 750), on which see his *Orthodox Faith*, 35–36, 79–81 (ch. 8), 95–96 (14), 170–73 (48–49), 180–81 (51–52), 200 (59), 211 (61), 216 (63), 237 (81b), 269 (91).

[55] Notice the following crowd reaction report that confirms the author's point (John 10:41–42). The significance of Jesus's God-empowered works has been the issue all along; see 10:24–25, 33 and 5:19–20, 30–38.

The author also expects the reader to remember this exchange:

> [Jesus said,] "And you know the way to the place where I am going."
>
> Thomas said to him, "Lord, we do not know where you are going. How can we know the way?"
>
> Jesus said to him, "I am the way and the truth and the life. No one comes to the Father except through me. If you know me, you will know my Father also. From now on you do know him and have seen him."
>
> Philip said to him, "Lord, show us the Father, and we will be satisfied."
>
> Jesus said to him, "Have I been with you all this time, Philip, and you still do not know me? Whoever has seen me has seen the Father. How can you say, 'Show us the Father'? Do you not believe that I am in the Father and the Father is in me? The words that I say to you I do not speak on my own, but the Father who dwells in me does his works. Believe me that I am in the Father and the Father is in me, but if you do not, then believe because of the works themselves." (John 14:4–11)

Jesus claims here to provide his disciples with knowledge of God (a claim already made by the narrator, John 1:18). How? By the works of God that God is doing through and so with Jesus. Witnessing those works counts as "seeing" and "knowing" God. Notice that Thomas is one of the questioners. Now in chapter 20, after meeting the risen Jesus, he's ready to confess Jesus as his Lord in whom God has been working all along. He literally says "My Lord and my God" *to Jesus* (20:28), but he's acknowledging Jesus as his Lord and the Father in Jesus as his God—he recognizes the Messiah and the God at work in him.

Lest the reader confuse Jesus with God based on Thomas's confession, the author has just shown Jesus confessing that his Father and God is the same as ours (20:17)—being under God implies that Jesus is not God Almighty, the one true God (17:3). And immediately following Thomas's confession, the author tells us the central thesis of his book: "that Jesus is the Messiah, the Son of God" (John 20:31). This is not what the author would write were his primary purpose to teach that Jesus is God, a divine Person, fully divine, or a coequal member of the Trinity.

In conclusion, is Jesus being addressed as "God" here? It's possible but unlikely, for the reasons above. But even if that was his intention, we can rule out that the author's point would be to assert Jesus to be as divine as the one God is or to be the one God himself.[56]

---

[56] For one thing, this author would have assumed God to be essentially immortal, but he tells us that Jesus died (John 19:30), which implies not being essentially immortal.

1.4.3 ROMANS 9:5

Here Paul writes, "to them [the Israelites] belong the patriarchs, and from them, according to the flesh, comes the Christ, who is over all, God blessed forever. Amen." Some translators openly admit (while others choose to conceal) that this text is unclear due to the ambiguity of the original Greek regarding its punctuation.[57] One of our most esteemed literal-leaning major translations, the NRSVUE, puts a footnote here with a plausible alternative translation: "[comes the] Messiah. May he who is God over all be blessed forever."[58] If this is the better translation, then Paul is referring to two beings rather than one, Christ and his god, not using a form of the word *theos* in reference to Jesus.

But according to many translators Paul here calls Jesus "God," and many interpreters infer that Paul assumes that Jesus is God himself or a fully divine Person.[59] Such interpretations are suspect, though, as Paul's topic is not the nature or status of Christ but rather the continuing status of Israel as God's chosen people. What is the chance Paul would drop a christological bombshell without comment, asserting Christ to be God or a divine Person, someone with all the essential divine attributes? Further, Paul's theology is well-known; for him, the one God and the Father are one and the same, and he is the god over the Lord Jesus Christ.[60] And just a few verses earlier (Rom. 8:31–34), Jesus is clearly portrayed as *the Son of* God, whereas the title "God" nearly always refers to the Father of this Son.

Trinitarian scholars have moved heaven and earth, in countless book chapters, articles, and commentaries, to show that Paul is here calling Jesus "God," in the hope that this supports the full deity of Christ.[61] But even if they're right, the verse is a doubtful instance, and too much weight should not be put

[57] Although the earliest New Testament texts lack most punctuation, as time went on, scribes added more. But as Harris explains, what we find there doesn't resolve this issue, and moreover "in the early centuries the scribes responsible for the transmission of the NT used marks of punctuation in an inconsistent and erratic fashion" (*Jesus as God*, 149).

[58] Rom. 9:5 translators' footnote.

[59] When referring to alleged Persons within a triune God, I usually capitalize "Person" to signal that the term is being used in a technical sense. Some trinitarians think that these "Persons" are persons (selves, literal someones), but others think they are something like ways God lives or roles that he plays.

[60] See the start of all the New Testament letters attributed to Paul. See also Rom. 1:1–7; 1 Cor. 8:6, 11:3, 15:20–28; Eph. 1:17, 4:6; 1 Thess. 1:9–10. An older but still helpful overview of Paul's views is Caleb Stetson's 1828 tract "The Apostle Paul a Unitarian" presented in Tuggy, "Podcast 253."

[61] Harris, *Jesus as God*, ch. 6; Craig, "Tri-Personal," 32–34.

on it. Further, even if Paul here calls Jesus "God," this would not really change our overall view of his theology and his Christology. In light of his other writings, we would take him to mean the sort of "God" who can be a mortal human who is subject to God.

1.4.4 TITUS 2:13

This verse is often translated something like: "while we wait for the blessed hope and the manifestation of the glory of our great God and Savior, Jesus Christ." Yet there's a translation problem here, so these translators give a footnote with the alternative translation: "of the great God and our Savior"—so that the mentioned glory is shared by both of them, God (a.k.a. the Father) and the man Jesus.[62] Many conservative scholars appeal to "Sharp's Rule" to support the first translation. This controversial grammatical rule for New Testament Greek was "discovered" by an amateur, error-prone apologist in the late 1700s to maximize the number of times *theos* is applied to Christ in the New Testament, so as to support a traditional full deity of Christ doctrine. Having been repeatedly falsified by counterexamples, its defenders have made a gerrymandering defense by simply adding exception clauses to the proposed "rule."[63] With no hint of this very controversial background (what's the chance that a rule of ancient Greek grammar is going to be discovered in the late 1700s?), apologist William Lane Craig presents Daniel Wallace's version of it as authoritative:

> In native Greek constructions (i.e. not translation Greek), when a single article modifies two substantives connected by *kai* ["and"] (thus, article-substantive-*kai*-substantive), when both substantives are
> i. singular (both grammatically and semantically)
> ii. personal, and
> iii. common nouns (not proper names or ordinals), they have the same referent.[64]

Appealing to this, Craig concludes that in this verse, "God" and "Savior" must have the same referent; thus, Jesus is being called "God."

Let's suppose this is correct, that Paul is calling Jesus "the great God." If so, then presumably his thought would be that as exalted, Jesus is now over all others—of course, God excepted (1 Cor. 15:20–28). But there is something in

[62] Titus 2:13, translators' footnote.

[63] For the unintentionally funny story of its "discovery" and its increasingly complex definitions by trinitarian scholars, see Wallace, "Sharp Redivivus."

[64] Craig, "Tri-Personal," 36.

the context that suggests that the word "God" is not being used in the highest sense. In the very next verse Paul writes, "He [Jesus] it is who gave himself for us that he might redeem us from all iniquity and purify for himself a people of his own who are zealous for good deeds" (Titus 2:14). The reader knows that Paul means Jesus gave himself *by willingly dying on the cross for us* (Rom. 5, Phil. 2:5–8), which rules out his being fully divine—divine in the way the only god is divine, which implies essential immortality.[65] Given this, even if it should be translated as trinitarians prefer, it does nothing to support their belief in the full deity of Christ. Craig and many others are content to argue that in this text the word "God" is applied to Jesus, merely assuming that *somehow* this supports their view that in the New Testament Jesus is fully divine, as claimed in Nicene orthodoxy.[66] But as we've seen, his being called "God" is consistent with the author thinking that, but it hardly implies that the author is committed to Jesus's full deity.

On the other hand, it is unexpected that Paul should call Jesus *the great* God.[67] And given the contextual reasons that weigh against Paul's commitment to the full deity of Christ, we may prefer instead to view this as a text that provides a counterexample to Wallace's alleged rule.

Independent of that controversial rule, Craig, Wallace, and others argue that the phrase "God and Savior" was a stock compound title that the Jews of this era used for Yahweh, so that the two terms refer to the same god and person.[68] But if this is what Paul is doing, he would be assuming the numerical identity of Yahweh and Jesus, which is a christological disaster, as that would imply that Yahweh and Jesus could not possibly simultaneously differ in any way.[69] But any Christian, trinitarian or not, thinks that Yahweh and Jesus have differed. If God is the Trinity, Yahweh would be tripersonal, but Jesus would not be. Or, aside from any Trinity speculations, Jesus is supposed to be the Son of Yahweh, but Yahweh himself is not. Thus, suggesting that Paul is assuming the numerical sameness of Yahweh and Jesus is ill-advised.[70]

---

[65] For the texts in which God is said to be immortal and for arguments that this should be understood as *essential* immortality, see my "Podcast 145"; "Nineteen," sec. 2, and section 5.10, p. 179, footnote 45.

[66] *NET Bible*, 2282, 2316; Craig, "Tri-Personal," 36–37; Harris, *Jesus as God*, ch. 7.

[67] The reader would expect him to reserve such a title for the Father, whom Paul believes to be the one true God himself, on which see the references in p. 19, footnote 60.

[68] Craig, "Tri-Personal," 37.

[69] Sections 8.3.3, 8.3.6.

[70] Tuggy, "Podcast 124."

1.4.5 HEBREWS 1:8–9

In Hebrews 1 the author is contrasting Jesus's current position with that of angels, arguing that Jesus's is greater. In part, he writes:

> But of the Son he [God] says, "Your throne, O God, is forever and ever, and the scepter of righteousness is the scepter of your kingdom. You have loved righteousness and hated lawlessness; therefore God, your God, has anointed you with the oil of gladness beyond your companions." (Heb. 1:8–9)

Once again, the translation can be contested. Another translation, offered in the translators' footnote, is not "Your throne, O God" but rather "God is your throne."[71] This ambiguity also exists in the Hebrew text quoted here.[72] Even if the former translation is preferred, this passage does not prove that Jesus is being called *theos* in the sense of God himself or full divinity or divine personhood, since (in v. 9) he has a god over him, namely, the one God, the Father (1:1–2). The just-mentioned senses of *theos* would rule out being under any god; the one God of the Bible can't be under any other. Thus, if "God" is referring to Jesus in this passage, then it is being used in a lower sense that doesn't imply being the only true god.

About the original text (Ps. 45:6), even trinitarian interpreters agree that "The king is clearly the addressee here"[73]—that is, an ancient king of Israel, as this poem has been composed for a king on the occasion of his wedding.[74] Jesus, to whom this text is now reapplied, is of course a king too, and a much greater one. Thus, given the majority translation, it makes sense that as a man who has appeared in these last days, God's unique, human Son and Messiah (Heb. 1:2, 2:11–14), Jesus is here referred to as a "God" in the sense of one who is *under* the one God.[75]

---

[71] Heb. 1:8, translators' footnote.

[72] A recent Jewish translation has "Your divine throne is everlasting," although in a note they give an alternate translation: "Your throne, O God" (Berlin and Brettler, *Jewish Study Bible*, 1332). A Catholic translation has "Your throne is from God forever" (NJB). Both note that the ancient Greek Septuagint translators chose instead "Your throne, O God."

[73] *NET Bible*, 956.

[74] *NET Bible*, 955.

[75] Trinitarian traditions insist here that Jesus was involved in the creation of the world, citing Heb. 1:2. In my view that is a doubtful interpretation, all things considered (Tuggy, "Podcast 258"; Tuggy, "Podcast 259"), but granting, for the sake of argument, that the author is asserting God to have created the world through the prehuman Jesus, that would *rule out* his being fully divine, which implies being *the ultimate* source of anything else there is (Tuggy and Date, *Is Jesus Human*, 101–2, 145–48).

As we've seen, the word "God" is ambiguous. If, as I assume, the majority translation "Your throne, O God" is correct, then "God" is verses 8–9 is being used in both a higher and a lower sense. The one who is "God" in the highest sense is the god over the other, who is "God" in a lower sense. What is that sense? That of the human Messiah, which is not unlike the usage for an ancient, lesser king, although of this greater king the author points out that God has said, "Let all the angels of God worship him" (Heb. 1:8, NET).

1.4.6 2 PETER 1:1–2

The second New Testament letter attributed to Peter begins,

> Simeon Peter, a servant and apostle of Jesus Christ,
> To those who have received a faith as equally honorable as ours through the righteousness of our God and Savior Jesus Christ: May grace and peace be yours in abundance in the knowledge of God and of Jesus our Lord. (2 Pet. 1:1–2)

If this translation is correct, then in the second half of the first sentence, Jesus is called "our God and Savior." Yet there is a translation difficulty, so the translators of the version above put in a footnote: "of our God and the Savior Jesus Christ"—reflecting the assumption that this righteousness pertains to both.[76] Notice how in the very next verse the author does something similar: there the knowledge is of God *and* of the Lord Jesus. This author habitually groups them together with some one blessing ("righteousness"—v. 1, "knowledge"—v. 2). This suggests also that the author is *not* saying in verse 1 that Jesus is "our God." As with other New Testament authors, that is the Father. Jesus is rather the unique Lord under that one God (2 Pet. 1:17, 1 Cor. 8:4–6, Eph. 4:4–6).

Still, some insist that for some grammatical reason(s) we should think that "our God" and "Savior" refer to the same one.[77] Let's suppose they're right. Would there be, in such a case, any contextual reason to think that "God" or "god" was being used here of Jesus in a lesser sense? Yes, there is: this one is *the*

---

[76] 2 Pet. 1:1 NRSV footnote; similarly, NJB, RSV. The ASV prefers what these others footnote, rendering, "the righteousness of our God and the Saviour Jesus Christ." The KJV has "the righteousness of God and our Saviour Jesus Christ." Phillips translates "the righteousness of our God, and saviour Jesus Christ." There does seem to be a trend of newer translations simply hiding this ambiguity in the Greek from the reader: ESV, HCSB, LEB, NABRE, NRSVUE, NIV.

[77] This is the other verse to which Sharp's (really, Wallace's) "Rule" is applied (Craig, "Tri-Personal," 37–38).

Son of God who received God's endorsement at the Transfiguration.[78] And as with the previous verse, one may view this very text as falsifying Wallace's alleged rule (p. 20). Either way, there is no support here for "the deity of Christ" in any sense trinitarians want.

1.4.7 JOHN 1:18

"No one has ever seen God. It is the only Son, himself God, who is close to the Father's heart, who has made him known." This verse suffers from both textual and translation difficulties.[79] The NRSVUE translators' footnote tells us that instead of "the only Son, himself God," other ancient authorities read "*is the only Son who.*" Those scholars who stick rigidly to the methodology of modern textual criticism accept the reading *monogenes theos*, one-of-a-kind, unique, or only god.[80] On the other hand, some of the best commentators on the Gospel of John, scholars who are most attuned to the author's terminology and thought, judge that he must have written *monogenes huios*, one-of-a-kind, unique, or only son. The great Johannine scholar John A. T. Robinson writes,

> From the manuscript evidence there is every reason to believe that *monogenes theos* [only god] is the reading that reaches furthest back to source, and every modern edition of the Greek Testament properly gives it precedence. It is equally noticeable however that both the RSV and the NEB still prefer *ho monogenes huios* [the only son] in their text, as opposed to the margin, and I am inclined to judge that they are right. For the contrast with 'the Father' appears overwhelmingly to demand 'the only Son' (as in 1:14), and *monogenes theos* is

---

[78] "For he received honor and glory from God the Father when that voice was conveyed to him by the Majestic Glory, saying, 'This is my Son, my Beloved, with whom I am well pleased.' We ourselves heard this voice come from heaven, while we were with him on the holy mountain" (2 Pet. 1:17–18). Compare Mark 9:2–8.

[79] The term translated "only" here, *monogenes*, was traditionally translated "only begotten," which seems to fit hand in glove with the traditional speculation about the Father "eternally begetting" the Son.

[80] However, the textual-critical situation here is *very* difficult. Since other words in this verse vary as well, there are something like thirteen total textual variants (Wright, "Jesus," 241). And while it's true that the earliest manuscripts we have say *monogenes theos*, texts outside of the Alexandrian tradition overwhelmingly read *monogenes huios* (Ehrman, *Orthodox Corruption*, 92–93). And with an author as early as Irenaeus, c. 180, we find both readings ("Jesus," 241–42). Thus, the corruption must have occurred *before* our earliest surviving Greek texts. And while it is often suggested that it is most plausible that the hard reading of *theos* was corrected by scribes to the more normal *huios* in this verse, it is easy to imagine that some scribes, such as Modalistic Monarchians or those committed to Logos theology, would prefer Jesus to be called *theos* here, and so may have changed *huios* to *theos*.

literally untranslatable ('the only one, himself God' is a paraphrase to make the best of it) and out of line with Johannine usage (contrast 5:44 and 17:3 of the Father). In other words, I believe that *theos* may indeed be the best attested reading, and even go back to the autograph, but that it was a slip for *huios* (there is only the difference between *YC* and *QC*) and the author would have been the first to correct it.[81]

The author of this Gospel does *not* think that Jesus is the only *god*; as Robinson points out, he believes the only god is the Father.[82] Another major commentator agrees that "the only son" must have been the original reading, citing Bultmann.[83] While admitting that it's *possible* that the author is referring to Jesus using *theos*, Bultmann argues,

> Nevertheless, *theos* cannot be defended here, for it neither fits in with the preceding *theon* etc., nor can it take the appositional phrase *ho on* etc. The latter must have *huios*, which is what the Evangelist always writes (3:16, 18; 1 Jn. 4:9). *Theos* is most likely the result of an error in dictation.[84]

This requires some unpacking. By "*theon* etc." Bultmann is referring to the phrase "No one has ever seen God" (in Greek this starts with *theon*, the accusative form of *theos*). It seems unlikely that the author's thought is that while God is unseen, the only God (the "God" just mentioned before?) has made him known. It's not God self-revealing but rather his being revealed by someone else, the Son, who is close to the Father's heart. By "the appositional phrase *ho on* etc.," Bultmann is referring to the phrase "who is close to the Father's heart." An appositional phrase is one that refers to something mentioned before—in this case, either the only God or the only Son. But would the only *God* be "close to the Father's (that is, to God's) heart? That doesn't make sense, but it does make sense that his unique *Son* would be close to the Father's heart. And as Bultmann points out, this author in other places describes the Son as unique.

After referring to the aforementioned textual-critical consensus for the reading *monogenes theos*, Craig concludes,

[81] Robinson, *Priority of John*, 372–73. At the end he refers to the ancient Christian scribal practice of abbreviating words referring to God or to Jesus in Greek texts written in all capital letters.

[82] Sections 9.1–9.3.1.

[83] Ridderbos, *Gospel of John*, 59. Compare Haenchen, *John*, 109, 121.

[84] Bultmann, *Gospel of John*, 82. About the possible error in dictation, *huios* and *theos* sound very similar in Greek.

> We may proceed with confidence, if not certainty, that here Jesus Christ is called *theos.* By means of the stunning appellation "the only-begotten God" John differentiates Christ the Son from God the Father while regarding both as God.[85]

Here Craig attributes a trinitarian idea to the author, that the Father and the Son are the same god even while thinking they are different Persons. But this is an anachronism, a demonstrably later idea which the best commentators avoid attributing to the author.

Thus ends Harris's list of Jesus-as-*theos* passages. There appears to be scant support in these for the trinitarian claim that Jesus is as divine as the Father or "fully" divine. Before we move on, though, let's examine a passage that Harris rejects but which some conservative scholars have argued is a case of Jesus being called "God."

1.4.8 1 JOHN 5:18–21

At the end of John's first letter we read,

> We know that those who are born of God do not sin, but the one who was born of God protects them, and the evil one does not touch them. We know that we are God's children and that the whole world lies under the power of the evil one. And we know that the Son of God has come and has given us understanding so that we may know him who is true; and we are in him who is true, in his Son Jesus Christ. He is the true God and eternal life. Little children, keep yourselves from idols. (1 John 5:18–21)

Who does "He" (Greek: *houtos*) refer to in the second-to-last sentence? The nearest referent is Jesus, at the end of the previous sentence. Thus, one might think it is Jesus who is being called "true God." It is a general rule of thumb that a pronoun in this circumstance refers back to the subject last mentioned,[86] and yet, as Craig points out, "*houtos* may take a more remote antecedent [that is, something mentioned farther back] if it is uppermost in the author's mind," citing two examples of this from the letters of John, 1 John 2:22 and 2 John 7.[87]

That God *is* the main subject in the author's mind throughout this passage is shown by his subsequent warning against idols, which were habitually

[85] Craig, "Tri-Personal," 40.
[86] Harris, *Jesus as God*, 247.
[87] "Tri-Personal," 43.

contrasted with the true God.[88] The author has just twice referred to the Father (a.k.a. "God") as "him who is true," contrasting him with "his Son Jesus Christ." Isn't it natural to think, then, that when the author goes on to refer to "the true God" he has in mind the Father? Many interpreters have thought so. It's *possible* that the author should suddenly switch the main subject here from God to Jesus, but it's more likely that his main subject is God throughout.[89]

But the idea that John is calling Jesus "the true God" is irresistible for many trinitarian interpreters, since the Nicene Creed famously calls the Son and Father "true God from true God."[90] Although Jesus in John 17 seems to presuppose that *only* the Father has the status of *true God*, some argue that John *couldn't* have meant that, as here the same author also says that someone else is *true God*.[91] But that is a classic example of trying to understand a clear passage using an obscure one. And it merely passes on the old apologists' canard that in calling the Father "the only true God" this doesn't exclude the Son because the author did not write "*only* the Father is the only true God" or "only the Father is the true God."[92]

Returning to our text in 1 John, some traditionalists argue that grammatical points alone require their interpretation of this passage, but Daniel Wallace wisely observes that "The issue cannot be decided on grammar alone."[93] Wallace is right; grammar is one interpreter's tool among many. Are there extra-grammatical reasons that require Jesus to be called "the true God" here?

William Lane Craig thinks so. In a recent short treatment he argues against Harris's view that *houtos* refers to the Father here.[94] First, Craig argues that the

---

[88] Paul writes elsewhere, "you turned to God from idols to serve a living and true God" (1 Thess. 1:9).

[89] Harris, *Jesus as God*, 252.

[90] "Profession," 5.

[91] Craig, "Tri-Personal," 44–45.

[92] If the Father *is the only* true god, it logically follows that no else is; hence it is wrongheaded to suppose that to exclude others from that status the author would have had to move "only" to earlier in the sentence or include an extra "only" at the start. This talking-point is unfortunately passed on by Craig ("Tri-Personal," 45), who knows better, as he understands the logical form of what Jesus assumes in John 17:1–3, on which see sections 8.2 and 9.2. Since Athanasius partisans of the Nicene creed have labored to deny the obvious implication of what Jesus says here, that no one else, no one other than the Father, has the status "true God" (Pollard, *Johannine Christology*, 225–28).

[93] Wallace, *Greek Grammar*, 327. This is contrary to Craig, who, unlike Wallace, appeals to "Sharp's Rule" here (Craig, "Tri-Personal," 44).

[94] Harris, *Jesus as God*, ch. 11.

two Johannine texts in which the author uses a pronoun to refer back to a previously mentioned person are not analogous to 1 John 5:20, since in the former the referent of *houtos* is unambiguous.[95] While that may be true, it misses the point: the cited examples serve only to illustrate that this author occasionally uses *houtos* to denote a more distant antecedent rather than, as is customary, the nearest one. Craig then argues, plausibly, that in the sentence "He is the true God and eternal life," only one is being called both of those things, "the true God" and "eternal life." He points out that in John's writings, Jesus and (eternal) life are closely associated; he is even called "the life" (John 11:25, 14:6). But both the Father and Son are closely associated with eternal life; as Craig points out in the letter John writes, "And this is the testimony: God gave us eternal life, and this life is in his Son. Whoever has the Son has life; whoever does not have the Son of God does not have life" (1 John 5:11–12). The reader of John's Gospel knows that we get eternal life from Christ but also that in some sense Jesus received eternal life from his and our God: "For just as the Father has life in himself, so he has granted the Son also to have life in himself" (John 5:26).[96] For John, the ultimate source of our eternal life is God, and this comes to us through his unique human Son.

Craig also argues that "Many commentators have observed that taking *houtos* to refer to 'him that is true' makes the phrase into a tautology ('This True One is the true God') and functions poorly rhetorically at the letter's close."[97] But the statement here is *not* a tautology, not a sentence that is trivial (uninformative) and true by definition, like the sentence "Every isosceles triangle is a triangle." If someone can be called "true,"[98] it is a further question whether or not he can be called "the true God." Further, as Harris observes, read as a whole, the author's thought appears to be neither tautological nor simply repetitive. Harris notes that this *houtos* "gathers up all that has preceded in the verse," and he summarizes the author's thought here as

> this true one, whom believers now know because of his Son's coming and gift of insight and with whom they are now united in fellowship, this one (*houtos*) is the true God and life eternal.[99]

[95] Craig, "Tri-Personal," 43.
[96] On the Father being Jesus's god, see section 11.4.
[97] "Tri-Personal," 44.
[98] For the possible New Testament meanings of "true" (*alethinos*) see Danker, BDAG, 38.
[99] Harris, *Jesus as God*, 252–53.

In support of Craig's reading, many trinitarian interpreters contend that the Fourth Gospel begins and ends with affirmations of Christ's full deity (1:1, 1:18, 20:28), and they read 1 John as intentionally patterned the same way—with corresponding declarations in 5:20 and 1:1–3.[100]

But "full deity" interpretations of all of those Fourth Gospel passages are contentious—the Jesus of this Gospel is under God (20:17), gets his message from God (12:49, 14:24), was sent by God (5:36), needs the support of God's testimony on his behalf (5:32, 8:18), prays to God (ch. 17), follows God's lead (5:19), receives authority bestowed by God (5:27, 17:2), and dies (19:30). The cited opening of John's first letter neither asserts nor clearly presupposes the full deity of Jesus, dashing the trinitarian's hopes of finding a deity of Christ inclusio in this book. It's irrelevant that a final declaration of Christ's divinity would be a rhetorically exciting ending.[101]

Craig makes some other points, and Harris has more to say as well.[102] I'll focus here on the points that strike me as the most relevant. Craig ends his case with an appeal to authority.

> Most NT scholars, then, do not agree with Harris' judgment that in 1 John 5:20 it is equiprobable that *houtos* refers to God or to Jesus Christ. Indeed, many consider the reference to Jesus Christ to be more than merely probable. The preeminent Johannine commentators Raymond Brown and Rudolf Schnackenburg, for example, conclude respectively, "I think the arguments clearly favor *houtos* as a reference to Jesus Christ," and "There is no longer any doubt . . . that the following *houtos* . . . refers to Jesus Christ."[103]

There is nothing wrong with appealing to a clear consensus of recent scholars, but here there is no such clear consensus. As Harris observes in this case: "Scholarly opinion is more evenly divided over the question of whether *theos* is

---

[100] Craig, "Tri-Personal," 44.

[101] Other interpreters want to see an inclusio in this book not asserting the deity of Christ but rather calling Christ "life" (*NET Bible*, 2345). In reply, 1 John 1:1–3 does assert that "the word of life" and "eternal life" have come to us through Jesus. And *if* the author in 5:20 is calling Jesus "eternal life," then this could be seen as an inclusio together with 1:1–3. But the possibility of such an inclusio seems by itself a *very* weak reason to interpret the text as Craig and others prefer.

[102] "Tri-Personal," 44; Harris, *Jesus as God*, ch. 11.

[103] "Tri-Personal," 46. This is an odd mistake on Craig's part; Harris nowhere says that the two readings are equiprobable, and he argues at length that it is more likely that John means to refer to the Father with this *houtos*. It could be that Craig is misremembering what Harris says, quoted below, about the near-equal split among scholars when it comes to these clashing interpretations.

predicated of Jesus than is the case with any other verse discussed in this book."[104] The editors of the excellent yet reliably partisan evangelical *NET Bible* agree with Harris, noting, "It is far from clear whether it [*houtos*] should be understood as a reference (1) to God the Father or (2) to Jesus Christ."[105]

I've found very helpful in understanding the Johannine books an equally heavyweight scholar who disagrees with Craig: John A. T. Robinson. He writes,

> I find it difficult to be persuaded by such as Schnackenburg, Bultmann and Brown in their commentaries . . . that it is Christ who is being designated "the true God." Rather, I am convinced with Westcott, Brook and Dodd that the remaining Johannine usage (particularly "This is the true God, this is eternal life" [1 John 5:20] and "This is eternal life: to know thee who alone art truly God" [John 17:3], which I believe the former deliberately echoes) requires the reference to be to the Father.[106]

Just before this Robinson has noted the clear passages where John teaches that the only true God is the Father himself: John 5:44 and 17:3. Such texts lead us to expect that he's calling the Father "the true God" in the passage at hand, and Craig has not overturned this expectation. In my view, the lay reader need not be paralyzed by the disagreement of experts here; she has enough information in the context of the passage and of John's other books to determine for herself that the Father is in view in this verse, not his human Son.

In confirmation of this, the Anglican philosopher-theologian Samuel Clarke observes that "no writer before the time of the Council of Nicaea [325 CE] interprets the words 'This is the true God' to be about Christ."[107] As best I can tell, Clarke is correct; I haven't read *all* surviving writings of that time, but the index to the *Ante-Nicene Fathers* series contains no references to 1 John 5:20.[108] This would be shocking if pre-Nicene Christians generally viewed this text as obviously, or even probably, calling Jesus "the true God." The timing of this change of preferred interpretation is suspicious and suggests that theology is influencing exegesis rather than vice versa. Clarke also points out that the Nicene heresy-hunter Epiphanius, writing around the years 374–78, in the process of defending Christ's status as "true God" (like the Nicene and Constantinopolitan Creeds assert), simply admits that Scripture doesn't ever

---

[104] Harris, *Jesus as God*, 240.

[105] *NET Bible*, 2345. Having said this, they tentatively take Craig's side.

[106] Robinson, "Fourth Gospel," 175.

[107] Clarke, *Scripture Doctrine*, 30–31 (sec. 410), modernized.

[108] Coxe, *Bibliographical Synopsis*, 265.

call Jesus "true God."[109] So, even while Nicene polemicists like Hilary around 356–60 asserted, based on this passage, "there is no eternal life nor resurrection for him to whom He [Christ] is not the true God,"[110] even as late as 378, some remembered the earlier consensus about the meaning of this text.

1.4.9 LINGUISTIC FACTS VS. THEOLOGICAL ASSUMPTIONS

We have now examined the seven passages that Harris argues are the most likely cases of the word *theos* being applied to Jesus in the New Testament, plus one more urged by some scholars. We have seen that each is questionable due to textual variants, translation issues, difficulty in interpretation, or a combination of these factors.

This fact is telling. Main points in the New Testament (such as that Jesus is the Messiah, that he was raised bodily from the dead and that he is coming again) are stated clearly and in multiple locations. The Bible is not a secret code book; it is meant to be clear and understandable to anyone, at least in its main points. It would be surprising if these include the teachings that Jesus is God himself or that Jesus is fully divine and yet it is mainly or only taught through these difficult-to-understand passages. One would expect such an important point to be evident throughout the pages of the New Testament. Some scholars claim that Jesus's deity is a central teaching of the Bible, but the authors hint at it constantly rather than stating it explicitly—however, that's another topic for another time. Attempts to extract "the deity of Christ" from New Testament texts are legion, and in recent years trinitarian scholars have creatively invented many new ways of doing that.[111]

Harris holds that Jesus is called "God" in the New Testament somewhere between zero and seven times. Granting that, we should not lose sight of the fact that the term *theos* nearly always refers to the Father in the New Testament. Harris notes, "Customarily, (*ho*) *theos* [(the) god, God] denotes the Father, but exceptionally it refers to the Son."[112] A few pages later he says, "When (*ho*) *theos* [(the) god] is used, we are to assume that the New Testament writers have *ho pater* [the Father] in mind unless the context makes this sense of (*ho*) *theos* impossible."[113] For instance, the "God" who is under another "God" in

[109] Clarke, *Scripture Doctrine*, 30–31 (410); Epiphanius, *Medicine*, 2:360 (69.32.4).

[110] Hilary, *Trinity*, 213 (6.43).

[111] Chandler, "Early"; "Christological." I discuss and criticize some of these unhelpful recent interpretive strategies in my "Podcast 393" and in sections 7.3 and 9.4 and chapter 10.

[112] Harris, *Jesus as God*, 42.

[113] *Jesus as God*, 47.

Hebrews 1:8–9 (assuming that is the correct translation) could not be the Father because the Father does not and cannot have a god over him; thus, it must be referring to the Son. A unitarian has an easy explanation of why "God" nearly always refers to the Father in the New Testament: it reflects the assumption that the Father and God—the only true god—are numerically the same thing.

These facts about the New Testament usage of *theos* don't sit well with trinitarian theologies. One would expect the earliest Christians, being Jews, to reserve the title "God" mainly for the one true God, as monotheists typically do. If they thought the only god to be the Trinity, then we would expect them to use the word "God" primarily for the Trinity. But in fact, New Testament authors *never* use *theos* to refer to the Trinity! That is shocking, if one supposes these authors to be trinitarians, and so this lack of usage is strong evidence that they are *not* trinitarians.[114] It is possible, but incredibly unlikely, that these had the concept of a triune god without having a word or phrase that was then understood to refer to that triune god. But they neither used *theos* nor any other word(s) at their disposal in that way.

In summary, in the Old Testament there is little ambiguity regarding the plural Hebrew word *elohim*. In most cases the context provided by surrounding words removes the ambiguity and makes the author's meaning obvious—that is, whether he is talking about God or various "gods." Monotheism is a central teaching of both the Old Testament and the New Testament; often the writers just assume it, as if it is something everyone already knows and thus does not require explicit statement. In contrast, the biblical authors assume the falsity of monotheosism (that only one being can be referred to as "God" or as "a god"). Occasionally, god words are used for beings other than God. This does not mean that these other beings should be confused with the one true God. "God" in the New Testament almost always refers to the Father, unless the context indicates somehow that it could not mean the Father. This fact aligns with the view that these authors assume the only god is the Father, but it seems to be strong evidence against the idea that these authors assume God to be the Trinity. It is incredibly unlikely that trinitarian authors would use "God" overwhelmingly for the Father but never for the triune god who is in their view both the only god and the main object of their devotion and worship.

---

[114] And there is *much* more confirming evidence; see my "New Testament," 87–109.

1.5 WHAT THEOS MEANS IN THE NEW TESTAMENT VS. WHAT TRINITARIANS NEED IT TO MEAN

As we've seen, trinitarians argue that in the New Testament Jesus is at least several times called "God." By itself this doesn't support traditional claims that Jesus is fully divine since there was a long-established usage of calling beings lesser than God "God" or "god" or "gods." What were the available ranges of meaning for *theos* in the New Testament? The most authoritative lexicon for New Testament Greek gives the following five meanings:

1. "In the Greco-Roman world the term *theos* primarily refers to a transcendent being who exercises extraordinary control in human affairs … deity, god, goddess"
2. "Some writings … use the word *theos* with reference to Christ (without necessarily equating Christ with the Father, and therefore in harmony with the Shema of Israel Deut. 6:4; compare Mark 10:18 … though the interpretation of some of the passages is in debate. In Mosaic and Greco-Roman traditions the fundamental semantic component in the understanding of deity is the factor of performance, namely saviorhood or extraordinary contributions to one's society. *[The Epistle to] Diognetus* 10:6[115] defines the ancient perspective … 'one who ministers to the needy what one has received from God proves to be a god to the recipients' … Such understanding led to the extension of the meaning of *theos* to persons who elicit special reverence … compare passages under 4 below … *theos* certainly refers to Christ as one who manifests primary characteristics of deity, in the following New Testament passages … John 1:1b … Titus 2:13 … John 20:28 … Heb. 1:8–9 … Jude 5 [in at least one ancient manuscript]."
3. a title of "God in Israelite/Christian monotheistic perspective, God—the predominant use, sometimes with, sometimes without the article."
4. for "that which is nontranscendent but considered worthy of special reverence, god," e.g. various humans (John 10:34f), some peoples' bellies or appetites (Phil. 3:19), or even
5. "of the devil (2 Cor. 4:4)."[116]

Under meaning 3 the authors cite many more specific uses of *theos* in various grammatical cases, with and without the article and in combinations with other words. The fourth of these is the common New Testament use of *theos* in conjunction with the word "Father."

[115] *Epistle to Diognetus*, 144 (10.6).
[116] Danker, BDAG, 398–400, abbreviations expanded.

D. used with *pater* ["Father"] . . . "the God and Father of our Lord Jesus Christ" Rom. 15:6; 2 Cor. 1:3; Eph. 1:3; Col. 1:3; 1 Pet. 1:3. "our God and Father" Gal. 1:4; Phil. 4:20; 1 Thes. 1:3, 3:11, 13. "God and Father" 1 Cor. 15:24; Eph. 5:20; Jam. 1:27. "God the Father" (*theos pater*) Phil. 2:11; 1 Pet. 1:2 . . . "from God our Father" Rom. 1:7b; 1 Cor. 1:3; 2 Cor. 1:2; Gal. 1:3; Eph. 1:2; Phil. 1:2; Col. 1:2 . . . Philem. 3; "from God the Father" (*apo theou patros*) . . . Eph. 6:23; 2 Thes. 1:2; 2 Tim. 1:2; Tit. 1:4; "from God the Father" (*para theou patros*) 2 Pet. 1:17; 2 John 3.[117]

Meaning 3 is the dominant use in a monotheistic context; most monotheists reserve the title "God" primarily for whom they believe to be the one true god himself—in the New Testament this is the Father. With or without the word "Father," meaning 3 is *theos* being used as a title *for the Father*, whom the New Testament authors assume to be one and the same with Yahweh in the Old Testament, the one true God. Thus, if we're wondering about *theos* being applied *to Jesus* in the New Testament, 3 is not a relevant meaning; these authors never confuse the Father with the Son. Neither is meaning 5, so let's set that aside. The first meaning is notably ambiguous, as it could express either the concept of a mere deity (a supernaturally powerful self) or the concept of a god (a deity who is ultimate, the farthest back source of anything else there is).[118] As the lexicon editors explain, 1 is primarily a Gentile (non-Jewish) use, though it does occur a few times in the New Testament, although never of Jesus.[119] As we've seen, 4 is a long-established use from ancient Greek translations of the Hebrew Bible.

Meaning 2 is the use in question above when we discussed the 0–8 times *theos* is applied to Jesus in the New Testament. The lexicon authors speak obscurely here of *theos* being applied to Jesus because he manifests "primary characteristics of deity," and then, unfortunately, cite what we've seen to be controversial textual examples as if they were clear-cut cases. Their phrase "as one who manifests primary characteristics of deity" is what I call weasel-wording. It is deliberately ambiguous between the idea that Jesus, in being so-called, is being said or assumed to have divine attributes, which would make him God, as only God has those,[120] and the idea that the man Jesus manifests God's attributes since Christ is "the image of God" who is so like God that he says that

[117] Danker, BDAG, 399, abbreviations expanded and Greek words either transliterated or translated.

[118] On this important distinction see my "On Counting Gods."

[119] They cite Acts 28:6 and 2 Thess. 2:4.

[120] On this line of thinking see section 8.3.6.

if you've seen him you've thereby seen the Father (2 Cor. 4:4; John 14:9). Trinitarians and unitarians can agree that the New Testament teaches Jesus to be like his Father, and that if Jesus is called *theos*, this likeness could be a or the reason. But the lexicon authors' deliberately vague statement throws a bone to the catholic tradition of urging that *theos* being applied to Jesus implies or presupposes or at least suggests that Jesus is fully divine.

Trinitarian interpreters usually urge that when *theos* is applied to Jesus in the New Testament, this must be "in the highest sense," since they aim to support the Nicene claim that the Son is as divine as the Father: fully divine. But here the trinitarian interpreter must steer carefully. The "highest" sense of *theos* is that which implies being the one true god, Yahweh himself. But in the New Testament, as the lexicon authors note, this is the Father, not Jesus. Besides, if Jesus is called *theos* in this *highest* sense, that would imply the numerical identity of the one God with Jesus—something that commits the trinitarian either to incoherence or to the officially heretical view that Jesus and the Father are one and the same, given that the Father is called *theos* in that same sense.[121]

On the other hand, if Jesus is called *theos* in the "lower" sense 4, that will not assume, imply, or even suggest any claim that he has a (or the) divine nature. The trinitarian interpreter needs Jesus to be called *theos* in some sense that doesn't imply numerical identity with God and that rules out his being "a mere man"—in other words, a human who is not also fully divine. Is that sense 2 above? The lexicon authors are none too clear about just what sense 2 assumes or implies. The New Testament Jesus is most certainly a person who elicits special reverence—that would be an understatement (Rev. 5). And he is undeniably presented as a savior, and in that sense plays a godlike role.[122] And as we've seen,

[121] If God and Jesus are one and the same (numerically identical) then they can't differ from one another. But the trinitarian thinks God is tripersonal yet denies Jesus to be tripersonal. And if both Jesus and the Father are called "God" in a sense that implies being one and the same with God, then they would also be one and the same with each other—things identical to the same thing must also be identical to each other. This would make it impossible for them to ever differ in any way, yet the trinitarian believes that at one point the Son was dead, but the Father was not dead. See sections 8.3–4.

[122] Luke 1:69, 2:11; compare with 1:47. See also: John 4:42; Acts 5:31, 13:23; Eph. 5:23; Phil. 3:20; 2 Tim.1:10; Titus 1:4, 3:6; compare with 1 Tim. 1:1, 2:3, 4:10; Titus 1:3, 2:10, 3:4; 2 Peter 1:11; 2 Peter 2:20, 3:2, 18; 1 John 4:14; compare Jude 25. "Savior" is undeniably a title that is ambiguous in the New Testament, being applicable both to God and to his human Son. God asserts in Isa. 43:11 that "I, I am the LORD, and besides me there is no savior." But this unique saviorhood of God neither assumes, nor implies, nor even hints that

Jesus is undeniably taught in the New Testament to in some sense manifest God or make God known (John 1:16–18, 14:8–10), but this is compatible with Jesus being a man while not being a god or a divine Person.

Meaning 2 is a special case of meaning 4. The human Jesus of the New Testament is "nontranscendent" (of this world) since he is portrayed as and asserted to be a real man, and one the reader should know (whether or not he existed before his human life) *isn't* also fully divine, since he has many qualities that could not be had by God himself, or by one who is fully divine. The New Testament Jesus dies, gets tired and sleeps, has less than perfect knowledge, is tempted to do wrong, puts his faith or trust in God, prays to God, is worshiped to the glory of God, and his testimony can benefit from confirmation by other testifiers.[123] This makes him, as a human being, fundamentally like those other humans whom Scripture refers to as "God" or "god" or "gods," although of course his calling and status are *far* higher than theirs, or indeed of any other creature. He is called "God" in a *similar* way as ancient kings and people to whom the word of God came, but he, as Messiah, is functionally *much* greater than any of those, having been exalted to God's right hand, so that everything but God is subject to him.[124]

Let's review our results. The trinitarian assumes that her doctrine is supported by the New Testament authors calling Jesus "God" (*theos*). This is supposed to imply Jesus's full deity while not also implying that he is the Father. They need "God" in the New Testament to sometimes mean "divine Person in God." But that is not a New Testament meaning of *theos*. According to the lexicon, there are five meanings of *theos* in the New Testament, and we've seen that one of those should be considered to be a sub-case of another. Meaning 1 isn't relevant to the earliest Christians except when discussing the views of outsiders. Also, one who is "transcendent" or a deity in the sense of meaning 1 need not be fully divine, so this is not what the trinitarian needs. Meaning 5 is also irrelevant; they will not be calling Christ "god" in the sense that Satan is called "the god of this world."

---

no one else can truly be called "savior." Being a unique savior doesn't imply being the unique "savior" (the only one for whom that title can properly be used). Thinking so is an error parallel to supposing that monotheism implies monotheosism.

[123] Respectively: Matt. 27:50; Mark 4:38, 13:32; Matt. 4:8–10; Heb. 2:17, 3:2,6; Luke 5:16; Phil. 2:9–11; John 8:18. None of these texts is unclear in its meaning for any of the reasons we've been considering in this chapter. For many reasons why the New Testament authors think that no real human being can also be fully divine, see my "Nineteen."

[124] Acts 2:32–36, Phil. 2:9–11, Col. 1:15–20, Heb. 1, Rev. 5.

What about meaning 3? The lexicographers stipulate that when *theos* is used of Jesus, this is a different meaning than 3, where it is used of the Father, which is why one of the uses they list is in combinations with "Father";[125] for instance, "according to the will of our God and Father" (Gal. 1:4). Notice that the terms "God" and "Father" here are used in apposition (that is, as two ways to refer to the same one). *Theos* as applied to Christ can't mean 3. This leaves us with meanings 2 and 4. I argued on New Testament grounds that 2 should be viewed as a special case under 4. But no sub-use of meaning 4 can be what the trinitarian wants, as it does not imply full deity.

If this is right, then the trinitarian needs a sense of *theos* that is unrecognized by the leading Greek New Testament lexicon. The usage she needs is an anachronism: a meaning that was unheard-of when these books were written. How can the trinitarian reply? She could argue that the lexicon is leaving out a New Testament meaning of *theos*, but that seems unlikely. The only other reply would be to argue that use 2 is *not* a special case of 4, as I've suggested, but rather assumes that Jesus is divine *in the divine-Person way*, without being divine in the way that implies being the only god (sense 3). For their part, the lexicon authors don't explain this as the meaning of sense 2, and I can't see any way this could be argued. As best I can tell, most trinitarian interpreters simply carry on as is traditional, arguing that Jesus is called *theos* seven or eight times, then asserting (or merely assuming) that this supports the Nicene and later claim that Jesus is fully divine. But the New Testament use of *theos* for Jesus is, as we've seen, *not* the highest or central use of *theos*, and the in-between, lower-than-highest but higher than any "mere man" use that the trinitarian needs is not a recognized use of *theos* in the New Testament.

While it's unlikely anyone is going to find some new meaning of *theos* heretofore unrecognized by the lexicon authors, I shall be so bold as to suggest that the list of meanings could be better organized so that the various uses are more reasonably classified. I've already made one such suggestion. About 1 and 3, there is no need to separate Jewish vs. Gentile usages. In the New Testament era both can and did use *theos* as a title for God understood as in monotheistic religions.[126] And Jews and their fellow travelers are perfectly capable of using *theos* in the more typical Gentile usage, for a mere deity (or alleged deity) that is not a god (not an ultimate deity—Acts 7:40, 14:11, 19:26). It makes more

[125] Danker, BDAG, 399 (3.D).

[126] On pagan monotheism see Athanassiadi and Frede, *Pagan Monotheism*; Chandler, *Constantine*; Maximus of Tyre, *Philosophical*.

sense to separate these uses by their conceptual contents rather than by the crowd in which they were more popular. Thus I suggest the following scheme:

1. a god (that is, a deity who is ultimate, God as conceived in monotheistic religions)
2. a mere deity (that is, a supernaturally powerful self who is not an ultimate, and so not a god)

Meaning 2, in accordance with the Old Testament background of the New Testament and the usage of the Septuagint (reflecting the range of the Hebrew *elohim*), covers angels, demons, and Satan. Again, BDAG's meaning 2 should be considered a special case of their meaning 4. A better approach would be

3. something that is like God in some way(s)

This groups together BDAG's meanings 2, 4, and 5, thus:

3. something that is like God in some way(s)
   a. the human belly (being served by people)
   b. a king of the Jews (ruling God's chosen people in righteousness)
   c. a recipient of God's message (having that message)
   d. God's Messiah, Jesus (being a savior and godlike in his powers, moral qualities, and activities)

Meaning 3d is an extension of meanings 3b and 3c. The New Testament Jesus is a present and future king (Luke 1:32–33, 19:37–38) and he is also a prophet[127] and recipient of God's word.[128] Of course, he is so much more than these, such as the God-appointed future judge of humanity (Acts 17:31, John 5:22–29, Rom. 2:16.), the lamb of God who takes away the sins of the world (John 1:29, 36), and the one Lord under the one God[129] now exalted to God's right hand. He is "the image of God" (2 Cor. 4:4; Col. 1:15). As such he is *much more* similar to God than any of the beings mentioned in 3a–3c, so much so that he says that if you've seen him, you've "seen the Father" (John 14:8–10)—he's the greatest revealer of God to humankind (John 1:18). And yet for all that, he is a real human person, like those called *theoi* (gods) in senses 3b and 3c. Must one who is *theos* in sense 3d also be divine? The entry doesn't say, which is as it should be. A lexicographer's job is to catalogue word meanings, not to decide between competing theological and Christological theories.

---

[127] Matt. 21:11, Mark 6:3–4, Luke 24:19, John 4:43–44.
[128] John 3:33–35, 14:10, 14:24, 17:8, 17:14; Rev. 1:1.
[129] Eph. 1:2-3, 17, 4:4–6; 1 Cor. 8:6, 15:20–28.

Is this use 3d of *theos* for Jesus, as Craig objects, hyperbolic or figurative?[130] One may think it is non-literal, that "god" here is used metaphorically or analogically. When the author calls Jesus *theos* in Hebrews 1:8, is he describing him *as if* he were a god? It seems not. Linguists have long observed the phenomenon of dead metaphors. A good example of this is the current English expression "piece of cake." Presumably once upon a time "piece of cake" was a vivid metaphor; the author was comparing some task to the easy and pleasant activity of eating a piece of cake. But today when an English speaker says that some task is "a piece of cake," that simply means it's easy. The phrase doesn't evoke images of cake consumption in the listener. What was once a metaphor has now become a literal, idiomatic expression. In contrast, if I call someone's naughty four-year-old "a vicious little monster" or a league-leading NFL pass-rusher "an assassin," I am speaking both metaphorically and hyperbolically (as I'm employing extreme exaggeration).

Meaning 3a is a metaphorical usage of *theos*. Just as good people worship and serve God, so these wicked people "worship" and "serve" their own bellies, that is, their own desires—in other words, they do whatever they feel like doing. Meanings 3b–3c are akin to dead metaphors in New Testament times, being long established by their usage in Greek translations of the Hebrew Bible. A primary and popular meaning of *theos* is a deity. A human king is not ordinarily thought to be a deity. (There were, of course, ancient speculations that a nation's deity would in some sense incarnate in its king, but then this would be meaning 2.) But a non-divine king is deity-like in various ways; the country belongs to him, the people must bow to him and obey him, he holds the power of life and death, and he is aloof from the ordinary and hard to access. So presumably at some point some subjects started to metaphorically refer to their king as a *theos* (or as some equivalent title in other languages). This would have been heard as a claim that the king is godlike.

But in New Testament times longstanding scriptures simply authorized addressing or describing a king, at least, of God's chosen people, as *theos*. This doesn't assume the conviction that this king is the one true god or even that he's a mere deity. It's a different use, of something that is in some way(s) godlike—our meaning 3—but it is a literal use, not a metaphorical one.

A trinitarian may complain, in the common parlance, that 3d applied to Christ is "too low"—that is, it doesn't suggest that Jesus is as divine as catholic

[130] Craig, "In Defense," 235.

theology and Christology demand. But the trinitarian can't reasonably object that 3d is either hyperbolic or figurative. It's certainly "higher" than 3b and 3c in that Jesus is *much more* similar to God, more godlike, than those to whom the word *theos* applies in senses 3b or 3c; 3d is just not the meaning for *theos* that the trinitarian needs to support her theology. Sometime in the last thirty years someone coined a new definition for the English verb "to surf," meaning, to browse the internet using a web-browsing computer program. One cannot use this meaning to interpret uses of the verb "to surf" written, say, in the 1960s. The trinitarian's use of "God" to mean "a fully divine Person in God" is like this; that meaning is seen in catholic theologians just before and after the Council of Constantinople in the year 381, but not in New Testament times.

1.6 OLD "LORD" VS. NEW "LORD"

In the Old Testament God has a proper name, written with four Hebrew consonants. In English letters it is "YHWH" or "YHVH." We're not sure how this was originally pronounced. In early modern times many scholars thought the correct pronunciation was "Jehovah," which is still preferred by the Jehovah's Witnesses and others. But more recently the consensus has shifted to "Yahweh." (For some Christians, the correct pronunciation of God's proper name is a matter of controversy; I explain in section 1.8 why I'm not interested in such controversies.) This name is often combined with other titles, such as "Lord Yahweh," "Yahweh-Elohim" (Yahweh-God), and "Yahweh Sabaoth" (Yahweh of Hosts), and many other simple and compound titles are used to refer to him in these books as well.[131]

At some point the view prevailed that it was disrespectful to write or pronounce God's proper name. This is interesting since in the Hebrew Bible the word "Yahweh" occurs frequently, reflecting that in earlier times they had no reservations about using God's proper name. But when it became taboo to write or say this name, they started substituting other spoken and written words for it.[132] Whatever the reason, the same rule was observed by the first century New

---

[131] These are beyond the scope of this chapter. See "Comprehensive Guide" for a good overview of these titles.

[132] Mainly *Adonai*. Later, most Jews decided that *Adonai* was also too holy to use, so it was replaced with *HaShem* ("the Name"). Ancient Christian copies of the Greek Septuagint translation of the Old Testament substituted *kyrios* ("Lord") for the divine name YHWH, but it is less clear whether earlier Jewish copies did this, although the evidence is strong that in this era the divine name was not read aloud (DeLacy, "'One Lord,'" 191–94).

Testament authors and by many Christian translators of the Hebrew Bible since.[133] This is why you may have never encountered the proper name "Yahweh" in your English Bible: that Hebrew name doesn't occur in the Greek New Testament, and most modern translations follow the ancient practice of substituting words for God's Hebrew name in the Old Testament, usually "the LORD." Two major recent translations are exceptions to this rule: the Roman Catholic New Jerusalem Bible and the Protestant Lexham English Bible. I wish that more translations would return to using God's proper name in the Old Testament; it affects the flavor of the texts and, as we will see, can also help to clear up ambiguities.

About ambiguities, we need to discuss "lord," "Lord," "my lord," "the Lord," and "LORD" in English translations of the Old Testament. The words "lord" and "Lord" can translate the singular noun *adon*. This is used primarily of kings and other people worthy of respect, although it can also be used for angels or as a title of God; in English we capitalize it when used of God. The phrase "my lord" translates the word *adoni*, which is *adon* with a singular first-person possessive ending. It is used in addressing one's human superiors. This is to be distinguished from *adonai* (also transliterated as *adonay*). The form of *adonai* is plural, but its use with singular verbs and other words tells us that its meaning is singular. Grammarians call this a "plural of majesty" or "an emphatic plural."[134] The point is to intensify the word when it is used of God rather than of humans or angels. Thus, *adonai* is used only in reference to God. Even though, like *adoni*, it has the possessive ending, in its use as a title of God the "my" drops out, and it is translated as "the Lord" or "Lord."[135] Finally, there is "the LORD," which is neither a translation nor a transliteration but rather an English substitution for God's proper name YHWH. It reflects the ancient practice of pronouncing the Hebrew word *adonai* when encountering the name YHWH in the text.

In New Testament times more Jews read the Old Testament in Greek than in the original Hebrew. In these Greek translations it seems that the proper name "Yahweh" did not appear, and the substitute *adonai* was translated as

---

[133] This rule may have developed as a reaction against magical practices. In many religions people believe they are protected from harm by writing their deity's name on an amulet and carrying it with them. Again, often it is believed that verbally invoking a deity may automatically provide some benefit from him or her.

[134] See p. 3, footnote 6.

[135] It is similar to the English title "my Lord" used in the context of an English court of law. The one using that phrase is only respectfully addressing the judge, not assuming or asserting ownership of that judge.

ho kyrios (the Lord). Old Testament quotations in the New Testament were taken from Greek translations. Thus this linguistic pattern was reflected in the New Testament as well. And so, confusingly, *kyrios* (lord, or a lord, or Lord) and *ho kyrios* (the lord or the Lord) could be used of humans, angels, or God.

Let's turn again to the state-of-the-art New Testament Greek lexicon for a list of uses of the Greek word *kyrios* (lord):

1. "one who is in charge by virtue of possession, owner"
2. "one who is in a position of authority, lord, master"
   a. "of earthly beings, as a designation of any person of high position,"[136]
   b. "of transcendent beings,
      i. as a designation of God"
      ii. "closely connected with the custom of applying the term *kyrios* to deities is that of honoring (deified) rulers with the same title"
      iii. "*kyrios* is also used in reference to Jesus"
         1. "in Old Testament quotations, where it is understood of the Lord of the new community . . . Matt. 3:3; Mark 1:3; Luke 3:4; John 1:23."
         2. "Apart from Old Testament quotations, Matthew and Mark speak of Jesus as *kyrios* only in one passage (words of Jesus himself) Mark 11:3 = Matt. 21:3 . . . but they record that he was addressed as "Lord" . . . once in Mark (7:28) and more often in Matthew . . . Luke refers to Jesus much more frequently as *ho kyrios* ["the Lord"] . . . In John the designation *ho kyrios* occurs rarely . . . On the other hand, [the vocative form] *kurie* in [direct] address is extraordinarily common throughout the whole book . . . more than 30 times"
         3. "Even in the passages already mentioned the use of the word *kyrios* raises Jesus above the human level . . . this tendency becomes even clearer in the following places: *ho kyrios* ["the Lord"] Acts 5:14; 9:10f, 42; 11:23f; 22:10b; Rom. 12:11; 14:8; 1 Cor. 6:13f, 17; 7:10, 12; 2 Cor. 5:6, 8; Gal. 1:19; Col. 1:10; 1 Thess. 4:15b; 2 Thess. 3:1; Heb. 2:3; James 5:7 . . . Without the article: 1 Cor. 4:4; 7:22b; 10:21ab; 2 Cor. 12:1; 1 Thess. 4:15a; 2 Tim. 2:24 . . . So especially in combinations with prepositions"

[136] This is the use of *kyrios* as a form of respectful address to one perceived as of a higher social standing, like the English "sir." The lexicographers give the examples: husband, father, government official, any respected person.

iv. "In some places it is not clear whether God or Christ is meant, compare Acts 9:31; 1 Cor. 4:19; 7:17; 2 Cor. 8:21; Col. 3:22b; 1 Thess. 4:6; 2 Thess. 3:16"

v. "of other transcendent beings"

1. "an angel Acts 10:4"
2. "in contrast to the one *kyrios* of the Christians there are . . . 'many gods and many lords' 1 Cor. 8:5"[137]

What does it mean (2.b.iii) to include Jesus among the "transcendent" beings (2.b.v)? If he is God's human Messiah, does that make him "transcendent"? Or does being "transcendent" require having a divine nature in addition to a human nature? Unfortunately, the term "transcendent" seems chosen precisely because of this ambiguity, as is the phrase "above the human level" in 2.b.3.iii. They're trying to throw a bone to deity of Christ advocates without anachronistically loading later formulations—specifically, "fully divine," "divine nature," "true God from true God"—into their entry, which concerns only New Testament–era usage. But "transcendent" is not a term from that era, nor does it clearly express any concept from that time. "Above the human level" sounds like a suggestion that Jesus being called "Lord" rules out that he is "a mere man" (that he is human but doesn't have a divine nature). But as evidenced by the second- and third-century Dynamic Monarchians, there is nothing about the New Testament uses of "Lord" in reference to Jesus that implies or even obviously suggests that.[138] Later in the chapter I'll propose a better way of organizing these uses that cuts out the unhelpful term "transcendent." But first, let's look at what this entry has right, which is a lot.

Some of today's popular apologists urge that in calling Jesus "Lord," the New Testament authors are calling him "Yahweh," straightforwardly identifying Jesus with the unique God of the Old Testament.[139] But the lexicographers don't suggest this, as they understand the New Testament assumption of the numerical sameness of Yahweh with the Father. Because of this, to identify Jesus with Yahweh would be, for these authors, to identify him with the Father, collapsing the two into one—something they never do. Thus, correctly, the

[137] Danker, BDAG, 511–12, Greek transliterated or translated, abbreviations expanded, words in brackets added for clarity.

[138] For a comprehensive case that these Christians held to the earliest (and New Testament) Christology, see Gaston, *Dynamic Monarchianism*.

[139] That is, not merely closely associating them but rather assuming or asserting their numerical sameness.

lexicographers list no meaning of "Lord" as the equivalent of the Old Testament "Yahweh" as applied to Jesus. They also avoid the simplistic equation of the Greek *kyrios* with the Hebrew YHWH by giving all of their meanings except 2.b.i, and by their recognition that in the New Testament sometimes *kyrios* refers to God and sometimes to Jesus, and in a minority of cases the reader is not sure which is meant (2.b.3.iv).[140]

Further, in 2.b.3.i they recognize a usage of *kyrios* "in Old Testament quotations, where it is understood of the Lord of the new community," that is to say, passages where New Testament authors quote an Old Testament statement about "the Lord" but they mean it of Jesus, not of God, the one Lord *as opposed to* the one God (1 Cor. 8:6; Eph. 4:4–6). Thus, they avoid what I call "the fulfillment fallacy,"[141] where one looks at an Old Testament passage about Yahweh, finds it quoted in the New Testament in reference to Jesus, and concludes that the New Testament author thereby expresses his assumption that Yahweh and Jesus are one and the same. That's a fallacy, in short, because New Testament authors think that scriptural passages can have multiple meanings and fulfillments and that some passages originally about God are now understood to be (also) about God's human Christ.

While this entry is both contentious and unclear in classifying uses of "Lord" for Jesus as one who is "transcendent" and "above the human level," they are surely correct that there are uses of "Lord" for Jesus that are distinct from other uses. Their meanings under 2.b.iii might have been put as a special case of 2.a. After all, whatever else he may be, Jesus is a human being. And it is also clear that these uses are for Jesus *as distinguished from* God.

Why is this clear? Suppose you are talking to a friend after watching your favorite movie together, *The Sound of Music*. You say to your friend, "Tell me a few of *your* favorite things." Your friend replies, "These are my favorite things: my only bat, my New York Yankees baseball cap, my horse Larry, and my only baseball bat." How many things has he just listed, three or four? Did he count his baseball bat twice? Presumably not, unless he's very confused. He must mean

[140] Sometimes the New Testament authors, being aware of the ambiguity of "Lord," will add words to disambiguate it. When the *Shema* is quoted in Mark, "the Lord" clearly refers to Yahweh (Mark 12:29–30). Even in Peter's sermon in Acts 2, he speaks of "the Lord our God" (Acts 2:39)—obviously Yahweh/the Father/God, not Jesus. Notice that in both of these instances, the authors add the phrase "our God" or "your God" to disambiguate the term *kyrios*, making sure the reader knows which "Lord" they mean.

[141] Chapter 10.

"bat" in some other sense (perhaps he has a pet horse *and* a pet bat). You assume that your friend is not double counting any of his favorite things but is naming four things, not three, because generally someone would not speak that way.

The apostle Paul names a few of his favorite things in Ephesians 4. He is emphasizing things all Christians have in common, uniting believers regardless of their differences. Churches, which were just house churches at that time, had been founded by different apostles, and some were quite proud of their founder: Peter, Paul, Apollos, etc. This led to rivalries among them. Furthering the tendency toward division, each church likely had different parts of the New Testament at different times, since the canon had not yet been standardized, and in Paul's time it may be that not all of those books were yet written. To counter these dividing tendencies, in his letters Paul would remind the believers of all the things they had in common. Here Paul reminds us that "there is one body and one Spirit, just as you were called to the one hope of your calling, one Lord, one faith, one baptism, one God and Father of all, who is above all and through all and in all" (Eph. 4:4–6). In counting both "one Lord" and "one God and Father of all," does Paul name the same thing twice? Did he double count one Lord who is none other than the one God? If we are reading charitably, we assume not, just as you assume your friend is not accidentally double counting his baseball bat.

Suppose a family of four—a husband, a wife, and two children—sends Christmas cards to all their friends and family. Imagine that you receive a card, and it says, "Merry Christmas from Bob and Sally, Chester, Lulu, and Mrs. Johnson." The only problem here is that Sally *is* Mrs. Johnson; she is Bob's current wife. You would not expect them, in sending their greetings, to deliberately double count, mentioning the same person twice. An inscription like this would mislead some into thinking that Mrs. Johnson is someone other than Sally Johnson.

Keeping this in mind, examine the beginning of each letter attributed to Paul in the New Testament. In each he sends greetings from two. For example,

> "Grace to you and peace from God our Father and the Lord Jesus Christ, who gave himself for our sins to set us free from the present evil age, according to the will of our God and Father, to whom be the glory forever and ever. Amen" (Gal. 1:3–5).

A greeting sent from two presupposes that they are numerically two beings. Elsewhere Paul writes, "for us there is one God, the Father, from whom are all things and for whom we exist, and one Lord, Jesus Christ, through whom are all things and through whom we exist" (1 Cor. 8:6). Notice the "and" (*kai*) between these two clauses; this "and" would be out of place if Paul was merely calling God by two different titles. "Lord" in such passages doesn't refer to God (a.k.a. "the Father," "Yahweh"); it must mean someone in addition to him. We ought not read these authors uncharitably, as confusedly double counting. Nor can "the one God" and "the one Lord" be two "divine Persons" in the Trinity; this is an idea from the fourth century and later, which has no place in interpreting New Testament texts.

There is one Lord, a unique Lord, in the New Testament, but he is someone in addition to the unique God.[142] To put it differently, the Old Testament "Lord" is Yahweh, the one God, but the "Lord" in the New Testament is Jesus. There is *not* a unique "Lord" in the New Testament, as that title is commonly applied to two different beings: God and his human Son and Messiah. But there is a unique *Lord*, a unique human ruler under God. And of course God himself is a *top-level* Lord, also unique.

It is surprising that "Lord" (Greek: *kyrios*)—the word in this time most often substituted for the divine name by Greek-speaking Jews—should come to also be used for the man Jesus. Is this these authors' way of hinting that Jesus "is Yahweh"—that is, the same self as him, or that Jesus is one of three divine Persons in some sense "in" God? The first is a confusion that the New Testament authors never fall into, and the second is a clear anachronism and therefore a clear misinterpretation.

The key to understanding why "Lord" came to be used as the main title for Jesus is an Old Testament text that the early Christians took to be a prophecy about the post-resurrection exaltation of Jesus: Psalm 110:1. Originally this seems to have been a coronation psalm for one of the kings of Israel, or at any rate it is clear that it was addressed to a king who in some sense served in a priestly function too.[143] Hebrews 7 teaches this to be a prophecy that was fulfilled in Jesus. Translated from the Hebrew, the opening of the Psalm says, "The LORD says to my Lord, 'Sit at my right hand until I make your enemies your footstool'" (110:1). Here Yahweh (the LORD) addresses *adoni* (my Lord). The latter referred to the lord of the writer, the human king. God is telling the king to sit at his right hand. The idea is that this was *God's* throne over his chosen

[142] Dunn observes that "Paul speaks of God . . . as 'the *God* of our *Lord* Jesus Christ' [Eph. 1:17. Cf. 2 Cor. 1:3] . . . the *kyrios* title is not so much a way of *identifying* Jesus with God, as a way of *distinguishing* Jesus from God" (*Did the First*, 110, original emphases).

[143] "The LORD has sworn and will not change his mind, 'You are a priest forever according to the order of Melchizedek' " (Ps. 110:4).

people Israel, and thus God was the one who was really enthroning the king. In a sense, the king gained God's authority by ruling over the nation. This passage is quoted in the earliest recorded Christian sermon, as summarized by Luke, where Peter says, "The Lord says to my Lord, 'Sit at my right hand until I make your enemies your footstool'" (Acts 2:34b–35).

Recall that the name "Yahweh" does not appear in the New Testament; Luke here thus quotes from a Greek Old Testament translation that does not use it. Instead "*the* Lord" (*ho kyrios*) is God and "*my* Lord" (*kyrio mou*) is Jesus. This same verse is quoted or referred to more than twenty times in the New Testament. The early Christians believed it to be fulfilled in the exaltation of Jesus portrayed in Revelation 5; this is all the justification they needed to use *kyrios* in a new way, as a title for Jesus.

The very next verse of Peter's sermon states, "Therefore, let the entire house of Israel know with certainty that God has made him both Lord and Messiah, this Jesus whom you crucified" (Acts 2:36). This is the climax of Peter's message, and many of the hearers respond, becoming followers of Jesus. The word "Lord" cannot mean Yahweh in this context because someone cannot be made Yahweh by Yahweh; Yahweh eternally and necessarily *just is* Yahweh! But Jesus is made to be "both Lord and Messiah" by Yahweh, the Lord. He is made to be, as the lexicon entry says, "one who is in a position of authority, lord, master." For the New Testament authors, this man has been put in charge of the rest of creation and of the church. This theme of Jesus's post-resurrection exaltation to God's right hand is a prominent theme of the New Testament, although it has often been neglected due to traditional speculations about "the deity of Christ."

There is a sophistical argument about the term "Lord" that is continually passed around among recent apologists:

1. In the New Testament "the Lord" is sometimes used to translate (or more precisely, as a substitute for) the Hebrew name "Yahweh."
2. In the New Testament, Jesus himself says that "the Lord our God, the Lord is one" (Mark 12:29), quoting the ancient Jewish Shema.
3. Yet Paul teaches in 1 Corinthians 8:6 that Jesus is the "one Lord."
4. Therefore, in the New Testament, Jesus just is Yahweh, and vice versa.[144]

[144] Some will instead infer that Jesus is a "divine Person" who is somehow "in" God, but this no more follows from 1–3 than does 4 above, and the divine-Person concept (where this is something less than a god) is alien to and later than the New Testament.

The argument is invalid; the conclusion 4 does not follow from the truth of premises 1–3. Given that both God and his human Son are called "Lord" and "one," it cannot be concluded that they are the same being, since, as we've seen, the title "Lord" is ambiguous in the New Testament.

An example may help to illustrate the invalidity of the argument (that its conclusion doesn't follow from its premises). Both Bruce Springsteen and the manager of your local automotive garage can be called "the Boss." If we call Springsteen "the Boss" or "the only Boss," and we call the garage manager "the Boss" or "the only Boss," does this imply that Springsteen just is the garage manager and vice versa? Clearly not. There are obvious differences between Springsteen and the garage manager; these show us that they are different individuals even though the title "the Boss" is used to refer to each of them. Even in calling each "the only Boss," our point is almost never that *the word* "Boss" can only apply to him. Rather, we are asserting for each, in his own context, some kind of uniqueness in respect of bosshood. Perhaps Springsteen, as "the only Boss" is unique among classic rock artists, whereas "the only Boss" of your local garage is unique in being the owner and manager of that shop.

There are several clear differences between the old "Lord" and the new "Lord" in the New Testament. First, the former is explicitly the god over the latter (John 20:17, Eph. 1:17, Rev. 3:12). The old "Lord" (God/Yahweh/the Father) necessarily has no god over him, is inevitably provident over all else (if there is anything else), and can't die. Thus, the Lord God was never raised from the dead or exalted to the highest position under God but is eternally immortal and has enjoyed the highest position as ruler of the cosmos for as long as there has been a cosmos. In contrast, the new "Lord" is under God, and this new "Lord" did die and was then raised from the dead and exalted by God. Although he has now been made immortal, he was not always so, as evidenced by his real death. These are *clear* New Testament teachings, not inferred from controversial interpretations or complex arguments.[145]

---

[145] "Blessed be the God and Father of our Lord Jesus Christ . . . [I pray that] that the God of our Lord Jesus Christ, the Father of glory, may give you a spirit of wisdom and revelation as you come to know him, so that, with the eyes of your heart enlightened, you may know what is the hope to which he has called you, what are the riches of his glorious inheritance among the saints, and what is the immeasurable greatness of his power for us who believe, according to the working of his great power. God put this power to work in Christ when he raised him from the dead and seated him at his right hand in the heavenly places" (Eph. 1:3a, 17–20).

Finally, I suggest the following as a more logically organized framework for classifying meanings for *kyrios* in the New Testament:

1. one who is in charge by virtue of possession, owner
2. one who is in a position of authority, lord, master
    a. a designation of God
    b. a designation of any mere deity
        i. pagan deity
        ii. deified human ruler
        iii. angel
    c. a designation of any human person deserving respect because of their societal position
        i. a polite term of address, roughly equivalent to the English "sir"
        ii. a human who must be respected because of familial relations, such as a husband, father
        iii. a high but not top-level government official
        iv. a top-level human leader such as a king, queen, or emperor
        v. a designation of Jesus, expressing that he (1) was destined to be, and/or (2) now is, as the Messiah, the greatest human king and the highest ruler under God, now exalted to God's right hand and ruling in godlike position and power, reflecting uses 1 (inheritor of God's kingdom), and all of 2.a–c above.
            1. in Old Testament quotations, where it is understood of the Lord of the new community, that is, not Yahweh but rather Jesus, the Son of God.
            2. as a title of Jesus or a term of direct address (vocative form) to him in the New Testament Gospels, alone ("Lord") or in combinations ("Lord Jesus Christ," "Lord Jesus").

This adds 2.c.iii for completeness and captures all the BDAG meanings except their 2.b.iv, which is simply the failure to be clear about whether one is using meaning (in my numbering) 2.a or 2.c.v. Gone is the useless term "transcendent" and the vague phrase "above the human level." This way of organizing the meanings brings out the fact that the New Testament use of *kyrios* for Jesus, while a new and distinctive usage, is one that builds on or extends out from most of the previous uses, with 2.c.i–ii being the least relevant. Most specifically, the new Jesus usage builds off 2.c.iv since Jesus is literally destined to be the greatest of human kings.

If one wanted to organize the versions of meaning 2 according to "height" of position, then the Jesus uses would come directly after 2.a above, just under

God and over all the others. After all, even God's angels must worship him (Heb. 1:6), and certainly must any other unseen beings and any (even allegedly deified) human rulers. Does usage 2.c.v presuppose that Jesus is "more than a man," that he is not only human but also divine? The entry doesn't say either way, which is as it should be, for that is a matter of interpretation and not something for lexicographers to decide. The entry quite properly brings out that "Lord" is a title that applies to Jesus in virtue of his authoritative position, under God but over every other human ruler.

1.7 TWO LINGUISTIC PROPOSALS TO REDUCE GOD-JESUS AMBIGUITIES

In this section I offer a couple of linguistic suggestions to increase the clarity of Christian discourse about God and his Son in theology, preaching, and worship. In all of these realms God-Jesus confusions are undesirable. As things stand, Christians usually follow the New Testament practice of using "the Lord" most often for Jesus, but in our singing and preaching, we often quote the Psalms or other Old Testament texts that mention "the Lord" (or "the LORD") meaning God (a.k.a. the Father). This often leads to confusion, especially among the less educated. They confuse together the old "Lord" with the new "Lord," something the New Testament authors, and fully informed believers nowadays, never do.

But we can reduce this confusion by following the New Testament's preference for "the Lord" being the unique, human Son of God. We can further reduce the confusion of God with his Son by being even a little more scrupulous than the New Testament authors about reserving the title "Lord" for Jesus. After all, we have plenty of perfectly good titles that we can reserve only for God in addition to his proper name, such as "the Father," "God the Father," "the Almighty,"[146] and "God." Instead of "the Lord," let's call God "God," "the Father," "God the Father," "our Father," and "Yahweh" (or your preferred pronunciation of that name). Most modern Christians do not find it disrespectful to use God's proper name since nowadays these names are not generally misused for making oaths[147] or in attempts to work magic. We observe our Old Testament–era Jewish forerunners using this proper name for

[146] As Samuel Clarke pointed out, the title *pantocrator* (Almighty) is used in the New Testament only for the Father and never for anyone else (*Scripture Doctrine*, 31 [sec. 414]).

[147] This would violate the clear teaching of our Lord Jesus in Matt. 5:33–37, passed down by his half-brother in James 5:12.

God for centuries in the hundreds of occurrences of "LORD" or "Yahweh," depending on the Old Testament translation we're using. If this was permissible for them, why would it be impermissible for us?

Some Christians refrain from using God's name when interacting with non-Christian Jews, or because they have adopted the ancient scruple against using this name. In those instances, I would suggest using "the Lord," "the Lord Jesus," or "the Lord Jesus Christ" for God's Son and "the Lord *God*" for his and our god.

1.8 THE "CORRECT NAME" DISTRACTION

There are some Christians today who suppose that God demands (or at least strongly prefers) that we use his proper Hebrew name YHWH—and that it must be pronounced in a specific, correct way. This reminds me of when I was a professor of philosophy, teaching an Introduction to Philosophy course. Among the students was a young lady from China, a diligent student who always attended class and took copious notes. One day she raised her hand to ask me a question, and I couldn't help but notice that she couldn't properly pronounce "Dr. Tuggy." I responded firmly: "Say my name *correctly*!" She tried again, with the same botched result. I yelled at her, "Are you an ignoramus? You can't say *Dr. TUH-gee*?! Is that *hard* for you?" I glared silently at her, refusing to help her until she pronounced my name properly. She looked as if she were about to cry, but at least I made it clear to all present that my name must be pronounced using the correct, North American accent.

Thankfully, this story is fictitious. I'm not such an arrogant and heartless person that I would refuse to interact with someone who couldn't pronounce my name the way I'm accustomed to. But if I, being such a limited and flawed person, would never dream of treating a student in this way, surely the perfect God, our caring Father, is not a stickler for his Hebrew name or its correct pronunciation (whatever that is). We should not think that God cares much about whether you use an ancient Hebrew word to refer to or address him. If he did care, then why does the name YHWH appear nowhere in the Greek New Testament? The authors could have used Hebrew letters or transliterated their sounds using Greek letters, but they did neither.

We should instead think that our Father in heaven delights in the many ways the world's tribes pronounce his name or use their own distinctive words for him, such as *Dios*, *Gott*, or even *Allah*.[148] In my view, there is nothing wrong with calling God whatever is conventional in the human language you are using. Nor, I suggest, does our Lord Jesus care whether you refer to him as Jesus, *Yehoshua*, *Yeshua*, *Iesous*, *Jesu*, *Isa*, etc. Don't *you* enjoy how people with various accents say your name? I do! When my friends from the southern United States pronounce my name "Del," to me that's just part of their charm, as when an Irish classmate used to pronounce "Dale" with a musical lilt that is so beautiful that I can't reproduce it. These little things are endearing. Why should things be otherwise for Jesus and God? We should not obsess about names or think that we're more dear to God or to his Son because we know, as it were, some secret code words of which the masses are ignorant. Our special access to God is provided by our being "in Christ,"[149] as Paul says, not by the use of a special name for him.

1.9 POSTBIBLICAL USES OF BIBLICAL WORDS

Thus far the conclusions drawn in this chapter have been positive. In most cases, the meaning of the words "god" and "lord" in the Bible, despite the ambiguities, can be understood relatively easily by paying attention to the context. Yet this is not always the case; there is no easy way to sort out some of the ambiguities we'll discuss in this section, ones that developed in postbiblical Christian theology.

As we've seen, the word "God" in the New Testament almost always refers to the Father, and the context of each instance makes that clear—it is the Father unless the context rules him out as the referent. As we noted in section 1.4, in the New Testament, somewhere between zero and eight times (depending on the correct Greek text and its translation and interpretation), "god" or "God" refers to the Son. Some people think that once or twice "God" refers to the Spirit (Acts 5:3–4). The words we translate as "God" never mean the Trinity in the Bible. All things considered, the term *theos* is only *slightly* ambiguous in the New Testament; we can be sure who it refers to more than 99% of the time.

But as Christian history progressed, word usage evolved along with catholic theologies, and "God" became much more ambiguous. The well-known "Athanasian" Creed (c. fifth century CE) states that "the Father is God, the Son

---

[148] *Allah* is the equivalent in Arabic of the Koine Greek *ho theos* (the god, "God"); it was used for God before the advent of Islam and still sometimes today (Priest, "Wheaton," 3). Pointing this out doesn't presuppose any answer to the disputed question about whether Christians and Muslims worship the same god, on which see my "Podcast 122."

[149] Rom. 3:32, 6:11, 6:23, 8:1, 12:5, 15:17; 1 Cor. 1:4, 1:30, 15:22; 2 Cor. 1:21, 5:17; Gal. 1:22, 2:4, 3:26, 3:28, 5:6; Eph. 1:11, 2:10, 2:13, 4:32.

God, and the Holy Spirit God; and yet there are not three Gods, but there is one God."[150] If the phrase "is God" is not shorthand for "has the divine nature" but rather "God" here is a singular referring term rather than a description, the word "God" is used four different ways in this one sentence. That is, the four occurrences of "God" here refer, respectively, to the Father, the Son, the Holy Spirit, and God the Trinity. These four meanings are all still widely used.

Usage of the word "God" varies in different times and places and among various groups of Christians. Sometimes the biblical pattern of god-talk is observed (where "God" is usually the Father), but then again, often "God" has become a title for the imagined triune god of catholic orthodoxy. Very often both usages are, confusingly, jumbled together, such as in Anglican or Catholic liturgies.

Unfortunately, this increase in ambiguity is not unique. Another example is the phrase "true God." It appears in both testaments. The prophet Azariah prophesies to King Asa, saying,

> The LORD is with you while you are with him. If you seek him, he will be found by you, but if you abandon him, he will abandon you. For a long time Israel was without the true God and without a teaching priest and without law, but when in their distress they turned to the LORD, the God of Israel, and sought him, he was found by them. (2 Chr. 15:2b–4)

Here the "true God" is Yahweh, the only god. Jeremiah uses this phrase in the same way, to contrast Yahweh with the idols of the Gentiles:

> [The idols of the nations] are both stupid and foolish . . . they are all the product of skilled workers. But the LORD is the true God; he is the living God and the everlasting King. (Jer. 10:8a, 10)

The phrase "true God" is also found in the New Testament. In the High Priestly Prayer, Jesus says, "Father . . . glorify your Son . . . And this is eternal life, that they may know you, the only true God, and Jesus Christ, whom you have sent" (John 17:1b, 3). Here "true God" clearly refers to the Father, who is assumed to be the same one as Yahweh from the Old Testament. Similarly, the apostle Paul celebrates how Gentile believers have

> turned to God from idols to serve a living and true God and to wait for his Son from Heaven, whom he raised from the dead—Jesus, who rescues us from the coming wrath" (1 Thess. 1:9–10).

[150] *Athanasian Creed*, 18 (15–16).

It is clear that the "living and true God," in other words, the only real god, as contrasted with the dead idols constructed to represent fictional deities, is the one who has a Son: the Father. Finally, in 1 John we read,

> And we know that the Son of God has come and has given us understanding so that we may know him who is true; and we are in him who is true, in his Son Jesus Christ. He is the true God and eternal life. (1 John 5:20).

As we saw,[151] in 1 John 5 the phrase "him who is true" refers to the Father, the one who has a Son, Jesus Christ, and the Father is also apparently being referred to in the latter portion of the passage as "the true God."

While in the Bible the "true God" is always the Father (Yahweh), again, word usage grew more complex as Christian history and theology progressed. The creed approved by an emperor-convened council of catholic bishops at Nicaea in 325 CE reads in part:

> We believe in one God the Father all powerful, maker of things both seen and unseen. And in one Lord Jesus Christ, the Son of God, the only-begotten begotten from the Father, that is from the substance of the Father, God from God, light from light, true God from true God, begotten, not made, consubstantial with the Father.[152]

After the creed was first drafted in 325, mainstream Christians spent decades debating whether to use this new and ambiguous language.[153] It was and is unclear what that language meant. But they were clear that both Father and Son were supposed to be "true God." Thus, a term that wasn't ambiguous in the Bible was made to be so.[154]

Even the phrase "the Father" has become more ambiguous over time. In the New Testament, "the Father" is used interchangeably with "God" as two ways of speaking about the same one. The New Testament authors stylistically swap them just for the sake of variation. A text reads better with a mix of referring

---

[151] Section 1.4.8.

[152] "Profession," 5. Confusingly, a different but similar creed ratified in 381 at a council in Constantinople is nowadays commonly called "the Nicene Creed" (Tanner, "Exposition of the 150 Fathers," 24).

[153] For an overview of this lengthy and complex series of disputes see my "Exposing."

[154] Worse, the phrase seems inconsistent with the monotheism affirmed at the start of the creed, where it states the only god and creator is the Father. Presumably one who can truly be called "true God" is a god, so the Father is a god and the Son is a god. These can't be the same god, as they are numerically distinct (Sections 8.3.2, 8.3.4). This is why in the ensuing decades-long controversy many mainstream Christians objected to this creed as implying the falsity of monotheism.

terms than with one used repeatedly. To illustrate, if one is composing an article about Donald Trump, one wouldn't refer to him as "Donald Trump" every time he is mentioned. The author might begin with "Donald Trump," then switch perhaps to "Mr. Trump," "Trump," "the president," and so on. That is what the author of the Fourth Gospel is doing in the following passage. Notice how he switches back and forth between the co-referring terms "God" and "the Father":

> [Jesus said:] "It is written in the prophets, 'And they shall all be taught by *God*.' Everyone who has heard and learned from *the Father* comes to me. Not that anyone has seen *the Father* except the one who is from *God*; he has seen *the Father*." (John 6:45–46, emphases added)

If every instance of "the Father" in this verse were changed to "God" or vice versa, the meaning would be the same, since the Father and the unique God are supposed to be one and the same. The two terms are switched because such variation is better style.

In later usage "the Father" sometimes still meant the one God. But after the trinitarian creeds were developed in the 300s, "the Father" was also meant to be a Person *within* the one God. Therefore, from that time forward, the term "Father" could either mean God (as in the New Testament) or *someone within* the one God (as in trinitarian theology). Again, an important biblical term had been made more ambiguous. Theology "advances" in a catholic direction at the expense of clarity of terms. And in prayer nowadays, one will hear Jesus addressed as "Father," and the Father addressed as "Jesus," the assumption being that these are one and the same, contrary to the New Testament.[155]

The New Testament uses Greek phrases we translate as "God the Father" roughly eighteen times and "God our Father" around eleven times. There are additional instances where "God" and "Father" occur in close proximity, reflecting the assumption that God and the Father are one and the same. In postbiblical theology, "God the Son," "God the Spirit," and "God the Trinity" were introduced in addition to "God the Father." These new phrases do not appear in the New Testament. They became popular largely due to the creeds, although arguably the first expansion of Christian god-talk occurred in the mainstream, almost-all-Gentile churches of the 100s, when terms like "God" and "our God" were commonly applied by some to Jesus.

---

[155] Compare with the comments of eminent New Testament scholar James Dunn about Christian worship of Jesus and the danger of "Jesus-olatry" in his *Did the First*, 146–47.

1.10 NEW POSTBIBLICAL WORDS

Mainstream Christian tradition hasn't only coined new meanings for biblical terms; it has also introduced new and allegedly improved terminology. In my view, there is nothing wrong, generally speaking, with using non-biblical terms in theology, such as "omniscient," "omnibenevolent," and "omnipresent." Such post-biblical terms earn their keep by their clarity and usefulness. It is problematic, however, when new terms are ambiguous and thus confusing. The following subsections examine the ambiguities of several post–New Testament terms that continue to resist uniform understanding, even among today's most informed trinitarian scholars.

1.10.1 "TRINITY"

In the last quarter of the 100s, some mainstream, probably highly-educated Christians—seemingly in imitation of the triads of transcendent beings popular in Platonic philosophies of the time—began to use the Greek word *trias* and the Latin word *trinitas*. But those terms did not function as they usually do now.

To understand the difference, consider the fictional superheroes Batman and Robin, who collectively have the nickname "The Dynamic Duo." If someone asks which one of them is "The Dynamic Duo," this is a confused question; neither the middle-aged man in the costume nor the kid in the short-sleeved outfit is himself "The Dynamic Duo." It's a *plural* referring term, referring to the two of them together. Now imagine that the creators of Batman and Robin decide the franchise needs a refresh and that Batman and Robin, as separate characters, should be replaced by a new character, "Batman-Robin," a single person with the combined powers of both original superheroes. If this new superhero Batman-Robin is still called "The Dynamic Duo," that phrase changes from a plural referring term to a singular referring term. If this happened, it would initially confuse the fans. Does "The Dynamic Duo" now refer to Batman *and* to Robin, or to Batman-Robin?

The words we translate as "the Trinity" (Greek, *he trias*; Latin, *trinitas*) are like "the Dynamic Duo." The first known use of the Greek *trias* dates to around 180 CE.[156] It was coined as a plural referring term to mean a triad of three beings, namely God, God's Son or his *Logos* (Word), and God's Spirit. Referring to such

[156] Theophilus of Antioch, *Autolycus*, 52 (2.15). So far is this ancient bishop from being trinitarian that a prominent patristic scholar has argued that he was actually a Dynamic Monarchian (Grant, *Greek Apologists*, ch. 19; *Jesus*, ch. 5).

a triad does not presuppose that they are one being or that they are equal in status. Typically these early theologians thought that the Father was greater than the other two (only the Father is all-knowing and all-powerful, only the Father is eternal, only the Father is perfectly good or good through himself or independently of any other, only the Father is fully divine, and this through himself or independently, whereas the others are only divine to some extent somehow because of him).

All the uses of this term from the late 100s through the early 300s CE carried this meaning. The one God (the Father) was the founder and the greatest *member of* this triad of beings; you would have received a blank stare if you asked who or which one being "the Trinity" referred to. This would have been like asking which superhero is "the Dynamic Duo," given actual Batman lore. But as theology developed, the term "Trinity" came to refer to the one God, who *somehow* consists of the Father, Son, and Holy Spirit, all of whom share the divine nature or essence.[157]

This is still confusing because the word's older meaning was never phased out; the new meaning was simply added to it, often making it unclear which meaning is intended. You may hear a Christian theologian claim that "the Trinity is everywhere in the Bible." If the word "Trinity" here is being used to mean the triad (God, God's Son, and God's Spirit or spirit), then the statement is correct (making allowance for the exaggeration "everywhere") since in many places one or more of these is mentioned. But if the term "Trinity" in our theologian's statement means the triune God, then his statement is false, as that isn't mentioned anywhere in the Bible—because in those times there was no term or phrase that was understood to refer to the triune God. Since "the Trinity" came to be used for the one God, it has become ambiguous between a triad that includes God and a triune god that *just is* (supposedly) God. In other words, "Trinity" is now used as a plural referring term for three but also as a singular referring term for one. This is one of the most central confusions in Christian theology, and it's one that some trinitarian theologians find useful, as it enables them to give the impression that something that is never mentioned in the Bible (the triune god) is mentioned all over the Bible (as is the aforementioned triad).

[157] For this crucial switch in the history of Christian theology see my "When and How."

Sir Isaac Newton's younger friend Samuel Clarke famously published *The Scripture-Doctrine of the Trinity* (1712).[158] This was a unitarian book that landed him in hot water as an Anglican minister, and it was attacked by a host of polemical authors as "Arian" heresy.[159] In the book Clarke uses "Trinity" to mean the triad of God, the Son of God, and the Spirit of God. Earlier, the English unitarian John Biddle had published *A Confession of Faith: Touching The Holy Trinity, According to Scripture* (1648)[160] and was jailed for it.[161] Here too we have the word "Trinity" being used not as a singular referring term for the triune or tripersonal God, but rather as a plural referring term for a triad or triple of beings, one of whom is the one God, the Father.

Why did unitarians like Biddle and Clarke use the word "Trinity"? Were they trying to disguise their beliefs, fooling their readers into thinking they were orthodox? Not at all. They used "Trinity" in this sense because some pre-Nicene Christian writers did, and these early modern authors were well-versed in the mainstream Christian theological writings which have survived from the first three centuries.[162] One of Clarke's favorite authors was Origen of Alexandria (c. 185–253), a brilliant and influential scholar who probably wrote hundreds of books, several of which still survive in part or whole. He died due to injuries sustained while being tortured for his faith during the persecution of Christians in the reign of the Roman emperor Decius (r. 249–51).[163] The martyr Pamphilus (d. 310) wrote a book called *Apology for Origen* to defend Origen from his postmortem critics. Notice how he describes Origen's "Trinity":

---

[158] The first edition was published in 1712 but the final and most authoritative edition is the posthumous fourth edition of 1738 in his complete works (*Scripture-Doctrine*).

[159] For the story see Ferguson, *Samuel Clarke*; Pfizenmaier, *Trinitarian Theology*; Whiston, *Historical Memoirs*. Clarke denied being an "Arian," as his views were inspired not by anything Arius or the fourth-century so-called "Arians" wrote but rather by mainstream theologians writing before the fourth century, such as Tertullian, Origen, and Novatian. While Clarke did believe in the prehuman existence of Jesus and in the Spirit as a self in addition to God and his Son, Clarke's book has rightly been recognized by later Christians as unitarian because of his central thesis that the one God and the Father are one and the same, together with his recognition that the idea of a tripersonal god is absent from Scripture. Clarke did not use the term "unitarian" of himself, as for him that recently coined word was a synonym for "Socinian," roughly, a unitarian who doesn't believe in the literal pre-existence of Jesus.

[160] Biddle, *Confession of Faith*.

[161] Tragically, John Biddle died from a disease he caught while imprisoned (Toulmin, *Review*, 100).

[162] See Lamson, *Church*. For Biddle's engagement with various pre-Nicene theologians, see his *Testimonies*.

[163] Trigg, *Origen*, 241–43; Eusebius of Caesarea, *Church History*, 234 [6.39].

> But let us move on to [Origen's] particular understanding of . . . the holy and blessed Trinity, that is, concerning the Father and the Son and the Holy Spirit . . . This is Origen's faith concerning the highest realities, that is, concerning the Holy Trinity.[164]

For Origen, the Father, Son, and Spirit are the "highest realities," that is to say, the three greatest beings, with God being the greatest, the Logos or Word (divine Son) of John 1 the second greatest, and the Spirit the third greatest. For him, as for other early adopters, "Trinity" was a plural referring term. Nowadays it would be more clearly translated as "triad."

In sum, when someone is discussing "the Trinity," we need to determine whether he means the triad of God (a.k.a. the Father), the Son, and the Spirit (however those are related) or rather the triune God posited by catholic theologies since the late fourth century. We could avoid this ambiguity by (contra Biddle and Clarke) using "Trinity" only as a singular referring term for the alleged triune god of orthodox theologies and the plural referring term "triad" for the Father, Son, and Spirit mentioned in the New Testament—whether or not these are supposed to be somehow all together the one God.

1.10.2 "PERSON," "ESSENCE"

Since the 381 Council of Constantinople the required trinitarian language has been that the Trinity in some sense "is" or consists of three *hypostases* (a Greek term usually translated as "Persons") with or in one *ousia* (essence, substance, or being). This does little to clarify the doctrine since these are technical, philosophical terms that have been used in many ways.[165] Unfortunately, this standard language about the triune God does not convey any one theology; different scholars mean different things even when using these same words. Some think that the three "Persons" are three beings (intelligent agents, selves, persons), while others think they are instead something like three personalities, or aspects, or ways that God lives—at any rate, not three beings. This is a very complex subject that we can't pursue further here.[166]

---

[164] Pamphilus, *Apology for Origen*, 61, 81 (secs. 38, 85). We'll look more closely at Origen's views in sections 1.11 and 7.4.

[165] On the many things that these might mean, see my *What is the Trinity*, chs. 6–7.

[166] For a survey of the many clashing Trinity theories articulated by recent analytic theologians, see my "Trinity."

1.11 MAKING SON-TERMS AMBIGUOUS

The terms "Jesus," "Messiah," and "the Son of God" in the New Testament are obviously co-referring terms, ways to refer to exactly one individual. About his own Gospel, John writes, "These are written so that you may come to believe that Jesus is the Messiah, the Son of God" (John 20:31). This is his thesis statement, the main point of his Gospel. "Jesus," "the Messiah," and "Son of God" are all used to refer to one and the same man, the star of this book. The other Gospels have the same central thesis. Mark, the earliest, begins with "The beginning of the good news of Jesus Christ, the Son of God" (1:1). This is clearly intended to be one character, not two. The high point of Matthew's Gospel occurs when Peter confesses, "You are the Messiah, the Son of the living God" (16:16). Again, it's clear that just one person is being described.

In Superman lore there are many names for Superman. His original name, given on his home planet, Krypton, was "Kal-El." He is also sometimes called "the Man of Steel." If someone were to say, "I like Superman, but I don't really like the Man of Steel," you would assume she didn't pay very close attention when reading the comics or seeing the movies. To think that Superman is one character and the Man of Steel is another is a mistake. It is just as obvious a mistake when reading the New Testament to think that Jesus is one character and the Christ is another.

Yet that mistake was repeatedly made in post–New Testament times. Some of the second-century Gnostics got the ball rolling by distinguishing the man Jesus from the Christ, the latter being an "aeon" or minor deity who abandoned Jesus at the crucifixion, hence Jesus's cry—it was thought, addressing that aeon—"My God, my God, why have you forsaken me?" (Mark 15:34).[167] Possibly influenced by them, or trying to one-up them—it must be remembered that in these decades many Gnostics participated in mainstream churches—the so-called "Logos theologians," beginning with Justin Martyr, distinguished between Jesus and the Word (Greek: *logos*) referenced in John 1:1: "In the beginning was the Word, and the Word was with God, and the Word was God." They read this as teaching that the Word was divine and that he was with God as one someone is with another. Thus he must be a divine being in addition to the Father, another "God."[168]

It seems that many naively believed we can detect both gods and humans by looking for their typical actions or the results of those actions. Thus, they

[167] Ehrman, *Lost Christianities,* 125.

[168] For why this is mistaken, see my opening statement in Tuggy and White, *John 1 Is Not.*

reasoned that Jesus's life showed the telltale signs of a god, such as miracles and divine teachings.[169] If one accepts such arguments, one may also reason that some of Jesus's other actions show the presence of a vulnerable man who is hungry, tired, worried, who needs sleep, and who can be killed. Thus, one concludes, there is New Testament evidence of a god and a man there—there *really* are two in what appears in the narratives as one self. These are shoddy arguments, but in fact this is what "two natures" originally meant, before the Chalcedonian "clarification" that there is one "Person" here.[170] The "two natures" were the Logos and the man.

So for the extremely influential Christian scholar Origen, the divine Logos is someone, and the man Jesus is someone else.[171] This is not always evident to readers, as Origen convinced himself that the Logos and the man Jesus are so functionally unified that they should be talked about *as if* they were one and the same—and so Origen does. But when you dig deeply into his works, you find that he believes in a narrative that we can summarize like this:

> Once upon a time, all human souls were without bodies. God awarded the most virtuous soul by unifying him closely with the eternal, divine Logos, thus imparting a degree of divinity even to that human soul. So unified, both of them eventually were born to Mary as what appeared to be a single self. But there were really two of them: the man and the lesser god, the Logos. The man Jesus was to be the object of interest for less spiritual people, those for whom Paul had to preach "nothing . . . except Jesus Christ and him crucified" (1 Cor. 2:2). But the more spiritual were meant to look past or through the man to behold the far more important Logos.[172]

While it must have appealed to some Origenists in the third and fourth centuries, this yarn was not accepted by later mainstream, catholic traditions. But in his era it was common at least for elite intellectuals to believe, like Origen,

---

[169] This is true, but in the New Testament, Jesus's actions are empowered by God's spirit, and he *says* that he received his teachings from God (John 8:40, 17:14). His actions are supposed to show not that he is a god (or that he has a divine nature, or that he is a god-man), but rather that God is working through him.

[170] For the fully spelled out medieval solution, see Pawl, *In Defense*, 47–64. For Christ's postulated "natures" interpreted as concrete realities in the fifth century, see *In Defense*, 39–42. I am aware of at least one contemporary analytic theologian who holds the man Jesus and the divine Son to be numerically distinct, although they are also supposed to be "the same Person" in the sense I explain in section 8.3.4 and 10.2; see section 11.5.

[171] Origen, *Against Celsus*, 73–74 (2.9), 364–65 (6.47), 482–83 (8.42–43).

[172] For Origen's christological views see Martens, "Origen's Christology."

in what scholars now call an anthropos-logos Christology, one with both a man and the Logos. We can see these two Sons, the human one and the (somewhat) divine one, in Tertullian as well, and also in Origen's Roman contemporary Novatian, who distinguishes "the Son of God" (the Logos) from "the Son of Man."[173] For these, the terms "Jesus," "the Son of God," "Christ," and so on had become ambiguous, referring either to the man (the human nature) or to the eternal divine person, the Logos (the divine nature).

And it didn't stop there. By the fourth and fifth centuries, terms like "Christ" and "Jesus" could also be used for what some call "the god-man," the one "Person" who has the "two natures." The picture is that the human nature, the one who suffered and hung on a cross, is a man, while the eternal divine Logos who was with God in the beginning is a divine person, and the god-man is what or who is composed of both of these natures. This god-man has also been called the "composite Christ" or "all of Christ." It appears that this Christology now contains three beings: the man or human nature, the Logos or divine nature, and the whole composite Christ, the god-man. Now, terms like "Christ," "Jesus," and "the Son of God" might refer to any of those three!

Sometimes the confusion goes a step further. Someone might say, for example, "I believe in Jesus, the Christian god, not Allah, the god of Islam."[174] In this case, the name "Jesus" is used to refer to the Trinity, the triune God of mainstream Christianity. At this point, there are four times as many Jesuses as one would expect from reading the New Testament alone: the man Jesus, the divine Logos, the two-natured Christ composed of those two, and the triune god. Again, mainstream traditions have taken an unambiguous New Testament name and made it very ambiguous.

Another problematic term is "nature." Some theologians think that a nature is a being, an individual thing. They ascribe the crucifixion and death to Jesus's human nature (by which they mean what we would normally call a man) and the miracles and divine teaching to his divine nature. These theologians, such as Origen, see the whole Jesus as two beings "joined at the hip," to put it simplistically. Others think that the nature of something is just the sum of the defining attributes of that sort of thing. As a human, you possess human nature, which consists of the attributes that make you a human being. In Jesus's case, after the Incarnation (when the Logos took on a human nature), he supposedly

[173] Novatian, *Trinity*, trans. DeSimone, 85–88 (ch. 24).

[174] A recent popular evangelical book uses "Jesus" as the name of the Christian god, as opposed to the Islamic god (Qureshi, *Seeking Allah*).

has all the divine qualities (eternality, omniscience, etc.) and also all the human qualities (being created, being limited in power and knowledge, etc.). A major problem with this view is that it seems one thing can't simultaneously have both of these natures. How can one thing be both all-knowing and not all-knowing, all-powerful and not all-powerful, and so on? These are apparently contradictory qualities.[175]

This point aside, when Jesuses start to proliferate, you should eliminate, keeping the number down to a reasonable *one* Jesus. To do this, many later theologians claim there is only one Jesus (the composite being) and the two natures are just attributes. This leaves just one person, although it is unclear whether this is actually a self, as some trinitarians seem to regard the "Persons" of the Trinity as something like three personalities of God or three ways in which he eternally lives. For others, the one person is the eternal divine nature, the Logos, and the human nature is just a body. (That is, the eternal Logos acquired only a human body). Again, this reduces the number of persons, but it's not clear how this works either. Would a divine being who comes to inhabit a body be a real human? This is a confusing subject, and many Christians are completely unaware of the historical and theoretical controversies, which we can't fully resolve here.

Some even claim that the name "Yahweh" is ambiguous in the Old Testament. Justin Martyr (d. c. 165 CE) was a Christian who was beheaded for refusing to worship the Roman gods. Justin seems to have been the initiator of Christian Logos theologies. He wanted to find the Son not only in the New Testament but also in the Old. Even though Hebrews 1:2 declares that God has only spoken to us "in these latter days" through Jesus (previously it was through the prophets), a tradition arose of trying to find the Son (the Logos or the prehuman Jesus) active somewhere in the Old Testament.

One place they turned to is Genesis 19, the episode involving Abraham and the destruction of Sodom and Gomorrah. In chapter 18 God and two angels come to talk to Abraham; the angels are then sent to investigate Sodom. After determining that they will indeed destroy it, we read that "the LORD [Yahweh] rained on Sodom and Gomorrah sulfur and fire from the LORD [Yahweh] out of heaven" (Gen. 19:24). Justin and others read this as claiming that there was one "Yahweh" on earth (the prehuman Jesus) and another "Yahweh" in heaven

[175] Tuggy, "Craig's Contradictory Christ"; "Nineteen."

(the Father).[176] It is not clear that the text must be read in this sense. The author may have just said "Yahweh" one too many times, which is a bit odd but certainly not indicative of there being two of them. Why can't God, like others, speak of himself in the third person?[177] And why couldn't the one Yahweh, the omnipresent, omnipotent, and omniscient God, manifest simultaneously on earth and in heaven? In fact, Old Testament–era people, including the Jews, assumed that a god could manifest in different ways in different places, even simultaneously.[178]

Another instance is found in Exodus 3.

> There the angel of the LORD appeared to [Moses] in a flame of fire out of a bush ... When the LORD saw that [Moses] had turned aside to see, God called to him out of the bush ... "I am the God of your father, the God of Abraham, the God of Isaac, and the God of Jacob." And Moses hid his face, for he was afraid to look at God. (Exod. 3:2–6)

It seems there are two non-human beings in this scene, an angelic messenger through whom God speaks and God himself, present and speaking through the angel. Some people in the 100s and 200s (and even some Old Testament scholars today) have also thought there are two here being called "God" and "Yahweh," the angel of Yahweh and Yahweh himself.

But not all trinitarian scholars agree. The esteemed evangelical New Testament scholar Ben Witherington III was asked:

> This "angel" of the LORD is later clearly identified as the LORD. How can the LORD be "of the LORD"? (Unless the Scriptures here teach one God in more than one person?)

He answers,

> The Trinity is not really mentioned in the Old Testament. The angel of the Lord is just that—an angel. The angel of the Lord is a special representative or messenger of God to God's people, and according to the ancient concept of agency, he could be considered to be the Lord who sent them, and was to be treated as if he were the one who sent him.[179]

That is, the messenger is treated like the one who sent him. The messenger can, like a human prophet, speak in the first person on behalf of the sender.

---

[176] Justin Martyr, *Dialogue with Tryhpo*, 55–56 (chs. 82–88).
[177] Malone, "God the Illeist."
[178] Sommer, *Bodies of God*, chs. 1–2.
[179] Witherington, *Living Word*, 224.

Plausibly then, only God in the passage above is being referred to as "God" and as "the LORD." He simply appears and speaks through his angel.

One motivation for understanding God-terms in the Old Testament as equivocal between the Father/Yahweh/God and another is reading John 1:18 in an absolute sense: "No one has ever seen God. It is God the only Son, who is close to the Father's heart, who has made him known." If no one has ever in any sense seen God, then anyone who is somehow seen in the Old Testament must be someone other than God.

I suggest that we should not take this statement in such an absolute sense. John probably means something else by "seeing" God here because, at least on the face of it, people did see God in the Old Testament, such as the prophet Isaiah: "In the year that King Uzziah died, I saw the Lord [*adonai*] sitting on a throne, high and lofty; and the hem of his robe filled the temple" (Isa. 6:1). As we saw in section 1.6, "the Lord" (*adonai*) refers to God (Yahweh) in the Old Testament. That is who Isaiah saw, whether literally or in a dream or a vision. Elsewhere we read, "Micaiah said, ' . . . I saw the LORD [Yahweh] sitting on his throne, with all the host of heaven standing beside him to the right and to the left of him' " (1 Kings 22:19). Again, the prophet Amos says, "I saw the LORD standing beside the altar" (Amos 9:1). And in Exodus we read,

> Moses and . . . seventy of the elders of Israel went up, and they saw the God of Israel. Under his feet there was something like a pavement of sapphire stone, like the very heaven for clearness. God did not lay his hand on the chief men of the people of Israel; also they beheld God, and they ate and drank. (Exod. 24:9–11)

The author of John surely knew these clear scriptural assertions of people seeing God. Perhaps he thought that one can't see God in the fullness of his glory, or that one can't see God directly but only through some appearance or intervening angel. Or perhaps he was loosely speaking, asserting a true but not universally true general statement, not unlike the statements, "You don't drink poison and live" or "No one survives falling from a plane." But I suggest that this author may mean "seeing God" in the sense of understanding or fully comprehending him. In other words, the "seeing" here is metaphorical and not literal. The point is that one cannot fully understand God, but the best way to understand and know him is through his Son, Jesus. This is, after all, a major theme of his book. And after he wrote "No one has ever seen God," he added "It is the only Son, who is close to the Father's heart, who has made him known" (John 1:18). In this book the Son does not make the Father literally visible, but he does enable us to better understand his and our god.

1.12 THREE OPTIONS FOR DEALING WITH THEOLOGICAL AND CHRISTOLOGICAL AMBIGUITIES

To summarize, certain biblical terms became more ambiguous as time went on and mainstream theology and Christology developed. We've seen this with the terms "true God" and "God the Father," which have just one meaning in the Bible but two or more meanings in later theology. And the term "God" went from being only slightly ambiguous, nearly always used for God, to four-way ambiguous (for the Father, the Son, the Spirit, or the Trinity). Other terms have become even more ambiguous, such as with "Jesus" and "Christ"; people nowadays may use these to refer to as many as five different things![180] Some even think that the proper name "Yahweh" is ambiguous in the Old Testament, sometimes referring to the Father and sometimes to the Son. And the New Testament uses of "Lord" (*kyrios*) are complicated enough that people have projected their own confusions onto those words.

Another trend is the introduction of new theological terms that are ambiguous and hard to understand, such as "Trinity," "God the Son," "God the Spirit," human and divine "natures," the "God-man," essence or being (*ousia*), and "Person" or "being" (*hypostasis*). These are difficult, and many people don't even try to make sense of them. At some point all the confusion leads one to question whether these developments were even necessary.

There are three ways to respond to this herd of new terms and new meanings for biblical terms: correlate, eliminate, or obfuscate. To correlate, whenever the word "God" appears in the Bible, mark it to show whether you think it means the Trinity, the Father, the Son, or the Spirit. For instance, you might obtain a set of colored highlighters or pencils, using yellow for the Father, blue for the Son, orange for the Holy Spirit, and green for the Trinity. Similarly, when it mentions the Son of God, decide whether you think it is referring to the eternal divine Son/Logos (red), the human nature, or man (blue), or the composite god-man, the Christ with two natures (purple). Do this with all the ambiguous terms we have discussed. Translate biblical language into later catholic language and see if it works. Truth must be consistent with truth. If later theological developments are correct, they must be consistent with what is taught in inspired Scripture.

---

[180] These are (1) a man/human person, (2) a "complete human nature" which is not a man (see pp. 156, 309), (3) an eternal, divine Person, (4) a two-natured god-man, and (5) the Trinity, understood as the Christian god, the tripersonal God.

In my view, the better option is to eliminate some of these alleged realities from one's theology and one's Christology. Believe in the explicit teaching of the New Testament that Jesus was a unique, virgin-born man, the Son of God; do not believe in the eternal divine Logos or the composite, two-natured Christ of later catholic traditions; they are mere products of Christian imagination.[181] Stick with the one biblical Jesus, the man. Similarly, believe in the triad of God, God's Son, and God's spirit, but not in the Trinity (the triune God), which is never mentioned in the Bible and doesn't best explain what is and isn't in the Bible. In the New Testament the one god is the Father. Believe that Jesus was a real human being and that God worked in him and gave his spirit to him, but don't believe in his having multiple natures. You can stick with explicit New Testament teachings and avoid the later confusions over two-natures and Trinity theories.

Unfortunately, many Christians choose not to correlate or eliminate but to obfuscate, kicking up a cloud of dust and trying to get away as fast as possible.[182] For example, people in this camp claim that the ideas of Christ's two natures and God as the Trinity are in the New Testament; the authors just didn't have the words to express them. But if all the ideas *are* there, it should be possible to carry out the correlation option, going through the whole New Testament to demonstrate exactly where these ideas are found. It isn't sufficient to claim they *are* there but run away without showing us where. Unfortunately, as best I can tell, this can't be done.[183] The remaining option is to eliminate, bringing your theology and Christology back to the clear teachings of Scripture. A more positive term for this is "reformation."

---

[181] Efforts to come up with a coherent two-natures Christology that also fits with the New Testament have not been productive; see my "Two Natures."

[182] Various ways Christians respond to apparent contradictions in theology are explored in chapter 6.

[183] Chapter 2.

CHAPTER 2

How to Argue That the Bible is Trinitarian

2.1 HOW IS THE BIBLE RELATED TO "THE DOCTRINE OF THE TRINITY"?[1]

Christians take one of three stances regarding how the Bible relates to "the doctrine of the Trinity" (and here we assume for the sake of argument that there *is* one such doctrine). These three stances can be understood by reflecting on the following inconsistent triad, a set of three claims that cannot all be true. If any two of them are true, it follows that the third is false.[2] Logical consistency requires believing at most two of these three claims:

1. Any core Christian doctrine must be clearly taught in the Bible.
2. The Trinity is a core Christian doctrine.
3. The Trinity is not clearly taught in the Bible.

Some Christians, especially Roman Catholics, deny 1. They do not think that *any* core Christian doctrine must be taught in the Bible, since in their view the authority of the Church is more fundamental and so can serve as the basis for core Christian doctrines not in Scripture.

Others—and this is typically the stance of Catholic and Protestant apologists—deny 3, asserting that, to the contrary, the Trinity *is* clearly taught in the Bible. But this stance requires either ignorance of the early history of Christian theologies or a simplistic and warped view of it. Clear-eyed familiarity with the views of Justin Martyr, Tertullian, Origen, Novatian, and Eusebius the

[1] An earlier version of this chapter is my "Podcast 260," which is the audio of my presentation on April 13, 2019, at the 28th Theological Conference put on by Atlanta Bible College and Restoration Fellowship.

[2] The reader should pause and read through the sentences until she understands the following to be true: If 1 and 2 are true, then 3 is false. If 2 and 3 are true, then 1 is false. If 1 and 3 are true, then 2 is false.

historian creates an insuperable problem for this stance.[3] *Clear* teachings of a text, even if they're only implicit, are understood immediately by many or most competent readers. But early Christian writings and historical evidence reveal that no author before around 359 CE thought that the Bible teaches the one God to be a Trinity of distinct and equally divine Persons. Though there were many interesting views in play, the Trinity (three equally divine Persons in the one God) was not one of them.[4] Perhaps, then, the Trinity is a teaching of the Bible, but it's not an *obvious* one. If it were, some early readers would have acknowledged it, but historical investigation reveals no such readers.

The final option is to deny claim 2, that the Trinity is a core Christian doctrine. This is the position taken by unitarian Christians like me, who believe that God and the Father are one and the same, and that Jesus is his human Messiah. We reject any tripersonal god doctrine as both unsupported by and contrary to the Bible.[5]

There are three ways a Trinity doctrine might conceivably be "in" the Bible. It may be directly stated, like the Bible's teaching about the resurrection of Jesus. Or it could be only implicitly asserted. A claim which is only implied but not said may nonetheless be a very clear assertion. (For example, Matthew 1:18–25 doesn't explicitly say but clearly implies that God miraculously caused Mary's pregnancy.) A slightly weaker position is that the authors' understanding that God is triune is not implicitly asserted but only assumed; perhaps they didn't bother to assert it, even implicitly, because everyone already agreed on it. For instance, monotheism is assumed in the New Testament. It is occasionally stated, but usually it's merely presupposed. Both the early Jesus movement and their Jewish critics agreed on it, so usually there was no need to assert it.

Every honest reader agrees that no Trinity doctrine is explicitly taught in the Bible. That it is implicitly asserted or assumed are more popular positions,

---

[3] Here are representative works from each: Justin Martyr, *Dialogue with Trypho*; Tertullian, *Against Praxeas*; Origen, *Commentary on John*; Novatian, *Trinity*; Eusebius, *Ecclesiastical History*. For an overview of the views of Tertullian, Origen, and Novatian, and the rival contemporary theologies they witness to, see my "Christian Theologies."

[4] A case in point is Novatian's short *The Trinity* (the original title may have been *The Rule of Truth*), which reveals the theological options then current at Rome around 240–50: Novatian's own logos theology subordinationism, modalistic monarchianism, and dynamic monarchianism. On these see my "Podcast 348." For when we finally see trinitarians in the history of theology and how we can detect them in the sources, see my "When and How." On the date 359 see note 33 below.

[5] For how any tripersonal god theory conflicts with Scripture, see chapter 3.

particularly among trinitarian apologists. Theologians, however, do not for the most part care to argue about this issue at all. They regularly presuppose that *somehow* the Bible teaches the Trinity, but they neither argue for this claim nor do they make clear in which of the three above senses the Trinity is "in" the Bible. They may claim that the Trinity is found in the whole Bible rather than in a few passages or that you can observe the Trinity in action in a few places. For instance, an article in a popular evangelical study Bible claims that the Trinity can be seen at Jesus's baptism or in the famous Great Commission text, Matthew 28:18–20.[6]

But where are the "three Persons in one essence" in these scenes, the tripersonal god? Such broad, simplistic claims are not enough. If we want to show that biblical teachings imply a triune god, we must start with undisputed biblical teachings and then draw out their logical implications, ultimately showing how these amount to a tripersonal god doctrine. Showing that the authors merely assume that God is the Trinity will be similar; even if they don't assert that claim, not even implicitly, we should be able to see that they are indeed committed to the truth of the doctrine of the Trinity by what they say on various topics. But the prior question is, what *is* this doctrine that we will be showing to be implied or assumed? To establish that it is either implied or assumed, we will need clarity about specifically what claims it consists of.

2.2 WHAT MUST BE DEDUCED? AND WHAT IS DEDUCTION?

Let us start with the claim that the New Testament authors imply (implicitly assert) a doctrine of the Trinity. How many claims would be required for that? And exactly what are those? One standard would be the famous Westminster Confession of Faith, a creed beloved by Presbyterians. Here it is with my numbering of its claims.

> [1] In the unity of the Godhead there be three Persons [2 and these three are] of one substance, [3 and these three share one] power, and [4 and these three share one] eternity: [5 and one of these is] God the Father, [6 and one of these is] God the Son, and [7 and one of these is] God the Holy Ghost. [8 Further,] The Father is of none, neither begotten nor proceeding; [9 and] the Son is eternally begotten of the Father; [10 and] the Holy Ghost eternally proceeding from the Father and the Son.[7]

[6] "Biblical Doctrine," 2514.

[7] *Westminster Confession*, 9 (sec. 2.3). Material in brackets added.

It is no simple matter to go about deducing all of these from actual scriptural sentences. This is a reason many shy away from the task.

We need to think carefully about deduction here, as this is typically the kind of reasoning apologists deploy to derive a Trinity doctrine from the Bible. This is the form of argumentation taught in introductory logic courses in universities.[8] A deductive argument should be valid, which means that *if* all the premises are true, *then* the conclusion must also be true. Put differently, there's a necessary link between the truth of all the premises and the truth of the conclusion. Consider, for instance, this valid argument:

1. If God exists, there is no evil.
2. There is evil.
3. Therefore, it is not the case that God exists.

If 1 and 2 were true, then the conclusion 3 would also be true. This argument is valid because it has a truth-transmitting structure. All parties agree on this, even though we, as Christians, think that premise 1 is false.

Deductive arguments are extremely useful for focusing a conversation between parties who disagree, since with a valid argument the only ways to avoid its unwelcome conclusion are to deny or cast doubt on a premise, or to show that the conclusion does not follow from the premises (so that the argument is *in*valid). Thus, to avoid atheism, Christians deny premise 1.

Here's another example:

1. According to the Old Testament, there is some sort of plurality in God.
2. According to the Old Testament, monotheism is true.
3. Therefore, according to the Old Testament, the one God is multiple Persons.

This is a clear case of an invalid argument; it could be that the conclusion 3 is false even though the premises 1 and 2 are each true. When an argument is invalid, a person would be consistent in affirming all the premises while denying the conclusion. Invalidity is one way in which deductive arguments fail: the premises, even if true, would not imply the truth of the conclusion.

Of course we want *more than* validity; we also want deductive arguments to be sound. A sound argument is a valid argument in which each of the premises is true. Because by definition a sound argument is valid, its conclusion must be true too. Thus, a sound argument constitutes a reason to believe the conclusion. Here is an example of valid and sound argument:

[8] For a primer on validity and soundness consult any university logic textbook or "Validity and Soundness." We will explore various deductive arguments in chapter 8.

1. If God exists, there is no absolute privacy.
2. God exists.
3. Therefore, there is no absolute privacy.

Christians agree that premise 1 is true because God, as essentially omniscient, must know everything everyone is doing. There is always at least one other who knows about your activities; thus, there is no absolute privacy. Even an atheist should accept the validity of this argument, though he would deny its soundness by rejecting 2. Theists agree on the soundness of this argument because we agree that all the premises are true, thus implying the truth of the conclusion.

If a deductive argument is going to persuade anyone, the premises must be plausible to them. Ideally, we want to point out to our interlocutor that, *according to her*, premises *A*, *B*, and *C* are true, and then help her to see how conclusion *D* follows from those, so that she ought to accept it. In that case the opponent must either deny a premise, show that the argument is invalid, or be persuaded by the argument to accept its conclusion.

The strength of using valid deductive arguments is that their premises don't merely make the conclusion likely or increase the probability that it's true; rather, the conclusion *must* be true if the premises are. These are "all or nothing" arguments; the premises either logically imply the conclusion, or they don't support it at all.

A weak point of any deductive argument is that in some sense the information in the conclusion must already be "in" the premises. Someone with an eye for logic will already know the conclusion of a simple, valid deductive argument just by knowing the premises. In other words, generally speaking, we don't obtain new information from deductive arguments; rather, they help us to draw out the logical consequences of what we believe. To illustrate, consider this argument:

1. All philosophers are godless heathens.
2. Dale is a philosopher.

As soon as someone asserts these premises, his point is already made. The audience already "hears" the conclusion within their minds. They understand that the unstated conclusion is:

3. Dale is a godless heathen.

The information in 3 is already encoded in the conjunction of 1 and 2. This is a feature of all deductive arguments, that their conclusion(s) merely draw out information already contained in their premise(s). Because of this, when a deductive argument is simple and its premises are easily understood, the whole argument can be communicated clearly even without explicitly stating a premise or the conclusion.[9] A merely implicit premise or conclusion can be as clearly asserted as an explicitly stated one.

2.3 WARFIELD'S SHORTCUT

With this understanding of deductive arguments in hand, let's turn to arguments from two scholars who have constructed deductive arguments purporting to show how biblical teachings imply the doctrine of the Trinity. The first is found in the influential "Trinity" entry in the 1915 *International Standard Bible Encyclopedia* written by the Reformed theologian B. B. Warfield (1851–1921).

> When we have said these three things, then—[1] that there is but one God, [2] that the Father and the Son and the Spirit is each God, [3] that the Father and the Son and the Spirit is each a distinct person—we have enunciated the doctrine of the Trinity in its completeness.[10]

In other words, if the Bible implies those three statements, the doctrine of the Trinity is true. Warfield is essentially giving us this deductive argument:

1. There is only one God.
2. The Father and the Son and the Spirit are each God.
3. The Father and the Son and the Spirit are different Persons.
4. Therefore, the doctrine of the Trinity is true. (1–3)

This is an invalid argument; one may consistently accept 1–3 while denying 4. If anything like the Westminster Confession is the standard of "the doctrine of the Trinity," then not enough has been derived from the Bible to constitute such a doctrine. There simply isn't enough content in Warfield's premises. Four claims are not ten claims; that much is clear. Worse, Warfield mis-formulates his claims in order to minimize their number. His three sentences express seven claims or assertions. To critically evaluate his claims about what can be deduced from the Bible, we must expand his tightly packed sentences to reveal the actual number of claims being made. Thus, we get the following eight-step argument:

---

[9] Here is a classic example of an enthymeme, a deductive argument with an unstated premise: 1. Socrates is a human. 2. Therefore, Socrates is mortal. The unstated premise is "All humans are mortal." This premise was true before, but since the resurrection of Jesus it has been false, since the raised Jesus is presently immortal while remaining human.

[10] Warfield, "Trinity," sec. 9.

1. There is only one God.
2. The Father is God.
3. The Son is God.
4. The Spirit is God.
5. The Father is not the Son.
6. The Son is not the Spirit.
7. The Spirit is not the Father.
8. Therefore, the doctrine of the Trinity is true. (1–7)

If one compares these to the ten claims of the Westminster Confession, then there still is not enough content in these seven claims to count as the doctrine of the Trinity. Glaring by their absence are the traditional claims that each of the three Persons has the divine *essence*, and that the Son and Spirit, respectively, are eternally generated and eternally proceed from the Father. Missing too is the key concept of a tripersonal god.[11]

But maybe the Westminster Confession includes too much; this is what some present-day trinitarian theologians think. (Others, though, would say that it does not include enough!)[12] Perhaps a "mere" trinitarianism, a bare-bones set of claims, is the way to go. Granting this for the sake of argument, still, the above seven claims are not enough. Trinitarians, by definition, agree that the doctrine of the Trinity is not any form of modalism or subordinationist unitarianism. "The" doctrine—as much as we can say that there is one—was crafted precisely to rule out all such views. But such heretical theologians could easily accept all of 1–7.

A modalist may agree with 1, that there is precisely one God, this being the Father-Son-Spirit. Each of those is a mode of the one God, so in that sense she will affirm 2–4. How can 5–7 be true? Each of the three is a distinct mode from the other two. This sort of modalist denies 8 but can affirm all of 1–7. Thus, affirming 1–7 is not sufficient for being a trinitarian. The argument is invalid, as 1–7 fail to imply 8.

---

[11] "On the Christian view, God is not a single person . . . but is tripersonal." "While the persons of the Trinity are divine, it is the Trinity as a whole that is properly God" (Moreland and Craig, *Philosophical*, 575, 588).

[12] Some theologians build in the notoriously difficult and patently unbiblical doctrine of divine simplicity (Barrett, *Simply Trinity*, ch. 5). On the many difficulties of divine simplicity see Mullins, "Divine Simplicity"; Mullins and Bird, "Modal Collapse." For a striking contrast in how complex various trinitarians think "the" Trinity doctrine is, see Hasker, "Knowing God"; Tuggy, "Faith"; Craig, "Tri-Personal"; Tuggy, "Changing."

Consider too the influential subordinationist unitarians Tertullian and Origen. They agree with 1, that there is one God—and this is the Father himself, not the Trinity. They agree with 2 also; for them the Father just is God. They will gladly say, with 3 and 4, that the Son "is God" and that the Spirit "is God." For them, each is divine in a lesser way, since they exist because of God, who bestows a lesser degree or kind of divinity on them. They affirm 5–7 too, as these are numerically three beings, the Father being the greatest one, the Son (or the Word) being the second greatest, and the Spirit being the third greatest.[13] And yet 8 does not follow. With such theologies there is no tripersonal God. It is possible for 1–7 to be true even though 8 is false; the argument is invalid.

You might think that slam dunking in basketball is difficult, but with a child-sized backstop and hoop, it's easy. Similarly, when it comes to showing that biblical theology is trinitarian, if the bar is low enough, one can point out a few arguably biblical claims, spike the ball, and declare victory, hoping that no one noticed the bar-lowering. Where does the idea come from that it's easy to show the Bible is trinitarian, needing just three or four or seven claims? It may go back to the Trinity shield diagram, which dates to the high Middle Ages and was popularized in the early modern era.[14] But such a pedagogical tool can't tell us which claims are essential to this doctrine.

2.4 BOWMAN ON THE BIBLICAL BASIS OF THE TRINITY DOCTRINE

Our next example of an apologist trying to show that the Bible implicitly teaches the Trinity is an article by Dr. Robert M. Bowman Jr.[15] The overall structure of his argument is:

---

[13] In the words of early Origenist Pamphilus (d. 310), for Origen the Trinity (the triad) are "the highest realities," the greatest of whom is the only god, "the Father of our Lord Jesus Christ . . . who is the God both of the apostles and of the Old and New Testaments" (*Apology*, 81 [sec. 85], 49 [sec. 23]). On the Son being lesser than the Father and the Spirit being lesser than the Son, Origen is quoted as saying that "the God and Father, holding all things together, is superior to every being, giving to each, from his own, to be whatever it is; the Son, being less than the Father, is superior to rational creatures alone, for he is second to the Father; and the Holy Spirit is still less . . . the power of the Father is greater than the Son and the Holy Spirit, and that of the Son is greater than the Holy Spirit, and again the power of the Holy Spirit differs greatly from other holy beings" (Justinian, *Letter to Menam*). All of this fits neatly together with his discussion of the different senses of the word "God" (*theos*) in his *Commentary on John*, 98–103 (2.12–35). See also section 7.4 below.

[14] "Shield of the Trinity."

[15] Bowman, "Biblical Basis."

1. All the elements of the doctrine are taught in Scripture.
2. The New Testament presents a consistent triad of Father, Son, Holy Spirit (God, Christ, Spirit).
3. Therefore, the Bible does teach the Trinity.[16]

The argument is valid. However, the second premise is not needed; it is idle in this argument, contributing nothing, since the conclusion 3 is implied by premise 1 alone.[17] Simplifying, this is the real core of the argument:

1. All the elements of the doctrine are taught in Scripture.
2. Therefore, the Bible does teach the Trinity.

This little argument *is* valid; if 1 is true, then 2 is true. But we must now ask: What *are* all the elements of the doctrine? If Bowman has not shown that *all* the elements are included, then he has not done enough to show that the Trinity is implied by the New Testament. We want to know if the argument is sound—that is, if, in addition to being valid, the one premise is true.

According to Bowman, all the elements of the doctrine of the Trinity are:

1. There is one God who is one divine being.
2. The Father is God.
3. The Son is God.
4. The Holy Spirit is God.
5. The Father, Son, and Holy Spirit are three Persons—they are not each other, nor are they impersonal; they relate to one another personally.

---

[16] Bowman, "Biblical Basis," sec. 7.

[17] The argument is valid with just premise 1, and it is not any more valid when 2 is added. Oddly, when I pointed this out to Dr. Bowman ("Podcast 260"), he insisted that 2 should be in the argument, as it "is needed not because my argument would not work without it but because it anticipates and refutes a possible objection. Specifically, the point about the consistent triadic teaching of the New Testament shows that the doctrine of the Trinity is not cobbling together unrelated elements of biblical teaching. The Father, Son, and Holy Spirit are coordinated as divine persons in numerous passages throughout the NT in such a way as to confirm that the finding that the NT teaches the deity of each person (established in earlier parts of my outline) is not an accident or a misreading. These three persons—and only these three—are presented to us in the NT as true deity" ("Biblical Basis Part 2"). But well-constructed deductive arguments do not have premises whose only function is to anticipate and answer an objection. I take it that Bowman is here is making a cumulative case that (his understanding of) the Trinity is overall a better explanation of the scriptural data than is any non-trinitarian view. As I argue later in this chapter, it is very important to show that, but not in this little argument, the function of which is to show how, allegedly, the Bible *logically implies* a Trinity doctrine, which if true would render any cumulative case argument unnecessary.

Bowman claims that "anyone who affirms ... these propositions is affirming what is essential to the doctrine of the Trinity, since this is just what the doctrine of the Trinity says.[18] Those five elements are indeed things that many trinitarians say. But note also what has gone missing. There is no mention of a tripersonal God;[19] it is not clear what has become of the ancient claim that God is "three *hypostases* in one *ousia*." Lacking too are the eternal generation and procession of the Son and Spirit, respectively, and the Father being "of none" (not existing because of any other). The very claims that are the hardest to find in the Bible have been left out. This looks like a case of conveniently lowering the bar.

Additionally, what are we to make of Bowman's "is God" statements? Someone who "is God" might represent God, be a proper part of God, have the or a divine essence, be a mode of God, be a divine "Person" somehow "in" God, or be the one God himself. Many present-day evangelicals, when saying that "Jesus is God," mean that Jesus and God are one and the same (that they are numerically identical). Let's try out that interpretation of Bowman's phrase "is God," expanding his compressed sentences in order to reveal the actual number of claims being made.

1. There is exactly one God, that is, one divine being.
2. The Father just is God.
3. The Son just is God.
4. The Spirit just is God.
5. It is false that the Father just is the Son.
6. It is false that the Son just is the Spirit.
7. It is false that the Spirit just is the Father.
8. The Father is a Person.
9. The Son is a Person.
10. The Spirit is a Person.
11. The Father and Son enjoy an interpersonal relationship.
12. The Son and Spirit enjoy an interpersonal relationship.
13. The Spirit and the Father enjoy an interpersonal relationship.

A few comments on this set of claims are in order, because not all trinitarians agree with all of them. Claims 11–13 clarify the meaning of "Person" in 8–10. A "Person" here is a self, an intelligent agent who can engage in friendships with other selves. All of claims 8–10 and 11–13 are denied by some trinitarian

---

[18] Bowman Jr., "Biblical Basis," sec. 7, his numbered propositions slightly rephrased.

[19] Notice that in premise 1 ("who") the one God is described as if God were a single self.

theologians, even some famous and influential ones.[20] In general, present-day theologians who repeat the common line that the Persons of the Trinity "are not persons in the modern sense of the term" would deny 8–13. Alas, what the doctrine of the Trinity amounts to is and always has been something mainstream Christians disagree about.[21] But perhaps Bowman is right about what "the doctrine of the Trinity" means and these others are wrong.

Granting that, this set of claims faces an insurmountable problem: anyone can "see" that they can't all be true! The problem is with the subset of claims 2–7. Things that are numerically identical with the same thing are, for that reason, numerically identical with each other.[22] Claims 2–4 tell us that each of the Persons is numerically the same with God. But then those Persons would be numerically the same with each other,[23] and so 5–7 would be false. *If* biblical teaching on the Father, Son, and Spirit includes claims 2–7, it implies contradictions and so can't be true.[24] This fact should send a trinitarian scholar back to the drawing board to reconsider and try to understand the texts in a way that is self-consistent.

But some trinitarians claim that the "is God" statements do *not* numerically identify each Person with God. Rather, to say someone "is God" is to say he is divine.[25] If they're correct, Bowman's claims would amount to:

1. There is exactly one God, that is, one divine being.
2. The Father is divine.
3. The Son is divine.
4. The Spirit is divine.
5. It is false that the Father just is the Son.
6. It is false that the Son just is the Spirit.
7. It is false that the Spirit just is the Father.

---

[20] Tuggy, "Trinity," sec. 1.

[21] That is, since there has been a required tripersonal god doctrine, around the year 381 CE, on which see my "When and How."

[22] Section 8.4.

[23] That is, the Father and Son are numerically one, the Son and Spirit are numerically one, and the Spirit and the Father are numerically one.

[24] I am convinced that all contradictions (statements of the form *P and not-P*) are false and that none of them are true. Incredibly, this has recently been denied by a few would-be defenders of catholic Trinity and Incarnation claims, who have urged that some contradictions are both false and true. See my "Trinity," sec. 5.3 and the sources cited there, my "Two Natures," sec. 5 and section 6.4.2 below for some objections to this sort of defense.

[25] Moreland and Craig, *Philosophical Foundations*, 588–91.

8. The Father is a Person.
9. The Son is a Person.
10. The Spirit is a Person.
11. The Father and Son enjoy an interpersonal relationship.
12. The Son and Spirit enjoy an interpersonal relationship.
13. The Spirit and the Father enjoy an interpersonal relationship.

What is meant by 2–4? We can rule out that each Person is said to be "divine" only in the way that an attribute, or mode, or event involving God might be said to be "divine," since each is a divine Person and is capable of entering into interpersonal relationships (8–13). Conceptually, a person or self is a certain sort of being who can think, choose, and relate to other persons. So we're being told that each person of the Trinity is a divine being (2–4), namely a divine person or self (8–13), that they really are three (5–7), and that there is exactly one divine being (1). But such claims—specifically 1–10—could not all be true! They imply the patently false claim that there is and is not one divine being.

So far, the project of deducing a doctrine of the Trinity from the Bible is not going well. One difficulty is deducing enough claims, but we must also steer around any evident contradictions, as we're aiming to find a doctrine that is not only taught in the Bible but also might possibly be true.

2.5 A LESS "SOCIAL" TRINITY?

Some will suspect that the problem with the above formulations is Bowman's "social" trinitarianism, his siding with what I call "three-self" trinitarians, who hold the Persons of the Trinity to be so many selves (someones, persons). But there are also "one-self" trinitarians.[26] A pastor searching online for sermon ideas may run across this material by Presbyterian pastor John A. Huffman, Jr.

> We see God in the person of the Father, Creator of all that is. We see God in the person of the Son ... our Redeemer ... We see God in the person of the Holy Spirit, the One who turns our thoughts to God through his revelation ... The word "persona" in Latin literally means a mask ... As God the Father, He is Creator. As God the Son, He is Redeemer. As God the Holy Spirit, He is Sustainer.[27]

Huffman then explains a realization that he had while at a relative's birthday party: "I realized that I was one unified human being, but a different person to

[26] Tuggy, "Trinity," sec. 1.
[27] Huffman, "Holy Spirit," sec. 1.

each of these [people]." Relative to various people, he was a son, a husband, a brother, a father, and a student. "I am still one, yet I am many persons. There is great diversity in the way I am perceived and the way I have functioned through the years to each of these other persons."[28] Huffman seems to think that "the doctrine of the Trinity" is something like the following claims:

1. There is one God, that is, one being who is God himself.
2. The Father is a persona of God.
3. The Son is a persona of God.
4. The Spirit is a persona of God.
5. The Father is not the same persona of God as is the Son.
6. The Son is not the same persona of God as is the Spirit.
7. The Spirit is not the same persona of God as is the Father.
8. Each persona of God includes the one God himself.

The idea behind 8 is that a persona of God will be analyzable as God existing or living in a certain way. I don't see any logical or metaphysical problems in a theology committed to 1–8. One may object that this is a form of heretical modalism, but it is consistent with saying that these personae of the Trinity are coeternal and essential to God, so I don't see why it can't be a one-self Trinity theory. But I do see serious biblical problems, one of which is that if 2, 3, and 8 are true, then the Father and the Son can't enjoy the sort of interpersonal relationship portrayed in many ways in the New Testament.[29]

Further, 2 demotes the Father of the New Testament from being the one God himself to being a way God exists or lives. And, linguistically, it is odd if "the Father," "the Son," and "the Holy Spirit" equally well include, as mode-terms, the one God, yet in the New Testament only the term "the Father" is normally interchangeable with the term "God."[30]

Finally, if Bowman's doctrine is true, then Huffman's is false, and if Huffman's is true, then Bowman's is false. And according to some learned trinitarians, both are false but some other "doctrine of the Trinity" is true.[31] Some theologians imagine that differences concerning this doctrine are a mere

[28] Huffman, "Holy Spirit," sec. 1.

[29] John 5:19, 6:35–40, 11:40–42; Matt. 3:17, 17:5; Luke 6:12; Mark 14:32–42. See also pp. 232–33.

[30] Harris, *Jesus as God*, 42, 47.

[31] These include relative-identity theorists like van Inwagen, Brower, and Rea, Positive Mysterians like James Anderson, and four-self theorists like Chad McIntosh, on all of which see my "Trinity."

matter of emphases or "starting points," but in fact "the doctrine of the Trinity" is more like a research program—an explanatory project—which contains mutually exclusive variants. Under the widespread verbal agreement there remains considerable disagreement within the camp of trinitarian theologians.

2.6 THE DEAD END OF DEDUCTIONISM

In sum, there are difficulties all around. With some interpretations, the suggested set of claims is incoherent. With other interpretations, many trinitarian theologians will disagree that those are what the doctrine of the Trinity amounts to. All such collections are bedeviled by the question of whether enough claims have been included. As currently interpreted, there is broad agreement that the New Testament books, as originally understood, say nothing about eternal generation and procession. But, again, there is disagreement among today's trinitarians over whether the doctrine of the Trinity requires such claims.[32]

Although these are serious problems, to my mind the *most* difficult is the historical one. In theory, we might resolve all the other problems we've discussed, but at the end of the day, if the doctrine of the Trinity involves some rather obvious deductions from a handful of clear biblical teachings, then it would have been grasped by many or most competent readers in the first three hundred years following Jesus's resurrection. But the historical record reveals no such theologian! The earliest trinitarian—that is, triune-God-involving—passages I've been able to find are arguably from the years 359–64.[33] This renders it highly unlikely that getting from the Trinity to the Bible was always just a matter of a few clear deductions. Deductionism about the Trinity, the claim that a doctrine of the Trinity is logically implied by scriptural statements, is a dead end.

---

[32] See Mullins, "Hasker"; "Trinitarian Processions"; Hasker, "In Defense."

[33] Athanasius, *Letters to Serapion*, 79 (1.17.1); Gregory of Nazianzus, *Oration 25*, 13 (6.13). I say "arguably" about the dating because we know that Gregory of Nazianzus collected and edited all his writings toward the end of his life, and he may have made this earlier letter more trinitarian than it was at the time. Similarly, one may suspect that these letters by Athanasius, dated to no later than 361, are a bit early to be mentioning the one God as identical with the Trinity, something that becomes common, though not universal, even among Nicenes, only in the 370s. It has been suggested that *On the Trinity*, written c. 359–60 by Hilary of Poitiers, should be considered the first truly trinitarian book, but I don't see that he there refers to the Trinity as the one God, although he says that the Father and Son are the same god because of their shared divine nature (*Trinity*, 278 [8.4]).

What if the trinitarian surrenders her claim that these authors implicitly assert "the" doctrine, retreating to the claim that they instead *assume* it? If they merely assume it, this would explain why there is no New Testament passage that implicitly teaches that God is tripersonal. If they assume but don't assert it, it would still be the case that these authors' commitments imply some such doctrine—but this is what no one has been able to show. In fact, there is strong evidence against their being so committed.[34] And moving to the weaker assumption claim doesn't help with the serious problems we've explored here in sections 2.2–2.5.

2.7 A WAY FORWARD: INFERENCE TO THE BEST EXPLANATION

The problem is the assumption that deduction is the tool needed. As I see it, the most historically informed and theologically sophisticated trinitarian scholars are turning to inference to the best explanation, setting aside the deductive approach.[35] Here is a way forward.

Trinitarians should acknowledge that there is no one *doctrine* of the Trinity. In 381 CE, at the Council of Constantinople, the bishops (with an assist from the emperor) made newfangled trinitarian language mandatory. However, it was unclear exactly what that language meant. Today's trinitarians are still trying to figure that out. Relatively united in language, they remain profoundly divided about interpreting the required sentences, and even among the most informed scholars, incompatible interpretations are still defended.[36] Thus, to argue that the Bible teaches "the doctrine of the Trinity," one first must define what is meant by that phrase. This is the first step in showing that biblical theology is trinitarian; hand-waving references to "the doctrine" or "trinitarian" theology will not do. Until this is done, one has not put an actual *explanation* on the table, one that can be compared with others to see whether or not it's the best available. Further, the responsible trinitarian must take care that her supplied definition doesn't include the crippling ambiguities discussed in sections 2.4 and 2.5 above.

Apologists should abandon deductive arguments from the Bible to support or prove the Trinity. More content is contained in any Trinity theory

[34] Tuggy, "New Testament."

[35] Tuggy, "Facts are Facts," 258; Hasker, "Knowing God," 3–12.

[36] One may compare, for instance, the clashing Trinity theories championed by two leading analytic theologians, Brian Leftow and Richard Swinburne (Tuggy, "Trinity," 1.4, 2.4). If one is true, the other is false. And of course both could be false.

than is found in the Bible. This is clear not only from the absence of ideas relating to eternal generation and eternal procession, or that each Person shares the same *ousia* (substance or essence), but, more fundamentally, there is no word in either testament that was then understood to refer to a tripersonal God.[37] This is *strong* evidence that no such concept or idea was present in the minds of those authors; had they had such an important idea, they would have come up with some word or phrase by which to express it. Thus, even in the central trinitarian claim that there is a tripersonal God, we have stepped beyond the contents of the biblical writings, whether we're talking about assumptions, implications, or explicit statements.

The only hope for one who would prove the Bible to be in some sense trinitarian is a different style of argument: inference to the best explanation. Here, instead of deducing the claims constituting the doctrine of the Trinity from the Bible, which wrongly assumes that all the contents (concepts and claims) of a Trinity theory are already in the Bible, one argues that, all things considered, a certain Trinty theory is the *best explanation of* what we see and don't see in the Bible, that it best makes sense of what is and what is not written there, and of any other relevant facts. Whereas the conclusion of a valid deductive argument will contain no more information than is contained in the premises, in contrast, there will be more information in the best explanation than there is in the sentences describing what is being explained. One may suggest that God intended the biblical writings to produce trinitarian belief not right away but rather in the fourth century. Any Jew or Christian must agree that God, the ultimate author of Scripture, could, in principle, intend the Bible to teach things that never entered the minds of its human authors. But has he in fact done this when it comes to the Trinity?

The apologist cannot merely *assert* that his explanation is the best and leave it at that. He must first separate the uncontroversial facts from suggested explanations of those facts. Then he must compare the rival explanations of those facts to determine which is the best overall explanation. This is no small task, and, as best I can tell, it has never been attempted.[38] It would require too much work, too much careful and fair consideration of the range of competing theories. It detracts too much from the self-righteous denunciations so popular with heresy-hunters going back to the second century.

---

[37] See sections 1.5 and 1.6 and my "New Testament."

[38] I have taken some steps toward this in my "Podcast 189," "Unfinished Business of the Reformation," and my contributions to McIntosh, *One God.*

A search for the best explanation often takes some hard turns. If some relevant information is left out, one's view of what the best explanation is can be skewed. When that information is added one's ranking of the competing explanations shifts. Inference to the best explanation is how crimes are solved. Suppose the police find a dead body in a bed. They see no wounds and no evidence of foul play. Their best explanation at this stage would likely be that the victim died in his sleep of natural causes. Then they see an empty pill bottle on his nightstand. Now the investigators wonder if he committed suicide by overdose. Later they learn from his friend that the bottle had been sitting there empty for months since he ran out of his medication. The friend adds that the dead man and his ex-wife had been fighting a lot. This new information changes the range of plausible explanations. The detectives now must ask whether or not she brought about his death.

As this example makes clear, inference to the best explanation often does not progress in one linear direction. Different explanations are "tried on for size," and one new piece of evidence can send the investigation in a different direction. This is why it is so important to put *all* the relevant facts on the table. A main failure point for this sort of reasoning is failure to consider all the relevant facts. In our theological and exegetical case, the facts are about what the Bible says and does not say and historical facts about the development of Christian theologies and christologies. Once all the relevant and available facts are in view, the rival explanations of those facts must be carefully delineated and compared with one another, to see which is, all things considered, the best. Another failure point of this sort of reasoning—in crime-solving called "tunnel vision"—is focusing on too narrow a set of explanations, such as considering only one or two suspects. In the case at hand there are at least four contending families of explanations for this data: one-self trinitarianism, three-self trinitarianism, biblical unitarianism, and subordinationist unitarianism.[39]

Someone who would show that some Trinity theory best explains the data must get into the trenches and do the hard work of fairly weighing rival explanations. There is a lot of partisan rhetoric in theological circles on all sides. For instance, you may hear statements such as "The Trinity is something that all Christians have always believed." That is demonstrably not the case. The available evidence confirms there were no believers in a triune God in the years 180 or 240 CE.[40] Non-trinitarians are denounced as Bible-hating skeptics or as

[39] Alas, these are not all the options. But in my view these are the best contenders, and I would argue that this is supported by the history of Christian theologies.

[40] On the latter era, see my "Christian Theologies" and my "Trinitarian 'Fool's Gold'".

rationalists who are allergic to things they can't fully understand or explain. Meanwhile trinitarians are denounced as deniers of monotheism or as devotees of Greek philosophy. The biblical unitarian, it is said, is merely assuming unitarianism. Weighing the competing theories requires setting aside such useless rhetoric in favor of careful, fair-minded comparisons of plausible rival explanations. This is as hard as popular denunciation is easy, but it must be done if Christians as a community are interested in the truth of the matter.

There is no simple, quasi-mechanical procedure one can follow to determine which of a batch of plausible explanations is, all things considered, the best. In about the last sixty years, philosophers of science have investigated how scientists sort through rival explanations to find the overall best one, and their insights are applicable to historical investigation and to historical-grammatical interpretation of the Bible. As they point out, these sorts of reasoning are employed in everyday life; they can be thought of as part of "common sense," so there is no avoiding them.[41] But this style of reasoning is not taught to students of theology or biblical studies. Still, one can sometimes observe these kinds of thinking in the best scholars, just under the surface of their prose.

Back to the philosophers who have thought deeply about inference to the best explanation—they have described a number of desiderata we are looking for in an explanation. There doesn't seem to be any simple way to rank these, or to adjudicate cases in which one explanation is much better than a second when it comes to a certain desideratum, while the second one is much better than the first one with respect to another desideratum. Nonetheless, it is helpful to keep in mind these qualities that we want in an explanation or "explanatory virtues" (factors that make an explanation to some degree and in some way good). Philosopher Peter Lipton writes,

> there are a number of plausible candidates for the explanatory virtues, including [1] scope, [2] precision, [3] mechanism, [4] unification, and [5] simplicity. [That is, in order,] [1] Better explanations explain more types of phenomena, [2] explain them with greater precision, [3] provide more information about the underlying mechanisms, [4] unify apparently disparate phenomena, or [5] simplify our overall picture of the world.[42]

---

[41] Douven, "Abduction," sec. 1.2.

[42] Lipton, "Inference," 197, bracketed numbers added. See also Cabrera, "Inference," sec. 6. These desiderata have only been discussed since around the 1960s and 1970s, when philosophers of science were trying to understand scientific revolutions, and more generally, how scientists choose between competing theories.

Trinitarians who want to move beyond the sloppy and unconvincing modern arguments attempting to deduce "the Trinity" from the New Testament would do well to articulate precisely what "the Trinity" amounts to, and then, using the above criteria, show that it is better than its rival explanations when it comes to the data of the New Testament and of history.

One must admit that the history of theology is a problem regardless of one's preferred explanation. Whether you are a trinitarian or a biblical unitarian, many non-Gnostic, mainstream Christians held *other* views during the first four centuries. Biblical unitarians must explain why people were calling Jesus by the title "God" and advocating subordinationist, literal-prehuman-existence Christologies so early after his death. Trinitarians need to explain why it took more than three hundred years for any required triune God doctrine to appear in mainstream Christianity. And if either view is correct, they ought to explain the popularity of modalistic views from the late 100s into the 300s.

Finally, an informed trinitarian scholar should get the timing right regarding the alleged divine revelation of the Trinity. We can see that no Trinity was revealed in Old Testament times; when God reveals something, people actually believe it. As far as we know, no one in the Old Testament era believed that God was the Trinity or three Persons in one essence.[43] We have no evidence of any trinitarians prior to the second half of the 300s CE. The books that compose what we now call the Old Testament were widely read and studied. That (as best we can tell) for many centuries *no one* came up with a trinitarian theology based on them is powerful evidence that they don't contain any trinitarian theology. Honest and competent scholars do not assert that the Trinity is explicit or even implicit in the Old Testament. Some urge that there are divinely dropped hints (or to sound more impressive, "adumbrations," vague foreshadowings) about the Trinity in the Old Testament, but they will admit that properly speaking, the original writers and readers of those texts were not adherents of any trinitarian theology. Such scholars hypothesize that now that the fullness of truth has been revealed, those who think that God is triune can look back and make better sense of certain facts than the people of that era. That is, what was revealed about God in the Old Testament makes better sense to us now than it did to them. There is an explanation of what was revealed to them, but they didn't know it. But we have finally understood it.

[43] Walton, *Old Testament Theology*, 286, 289.

But if not in the Old Testament era, *when* did this revelation of God as the Trinity happen? Was it during the earthly ministry of Jesus or the writing of the New Testament books? Or was it in 381 when the second "ecumenical" council propounded what is arguably the first truly trinitarian creed? Or was it some time in between? The theology in question will need to fit together with the facts of the era of its revelation, whatever that is decided to be.

A popular view with apologists, including Bowman, Warfield, and James White, is that the Trinity was revealed during the earthly ministry of Jesus and shortly thereafter.[44] By the time the New Testament was written, the authors were all assuming that God is a Trinity. This would explain why there is no passage in the whole New Testament that succinctly educates Christians about God's triunity, his comprising three divine Persons. A reader of a modern translation of the Bible will notice that there is no section header (supplied by the translators or editors) that reads "The Trinity" or "The Doctrine of the Trinity" or "That God is Triune." What is known by all the community doesn't need to be explicitly stated and can just be assumed.

But what evidence is there that New Testament authors assume trinitarian theology? Presumably the apologist will appeal to so-called "triadic" passages in which God, his Son, and his S/spirit are mentioned together.[45] He would probably also try to prove that things are said about the Son and the Spirit that require them to be "Persons" and fully divine. But this Trinity-as-assumed position can't be sustained, for there is much stronger evidence against it than for it, when one looks at the totality of the textual and historical evidence.[46]

Further, if the Trinity had been revealed in the New Testament era or just before, smart people in the first few Christian centuries would have perceived that it is assumed or implied in those books. But our evidence shows that they

---

[44] White says, "I always teach that the doctrine of the Trinity is taught in the 'gutter' between Malachi and Matthew. What I mean by that is, it is in the incarnation of the Son and the outpouring of the Holy Spirit that we have the full doctrine of the Trinity revealed to us" ("Conversation"). Earlier Warfield wrote, "We cannot speak of the doctrine of the Trinity . . . as revealed in the New Testament, any more than we can speak of it as revealed in the Old Testament. The Old Testament was written before its revelation; the New Testament after it. The revelation itself was made not in word but in deed. It was made in the incarnation of God the Son, and the outpouring of God the Holy Spirit" ("Trinity," 8 [sec. 8]). My thanks to C. S. Lakin for pointing out this passage.

[45] Bowman Jr., "Triadic."

[46] For a consideration of the evidence of twenty classes of relevant New Testament or historical facts, including the so-called "triadic" passages, see my "New Testament."

did not.[47] Even in the mid-300s there were still large numbers of non-Nicenes, in many areas a majority of the Christian population. Again, people *get it* when God reveals something; this follows from his being competent to accomplish the revelatory task, which is implied by his essential omniscience and omnipotence. Yet clearly and explicitly trinitarian (triune-god-involving) theology doesn't really appear until around the time of Augustine, in the late 300s, soon after the Council of Constantinople in 381.[48] It is awkward for a Protestant to claim that the pinnacle of divine revelation regarding the Trinity occurred around 381 or later and not in the New Testament era!

This fair-minded comparison of rival explanations is as hard as popular denunciation and question-begging assertions are easy, but it must be done if Christians as a community are interested in the truth of the matter. It is not sufficient to *claim* that one explanation is the best without *showing how* it is superior to its competitors. I would love to take part in a dialogue comparing the four aforementioned rival explanations (p. 85). In my view biblical unitarianism—that the one God is the Father alone, not the Trinity, and that his unique Son is the man Jesus—is by far the best explanation of the relevant textual and historical facts. It remains to deploy our desiderata for explanations (p. 86) to show in what respects it is better than its rivals.

---

[47] For the non-trinitarian theologies we find in the first half of the 200s, see my "Christian Theologies," my "Podcast 384," Novatian, *Trinity*, Lloyd, *Novatian's Theology*.

[48] I have argued that the creed from the 381 council assumes a trinitarian theology because in my view at least some leading Nicenes at that time assumed that the shared "nature" of the "Persons" implied they were in some sense one god ("When and How"). But in any case, that council's surviving documents are certainly not explicitly trinitarian. Things are surprisingly different in the many works of Augustine, who converted to Nicene, catholic Christianity just a few years after that council, in 386; he wears his trinitarianism on his sleeve, saying for example that "This Trinity is one God" and "we indeed recognise in ourselves the image of God: that is, of the supreme Trinity" (*City of God*, 462, 483 [11.10, 11.26]). See also Augustine, *Trinity*, 69 (1.2.7), where he reveals his false assumption that mainstream tradition has always taught God to be the Trinity.

CHAPTER 3

How Trinity Theories Conflict with the Bible

3.1 INTRODUCTION[1]

While there are many Trinity theories, they share the claim that the one God just is the Trinity. But in the New Testament, the one God just is the Father. One can't consistently affirm both claims. There is a logical clash between trinitarian traditions and the New Testament, and when these conflict, Protestants should side with Scripture. But for the theologically educated there are extreme social pressures against deviating from longstanding Catholic and Protestant traditions. For many, it is unthinkable that the mainstream could have made such a big mistake; the New Testament *must* be consistent with catholic Trinity traditions.

But a Protestant should remember that Protestantism arose because of the widespread conviction that the mainstream had gone seriously off track over the centuries, with its teachings and practices such as the papacy, transubstantiation, the veneration of Mary and other saints, the authority of bishops, clerical celibacy, and purgatory. Protestants, of all Christians, should be able to admit that the mainstream can and has gone wrong on serious matters of doctrine and practice. Trinity speculations are just one of them.

It is *demonstrably* a mistake to think you can coherently affirm both that God is the Father and that God is the Trinity. I will supply the demonstration in section 3.3. I use the word "demonstration" very deliberately. I mean that there is a proof of inconsistency that any trinitarian can see to be valid (it contains no mistake in reasoning), and it employs only premises to which the trinitarian is committed simply by being a trinitarian. This proof puts the trinitarian in a tough spot. She can either (1) embrace the apparent contradiction, which looks very foolish when that contradiction is stated

[1] An earlier version of this chapter was my "Podcast 248."

(instead of obliquely gestured at), (2) deny obvious biblical teachings, or (3) deny obvious, self-evident truths. Any way she turns, her Trinity theory comes at an unacceptably high price.

3.2 CLARITY ABOUT NUMERICAL IDENTITY

First, I will briefly draw your attention to a foundational, unanalyzable concept that you already possess and regularly use: the concept of numerical identity, or numerical sameness, or being-the-same-thing-as. I will explain it by describing scenarios in which you habitually employ that concept.

Suppose you've just moved to a new city and are considering attending a party to meet some new friends. As you're deciding whether or not to go, you consult with your one friend in town, who happens to know everyone who will be at the party. This friend knows you are looking to make friends with people who are both smart and kind. You ask her, "Will any such people be there?" Consider two things the friend might reply:

1. Someone there will be smart and kind.
2. Someone there will be smart and someone there will be kind.

Both pieces of advice, if true, imply that the party-goers include at least one smart person and at least one kind person. But the first requires that at least one person there will be both. If you hear 1, you will probably go to the party. But if you hear 2, you will still be wondering if it is worth your time—smarts alone and kindness alone are not enough for you, and 2 doesn't imply that anyone there is both. That you understand the difference between these answers shows that you grasp the concept of numerical identity. If 1 is true, then at least one of the smart people there will be one and the same with one of the kind people there. Option 2 requires no such overlap of the smart ones with the kind ones (however many there are); 2 is compatible with there being no one there who is both smart and kind.[2]

Again, in a theological conversation, you say, "Only God is uncreated." You have used one sentence, but you have asserted two claims. What you're saying is that God is uncreated, and also, for any *x* whatever, if *x* is uncreated then *x just is* God (is numerically identical with God). In other words, God is uncreated and nothing else is. Whatever the subject-matter, in "all" or "only" statements of this sort, you're employing the concept of numerical identity.

[2] I owe this sort of example to Hawthorne, "Identity," 100.

Suppose you're reading Genesis for the first time and not paying close attention to the text. You think Abram is one character and Abraham is another. But eventually, as you reread, you realize your mistake and, as it were, collapse "the two of them" into one. You now see that Abram *just is* Abraham and vice versa (Abram = Abraham and Abraham = Abram).

Now imagine that you're reading an unusual Old Testament translation in which the translator sometimes uses the name "Abe" for that man. Now there are now three co-referring names in play in the text. But you realize that this is supposed to be the same character as Abraham; the translation assumes that Abe = Abraham. You realize that in this translation it must also be that Abe = Abram, because things identical to the same thing must also be identical to each other. (Abe just is Abraham. And Abram just is Abraham. Thus, Abe just is Abram. This is all just *one being* we're referring to via three different names.)

Back to our standard translations (with only "Abram" and "Abraham"), Christians don't think this variously named fellow is a fictional character; we think this is a true narrative. In our view, Abraham and Abram are the same man. This is to make three claims: (1) Abraham is a man, (2) Abram is a man, and (3) Abraham just is Abram (they are numerically identical, one and the same thing).[3]

We must distinguish between *numerical* identity (sameness) and *qualitative* identity/sameness or similarity.[4] Human identical twins are by definition (normally) qualitatively the same (to a high degree), but they can't be numerically the same. (As twins, they are two similar things, not one thing.) In principle, *two* things can't be *numerically* the same. If we say that this and that are numerically identical, then some one thing is being referred to in two different ways. Qualitative sameness (similarity) comes in degrees and kinds. For instance, things may be qualitatively similar with respect to height, but not similar with respect to intelligence. And a novel with 1,000 pages is more similar in respect to size to one that is 900 pages than it is to one of 100 pages. In contrast, numerical sameness is all-or-nothing; it doesn't come in kinds or degrees.

Both relations can be reflexive. Just as one thing can be similar to another, so everything surely is (at any given time) similar to itself, and maximally so.

[3] Nothing is special about the word "man" here. We could also truly say that Abraham and Abram are the same patriarch, the same husband, the same son, the same brother, the same carnivore, and so on.

[4] Both concepts are explored more thoroughly in chapter 8.

However, only numerical sameness is *necessarily* reflexive. In other words, what are really two things can be similar, but they can't be numerically the same. Only a single thing (entity, being) can be numerically the same with itself. In any true statement of numerical sameness, we're just referring to one and the same thing twice using two co-referring terms, names, or expressions. For example, those familiar with nicknames for recent American presidents will recognize that Slick Willy = Bill Clinton and Dubya = George W. Bush Jr.

3.3 THE ARGUMENT FOR THE INCOHERENCE OF BIBLICAL TRINITARIANISM

The proof to follow employs *only* the concept of numerical identity; it does not directly make any claims about qualitative identity (similarity). This argument doesn't try to show, nor does it presuppose, that the idea of the Trinity (supposing that is one idea) is incoherent. It is neither presupposing nor attempting to prove that the concept of the Trinity implies a contradiction, like the concept of a square circle.

Instead, the argument shows that some clear claims of biblical theology together with claims needed by any Trinity theory are incoherent, as they imply a contradiction.[5] This is a proof of inconsistency, what logicians call a *reductio ad absurdum*—a reduction to absurdity. The point is not that you're supposed to believe the last line. Rather, the point is that you must deny one or more premises to avoid committing to the contradiction (here 5 together with 6).

1. God just is Yahweh.	premise
2. Yahweh just is the Father.	premise
3. God just is the Father.	from 1, 2
4. God just is the Trinity.	premise
5. It is not the case that the Trinity just is the Father.	premise
6. The Trinity just is the Father.	from 3, 4[6]

[5] Trinitarian apologists tirelessly point out that "the doctrine of the Trinity" is not incoherent because it's not that God is three and one *in the same way* but rather that God is three *Persons* but one *essence or being*. This standard opening defensive move is not, in the end, very helpful (Tuggy, "Standard Opening Move"). But what's important here is that it's *completely irrelevant* to the argument at hand.

[6] Here are the sentences in logical notation using the standard symbol "=" for numerical identity, *g* for the one God, *y* for Yahweh, *f* for the Father, *t* for the Trinity, and "¬" for the negation operator (it is not the case that).

Claims 5 and 6 together are a formal contradiction, a denial and affirmation of the same claim. Whatever the letters refer to, we all know that no pair of sentences with the structure *P and not-P* can simultaneously be true.[7] Let's walk through the argument now and examine the justification for each step.

1. "God just is Yahweh" is a premise that is clearly taught throughout the Old Testament. "Yahweh" is the proper name of the only god. Yahweh is not supposed to be one being while God is another![8]

2. "Yahweh just is the Father" is a premise assumed throughout the New Testament. The New Testament doesn't use the Hebrew name "Yahweh" or any Greek transliteration of it because, at that time, it was considered improper or impious to write or speak God's name. The New Testament authors call Yahweh "God" (Gr: *ho theos* or *theos*) or "the Lord God." It is clear that this one is none other than the Father, as expressed in the title "God the Father" and the phrase "one God, the Father" (John 6:27, 1 Cor. 8:6). Notice how the author of the

---

1. $g = y$
2. $y = f$
3. $g = f$ from 1,2
4. $g = t$
5. $\neg(t = f)$
6. $t = f$ from 3,4

[7] I hold it to be self-evident that any sentence of the form *P and not-P* (in symbols, $P \wedge \neg P$—in other words, an affirmation and negation of the same claim, a contradiction) is false and not true. Unfortunately, as with many other obvious truths, some philosophers deny it. The logician and philosopher Jc Beall (*Contradictory Christ*) has argued that Christ is a contradiction, in other words, a reality about which one or more contradictory statements are true. In a following book (*Divine Contradiction*) he has extended this approach to a *very* sophisticated interpretation of the doctrine of the Trinity based on his reading of the "Athanasian" Creed. I'm not engaging with it here because, among other reasons, I can't fathom how Beall would respond to the main argument of this section. Readers wanting a brief introduction to what Beall is doing regarding the Trinity can see Molto, *Review*. I interact briefly with Beall's defense of Christ as a contradiction in my "Two Natures," sec. 5 and in section 6.4.2 below.

[8] This point is granted by all Christians. One way to see this commitment of the Old Testament authors is by their use of terms in apposition. Suppose that a journalist wrote in 2011, "Barack Obama, the president of the United States, is an articulate guy." This statement presupposes the numerical sameness of Barack Obama and the president in office in 2011; the proper name refers to a man, and the description "the president of the United States" referred in 2011 to that same man. Similarly, in Exodus we find Moses in his capacity as prophet saying, "Thus says the LORD, the God of Israel" (Exod. 5:1). Here he refers to the same thing twice, first via God's proper name "Yahweh" (hidden here under that traditional substitute "LORD"), and second by the description "the God of Israel." Just as clearly, this statement presupposes that the LORD *just is* the god of Israel, and vice versa.

Fourth Gospel, seemingly just for stylistic reasons, swaps the terms "God" and "the Father."

> "Not that anyone has seen *the Father* except the one who is from *God*; he has seen *the Father*." (John 6:46, emphases added)

> "Can you say that the one whom *the Father* has sanctified and sent into the world is blaspheming because I said, 'I am *God*'s Son'?" (John 10:36, emphases added)

> Jesus, knowing that *the Father* had given all things into his hands, and that he had come from *God* and was going to *God*. (John 13:3, emphases added)

This term-swapping is not confusing because both author and audience assume that those terms normally co-refer. It is better style to vary the ways in which one refers to someone.

3. "God just is the Father" is a conclusion implied by premises 1 and 2. Like the relation *bigger than*, the relation of numerical identity is transitive: just as if $a > b$ and $b > c$, then $a > c$, so if $a = b$ and $b = c$, then $a = c$. In this case, $g = y$ (1) and $y = f$ (2); therefore, $g = f$ (3). Happily, the claim that $g = f$ is also a clear assumption throughout the New Testament independently of the above reasoning. Consider this passage:

> [Jesus said,] "I have come in my Father's name, and you do not accept me; if another comes in his own name, you will accept him. How can you believe when you accept glory from one another and do not seek the glory that comes from the one who alone is God?" (John 5:43–44)

Here "the one who alone is God" is supposed to be one and the same with the one Jesus refers to as "my Father."

4. "God just is the Trinity" is a premise that is neither directly nor clearly taught or presupposed anywhere in the Bible, but it is the core thesis of any trinitarian theology. If you're a trinitarian, for you the one God *just is* the Trinity, the tripersonal God, so as a trinitarian you are committed to 4.

5. "It is not the case that the Trinity just is the Father" is also a premise to which any trinitarian is committed. It is self-evident that nothing can, at one time or in eternity, be and not be the same way (that is, qualitatively differ from itself). Abstractly put, numerical identity implies indiscernibility at a time or in timeless eternity (if there is any such thing). If there is a triune god, this god can't be numerically one with the Father because those would eternally (either timelessly or at all times) differ from one another. How? The Trinity is supposed to have the Father as one of its three "Persons," but the Father is not supposed to have the Father as one of its three "Persons." The Trinity is supposed to be

tripersonal, but the Father is not, according to any catholic or orthodox Trinity theory. Again, for most trinitarians, the Father is supposed to eternally generate the Son, but the Trinity does not.

6. "The Trinity just is the Father" is a conclusion implied by 3 and 4. It is self-evident that things identical to the same thing must be identical to each other.[9]

In sum, we started with uncontroversial scriptural teachings (1–3). We added two unavoidable commitments of any trinitarian theology (4–5), and 6 follows. But 6 affirms the same claim that 5 denies; together, the two form a contradiction. If a set of claims implies a logical contradiction, at least one of those claims must be false. We therefore *know* that at least one of 1–5 is false; it can't be that each of 1–5 is true (and not false).

What premise(s) should be denied in order to avoid the contradiction? Claims 1 and 2 are clearly taught in Scripture. The committed trinitarian will try to protect 4 at all costs. Perhaps the first thought for many will be to deny 5, the most obviously non-scriptural or "philosophical" premise. But any trinitarian, as such, is committed 5, as revealed by this supporting argument.

5-1. According to any trinitarian theology, the Father and the Trinity will simultaneously (at the same time, or in timelessly eternity) differ.
5-2. Things that simultaneously or timelessly differ are numerically distinct.
5-3. Therefore, according to any trinitarian theology, the Father and the Trinity are numerically distinct.

There's nothing to find fault with here. The conclusion 5-3 follows from 5-1 and 5-2. A trinitarian should agree with premise 5-1. She must accept that there are some things that are true of the Trinity that are not true of the Father (such as being tripersonal and not being a single Person), and vice versa (such as generating the Son or being a single Person). And 5-2 (the distinctness of discernibles) is self-evident. Going back to the main argument, one is committed to 5 just by being a trinitarian.

For a trinitarian, then, 4 and 5 must be affirmed and not denied. And 1 is off the table too. No Christian should deny 1, for it is evident by simple reading comprehension that in the Old Testament that "Yahweh" ("the LORD") and (most uses of) "God" are co-referring terms. It appears that the only ways to save some trinitarian theology (which requires commitment to 1, 4, and 5) are to

[9] That is, if $a = c$, and $b = c$, it follows that $a = b$. Here, $g = t$ and $g = f$, so $t = f$. This follows from the symmetry and transitivity of =. The reasoning is: $g = t$, so therefore by symmetry it follows that $t = g$, and adding the premise that $g = f$, by transitivity we get $t = f$.

deny 2 and/or 3. Notice that 3 follows from 1 and 2. We don't want to deny 1. The only option left is to attack 2, either denying or at least casting doubt on the premise that the "Yahweh" of the Old Testament is the same one called "Father" in the New Testament. This claim (premise 2) that Yahweh just is the Father is not something that surfaces explicitly in the New Testament. It's rather a shared assumption, something that the authors thought didn't need to be argued for. Still, it comes *pretty close* to the surface at times.

3.4 EXHIBIT A: LUKE IN ACTS

In chapter 2 of Acts, Luke has Peter say,

> "This Jesus *God* raised up, and of that all of us are witnesses. Being therefore exalted at the right hand of *God*, and having received from *the Father* the promise of the Holy Spirit, he has poured out this that you both see and hear." (Acts 2:32–33, emphases added)

Do you see what Luke has done here? He's just used "God" twice. He could have just as easily used "God" a third time. But, presumably just for variety, the third time around he substitutes the phrase "the Father." He can do that because, for him, "God" and "the Father" are normally co-referring terms; he assumes the identity of God with the Father (and vice versa). He knows his readers assume this too, so this switch will not confuse them.

In the next chapter, in another sermon by Peter, he says:

> "You Israelites, why do you wonder at this, or why do you stare at us, as though by our own power or piety we had made him walk? The God of Abraham, the God of Isaac, and the God of Jacob, *the God of our ancestors* has glorified his servant Jesus, whom you handed over and rejected in the presence of Pilate, though he had decided to release him." (Acts 3:12–13, emphases added)[10]

"The God of our ancestors" is the god of the Jews, Yahweh, and the one to whom Jesus is a servant (and Son [Acts 9:20, 13:30]). He is the Father. Here we see Luke and Peter assume that Yahweh and the Father are numerically the same. Luke doesn't use the phrase "the Father" in this context, but the reader knows from the rest of the book that this is a way to refer to God (Acts 1:4, 7, 2:33).[11]

---

[10] Compare Acts 5:29–31, 7:32, 26:6.

[11] The astute reader will also find this use of "Father" for the one God in Luke's prior volume: Luke 2:49, 6:36, 9:26, 10:22, 11:2, 11:13, 12:30, 12:32, 22:29, 22:42, 23:34, 23:46, 24:49. Perhaps most tellingly, in Luke 10:21 Jesus, while praying, uses the terms

3.5 EXHIBIT B: PAUL IN EPHESIANS 1

Paul repeatedly calls someone the god of (that is, the god *over*) Jesus. Surely, given the first-century Jewish context, this is the god of the Jews, Yahweh. And for Paul this god is none other than the Father. Thus to the Ephesians he writes:

> Grace to you and peace from *God our Father* and the Lord Jesus Christ. Blessed be *the God and Father of our Lord Jesus Christ, who* has blessed us in Christ with every spiritual blessing in the heavenly places, just as *he* chose us in Christ . . . I do not cease to give thanks for you as I remember you in my prayers, that *the God of our Lord Jesus Christ, the Father of glory*, may give you a spirit of wisdom and revelation as you come to know *him.* (Eph. 1:2–4, 16–17, emphases added)

It's just basic reading comprehension that Paul is using the italicized words to refer to the same one here—Yahweh, the one true god of the Jewish Scriptures.

3.6 CONCLUSION

Given your commitment to 1, in order to deny 3, you must also deny 2. But in denying 2, you are denying a clear, implicit New Testament teaching. God (a.k.a. the Father) in the New Testament is supposed to be none other than Yahweh himself, the unique god of the Old Testament, the creator. This is foundational to understanding the New Testament. It looks like a trinitarian must commit to all of 1–5. But then she is in the teeth of a clear contradiction (5 and 6).

Don't intone "mystery" here and expect us to think that is a reasonable escape. *How* is this a mystery? The meaning of each claim in steps 1–6 is clear; there is no dark, barely intelligible, mysterious claim here. Your point, if you're going to play the mystery card, must be that there is an apparent contradiction in 5 and 6. Indeed, there is! If you reply with the obvious truism that not every apparent contradiction is a real one, we will nod in agreement but point out that this sure looks to be a real one! It has the form *P and not-P*, which anyone can see is a contradiction and which therefore is false.

If you're really going to die on the mystery hill, say out loud what the mystery is. Own it. Say, "It is *and* isn't the case that the Trinity just is the Father." Or, if you prefer: "The Trinity and the Father are *and are not* the same—and, yes, I mean 'same' in the same sense both times." You don't want to assert things like these? Good! I don't want you to either, because it is ridiculous to do so.

"Father" and "Lord of heaven and earth" in apposition, and the reader knows that the latter is a title unique to the one true god.

Here's another way to look at it, one that seems more reasonable than mystery-mongering. If one can't hold on to all of a group of statements, one should let go of the one with the least supporting evidence. So let's consider the various steps in our argument in light of their differing degrees of evidence. I'll call those degrees "level 1" and "level 2." To have level 1 evidence is to be somewhat plausible in light of all relevant considerations. Level 2, a higher level, is something you're more sure of because it is plainly biblical teaching (we'll assume you know the Bible to be inspired). Plausible but speculative theories are level 1, while straightforward biblical teachings are level 2. Here again is the argument:

1. God just is Yahweh.
2. Yahweh just is the Father.
3. God just is the Father. (1, 2)
4. God just is the Trinity.
5. It is not the case that the Trinity just is the Father.
6. The Trinity just is the Father. (4, 5)

We can't reasonably agree with both 5 and 6, since they can't both be true. If you're a trinitarian, as we've seen, you're committed to 5. So you need to deny 6. But 6 is implied by what came before. Where, then, is the weak link in 1–4?

What grounds are there for 4? It is a piece of speculative theology. There may be some chain of argument that leads one from the Bible to the Trinity. But the Trinity itself is neither an explicit nor an implicit but clear biblical teaching, nor does it seem to be an assumption of the New Testament authors. It is not even a clear or obvious inference from Scripture, since it does not appear in Christian theology until the latter half of the fourth century.[12] The argument will be *much* more complex than the simple argument we've been exploring in this chapter. It will be controversial, and other trinitarians will likely disagree with it. It will depend on contentious New Testament interpretations. Even if there are some New Testament grounds for claiming that God is the Trinity, in the end such a doctrine is still speculative, so will have a lesser degree of justification than 1–3.

Clearly the weak link in our argument is premise 4. That God is the Trinity is neither an explicit nor a clear teaching of the Bible. It has *at most* level 1 justification. Claims 1–3 have level 2 justification. Premises 1 and 2 are each taught in Scripture, and 3 logically follows from them. Theory must bow to fact. Deny 4, and there is no longer any basis on which to infer 6. Problem solved.

---

[12] See p. 82 and my "When and How."

The price of this denial is that you can no longer in good conscience remain in what I call the "Trinity club."[13] But what you've bought is a truly biblical theology that makes sense on its own, without the many agonies of trinitarian theorizing. If you believe that the New Testament is divinely inspired and the writings (or at least most of them) accurately represent apostolic teaching, you should go with their theology rather than the theology of bishops from the late 300s. Why? Because as we've just seen, those theologies conflict; they can't both be true.

I offer this argument in the hope that it will help you make the right choice. Do you agree that 4 is the weak link? Why or why not? Protestants have been making the discovery ever since the Reformation that according to Scripture, God is one person or self, the Father, and so not a Trinity. I hope that you will make this discovery as well.

3.7 POSTSCRIPT: TRINITARIAN WAYS TO DENY PREMISE 4?

Analytic theologians—scholars writing on theological topics who have been trained in the methods of recent analytic philosophy—are more skilled than other theologians when it comes to detecting logical contradictions and then avoiding committing to them by making fine distinctions.[14] I agree with these scholars that simply by being a theoretical project, any theology will assume various philosophical concepts and claims, and that recent analytic theology is in many ways an advance on the ancient, medieval, and early modern "continental" philosophies that underlie other traditions of theology. But not every fine distinction is a reasonable one, and sometimes a fancy use of words is deployed that tends to hide rather than to solve the problem at hand.

3.7.1 CRAIG'S USE OF THE WORD "TRINITY"

In recent work on the Trinity, apologist, philosopher, and theologian William Lane Craig has suggested that the term "the Trinity" should be understood not as a singular referring term but rather as a plural referring term for the Father, the Son, and the Spirit, as three referents.[15] In this he is, confusingly, going back

[13] Tuggy, "Podcast 232."

[14] On this approach to Christian theology see Arcadi and Turner, *Handbook*; McCall, *Invitation*; Crisp and Rea, *Analytic Theology*.

[15] This seems to be assumed in his contributions to McIntosh, *One God*, but it comes out

to the older usage.[16] Because of this, he would, although confessedly a trinitarian (of his own unique sort), deny 4 above. If "the Trinity" is a *plural* referring term, there is no one thing it refers to, and thus it could not be true that the Trinity is one and the same thing as God, as premise 4 says.

Nonetheless, Craig's theology features a tripersonal god; it's just that he doesn't call this god "the Trinity." He instead refers to this god as a soul with three cognitive faculties.[17] But this theology contradicts the New Testament just as much as theologies that call their triune god "the Trinity." The argument of section 3.3 can easily be adapted to show the clash between Craig's speculative trinitarianism and biblical theology. We need only to slightly modify premises 4 and 5.

1. God just is Yahweh.
2. Yahweh just is the Father.
3. God just is the Father. (1,2)
4. God just is the Tripersonal Soul.
5. It is not the case that the Tripersonal Soul just is the Father.
6. The Tripersonal Soul just is the Father. (4,5)

As before, the weak link is 4. I believe that, given premise 1, Craig may attack 2. If so, he'd be choosing to double down on his theory rather than yield to clear biblical teaching, as discussed in sections 3.4 and 3.5.[18]

3.7.2 "MONARCHICAL TRINITARIANISM"

This neologism was coined by Beau Branson and has since been taken up by Joshua Sijuwade. Both are analytic theologians and adult converts to Eastern Orthodoxy. Both have been active on YouTube, so several popular apologists have also brandished this label. As I'll explain, to me the term "Monarchical Trinitarianism" is unfortunate, as the theology it refers to is not, properly speaking, trinitarian. "The Monarchy of the Father" is an abstract phrase that can mean different things. For some, it means that the Father is the source of the

---

more clearly in a conference discussion with his co-authors (Tuggy, "Podcast 372"; Tuggy, "Podcast 373"). In this it seems Craig is following Michael Rea, on which see my "Constitution Trinitarianism," sec. 2. On the plural vs. singular referring terms distinction, see section 1.10.1 above.

[16] See section 1.10.1, section 7.4, or Tuggy, "When and How."

[17] Craig, "Tri-Personal," 52–54.

[18] In addition to those sections, that a denial of 2 clashes with the theology of the New Testament authors is shown by many other facts (Tuggy, "New Testament").

unity of the triune God because he's the eternal source of the other two Persons, as he eternally generates the Son and eternally spirates the Spirit. Branson circulated a paper online for several years that defined "Monarchical Trinitarianism" as including the claim that the one God just is (is numerically the same with) the Father alone. When the paper was published, even though, as best I can tell, Branson still held to the numerical identity of the only god with the Father, he had changed that definition.[19]

For his part, Sijuwade ran with "Monarchical Trinitarianism" as implying the numerical identity of God with the Father alone.[20] He has recently rebranded this view as "Conciliar Trinitarianism,"[21] the idea being that this is the teaching of the seven "ecumenical" councils that Sijuwade, as Orthodox, considers authoritative. The variously named theology here is a conjunction of the defining thesis of any *unitarian* theology, the identity of God/Yahweh with the Father alone, and the traditional catholic claims that eternally the Father (via generation and procession) shares his *ousia* ("essence" or "substance") with two other divine "Persons," the Son and Spirit.[22] As with Craig (section 3.7.1), I understand Sijuwade to be using the word "Trinity" as a plural referring term but in contrast to Craig, for Sijuwade, Yahweh is one of the three things that term refers to.

On the face of it this theology is a remarkable retreat from the full claims of trinitarian traditions; the key idea of a tripersonal God has been discarded. How many in trinitarian traditions will agree that the doctrine of the Trinity is true but there is no such thing as the triune God? But Branson and Sijuwade have

---

[19] In the published version Branson says he wants to defend a "Monarchical" view of the Trinity, which is any view according to which "(1) the Father is the *arche anarchos* [source without source], and (2) there is a use of "God" as a singular term, such that it refers particularly to the Father because He is the *arche anarchos*" (Branson, "One God," 23). For the oddities of this definition, see my "Ancient," 184. As far as I know, Branson has not publicly explained the change, but I hypothesize that the new definition is preferred because it allows not only people who think the one God is the Father but also people who think the one God is the Trinity to count as "monarchical trinitarians." Today's Eastern Orthodox theologians are split into those camps (Tuggy, "When and How," 44–46).

[20] Sijuwade, "Monarchical Trinitarianism," 43; "Building the Monarchy," 436.

[21] Sijuwade, "Conciliar Trinitarianism," 498 n. 1.

[22] Sijuwade, "Nature of Monotheism," 113–14. Sijuwade and I disagree about what the 381 council was asserting; I see them as also presupposing that *ousia*-sharing implies that the Trinity is God, and so they mean to teach—though they don't explicitly say this—that God just is the Trinity; for my reasons, see my "When and How," 33–43. Sijuwade also holds to what I have called "the Western Misunderstanding Narrative," according to which "Western" or Latin-speaking theologians starting especially with Augustine misconstrued the councils to be teaching a tripersonal God (Tuggy, "When and How," 29–32).

discerned the clash between New Testament theology, according to which the unique God is the Father, and tripersonal God theories, on which the only god is the Trinity. That so many trinitarians are willing to take this sort of "trinitarianism" seriously is a testament to how "the doctrine of the Trinity" functions as a shibboleth in mainstream Christianity.[23] As it discards the core thesis of any trinitarian theology—that the one God is the Trinity—while affirming the defining thesis of any *unitarian* theology—that the one God is the Father alone—this "Monarchical Trinitarianism" should be considered a kind of unitarian Christian theology.

But it's not a plausible unitarian theology! While it asserts monotheism, it also implies the falsity of monotheism by implying the existence of two other gods—beings with the divine essence. In Sijuwade's view the doctrine of the Trinity teaches "the existence of three deities (divine persons) . . . with the Father being the sole fundamental deity."[24] Such a theology is a nonstarter for any biblically faithful Christian. According to the assumed theory of essences, an essence is what makes the owner (or subject) of it an individual of a certain natural kind. Thus, you and I each have the essence *humanity*; this is what makes each of us a human being. What does the Father have, by virtue of which he is the only god? *Divinity*. What else, beyond that, is required for being a god? Nothing. An essence, by definition, is sufficient for its owner being an (or the) example of a certain kind. Following Nicene catholic tradition, Sijuwade insists that the Son and Spirit have that very same *ousia* the Father has. It follows that the Son is a god and the Holy Spirit is a god; each has all it takes to be a god, namely, the essence *divinity*.

Sijuwade has tried out various responses to this problem.[25] One is to characterize monotheism as what I've called "monotheosism," the claim that only one being can rightly be referred to as "God" or "god."[26] But conceivably, a tritheist may, for some reason, decide to dub one of the gods but not the other two "God"—and this word use would not make his theology monotheistic. The main solution Sijuwade offers is redefining the term "monotheism" so that it's not the claim that there is exactly one god but that there is exactly one "fundamental" god, and in his theology, only the Father is a fundamental god—that is, a god who is

[23] Tuggy, "Podcast 232."

[24] Sijuwade, "Nature of Monotheism," 113.

[25] Sijuwade (in my view correctly) rejects relative identity solutions ("Conciliar Trinitarianism," 516 – 17), on which see section 8.3.4 and chapter 11.

[26] Section 1.3. "Monotheism . . . [is defined as] The belief that there is only one 'god'" ("Nature of Monotheism," 88). See also Sijuwade, "Building the Monarchy," 438.

not "grounded" (in a technical, metaphysical sense) but who "grounds" the existence of all else, including the Son and Spirit.[27]

But this is merely an arbitrary, theory-saving redefinition of the term "monotheism"—the claim that there is exactly one god. Imagine that a society practices polygamy, and in their tradition the first wife a man marries is called the "primary wife," who uniquely among the wives gets veto-power over any further proposed wives. Jethro, let's imagine, has seven wives, one of whom is his primary wife. Is Jethro a polygamist? He may urge that he is not, on the grounds that polygamy is the practice of having more than one *primary* wife. This defense against the charge of polygamy is as plausible as Sijuwade's redefinition defense against the charge of polytheism.[28]

In a recent piece Sijuwade has added to "Conciliar Trinitarianism" the claims that each divine "Person" is numerically identical with the one divine substance that God is or has.[29] If that's so, then the councils are committed to the numerical identity of each Person with the other two, since things identical with the same thing must therefore be identical with one another.[30] But this runs contrary to catholic traditions, which have long required the numerical distinctness of the Persons, in opposition to "Sabellianism" or modalistic monarchianism.[31]

As I read him, Sijuwade, sensing the inadequacy of his other replies to the objection that his views contradict monotheism, has developed an extremely speculative interpretation of that conciliar doctrine, a rational reconstruction of it.[32] He calls this "Conciliar Aspectivalism," and it is admittedly similar to Brian Leftow's one-self Trinity theory.[33] According to "Conciliar Aspectivalism," "the single divine substance is conceived as a 'multiply located trope [the individual yet abstract property *divinity*],' whose identity remains fully one while also being irreducibly manifested in three relationally distinct ways,"[34] which are the Persons. Space prevents discussing the metaphysical details, which are legion, but the

---

[27] Sijuwade, "Building the Monarchy," 439–46; "Conciliar Trinitarianism," 509–14; "Nature of Monotheism," 99–105.

[28] Sijuwade is not the first analytic theologian to redefine "monotheism" to head off their Trinity theory's implication of tritheism; see p. 234 below.

[29] "Conciliar Trinitarianism," 500.

[30] Section 8.3.1.

[31] See for instance sections 2.3–4, pp. 75, 77–79.

[32] Section 6.5.1.

[33] "Conciliar Trinitarianism," 501, note 7; Tuggy, "Trinity," sec. 1.5.

[34] "Conciliar Trinitarianism," 501. On the relevant concept of a trope see Sijuwade, "Logical Problem," 7–15; "Conciliar Trinitarianism," 502–6.

theory includes the numerical identity of the divine nature with each Person, and so the numerical identity of each Person with each of the other two. Despite being one and the same thing, though, appealing to the technical concept of aspects as developed by Donald Baxter and other metaphysicians, Sijuwade holds that each Person can qualitatively differ from each of the others—which is to say that the theory requires that one and the same thing can at one time have and lack a property by having aspects.[35] The account doesn't embrace true contradictions; rather, the divine substance manifests differently in different spatial regions, and these manifestations each have a first-person perspective and can act in different roles despite being "differing aspects of the one multiply located trope, Divinity."[36]

Here, on the face of it, is the gist of another, more traditional defense of "the doctrine of the Trinity" as monotheistic. Why not say that the divine substance, as so described, is the triune God, the Trinity? At one point Sijuwade says that "what might appear externally as multiple agents (Father, Son, Spirit) is, in fact, one agent, Divinity . . . playing different roles . . . preserving the indivisible oneness of God."[37] This sounds like a one-self Trinity theory on which the "Persons" are not strictly selves/someones, but rather the triune God is. But in the most recent work I've seen, Sijuwade instead maintains that monotheism is secured by "the one God being numerically identical to the Father as the *fundamental divinity-Aspect*—where this specific aspect of Divinity . . . is ontologically prior to all other things."[38]

For my part I don't see how the Father, being *a manifestation of* the divine substance, would be fundamental or ultimate, as opposed to that substance of which he or it is a manifestation. Nor do I see how a thing can be identical with its qualitatively different manifestation; for starters, the first isn't and the second is a manifestation. Whatever its benefits, this theory comes at a high price.

---

[35] Sijuwade, "Conciliar Trinitarianism," 514–17; "Logical Problem," 21–25. See Baxter, "Self-Differing," for the—to my mind wholly unconvincing—everyday scenarios involving conflicting desires which are meant to motivate the claim that a thing can at one time both have and lack some quality. This involves positing a new kind of linguistic reference such that "an expression . . . can refer to an aspect without referring to one numerically identical with it" (sec. 2). This, as well as the claim that a thing can simultaneously differ from itself, seems patently impossible; see section 8.3.2.

[36] "Conciliar Trinitarianism," 514. I can only give the barest sketch of this *extremely* complicated theory. For the many metaphysical details see his "Conciliar Trinitarianism," "Logical Problem," and a forthcoming academic monograph.

[37] "Conciliar Trinitarianism," 516. Earlier in this piece (502–3) Sijuwade approvingly quotes Augustine, who in my view clearly affirms the one god to be the Trinity.

[38] "Conciliar Trinitarianism, 513, original italics.

CHAPTER 4

Heretic! Traditional Approaches to Dropping H-Bombs vs. the New Testament

4.1 TRADITIONS OF HERESY-HUNTING[1]

For a long time now in mainstream Christian traditions, there has been a concern to label, classify, exclude, and refute heretics and the heresies they teach. There have been times and places where such labels could result in death for the recipient.[2] Thanks to the radical, reforming Protestants who revived religious freedom in the modern era, undoing centuries of disastrously intolerant catholic traditions, these days are past, at least in most Christian and formerly Christian realms. Still, to be labeled a "heretic" means being excluded from churches and mainstream Christian institutions such as conferences, universities, seminaries, publishing houses, and para-church ministries. Dropping the H-bomb (calling someone a heretic), while no longer a matter of life or death, is still very serious business, and the dropper should first think very carefully about what a heretic and heresy are supposed to be. That is the purpose of this chapter.

---

[1] An earlier and much shorter version of this chapter was a presentation in May of 2015 at the 24th Theological Conference organized by Atlanta Bible College and Restoration Fellowship. It was called "Heretic! Four Approaches to Dropping H-Bombs," and was later presented as my "Podcast 85."

[2] For Thomas Aquinas's argument for the death penalty for heretics, see his *Summa Theologica*, 440 (2.2.Q11.A3). Although catholic Christianity officially repudiated religious freedom in the decades following the 381 council, nonetheless, active persecution of those with nonstandard beliefs was far from continuous (Freeman, *A.D. 381*; Stark, *Triumph of Christianity*, 304–5).

4.1.1 "HERESY" IN THE NEW TESTAMENT

Someone steeped in longstanding traditions of heresy-denouncing will be surprised to learn that the New Testament says little about "heretics," "heresy," or "heresies." Some principal English translations, such as the GNT and the NRSVUE, don't employ those English words at all. Others use only one of them, and only once. The word in that one passage, which in four other places the KJV translates using "heresy" or "heresies,"[3] is the Greek word *hairesis*. Related to a verb whose primary meaning is "choice," this word, as a standard reference source explains, occurs nine times in the New Testament, six of them in Acts,

> where it always has the meaning, "party, sect," whether referring to the Pharisees and Sadducees ... or to the Christian community, which was perceived as a sect from a Jewish point of view.[4]

This was an extension of the preexisting secular use of the term, which applied to what we call "schools" of philosophy.[5] As such, this term carries no negative connotations. However,

> Paul uses the term twice with reference to "factions" within the church (1 Cor 11:19) ... Gal 5:20 [listed among works of the flesh]); these are viewed as invalid because they are violations of the unity and universal character of the church ... the adjective *heretikos* probably has the related meaning "divisive" in its only New Testament use ... Titus 3:10.[6]

Here there is a sin in view, that of being a factious or wrongly divisive person, someone who tries to divide a social group that ought to remain together. Here, a distinctively Christian use of *hairesis* and related words with a strongly negative connotation begins to arise.

2 Peter warns,

> But false prophets also arose among the people, just as there will be false teachers among you, who will secretly bring in *destructive opinions*. They will even deny the Master who bought them—bringing swift destruction on themselves. (2 Pet. 2:1, emphases added)

---

[3] Acts 24:14, 1 Cor. 11:19, Gal. 5:20, 2 Pet. 2:1.
[4] Silva, *New International 1*, 176.
[5] Danker, BDAG, 24.
[6] *New International 1*, 176, abbreviations expanded.

Many other translations have "heresies" here instead of "opinions." But the NRSVUE translators evidently take the view that "the negative sense [of the phrase] is expressed by *apoleia* . . . 'destruction' . . . and that *hairesis* by itself simply means 'course of thought, opinion, doctrine.' "[7] If the other translators are correct, then this "would be the first attested instance of [*hairesis* having] the meaning 'false doctrine.' "[8] Either way, they note that this text may have been the pointer that led to the Christian use of *hairesis* we see in the second century and beyond, "where it became a technical term for groups that opposed the church,"[9] and, I would add, for those groups' distinctive teachings.

4.1.2 WHAT NEW TESTAMENT AUTHORS BLAST

For a traditional Christian nowadays, a "heresy" primarily means "a fundamental error in religion, or an error of opinion respecting some fundamental doctrine of religion."[10] If one goes looking for New Testament guidance on heresies in this sense, one will get nowhere by looking for the word "heresy." Thus, when evangelical New Testament scholar Craig Blomberg turns to the New Testament for guidance on heresies, he ignores the word sometimes translated as "heresy" or "heresies" and instead focuses on "When Do Jesus and the Apostles Really Get Mad?"[11] In this insightful journal article, Blomberg reviews not so much negative-emotion-triggering things in the New Testament as errors so serious that they warrant strident, public opposition through strong rhetoric and argument. I'll call them "blastable" people, actions, and teachings.

The New Testament tends to focus more on bad people and their bad actions than on their false teachings. For instance, consider this warning from Jesus:

> "Beware of false prophets, who come to you in sheep's clothing but inwardly are ravenous wolves. You will know them by their fruits. Are grapes gathered from thorns or figs from thistles? In the same way, every good tree bears good fruit, but the bad tree bears bad fruit. A good tree cannot bear bad fruit, nor can a bad tree bear good fruit. Every tree that does not bear good fruit will be cut down

---

[7] Silva, *New International 1*, 177.

[8] *New International 1*, 177.

[9] *New International 1*, 177.

[10] Webster, "heresy." A more recent American dictionary gives too weak a meaning: "an opinion or doctrine contrary to church dogma" ("heresy"). But not all church dogmas are fundamental—that is, both essential and central to the faith; this definition is too broad.

[11] Blomberg, "New Testament Definition," 59.

> and thrown into the fire. Thus you will know them by their fruits. Not everyone who says to me, 'Lord, Lord,' will enter the kingdom of heaven, but only the one who does the will of my Father in heaven. On that day many will say to me, 'Lord, Lord, did we not prophesy in your name, and cast out demons in your name, and do many mighty works in your name?' Then I will declare to them, 'I never knew you; go away from me, you who behave lawlessly.' " (Matt. 7:15–23)

People, not teachings, are the target here—false messengers or prophets claiming to bring guidance from God, but whose actions are contrary to God's will, who will be judged and damned despite their real or alleged ministry exploits. Here their bad deeds—not their teachings—are in view. Thus, John the Baptist denounces "many of the Pharisees and Sadducees" as "a brood of vipers" who resist repentance (Matt. 3:7–10).[12]

As Maurice Wiles observed, the "archetypical" or paradigmatic heresy in catholic traditions is Arianism, which is pilloried for taking too "low" a view of Jesus, making him less than fully divine.[13] For these traditions, a paradigm and central heresy is teaching either that Jesus is "a mere man" (human but not divine) or that he's divine in a lesser way than the Father. A mainstream Christian reader, then, expects to find such errors blasted in the New Testament. But does she?

When a group of people is blasted by John the Baptist, Jesus, or the apostles in the Gospels and Acts, it is often but not always clear what their serious sin and/or harmful false teachings are. For the Pharisees and Sadducees, we can summarize their sin and error as supposing that their Jewish identity and practice, without repentance, make them right with God.[14] Also singled out are the sins of attributing God's miraculous works to Satan, claiming to be the Messiah or Christ returned, financial exploitation of Jewish worshippers in the temple, greed or inordinate love of money, and either trying to follow Jesus secretly, falling away after having started to follow him, or merely making a pretense of following him.[15]

Things get more specific in the Pauline letters. In his letter to the Galatians, Paul aggressively blasts a "different gospel" being promoted by unnamed teachers that imperils the salvation of those in the church (Gal. 1:6–9). In

---

[12] Blomberg, "New Testament Definition," 60.

[13] Wiles, *Archetypal Heresy*.

[14] Blomberg mentions their "covenantal nomism," "legalism," and focus on "badges of national righteousness" ("New Testament Definition," 60).

[15] "New Testament Definition," 60–66.

response to this teaching, they have been observing special days and months and seasons and years" (4:10)—that is, those required by the Law of Moses—and practicing circumcision or at least thinking about it (5:2). Paul exclaims, "I am afraid that my work for you may have been wasted" since "you who want to be reckoned as righteous by the law have cut yourselves off from Christ; you have fallen away from grace" (4:11, 5:4). In Christ, he reminds them, "There is no longer Jew or Greek" (3:28). As Blomberg observes, "The package of legalism, nomism, and ethnocentrism that made the key pharisaic leaders so inimical has intensified and triggers Paul's sternest warnings," and he adds that in chapters 5 and 6 Paul perhaps preemptively, lest they swing to the opposite extreme, "proscribes antinomianism."[16]

We should add that in contrast to countless later inter-Christian disputes, Paul expresses no concern about differing views on the metaphysical nature(s) of "the Lord Jesus Christ" (Gal. 6:3), the descendent of Abraham, God's "Son, born of a woman" (3:16, 4:4). And the "God" who is one (unique) is the Father himself,[17] not the later triune god of catholic orthodoxy. The latter is not mentioned in any Pauline letter.

In his first and second letters to the Thessalonians, there's not much about false teaching apart from the surprising circumstance that some think "the Day of the Lord" (Jesus's return) has already come (2 Thess. 2:2).[18] This is rather gently corrected; these letters feature no blastable teachings or practices. The same is true of Paul's long and theologically rich letter to the Romans.

Things are otherwise when it comes to his first letter to the Corinthians! In Blomberg's summary,

> this immature congregation ... have divided themselves into factions, focusing on human leaders ... have failed to deal with serious sexual sin in the camp ... are suing one another ... there is a group promoting celibacy as normative for all ... "weaker" and "stronger" brothers and sisters contend over idol meat, gender roles, the Lord's supper, and spiritual gifts ... and some disbelieve the bodily resurrection of Christ.[19]

---

[16] Blomberg, "New Testament Definition," 66.

[17] Gal. 1:1, 3, 3:19, 4:4.

[18] Blomberg observes, "This could have resulted from false teachers, but it is at least as likely that it merely reflected a misunderstanding of Paul's first epistle" ("New Testament Definition," 67).

[19] "New Testament Definition," 67.

While there's plenty of direct correction here, I see no blasting, even when it comes to the rather surprising falsehood that Jesus was not raised (ch. 15).

But in his next New Testament letter, as Blomberg observes, "Paul's language in 2 Corinthians 10–13 rivals that of Galatians in severity."[20] His target is again some group of Judaizers who

> preach a distorted gospel that Paul attributes to "a different spirit" (11:1–6); demand money for their ministry ... can be called servants of Satan masquerading as angels of light (11:13–15); and boast in their credentials, including ethnic ones ... these Judaizers similarly seduce the Corinthian congregation to adopt an unwarranted triumphalist spirit.[21]

In both Corinthian letters there is no hint of any controversy about who God and his human Son, Jesus, are. The only god is one and the same with the Father (1 Cor. 1:2–9, 8:6), who is the god over Jesus (2 Cor. 1:3), and "the one Lord" is his human Son "through whom we are," whom God has raised from the dead and exalted to the highest position under God (1 Cor. 8:6, author's translation; 1 Cor. 15:20–28).

In his letter to the Colossians, Paul again seems to be opposing Judaizers (2:11–23, 3:11), now together with what interpreters suppose to be some proto-Gnosticizing teachers, "perhaps with elements of local mystery religions and magical practices thrown in."[22] Again, the one God is the Father himself (Col. 1:3, 13, 3:17). But as Paul seems concerned with false teachers who may deceive them "with plausible arguments" (Col. 2:4), "philosophy and empty deceit, according to human tradition, according to the elemental principles of the world, and not according to Christ," having to do with "self-abasement and worship of angels" (Col. 2:8, 18), he emphasizes the current supremacy of Christ. Here many commentators see Paul pushing back against some Gnostic type of teaching. Readers familiar with the elaborate cosmologies and mythologies of second-century Gnostics can't help but notice that Paul in this letter sprinkles in terms used by them, such as "mystery," "knowledge," "wisdom," and "fullness." Christ is "God's mystery ... in whom are hidden all treasures of wisdom and knowledge" (Col. 2:2–3). The Colossian believers don't need any inside information about a *pleroma* (fullness) between God and humans

[20] Blomberg, "New Testament Definition," 68.
[21] "New Testament Definition," 68.
[22] "New Testament Definition," 68.

consisting of aeons,[23] since in Christ "the whole fullness of deity dwells bodily, and you have come to fullness in him, who is the head of every ruler and authority" (Col. 2:9–10). Those asserting a catholic two-natures theory about Jesus seize on this phrase as if it were equivalent to the claim that Christ has a divine nature in addition to a human one. But earlier Paul puts it differently, writing that "in him all the fullness of God was pleased to dwell, and through him God was pleased to reconcile to himself all things" (Col. 1:19–20).[24] The "deity" dwelling in Christ is God himself.

As Paul says elsewhere, "God was in Christ reconciling the world to Himself" (2 Cor. 5:19, NASB 1995), or as Jesus puts it in the Fourth Gospel, "the Father is in me . . . the Father who dwells in me does his works" (John 14:10). Jesus is "the image of the invisible God," that is, of the Father (Col. 1:15, 2), who now has "first place in everything" (1:18), of course, under God (3:1). Through him God has accomplished the new creation (1:15–20) and has "disarmed" and humiliated the ruling spirits of this age, making them as though dead to believers (2:15, 20). While Paul exalts the Lord Jesus Christ over any other proposed mediator(s) between God and humans, he doesn't engage in any blasting in this letter, though he briefly hints that these false teachings could imperil their salvation (1:23).

In his letter to the Ephesians we again find Paul teaching, not blasting, and no false teachers or teachings are clearly in view. The letter to the Philippians again features him blasting Judaizers (Phil. 3:2–16). They are dogs, evildoers, and mutilators, who put "confidence in the flesh" (3:2–3). While this book contains one of the most argued-over christological passages, nonetheless it is clear that here, as everywhere in Paul's letters, the one God is the Father (Phil. 1:2–3, 4:18–20) and Jesus is his human Son and Messiah, his human servant who obeyed him through a terrible death and consequently has been raised and exalted by God, to God's glory (Phil. 2:5–11).

As Blomberg observes, the "pastoral" letters (1 Timothy, 2 Timothy, Titus) don't add to what we've seen already. And, "Once again, probably to our surprise, factiousness emerges as an excommunicable offense (Titus 3:10) that

---

[23] Irenaeus, *Against the Heresies 1*, 24–27 (1.2).

[24] In a footnote the NRSVUE translators inform us that they've added "of God" to the translation for clarity.

is self-condemning (v. 11)."[25] Or, as the KJV translates the start of verse 10, "If a man is a heretic" (the Greek is *hairetikon anthropon*), "a person who stirs up division" (ESV), "a divisive person" (NIV, HCSB, NET), "factious man" (ASV, NASB). Or we might say, someone who is a "heretic" *in the New Testament sense.*

Moving beyond Pauline letters, the letter of James, the letter to the Hebrews, and 1 Peter are blast-free and seem not to be directed at false teachers. Beyond these, Blomberg observes,

> Jude and 2 Peter have defied the best scholarly attempts to identify the teachings they oppose ... We learn more from both letters about the false teachers' immorality than about their ideology.[26]

In contrast, there is broad agreement that the New Testament letters from John are directed against

> emerging Gnosticism, Docetism, and Cerinthianism (themselves considerably overlapping) ... Key doctrinal tenets opposed would then include perfectionism, antinomianism, and an inadequate Christology.[27]

Inadequate in what way? The false teachers, "antichrists" who "went out from us" since "they did not belong to us," seem to be denying that Jesus is God's Christ, his Messiah (1 John 2:18–19, 22). Reading between the lines, these teachers may have been peddling some special "knowledge" or "truth," as John writes to his flock,

> But you have been anointed by the Holy One, and all of you have knowledge. I write to you, not because you do not know the truth, but because you know it ... As for you, the anointing that you received from him abides in you, so you do not need anyone to teach you. But as his anointing teaches you about all things and is true and is not a lie, and just as it has taught you, abide in him. (1 John 2:20–21, 27)

How were they denying him to be God's Messiah? Seemingly by denying that Jesus is *a real human being*, for the Messiah must be that.[28] John has already noted that Christians have benefitted from the cleansing *blood* of Jesus, which

---

[25] Blomberg, "New Testament Definition," 69. This elaborates on Paul's command in Romans 16:17: "I urge you, brothers and sisters, to keep an eye on those who create dissensions and hindrances, in opposition to the teaching that you have learned; avoid them."

[26] "New Testament Definition," 70.

[27] "New Testament Definition," 70.

[28] According to several New Testament texts the Messiah is a descendent of King David (Matt. 1:1, 17, 9:27, 12:23; Luke 1:32; John 7:42).

requires him to be flesh-and-blood, a man, not some sort of spirit merely appearing to be a man (1 John 1:7). Later he writes:

> Beloved, do not believe every spirit, but test the spirits to see whether they are from God, for many false prophets have gone out into the world. By this you know the Spirit of God: every spirit that confesses that Jesus Christ has come in the flesh is from God, and every spirit that does not confess Jesus is not from God. And this is the spirit of the antichrist (1 John 4:1–3).

The real Jesus is a real man, but of course not "just a man"—rather, "Everyone who believes that Jesus is the Christ has been born of God . . . one who believes that Jesus is the Son of God" (5:1, 5).[29]

That John is combating some sort of docetic Christology is also suggested by his interesting argument in 1 John 5:6–11. Here is my interpretive paraphrase:

> God has given us three "testimonies" about Jesus. First, Jesus "came by water," in other words, by his baptism at the start of his ministry, when the great prophet John "testified that this is the Chosen One," who is "the Lamb of God who takes away the sin of the world" (John 1:34, 29). (And being immersed in water shows him to be a real human being, of flesh and blood.) The second divine testimony is "the blood" he shed for us at his crucifixion (1 John 5:6–8). Or perhaps the "water and blood" John has in mind here are the "blood and water" that gushed out of him when the soldier speared him to confirm that he was dead.[30] The third "testimony" is from the spirit which God has put into believers.[31] These all testify to Jesus, that he is God's human Son and Christ. Can a spirit be stabbed by a spear and bleed and ooze out water? Can a spirit be dunked in water?

The second letter of John confirms that it is such a serious error to "not confess that Jesus Christ has come in the flesh" that believers should "not receive and welcome this person into your house, for to welcome is to participate in the evil deeds of such a person" (2 John 7, 10). Such a teacher is blasted as a "deceiver" and "antichrist" (7). Third John calls out one "Diotrephes" for "spreading false charges against us" (3 John 9–10), but beyond that the situation

---

[29] Contrary to some interpreters, John does not later in this chapter describe Jesus as "the true God"—see section 1.4.8.

[30] "But when they came to Jesus and saw that he was already dead, they did not break his legs. Instead, one of the soldiers pierced his side with a spear, and at once blood and water came out. (He who saw this has testified so that you also may believe. His testimony is true, and he knows that he tells the truth, so that you also may continue to believe)" (John 19:33–35).

[31] 1 John 5:6–7, 10; 4:13; 2:20, 27.

is unclear. Some passages in Revelation have been put forward as supporting the deity of Christ,[32] but the book offers no clarification on what would constitute false teaching in the New Testament era.

After his review of blastable errors in the New Testament, Blomberg writes,

> The collection of false teaching and immoral behavior that NT authors most strongly oppose is an interesting one. A strong insistence on both the full deity and the full humanity of Christ naturally appears.[33]

But Blomberg has not shown any emphasis on the full deity of Jesus in the New Testament, and he overlooks that failure to teach that, surprisingly, is never blasted.[34] That is not what we would expect if, as evangelicals assume, the New Testament authors are committed to the full deity of Jesus, and so it is evidence that they had no such commitment. But as we saw, teachings that imply that Christ is not a real human *are* blasted.

Blomberg also observes that

> The harshest rhetoric is almost always reserved for the ultraconservative religious insider who transgresses key boundaries, especially leaders who should certainly know better.[35]

This profile of blastable errors changes in the second century in mainstream Christian tradition, where we can observe the birth of what scholars call the genre of heresiological writings.

4.1.3 JUSTIN MARTYR AND THE BIRTH OF HERESIOLOGY

At first glance, by later standards Justin Martyr seems remarkably mellow about *some* rival factions in the Christian camp. In his *Dialogue with Trypho*, his Jewish interlocutor pushes back on Justin's belief that Christ existed "as a god" (or "as God" or "as 'God' ") before becoming human, calling this belief "not only

---

[32] But see Rev. 1:1, 3:12, and Rev. 4–5.

[33] Blomberg, "New Testament Definition," 71.

[34] Blomberg is among the endorsers of Bowman Jr. and Komoszewski, *Putting Jesus*. As such, he probably assumes that the full deity of Jesus is rather obviously implied or assumed by various New Testament texts, and/or that there is an overwhelming cumulative case that these authors thought him to be fully divine, that is, to have all the essential divine attributes.

[35] "New Testament Definition," 71. See that same page for the rest of his summary of the teachings and behaviors that get blasted by New Testament authors.

paradoxical, but preposterous."[36] Justin replies that even if he can't prove this, nonetheless it would still stand that he has proven Jesus to be "the Christ of God."[37] Thus Justin writes,

> For, my friends, there are some of your race, who acknowledge that he is the Christ, but claim that he has a merely human origin.[38] I naturally disagree with such persons, nor would I agree with them even if the majority of those who share my opinions were to say so. For we have been told by Christ himself not to follow the teachings of men, but only those which have been announced by the holy prophets and taught by himself.[39]

There is a textual problem in the first sentence; some editors of the Greek text have thought that it should read "our" rather than "your." In that case it looks like Justin would be admitting that some Christians (or perhaps Gentile Christians) don't believe in the prehuman existence of Christ. If the correct text is "your," then Justin would be referring to some Jewish Christians who denied Jesus's literal prehuman existence. It is striking that Justin is even willing to consider the hypothetical that he can't prove literal preexistence from Scripture; this suggests that this was not a majority view in his day.[40] There are reasons to think that such views were tolerated in mainstream churches until the papacy of Victor at the end of the second century.[41] But Justin *may* here be only referring to Jewish-Christian groups that he does not reckon as true Christians but whose example in believing in the messiahship of Jesus he cites for the sake of persuading his Jewish interlocutor.

At any rate, there are certainly limits to Justin's tolerance. A recent monograph argues that this whole *Dialogue*, though outwardly engaging with non-Christian Jewish views, is also directed against the teachings of Marcion.[42] It is no surprise that Justin, as a Christian teacher, would be alarmed at the success of Marcion of Pontus, given his teaching.

---

[36] Justin Martyr, *Dialogue with Tryhpo*, 73 (48.1).

[37] *Dialogue with Trypho*, 73 (48.2–3).

[38] The Greek here says literally that he is "a man of men."

[39] *Dialogue with Trypho*, chs. 73–74 (48.4). This passage intrigued many early modern unitarian Christians, on which see Christie, *Dissertations*, 208–11.

[40] Christie, *Dissertations*, 210–11.

[41] Gaston, *Dynamic Monarchianism*, ch. 8.

[42] Den Dulk, *Between*.

Justin's *First Apology* (an "apology" in the ancient sense of a defense), written around 150–54,[43] is a public letter addressed to the three current emperors, the Roman senate, and the Roman people, defending the Christians against false accusations, explaining a few of their beliefs, and urging tolerance. As is well-known, early Christians met secretly, and consequently pagan imaginations ran wild, supposing that the Christians' "love feast" involved incest and that since someone's flesh was in some sense being eaten and their blood imbibed (the bread and the wine), cannibalism was being practiced. Various early Christian defenders deny these wild accusations, but Justin goes a step further, trying to deflect the fury onto others. In chapter 26 he explains that just as there are "philosophers" who are not true philosophers, so there are "Christians," people so-called, who are in fact *not* true Christians. Just before he'd mentioned Simon and his associates Helen, Menander, and Marcion of Pontus. He writes about Marcion that he is

> even now teaching his disciples to believe in some other god greater than the Demiurge [the "Craftsman," the maker of the cosmos]; who by the aid of the demons, has caused many of every race of men and women to speak blasphemies and to deny that God is the Maker of this Universe, and to profess another, who is greater than He, has done greater works.[44]

Justin proceeds to throw all three groups under the bus:

> And whether *they* commit the shameful deeds about which stories are told—the upsetting of the lamp, promiscuous intercourse, and eating of human flesh—we do not know; but we do know that they are neither persecuted nor put to death by you, at least for their opinions. But I have a treatise against all heresies which have arisen already composed, which I will give you if you wish to read it.[45]

Instead of calling out the accusations of incest and cannibalism as vicious and baseless rumors, he says that *for all he knows* it is these pseudo-Christians who are doing those things. He then offers, as Den Dulk puts it,

> to provide the Roman government with a 'black list' of sorts that could inform them about the kind of 'Christians' that falsely claimed that name and deserved

---

[43] Den Dulk, "Justin Martyr," 480–81.

[44] Justin, *First Apology*, 41 (sec. 26).

[45] *First Apology*, 41 (26), emphasis added. The "upsetting of the lamp" here means turning out the lights so that evil deeds may be done under cover of darkness.

> to be punished, in contradistinction to people such as Justin, i.e. the 'true Christians,' who ought to be tolerated by the Romans.[46]

That blacklist is believed by many scholars to be the first heresiological book, called the *Syntagma* after Justin's Greek word translated as "treatise" above. Although his statement is ambiguous, it seems reasonable to conclude that Justin is the author of this now-lost work,[47] a catalogue of the heretical groups. It seems likely too that he reuses or adapts material from this lost book elsewhere.[48]

In Justin's defense, perhaps he is genuinely wondering if there is any basis in fact for the standard vile accusations. If that's so, nonetheless, without adequate evidence, he is trying to redirect the imperial persecution of his group toward their religious rivals. Sadly, this will be far from the last time that various Christian or "Christian" factions try to enlist the empire to crush their rivals. Despite this effort, the imperial sword came for him; according to tradition, Justin and some associates were beheaded c. 162–67 by the Romans for refusing to sacrifice to the Roman deities.[49]

4.1.4 ANCIENT CATHOLIC HERESIOLOGY

This idea of cataloging and refuting all the false Christianities together, to facilitate their exclusion if not persecution, was much expanded by a slightly later author, who, like many, had read Justin's works. In his massive *Against Heresies* (or *Against the Heresies*),[50] written c. 182–88,[51] the bishop Irenaeus undertakes to document and refute the often-convoluted teachings of the many groups that existed in and around the mainstream churches in the mid to late 100s, most of which have been called "Gnostic" by later authors. Along the way Irenaeus expounds his own understanding of Christian teachings.[52]

---

[46] Den Dulk, "Justin Martyr," 477.

[47] "Justin Martyr," 477–83.

[48] Justin, *First Apology* chs. 26, 56, 58 (Den Dulk, 479–80).

[49] *Martyrdom of the Holy Martyrs.*

[50] Irenaeus, *Against the Heresies 1*; *Against the Heresies 2*; *Against the Heresies 3*; *Against the Heresies 4–5*.

[51] Irenaeus, *Condensation*, 2. Other scholars suggest that he wrote over a series of years perhaps more centered around the year 180 (*Against the Heresies 1*, 3–4).

[52] A recent condensation by Payton cuts out all the interactions with false teachers so as to present mostly only Irenaeus's own views (Irenaeus, *Condensation*). The best short introduction to Irenaeus's thought is Minns, *Irenaeus: An Introduction.*

While the New Testament, as we've seen, shows ample concern with false teachers and false teachings, Irenaeus's work set a new pattern. First, a heresy, a pseudo-Christian sect, is (usually) said to be founded by some heresiarch after whom it is named. Thus, as historian David Litwa puts it, "The internal others" are "ostracized through the power of relabeling."[53] The idea is that these people are not *Christians*; they are not disciples *of Christ*, but rather of some real or imagined heresiarch. Usually their error is diagnosed as being unduly influenced by this or that school of Greek philosophy (or some other pagan tradition), so despite their claim to be following Christ, they are *really* disciples of a pagan Greek philosopher.[54] It is even suggested that they're not only fake Christians but also pathetically unoriginal plagiarists. Litwa observes,

> For [Irenaeus] the bishop of Lyons, gnostic number speculation was perverted Pythagoreanism (*Haer.* 1.1.1), the Basilideans borrow their principles from astrologers (*Haer.* 1.24.7), and followers of Ptolemy the Valentinian took their theology from Homer (*Haer.* 1.12.1) . . . Irenaeus . . . lists the "real" sources of Valentinian thought as Thales, Homer, Anaximandros [Anaximander], Demokritos [Democritus], Epikouros [Epicurus], Plato, Empedokles [Empedocles], the Stoics, Hesiod, the Cynics, Aristotle, and the Pythagoreans (2.14.2–16).[55]

Modern scholars view most of these accusations as implausible. This sort of polemic is more religious than scholarly, and the genre as a whole exhibits several glaring defects. Litwa observes,

> The polemical features of heresiography include (1) the reduction of complex, nuanced teachings and practices to bare-bones, hostile, and disconnected opinions, (2) the grouping of otherwise unconnected figures into schools of thought characterized by genetic links of succession, (3) the practice of psychologizing[56] and character assassination, (4) the use of false inference[57] and

[53] Litwa, *Found Christianities*, 4.

[54] For example, the author of *Refutation of all Heresies* urges that the modalist Noetus is *really* a disciple of Heraclitus (*Refutation*, 639 [9.8].

[55] Litwa, *Found Christianities*, xlvi–xlvii.

[56] That is, shifting the focus away from a person's reasons or evidence for their view to their state of mind. For instance, one may argue that a person only holds a certain position because she is afraid, ambitious, or proud.

[57] That is, seizing on an alleged logical implication of a claim (perhaps even one that its

the polemical construction of "historical" details, all resulting in (5) the progressive distortion of reports as they were passed down, recopied, expanded, and contracted through time. As a result, virtually nothing heresiologists report can be readily or uncritically accepted.[58]

Going beyond (2), some later sources even try to classify all the heresies into a few basic families.[59] These manuals provide the reader with an illusion of breadth and depth of understanding; they offer to do the heavy lifting for the reader, claiming to give her all she needs to know about sorting the truly Christian groups and claims from their many counterfeits.

Many of Irenaeus's treatments get taken up and expanded or adapted in later heresiological works.[60] At least his treatments are better than most; patristic scholar Mark Edwards says about *Against the Heresies* that it is "perhaps the only one from the patristic age whose arguments against the rejected doctrines are not wholly devoid of intellectual or forensic merit."[61] The responsible historian of Christian doctrines, then, has his work cut out for him, as sadly these are pretty much our only sources of information about many historical figures and movements and their distinctive teachings, since their own writings have not survived.

Despite these glaring defects, it must be said that Justin and Irenaeus were justified in strongly opposing Marcion, and that Irenaeus was right in opposing most of the groups later scholars call "Gnostics." Why? Because they boldly contradicted central Christian claims, denying that God the Father (a.k.a. Yahweh) created the cosmos, and teaching that the "Christ" who really matters is a spirit who deserted the man Jesus on the cross. They taught various gospels of their own making, trying to hijack the traditions of Jesus and his apostles.[62]

---

proponents deny is an implication of it) and criticizing that implication as if it were the claim itself or a part of it. For instance, some Christian apologists urge that atheism implies that no action is right or wrong (ethical antirealism) and then criticize atheists for being ethical antirealists (which many of them *deny* is an implication of their atheism).

[58] Litwa, *Found Christianities*, 11.

[59] Writing in the eighth century, John of Damascus (*On Heresies*, 111 [Intro.]) claims that all heretical groups can be classified as examples of Barbarism, Scythism, Hellenism, and Judaism. In this he follows Epiphanius of Salamis, *Medicine Chest*, 1:9-12 (Proem 2.1).

[60] Most notably: the early third century *Refutation of All Heresies*, which used to be attributed to Hippolytus, and the late fourth-century *Medicine Chest* by Epiphanius of Salamis (c. 315–403).

[61] Edwards, *Catholicity and Heresy*, 42.

[62] Ehrman, *Lost Christianities*, chs. 5–6.

But once the various Gnostic groups had effectively disappeared from the scene, heresy-hunting traditions applied equal harshness to far more mainstream theological streams of thought. This took a terrible turn in the fourth century, when the emperor Constantine initiated a tradition of state-empowered persecution of every Christian not in the empire-endorsed mainstream.[63] A few generations later, under Theodosius I and his successors, religious freedom was extinguished, and this lasted until the early modern era, until around the time of John Locke.[64]

4.1.5 HERESIOLOGY TODAY

The heresiological tradition lives on today in countless encyclopedia entries, systematic theologies, apologetics materials, websites, social media posts, and theological reference works.[65] A heresiology, ancient or modern, is meant as a handy encyclopedia of theological and christological errors. It provides the reader with easy labels by which to pigeonhole and dismiss various sects, teachers, and teachings. ("Oh, *that's just* Marcionism," or "Valentinianism," or "Sabellianism.") Those are the "heresies," the pseudo-Christian sects that rival the correct, universal ("catholic") Church (however that is understood). Or one may call their *teachings* "heresies." Their founding heresiarchs, such as Sabellius, are "heretics," and so are the misguided souls who follow in their paths. One labels them in these ways to mark them to be set aside in one's search for the truth and to exclude anyone with similar views from the true church. While such books often argue that the heresies contradict Scripture, the whole genre presupposes that the catholic mainstream (or "historic Christian orthodoxy") has at least for the most part correctly interpreted the Bible.

Christians today still feel a need for help in distinguishing between false and true Christian teachings and groups. As theological scholarship has progressed, there has been a trend to distill the various errors into a scheme of abstract "isms," to a large degree setting aside the dubious biographical and historical accounts of the ancient heresiologies. Thus, on the topic of the Trinity, there are standard warnings against tritheism, modalism, and more recently, "partialism" (the Persons as proper parts of the Trinity), which popular apologetics sources

---

[63] Stark, *Triumph of Christianity*, ch. 10.
[64] King, *Emperor Theodosius*; Locke, *Locke on Toleration*.
[65] For example: Martin, *Kingdom*.

tirelessly pass around and reproduce. At least the scholarly standards of today's manuals are generally higher than ancient standards were.

But how, beyond blindly trusting in the classifications of such a manual, do we know *which* "isms" should be ruled out as non-Christian and which are required to be Christian? Most often in recent times it is simply asserted that this and that doctrine are "essential" (whatever that means) to "historic Christianity" (whatever that means). Lists of "heresies" are simply put forward, perhaps with a vague gesture at the Bible or a handful of proof texts. At least, that is the Protestant approach. The fully developed Roman Catholic approach is quasi-legal and, I shall argue, more behavior-oriented.

4.2 A ROMAN CATHOLIC APPROACH TO HERESY

As we saw, mainstream Christianity began in the 100s to define itself in distinction to rival groups; "heresies" at first were primarily groups. But as time went on, it was the rival, distinctive teachings of these groups that came to be called "heresies." To understand a traditional Roman Catholic approach to "dropping the H-bomb" (accusations of heresy), we need to see that the primary or foundational concept here is a "heresy" in the sense of a particular sin some people commit, not "heresy" in the sense of a false teaching. What does it take to commit that sin? In this, as in a great many other matters, Roman Catholics have an official definition: "Heresy is the obstinate denial or obstinate doubt after the reception of baptism of some truth which is to be believed by divine and Catholic faith."[66] Some have understood this definition to imply that "only a Catholic can be a heretic,"[67] while others have interpreted it as only requiring a valid baptism, which may have been outside the Catholic Church.[68] Some also see it as requiring that the person in question still professes to be a Christian, to rule out his being an "apostate."[69] The truths in question are restricted to a subset of all official Catholic teachings.[70] Note the all-important adjective "obstinate."

[66] "Code of Canon Law," can. 751. See also *Catechism*, sec. 2089.

[67] Kerper, "What Is," 10.

[68] Hardon, "Heresy"; "Session 7," 685.

[69] Hardon, "Heresy." "Apostasy" is defined as "the total repudiation of the Christian faith" ("Code of Canon Law," can. 751).

[70] Caridi, "Can a Pope." Then-Cardinal (and future Pope) Joseph Ratzinger gave examples of such truths in an official publication: "The articles of faith of the Creed, the various

What does it take to have a belief or doubt obstinately? One must have been confronted by some representative of the Church and refused to desist. Thus, Thomas Aquinas quotes Augustine as saying,

> In Christ's Church, those are heretics, who hold mischievous and erroneous opinions, and when rightly rebuked that they may think soundly and rightly, offer a stubborn resistance, and, refusing to mend their pernicious and deadly doctrines, persist in defending them.[71]

Sociologist Rodney Stark has observed a practical aspect of this. If the Roman Catholic Church doesn't consider you to be a threat, it may simply decline to confront you, allowing you to exist within it, despite your believing and even teaching claims that go against core Catholic teachings.[72] If they have not confronted you, you are not "obstinate," and so you are not a heretic, as you have not committed the sin of heresy.

In this way the Roman Catholic Church has simply absorbed many people into its churches and monastic communities who believed and taught ideas contrary to official doctrine. It chose not to make them heretics by refraining from confronting them. By their official definition, no one is a heretic until after they're confronted, and then only if they refuse to yield.[73] An ordinary Catholic lacks the authorization to declare anyone a heretic. The Church is the judge both of who needs to be confronted and of when the response is deemed stubborn. At least, this is the official, by-the-book way of understanding the Catholic concept of a heretic.

But there is another, more popular and less official way, a way that goes back to the second century. Perhaps you encounter some unfamiliar teacher or

---

Christological dogmas and Marian dogmas; the doctrine of the institution of the sacraments by Christ and their efficacy with regard to grace; the doctrine of the real and substantial presence of Christ in the Eucharist and the sacrificial nature of the eucharistic celebration; the foundation of the Church by the will of Christ; the doctrine on the primacy and infallibility of the Roman Pontiff; the doctrine on the existence of original sin; the doctrine on the immortality of the spiritual soul and on the immediate recompense after death; the absence of error in the inspired sacred texts; the doctrine on the grave immorality of direct and voluntary killing of an innocent human being" (Ratzinger, "Doctrinal Commentary").

[71] Aquinas, *Summa Theologica*, 439 (2.2.Q11.A2). Compare: Augustine, *City of God*, 898 (18.51).

[72] Stark, *One True God*, 120–22.

[73] Even then, whether one is guilty of the sin of heresy may depend on your motives (Wilhelm, "Heresy," sec. 1).

teaching and you're *not* inclined to humbly let Mother Church deal with the matter whenever she may get around to it. You may simply consult a manual of heresiology and based on what you read there try to fit that teacher or teaching into one of the provided slots. He'll end up being a "Sabellian," an "Arian," a "psilanthropist,"[74] or whatever. Never mind whether you understand those terms or the disputes in which they were coined by those who ended up on the catholic side of the argument. You may, on this basis, carry on with an *un*official denunciation.

Another less official way of proceeding is to trust the so-called "Athanasian" Creed to set the boundaries of what someone must believe to be saved.[75] Any group, then, that either contradicts or merely fails to teach those truths must be less than Christian. This shortcut seems to be preferred by many recent analytic theologians since that short document conveniently sets up puzzles that the clever logician or metaphysician can try her hand at solving by way of making fine distinctions.[76] All Christians, it is assumed and sometimes said, are committed to such claims, and so any solution will hopefully be relevant to all Christians. But this document's claims appear to be self-inconsistent—that is, logically incoherent.[77] Nor do they clarify matters; instead, they issue commands about which sentences should and should not be said. A host of competing theories have been generated in the attempt to show how such a Trinity doctrine is coherent after all.[78] This document just doesn't have what it takes to *clarify* what is orthodox and what is heretical.

4.3 TWO HISTORICAL PROTESTANT APPROACHES TO HERESY

Protestantism doesn't have one central organization, one network of ruling bishops, or one institutional church. Thus, Protestants can't define the sin of

---

[74] This is someone who teaches Jesus to be "a mere man" (*psilos anthropos*)—a derogatory term for the belief that Jesus is human but not also divine.

[75] This creed is not from the hand of Athanasius but is believed to be the product of the late 5th or early 6th century (Kelly, *Athanasian Creed*, ch. 7). It was endorsed by a pope and an official Catholic council in 1439 ("Session 8," 550–53).

[76] Regarding "the doctrine of the Trinity," a seminal treatment is Cartwright, "On the Logical." On the limits of this approach and its historical blindness, see my "Metaphysics and Logic"; Branson, "Ahistoricity."

[77] Tuggy, "Tradition and Believability," sec. 4. For an interpretation of the "Athanasian" Creed as incoherent by a friend of it, see Beall, *Divine Contradiction*, ch. 1.

[78] Tuggy, "Trinity"; Baber, "Trinity"; Howard-Snyder, "Trinity"; Werther, "Incarnation."

heresy as essentially defying the correction of the bishops or the one visible, institutional church, either directly or through some intermediary. A Protestant Christian might be in defiance of one ruling body, such as the Southern Baptists, but not another, such as the United Methodists. If a heretic is one who commits a sin of heresy, and this is essentially, as with the official Catholic approach, defying the correction of some authoritative leaders, then one may be a heretic relative to one organization while being a non-heretic in relation to others. But this whole tradition of talking about heresy and heretics doesn't grant that a teaching's status as a heresy or a person's status as a heretic are group-relative; what's heretical, outside the bounds of the true church and her teaching, just is so, whether or not a given group or body of leaders agrees.

Protestants take the concept of heresy as a belief as primary. The idea of a sin of heresy only makes sense in a quasi-judicial context, for instance, in a heresy trial conducted by a denomination. These are relatively rare in a Protestant context. Protestants prefer to think that a person is a heretic simply by teaching or believing (or disbelieving) certain things.

Protestants have embraced the approach of heresiology. They tend to adopt the same heresy labels developed by bishop-ruled catholic Christianity, mainly in the third through the sixth centuries. Thus, they in practice rely on heresiologists, but recent ones, be they seminary professors, independent apologists, or enthusiastic jousters on the internet. Speaking of enthusiastic jousters, Protestants are also painfully aware that heresy-hunting easily gets out of hand. Certain people love to accuse and habitually go off half-cocked. Accusations serve to burnish the image of the accuser as a Defender of the Faith, and the denouncer gets a self-righteous thrill and a social status boost when calling out the alleged theological sins of others. Human evil is all too quick to seize upon traditions of dropping H-bombs and use them to divide Christian communities.

It somewhat mitigates the damage that most Protestants follow the catholic tradition that not just any false teaching should count as heresy. Maybe a person has his own idiosyncratic scheme of reconstructing Jesus's life and so believes that Jesus was between forty and fifty when he was crucified.[79] This, most Protestants think, is false but not worth denouncing as heresy. After all, to declare someone a heretic has a practical aspect; you are saying that this person,

[79] Irenaeus convinced himself of this based on John 8:56–57 (*Against the Heresies* 2, 75 [2.22.6]).

unless they change their mind, should be excluded from Christian fellowship. Roman Catholics will, when they choose, excommunicate a heretic. Protestants will kick a declared heretic out of their church or denomination.

Heresy, then, is serious business; it concerns our intimate friendships with fellow Christians, and it may concern the salvation of the heretic or those whom he teaches. It's vitally important, then, to limit the dropping of H-bombs to the really serious cases. But which are those?

4.3.1 ESSENTIAL VS. NONESSENTIAL DOCTRINES

The most common answer given by Protestant theologians and apologists is to distinguish essential from nonessential doctrines. It is only by not believing or denying *an essential* doctrine that one becomes a heretic. One may err concerning nonessential beliefs and still be a Christian. But the essential ones must all be believed, and none may be denied. In this way, we won't have to declare every person with a false opinion to be a heretic, but we can root out the sorts of dastardly false teachers catalogued in traditional heresiologies.

The word "essential" here can not merely mean "important." An essence of something is a *defining* feature of it, a feature without which that sort of thing can't exist. It is essential to a triangle to have three sides. Arguably, it is essential to a quantity of water that it contains hydrogen and oxygen atoms. An essential feature is one that the owner of that feature cannot exist without having. A thing may come into or go out of existence, but at every moment of its existence it must have all of its *essential* properties. Thus, if a doctrine is essential to being a Christian, then no one is a Christian unless he believes that doctrine, and as long as there has been any Christian community, it has taught that doctrine. Christianity—the system of belief, the true theology—contains it as a core, defining part if it is an *essential* doctrine. And any group that ceased to teach or taught against that doctrine would be at best defectively Christian and at worst pseudo-Christian. A teaching, then, can't be recently minted, if it is an *essential* doctrine; it must be the same age as the system of belief to which it is essential. If it's really essential, it must have been there at the very heart of the faith in the beginning and in the minds of true believers ever since.

The early theologian, apologist, and heresiologist Tertullian of Carthage understood this point and used it as a weapon against the Gnostics in about the first quarter of the third century. Their teachings, he argued, were newly minted, but mainstream Christian teachings have been taught since the apostles, since there have been Christians, which is shortly after Jesus's resurrection.[80] Unfortunately for Tertullian, he was fragged with his own grenade. Many of Tertullian's own teachings about God and Jesus were not taught in the earliest days.[81] But the same point applies to present-day Catholic or Protestant apologists who argue that the Trinity and the two natures of Christ are essential doctrines, which therefore must have always been taught by Christians. This is *demonstrably* not so. No Christian confessed belief in a tripersonal god until sometime in the second half of the 4th century.[82] And no Christian confessed the two natures of Christ in its official, required form until the Council of Chalcedon in 451, although clashing speculations about Christ essentially being in some sense divine, in addition to being human, began in the second Christian century.

Still, it is undoubtedly correct that fellowshipping Christians may disagree about many things, and not only styles of music or politics but even theological matters. And surely there is in "the faith that was once and for all handed on to the saints" (Jude 3) a core set of essential teachings, the acceptance of which forms the basis for Christian community. But notice that we've only made a formal point: that, in theory, some teachings will be essential and others not, and only the essential ones are required to be accepted in our community. But which teachings are those exactly? Controversy rages over which beliefs are and are not essential, and it is unclear who gets to determine this. When Protestant theologians say that heresy is the denial of some essential doctrine, they are, in a sense, faking it. They usually have no actual list or procedure for deciding which claims are essential. And they are aware that there are serious disagreements about many such matters. For instance, some evangelicals strongly insist on biblical inerrancy, and various other evangelicals and other Protestants deny that inerrancy is essential, or even that it is true. Many of them boldly make things up about what is essential or how heresy should be understood.

In a recent book Anglican theologian Alister McGrath writes that heresy "is best seen as a form of Christian belief that ... ultimately ends up subverting,

---

[80] Tertullian, *Against Praxeas*, trans. Souter, 29 (2).

[81] For example, Tertullian's view that the prehuman Son of God is composed of a portion of the divine matter that composes God (*Against Praxeas*, trans. Souter, 46–47 [9]).

[82] The first known creed that arguably assumes that God is tripersonal is the one promulgated by the 381 council in Constantinople (Tuggy, "When and How," 42–43).

destabilizing, or even destroying the core of the Christian faith."[83] This is too unclear to serve as a definition. But notice that it is offered as a practical definition. A heresy is construed as a belief or teaching that sooner or later turns out to be harmful to Christian "faith," presumably true belief and/or faithful living. But this definition is idiosyncratic; it is unique to McGrath.

In an earlier textbook McGrath says that "heresy . . . is best understood as *an inadequate version of Christianity*," and that "it is a faulty or inadequate understanding of core Christian beliefs that arises within the context of faith itself."[84] "Core" here is probably a gesture at the idea of a belief that is essential to Christianity, but McGrath seems only to assume that catholic traditions have rightly determined Trinity and Incarnation to be essential ones.

As we've seen, the traditional Roman Catholic approach is to treat the concept of heresy as a sin as fundamental, basically, stubbornly defying the Church when it confronts you about matters of Christian belief. McGrath, a Protestant, doesn't recognize the authority of current-day Catholic or Eastern Orthodox bishops. But, strangely, like many Protestant theologians, it seems to be unthinkable for him that a true Christian should depart from the pronouncements by meetings of catholic bishops at Nicaea, Constantinople, or Chalcedon.

If not Mother Church or Catholic or Orthodox bishops, then who judges a teaching to be a heresy in McGrath's sense? Who decides that a teaching is long-term unhelpful or unhealthy for Christianity? He tells us, "the whole Christian church, not a party within that church."[85] But many seemingly Christian groups have ignored or denied many of the things insisted upon by the so-called "ecumenical" councils from 325–787. Recent ecumenical fashions being what they are, he will not lift a finger to help us decide what is included in and excluded from the true Church. In the end, McGrath merely reassures mainstream believers that the traditional condemnations are correct. He gives shallow brush-offs to serious Christian thinkers who would dare depart from the ancient creeds, pigeonholing them as mere revivers of ancient mistakes, brazenly ignoring their many carefully wrought theological and exegetical arguments.[86]

---

[83] McGrath, *Heresy*, 11–12.

[84] McGrath, *Christian Theology*, 254, 116, original italics.

[85] McGrath, *Heresy*, 216.

[86] See his casual brush-offs of the "Arians," Socinus, Newton, and Juan de Valdés (*Heresy*, 142–52, 185–86, 214). By far the deepest engagement here is with the "Arians," but McGrath seems to just uncritically accept Athanasius's polemical critiques of their views.

Many a unitarian Christian has been in a conversation like this:

> Unitarian: I don't see that Scripture teaches the one God to be the Trinity. To the contrary, I see that it teaches the one God to be the Father.
>
> Trinitarian: You're a heretic!
>
> Unitarian: What do you mean?
>
> Trinitarian: I mean that you're denying an essential doctrine of the historic Christian faith.
>
> Unitarian: But I don't agree that the Trinity *is* an essential doctrine. Like I said, I don't see it taught in Scripture.
>
> Trinitarian: But it *is* essential.

That last step is useless "table pounding"—merely repeating the same assertion but now more emphatically, thereby assuming the very point that is being challenged. This is so common, I suggest, because Protestantism doesn't provide any obvious way to delineate the essential from the nonessential teachings in a way that gets the correct, catholic answers, above all, making Trinity and Incarnation essential. Suppose one tried to appeal to "the consensus of the Church" in putting forth those dogmas as essential. But the Protestant, by definition, thinks that sometimes the mainstream consensus went wrong, very wrong, on important issues. Why should these not be among them?

Below I shall suggest a principled, Protestant way to separate the essential from the nonessential, but it is one that does not align with the catholic consensus on what the correct answers are.

4.3.2 NO CREED BUT THE BIBLE

All of this may give you a big, fat Protestant headache. Maybe we should have no doctrinal standards, or maybe we should just point to the Bible and say that, as a group, we adhere to whatever it teaches. Maybe "man-made creeds" produce only division and so should be avoided.

This approach was tried in the late eighteenth and nineteenth centuries in America, and it is one of several factors that killed American Congregationalist Unitarian Christianity as a Christian movement.[87] This stance was driven by the early American cultural disdain for authoritarian traditions. It was an overreaction to the state-controlled churches of Europe at that time.

---

[87] For some of the other factors see my "Podcast 168."

I will deal briefly with this approach. First, it is impractical if your aim is to live in a Christian community. With no standards, or with only gesturing at the Bible and saying, "We all accept *that*, however understood," what defense do you have when your pastor or a teaching elder stops believing in a personal God (choosing instead a "God" that is a transcendent, inconceivable who-knows-what), or asserts that the only essential message of the Bible is love of one's neighbor, or when he decides that baptism is no longer necessary? These things actually happened in nineteenth-century America.[88] The "free," creedless churches simply chose individual autonomy over fidelity to apostolic teaching, and over time they ceased to be a part of any Christian movement.

Second, this stance is hypocritical. Any like-minded religious community, in fact, has its own standards about what can be taught therein, even if they pretend not to. Try going into a Unitarian Universalist congregation and teaching that wives should submit to their husbands, that any sex outside of heterosexual marriage is a sin, or that George W. Bush was an excellent American president. You will soon find yourself unwelcome.

Third, this no-doctrinal-standards approach goes against apostolic practice. They did not simply accept any teaching, or pretend to have no doctrinal standards, or opine that it'll all work out if we just let everyone find his own way. On the contrary, they were capable of fiercely opposing certain teachings and expelling people from their churches. And they nagged us to hold tightly to the traditions they taught us. They did not value universal acceptance or individual autonomy above all else.

Finally, "No Creed but the Bible" is, unfortunately, not in the Bible; it is neither stated, nor implied, nor presupposed in any scriptural book. This stance appeals to some people, but it doesn't seem to have any justification.

4.4 A PRINCIPLED PROTESTANT APPROACH TO HERESY

We need, like the brave Protestants of the sixteenth century, to go back to the sources—to the books of the New Testament—and carefully rethink our approach to dropping H-bombs. The Reformation came up short in this area. Mainstream Protestants have traded the old Catholic approach for one that raises only further questions and invites confusion and unjustified speculations. We must continue to reform, to revise human traditions until they conform to

[88] Grodzins, *American Heretic*, ch. 9.

divine revelation. If we believe that God's revelation through Scripture is sufficient for Christian practice, shouldn't we expect it to give us sufficient guidance when it comes to heresy, and specifically to what exactly is essential for Christian belief?

The New Testament doesn't say much about heretics, heresy as a sin, or heresy as a false teaching. But as we saw, it warns us repeatedly about false teachers. And when viewed as a whole it provides a better way of thinking about false teachings and false teachers. As I see it, there are four relevant features of apostolic tradition; I will present these in the following four subsections.

But first, when someone asks, "Is this belief essential?" we should ask, "Essential *for what*?" What goal can't be reached, what purpose can't be achieved, what state of affairs can't be realized *unless* a person believes that? The catholic heresiological traditions presuppose that it is fully catholic, orthodox belief that should be our concern, because "whoever wills to be saved, before all things it is necessary that he holds the catholic faith. Unless a person keeps this faith whole and undefiled, without doubt he shall perish eternally."[89] (However, as we saw above,[90] one might not believe this and yet remain a member of the Roman Catholic church in good standing.) Nonetheless, this fully catholic "faith," which includes the Trinity and the Incarnation, is part of what it means to be a properly instructed church member in good standing, and as the traditional slogan says, "There is no salvation outside the church" (Latin: *Extra Ecclesiam nulla salus*). Which church? When first promulgated[91] this slogan referred to the bishop-ruled mainstream network of churches, the network that eventually split into the Roman Catholic and the Eastern Orthodox churches. And later, when that Latin slogan was used, it meant outside of the Roman Catholic Church. Thus, another goal is to remain a member of the Church, whose membership is strictly necessary for being saved.

There are two issues here that should be separated: whether there is any Christian monopoly—a visible, institutional church that you must be a member

---

[89] "Session 8," 551. This statement from the Roman Catholic Council of Basel-Ferrara-Florence-Rome, in its Basel phase in 1439, is also a bull from Pope Eugene IV, as he presided over this session in person. They are explicitly quoting "that compendious rule of the faith composed by the most blessed Athanasius" (550). This is the "Athanasian" Creed, which we now know was not composed by Athanasius (Kelly, *Athanasian Creed*).

[90] Section 4.2.

[91] The idea (but not the phrase) was asserted in the year 251 by the bishop Cyprian of Carthage (*Unity*, 157 [ch. 6]).

of to be saved—and what exactly is the bare minimum that must be believed by a person in order to be saved. I shall argue that in the New Testament there are no grounds for any institutional monopoly on God's grace, and that the strictly required beliefs required are surprisingly simple.

4.4.1 MINIMALISM ABOUT SALVATION-ESSENTIAL DOCTRINES

A salvation-essential doctrine is one that, if you don't believe it, bars you from being considered a Christian, even if you are a child, uneducated, or mentally handicapped. We should be afraid of adding to or changing the conditions of the new covenant proclaimed by Jesus and the apostles; we dare not make it harder for people to be saved by demanding assent to too much. A strong case for this is argued by the great Christian philosopher John Locke. He was disturbed by the acrimonious disputes of his day between Calvinists and Arminians and between trinitarians and unitarians. He knew that in many cases mere well-intentioned speculations were being foisted on Christians as essential beliefs. Being a Protestant, in the winter of 1694–95, he searched the New Testament to find out what was essential, to determine how much or how little one must believe to become a Christian. What he found astounded him. To a friend he wrote,

> From an intent and careful reading of the New Testament the conditions of the New Covenant and the teaching of the Gospel became clearer to me, as it seemed to me, than the noontide light, and I am fully convinced that a sincere reader of the Gospel cannot be in doubt as to what the Christian faith is.[92]

This is what he found:

> This was the great proposition that was then controverted concerning Jesus of Nazareth: "Whether he was the Messiah or no?" And the assent to that, was that which distinguished believers from unbelievers.[93]

In the next chapter I will follow in Locke's steps and show this in the book of Acts, adding some important details and nuances. For now I will review some of the texts Locke does, showing that this "great proposition" lies on the face of all four Gospels.

---

[92] Locke, *Letter to Limborch*, quoted in Locke, *Writings*, xlv.

[93] Locke, *Reasonableness of Christianity*, 17 (sec. 28). Older editions are available at books.google.com and archive.org, but this modernized paperback edition edited by Ewing is particularly accessible. The interested reader can also peruse an anonymous, nineteen-page summary of this book that Locke seems to have endorsed (Nuovo, "Extract").

But first, it is undeniably the main thesis of all four New Testament Gospels that Jesus is God's Messiah. These are practical, not theoretical, books; their aim is to empower the reader or hearer to follow Christ, to enter into God's new covenant through him. To so empower you, they must tell you what you need to believe—and they do. To review Locke's texts,[94] the author of the Fourth Gospel tells us that "whoever believes in the Son has eternal life" (John 3:36). But what does this trust in Christ require believing about him? The reader finds out in the next chapter, in Jesus's conversation with the Samaritan woman. After some conversation with Jesus in which he displays supernatural knowledge of her past and makes other prophetic statements, she brings up God's Messiah, and he confirms her suspicion.

> The woman said to him, "I know that Messiah is coming" (who is called Christ). "When he comes, he will proclaim all things to us."
> Jesus said to her, "I am he, the one who is speaking to you." (John 4:25–26)[95]

She runs off and tells this to her Samaritan friends, and we learn that

> many Samaritans from that city believed in him because of the woman's testimony, "He told me everything I have ever done." So when the Samaritans came to him, they asked him to stay with them, and he stayed there two days. And many more believed because of his word. They said to the woman, "It is no longer because of what you said that we believe, for we have heard for ourselves, and we know that this is truly the Savior of the world." (John 4:39–42)

These Samaritans respond in the way the Gospel authors want every reader to respond. Upon encountering Jesus's divinely empowered miracles and teachings, they believe him to be the Messiah, in other words, "the Savior of the world."

When Jesus deliberately said obscure and off-putting things, driving many away, he asked his disciples if they were going to leave him too (John 6:22–66). Peter spoke for them: "Lord, to whom can we go? You have the words of eternal life. We have come to believe and know that you are the Holy One of God" (John 6:68–69)—in other words, God's Messiah. In the other three Gospels, when Jesus asks his inner circle who they think he is, they give the same answer: "the Messiah, the Son of the Living God," "the Messiah," "the

---

[94] Locke, *Reasonableness of Christianity*, 15–20 (25–30).

[95] "I am he" here translates the Greek *ego eimi*, literally "I am," providing an interpretive key the author expects the reader to have in hand when she comes to John 8:58.

Messiah of God" (Matt. 16:16, Mark 8:29, Luke 9:20). In the Fourth Gospel the central purpose of the book is laid out with maximum clarity.

> Now Jesus did many other signs in the presence of his disciples that are not written in this book. But these are written so that you may continue to believe that Jesus is the Messiah, the Son of God, and that through believing you may have life in his name. (John 20:30–31)[96]

Notice that as with the quotation from Matthew, the author seems to equate being God's Messiah with being the Son of God. In the use of this latter title, there is no idea, like we see in catholic traditions from Athanasius on, that Jesus must be "a *real* Son," one with the same metaphysical nature or essence as his parent. The Son of God, being God's Messiah, is therefore a man.

According to Luke this message that Jesus is God's Messiah was proclaimed by the angel Gabriel to Jesus's mother even before his miraculous conception.

> "And now, you will conceive in your womb and bear a son, and you will name him Jesus. He will be great and will be called the Son of the Most High, and the Lord God will give to him the throne of his ancestor David. He will reign over the house of Jacob forever, and of his kingdom there will be no end." (Luke 1:31–33)

This same thesis was announced by an unnamed angel on the day of Jesus's birth: "To you is born this day in the city of David a Savior, who is the Messiah, the Lord" (Luke 2:11). This savior, this Messiah, is of course a man, the son of Mary, though one without a biological father; one finds no concern in these texts to assert his divinity. Nor is there the slightest hint of an eternal, divine Person coming down to "assume" a complete human nature.[97] The reader gathers that, as with other human beings, Jesus's existence began at some point in Mary's pregnancy, either at conception or a bit later. The text is a problem for believers in an eternally existing Son.

This good news doesn't change as we read through the four Gospels. Four days after the death of his friend Lazarus, we find Jesus discussing eternal life with Martha.

---

[96] Many commentators point out that this was probably the original ending of the book; chapter 21 seems to be an addition, for all we know, part of a second edition produced by the original author.

[97] Brown, *Birth of the Messiah*, 138–50, 290–91, 310–16.

> Martha said to Jesus, "Lord, if you had been here, my brother would not have died. But even now I know that God will give you whatever you ask of him."
>
> Jesus said to her, "Your brother will rise again."
>
> Martha said to him, "I know that he will rise again in the resurrection on the last day."
>
> Jesus said to her, "I am the resurrection and the life. Those who believe in me, even though they die, will live, and everyone who lives and believes in me will never die. Do you believe this?"
>
> She said to him, "Yes, Lord, I believe that you are the Messiah, the Son of God, the one coming into the world." (John 11:21–27)

In this passage the author presents Martha as a model of trusting in Jesus. What does that require? Believing him to be God's Messiah, a.k.a. the Son of God. Much earlier in the book we're given the example of two of Jesus's apostles.

> Philip found Nathanael and said to him, "We have found him about whom Moses in the Law and also the Prophets wrote, Jesus son of Joseph from Nazareth."
>
> Nathanael said to him, "Can anything good come out of Nazareth?"
>
> Philip said to him, "Come and see."
>
> When Jesus saw Nathanael coming toward him, he said of him, "Here is truly an Israelite in whom there is no deceit!"
>
> Nathanael asked him, "Where did you get to know me?"
>
> Jesus answered, "I saw you under the fig tree before Philip called you."
>
> Nathanael replied, "Rabbi, you are the Son of God! You are the King of Israel!"
>
> Jesus answered, "Do you believe because I told you that I saw you under the fig tree? You will see greater things than these." (John 1:45–50)

The reader is to believe that Jesus is God's Messiah. This is what he was implicitly claiming all along (and he sometimes explicitly says it)[98] and, as he points out, his testimony about himself is strongly confirmed by the miracles God does through him and by the testimony of the great prophet John the Baptist.[99]

Simply put, in the Gospels, the belief that separates believers from unbelievers is that Jesus is God's Messiah.[100] I would add that this is more a

---

[98] For example: Mark 14:61–62.

[99] John 1:15, 29–34, 3:32, 5:31–33, 8:17–18.

[100] C. S. Lakin pointed out to me that Paul agrees: "If you confess with your mouth that Jesus is Lord and believe in your heart that God raised him from the dead, you will be saved"

confession, a kind of public commitment to basic Christian teaching, than a single belief. If you believe that Jesus is the Son of God, that is, God's Messiah, then it follows that you should also believe a number of related truths: that the one God is the god of Israel, the Almighty Creator, who sent and empowered Jesus to teach us about God and to willingly give himself as a once-and-for-all sacrifice for sin. You must also believe that Jesus—a real man, God's anointed—died and was brought back to life and then was exalted to God's right hand. All of this is in the job description, as it were, of the Messiah, as provided by the prophets and the authors of the New Testament. So, confessing Jesus as Messiah, or as the exalted Lord, involves believing these things as well. (In the next chapter I'll explore more of what is in this package of beliefs signified by the confession that Jesus is God's Christ/Messiah.)

This minimalism about salvation-essential doctrine is presupposed by the conversion practices of most Protestants. Most of us have always thought that children, the uneducated, and those with low intelligence can become believing Christians, and those of us who hold to believers' baptism do baptize such people, *because* we think they have what is needed to accept Jesus as their Lord, as the risen Messiah, the mediator between God and humans. We don't quiz them first on the "Athanasian" Creed, the communication of attributes, or the particulars of the definition of Chalcedon, or on whether or not there are three *hypostases* who share one *ousia*, and it seems absurd to require commitment to such things for a person to gain entrance to the Christian community.

The catholic answer to which beliefs are strictly required for salvation unfortunately underwent a massive and unjustified expansion as their official doctrines expanded, particularly in the fourth and fifth centuries, but even beyond. In contrast to these famous later statements, the earliest creeds were short and devoid of paradoxes and technicalities. For instance, here is a short interrogatory creed from the early third century, to be used when baptizing:

> "Do you believe in the Father Almighty?"
>
> And he who is being baptized should reply, "I believe" . . .
>
> "Do you believe in Christ Jesus, the son of God, who was born under Pontius Pilate and was dead and buried and rose on the third day alive from the dead and ascended in the heavens and sits at the right hand of the Father and will

---

(Rom. 10:9). An examination of Paul's writings shows that confessing Jesus as "Lord" is not confessing him to be Yahweh but rather God's unique Messiah and Son (Rom. 1:4, 5:8–21; 1 Cor. 11:3, 15:20–28; Eph. 1:3, 17). On the title "Lord" in the New Testament see section 1.6.

> come to judge the living and the dead?" ... "Do you believe in the Holy Spirit and the holy church and the resurrection of the flesh?"[101]

In contrast, in 380 Emperor Theodosius I enshrined in Roman law that all Christians must believe in the baffling views that emerged toward the end of the so-called "Arian" controversy, what scholars call Neo-Nicene or Pro-Nicene theology. He decreed, in part,

> It is Our will that all the peoples who are ruled by the administration of Our Clemency shall practice that religion which the divine Peter the Apostle transmitted to the Romans ... It is evident that this is the religion that is followed by the Pontiff Damasus and by Peter, Bishop of Alexandria, a man of apostolic sanctity; that is ... we shall believe in the single Deity of the Father, the Son, and the Holy Spirit, under the concept of equal majesty and of the Holy Trinity.[102]

Here the emperor effectively ended the long-running controversy about the new language introduced at Nicaea in 325, declaring the Pro-Nicene party correct. Shortly after he called and hosted the 381 meeting in Constantinople, which seems to have promulgated two creeds, one of which was eventually affirmed as authoritative by the 451 council.[103] What exactly are the required beliefs here? The emperor gestures vaguely at them, describing them as what two prominent Pro-Nicene bishops believe, but we have good reason to believe that Damasus was an early adopter of the then-new trinitarian theology.[104]

The inflation continued; catholic tradition soon demanded much more, saddling the believer with baffling paradoxes. The "Athanasian" Creed, which seems to have been inspired by the trinitarian theology of Augustine (354–430) states that "we are obliged ... to acknowledge each person separately [as] ... God" and "the Father is God, the Son God, the Holy Spirit God; and yet there are not three Gods, but there is one God."[105]

What does do these sentences mean? The early modern unitarian polemicist Stephen Nye (1648–1719) brings about their absurdity in a famously vivid and humorous way:

---

[101] Hippolytus, *Apostolic Tradition*, 134 (21.12–17).

[102] Pharr (trans.), *Theodosian Code*, 440 (16.1.2).

[103] For the difficult historical evidence here see Kinzig, *History*, chs. 7–9. Oddly, it is this creed that nowadays is called "the Nicene Creed."

[104] Damasus of Rome, "Tome," 146 (sec. 24).

[105] *Athanasian Creed*, 18 (15–16, 19).

> that [faith] of the *Trinitarians* is absurd, and contrary both to Reason and *to Itself*; and therefore not only false, but *impossible*. For [they] . . . teach, That there are Three *Almighty, most Good and most Wise* Persons, and yet but One God; as if every *Almighty most Wise and Good Person* were not a God, a most Perfect God; and consequently Three such Persons, Three Gods. You add yet more absurdly, That there are Three Persons who are *severally and each of them true God,* and yet there is but One true God. This is *an Errour in counting or numbring; which,* when stood in, is of all others the most brutal and inexcusable: and *not to discern it, is not to be a Man.*[106]

There is a terrible and tragic injustice in this inflation, a violation of God's will concerning his new covenant through Christ. What was meant to be easy has been made hard. How exactly might one go about *believing* such claims? Repeating them out loud, with some embarrassment, is doable for many people, given enough social pressure. But actually *believing* them . . . how does one do that? I don't know!

Since people are desensitized to nonsense in Christian theology, the point may be easier to see with a mundane parallel. Let me tell you about my pets. First, there is Barron, a quiet, thin, black cat. Second, there is Melania, a beautiful, friendly gray cat. Finally, there is Donald, and he is a fat, mean, noisy, orange cat. Also, I don't have three cats; I have only one cat.

Faced with testimony like this, what are you to believe? You will probably think I'm joking and that I'm not trying to get you to believe anything in particular. But suppose I convince you that I'm wholly serious. You may conclude that I'm suffering from some sort of cognitive malfunction that interferes with cat counting. But as our conversations continue, you rule that out. Will you *agree with* what I have said about my pet ownership? You don't even know what it would mean to agree with what I said. In the first part, I confessed to having at least three cats, each with distinctive qualities that the other two lack. But then I explicitly asserted that I own exactly one cat, which rules out my having at least three.

Perhaps I could somehow impress you so much that you can't bring yourself to believe that I could be mistaken about my own pet ownership. Perhaps I could convince you to have "implicit faith" in my testimony so that you will in some sense commit yourself to *whatever it is* I just said about my pets. But this

[106] Nye, *Brief History*, 9 (1.7).

isn't really to agree with or to believe what I said. You might think this is the best you can do since you can't get yourself to actually believe that, at the same time and in the same way, Dale has and does not have three cats, or that Dale has and does not have exactly one cat. Or perhaps you would give up on any attempt to evaluate what I testified about my own pet ownership, concluding that you simply do not understand what I was asserting, if anything.

Try to imagine the terrible situation you would be in if your eternal destiny somehow depended on your agreement with what I said! If you really thought something important hinged on your agreement, you might decide to habitually parrot my words, hoping against hope that at some point it would start to make sense to you (as it *seemed* that it made sense to me when I said it) so that you would then have something in your mind to agree with. This imaginary setup is extremely cruel.

But so is this situation: either believe in the seemingly incoherent claims of the "Athanasian" Creed or burn eternally in hell, suffering for an infinitely long time, with no hope of escape. The catholic traditions have made a monumental error in making such impossible demands, and Bible-believing Christians should return to the mystery-free, paradox-free standard of the New Testament.

John Locke rightly points out that we have no right to make the new covenant and Christ's church harder to enter into.

> The law of faith, being a covenant of free grace, God alone can appoint what shall be necessarily believed by everyone he will justify. What is the faith which he will accept and account for righteousness depends wholly on his good pleasure. For it is of grace, and not of right, that this faith is accepted. And therefore he alone can set the measures of it, and what he has so appointed and declared, is alone necessary. Nobody can add to these fundamental articles of faith, nor make any others necessary, but what God himself hath made and declared to be so.[107]

In a follow-up writing Locke has this stern warning for those who concoct puzzling, paradoxical, or very complex and speculative creeds that must (allegedly) be believed by anyone to become a Christian.

> I tell him [the creed maker], and I desire him to take notice of it, God has nowhere given him an authority thus to garble the inspired writings of the Holy

[107] Locke, *Reasonableness of Christianity*, 191 [250].

> Scriptures. Every part of it is his word, and ought, every part of it, to be believed by every Christian . . . according as God shall enable him to understand it.[108]

With so many clashing creeds afoot, the result is widespread confusion:

> While almost every distinct society of Christians magisterially ascribes orthodoxy to a select set of fundamentals, distinct from those proposed in the teaching of our Savior and his apostles, which in no one point must be questioned by any of its communion. By this means their people are never sent to the Holy Scriptures, that true fountain of light, but are hoodwinked; a veil is cast over their eyes, and then they are bid to read their Bible. They must make it all chime to their church's fundamentals, or else they were better to let it alone. For if they find anything there against the received doctrines, though they hold it and express it in the very terms the Holy Ghost has delivered it in, that will not excuse them. Heresy will be their lot, and they will be treated accordingly. And thus we see how . . . creed-making always has and always will necessarily produce and propagate ignorance in the world, however each party blame others for it.[109]

Elsewhere Locke suggests that making a creed can make sense *if* its words are as clear as or clearer than what is in Scripture.[110]

4.4.2 NO INSTITUTIONAL MONOPOLY ON SALVATION

In the beginning there was no idea of a monopoly on God's grace in the new covenant era, as there was no institutional church. But given human nature, early Christians had a propensity to idolize their leaders and so to factionalize around them. In his first letter to the Corinthians Paul writes,

> Now I appeal to you, brothers and sisters, by the name of our Lord Jesus Christ, that all of you be in agreement and that there be no divisions among you but that you be knit together in the same mind and the same purpose. For it has been made clear to me by Chloe's people that there are quarrels among you, my brothers and sisters. What I mean is that each of you says, "I belong to Paul," or "I belong to Apollos," or "I belong to Cephas," or "I belong to Christ." Has Christ been divided? Was Paul crucified for you? Or were you baptized in the name of Paul? I thank God that I baptized none of you except Crispus and Gaius, so that no one can say that you were baptized in my name. I did baptize also the household of

---

[108] Locke, *Second Vindication of the Reasonableness of Christianity*, sec. 45, quoted in *Reasonableness of Christianity*, 210–11.

[109] Locke, *Second Vindication*, sec. 28, quoted in *Reasonableness of Christianity*, 211.

[110] Locke, *A Third Letter for Toleration*, 154, quoted in *Reasonableness of Christianity*, 212.

Stephanas; beyond that, I do not know whether I baptized anyone else. For Christ did not send me to baptize but to proclaim the gospel—and not with eloquent wisdom, so that the cross of Christ might not be emptied of its power. (1 Cor. 1:10–17)

The story of Acts is not about the founding and expansion of an institutional church but rather the spreading of God's word/message.[111] Wherever that message goes and is believed, we have members of the universal church, the "body of Christ" (1 Cor. 12:27). The New Testament authors never envision the rise of a ruling class of bishops whose domains define the boundaries of the institutional catholic church. The earliest churches seem to have been led by a plurality of leaders variously called "elders" or "presbyters" (*presbyteroi*), "overseers" or "bishops" (*episkopoi*),[112] "pastors" or "shepherds" (*poimenes*), or teachers (*didaskaloi*). In addition to these teachers and leaders, there were "deacons" (*diakonoi*) in various service roles, following the apostolic example (Acts 6:2–4).[113] Churches were also served by the itinerant ministries of apostles, prophets, and evangelists (Eph. 4:11).

If we follow the current consensus and accept the problematic seven middle-length letters attributed to Ignatius as genuine,[114] then at the very most they show that the one-bishop system, the monarchical episcopate, began in some

[111] Acts 4:4, 29; 6:2, 7; 8:4, 25; 10:44; 11:1, 9; 12:24; 13:5, 7, 44, 46, 48; 13:49; 14:3, 25; 15:35–36; 16:32; 17:13; 18:5; 19:10.

[112] These terms seem to be used to refer to the same groups of people in Acts 20:17, 28.

[113] Whether or not women served in the other capacities, there were female deacons early on (Rom. 16:1). This continued for some time. "Churches stopped ordaining women to the office of deacon . . . during the sixth century in the West and much later in the East" (Collins and Walls, *Roman*, 172). The only "priest" in New Testament ecclesiology is the permanent high priest, the exalted man Jesus (Heb. 2:17, 3:1, 4:14–15, 5:1–5, 6:20, 8:1–3, 9:11). What happened in catholic history is that the bishop job came to be so high-level and laden with other responsibilities that the task of presiding over services was handed to underlings, to elders/presbyters. Old Testament "priest" terminology was applied in the late second and early third centuries both to bishops and to presbyters, and later mainly to the latter, who normally presided over services (Collins and Walls, *Roman*, 174–79).

[114] For the wide range of positions scholars take on these letters, see Schoedel, *Ignatius*, 4–7; Brent, *Ignatius of Antioch*, ch. 5. I am agnostic on how many of the seven middle-length letters are genuine, but any that are have suffered from significant corruption. Paul Gilliam (*Ignatius of Antioch*) persuasively argues for Nicene-controversy-era corruptions of these in increasing the God-language used in reference to Jesus. Some of the language in these letters strikes me as modalistic, and I would not rule out corruption at earlier stages as well, perhaps even relating to the topic of bishops.

places surprisingly early, in the early second century.[115] But while the author presupposes that every church will be under one bishop/overseer, it is not clear whether this one governs all the churches in his region rather than a single church. Nor does Ignatius assume or imply the later idea of apostolic succession, that the apostles designated monarchical bishops as their replacements. In fact, it could be that a single top church leader was a new development, which would explain why the author so strongly insists on it.[116] Whether or not these letters are genuine, they do attest to the three-fold leadership structure we see arising throughout the second century.

> Let everyone respect the *deacons* as Jesus Christ, just as they should respect the *bishop*, who is a model of the Father, and the *presbyters* as God's council and as the band of the apostles. Without these no group can be called a church.[117]

In contrast to these letters, other late first- and early second-century writings seem to presuppose the New Testament model of multiple elders/overseers and deacons.[118] Current historians view the one-bishop system as slowly and unevenly establishing itself in the second and third centuries.[119] And even where that system was in place, there could be disputes about who the bishop was, as seen famously in third century Rome, where at times the unknown author of *Refutation of All Heresies* and Novatian led rival factions,[120] sometimes being anachronistically described in later times as "anti-popes."

At least by the fourth century a one-bishop system seems to have been universal in the churches of the Roman Empire. These considered themselves to be the true successors of the apostolic tradition. In their eyes the only legitimate Christian churches, the only "catholic" (universal) churches, were those under their control.

---

[115] The author strongly emphasizes obedience to a single bishop, referencing Eph. 6:1 (Ignatius, *Trallians* 215 [2:1]; *Smyrneans*, 257 [9:1]).

[116] Ortlund, *What It Means*, 125–26.

[117] Ignatius, *Trallians*, 217 (3:1), emphases added. And earlier we see a mention of these three but without any indication that there was only one bishop who ruled over all the churches in his area (215–17, [2:2–3]).

[118] Ortlund, *What It Means*, 122–25.

[119] For the historical case against Roman Catholic claims that Jesus made Peter the first Pope and that the papacy (and the one-bishop system) go back to the beginning, or at least to a point when the apostles made the bishops their successors, see Ortlund, *What It Means*, chs. 7–8; Collins and Walls, *Roman*, chs. 10–13; Lampe, *Paul to Valentinus*, ch. 41.

[120] *Refutation*, xl–xlii; Novatian, *Trinity*, trans. Papandrea, 10–16.

The question then arises: must one be a member in good standing of such a church to be saved? As with so many issues in early catholic Christianity, the answer was unclear; one can appeal to patristic texts for and against it.[121] But as the centuries passed, a clear trend toward extreme monopoly claims over salvation emerged. An African bishop writing in the 520s tells us that

> not only all pagans but also all Jews and all heretics and schismatics who end this present life outside the Catholic Church are about to go into the eternal fire that was prepared for the Devil and his angels.[122]

This extreme claim was affirmed at the Roman Catholic Fourth Lateran Council in 1215[123] and was asserted in no uncertain terms in a papal bull in 1302.[124] In 1442 this position was strongly affirmed in another papal bull by Pope Eugene IV (r. 1431–47):

> all those who are outside the catholic church, not only pagans, but also Jews or heretics and schismatics, cannot share in eternal life and will go *into the everlasting fire which was prepared for the devil and his angels,* unless they are joined to the catholic church before the end of their lives ... nobody can be saved, no matter how much he has given away in alms and even if he has shed his blood in the name of Christ, unless he has persevered in the bosom and the unity of the catholic church.[125]

The phrase "even if he has shed his blood" denies the doctrine that one who is martyred for their faith before their baptism has something as effective—a "baptism of blood"—so that they are saved. No, the pope is insisting that an intention to be baptized, and even martyrdom, are not enough. What—you say

---

[121] Mazza, "*Extra Ecclesiam.*"

[122] Fulgence of Ruspe, *Rule of Faith*, 298 (sec. 81).

[123] "There is indeed one universal church of the faithful, outside of which nobody at all is saved" ("Constitutions," 231 [sec. 1]).

[124] "The Church is one, holy, catholic, and also apostolic ... outside of her there is neither salvation nor the remission of sins ... There had been at the time of the deluge only one ark of Noah, prefiguring the one Church, which ark ... had only one pilot and guide, i.e., Noah, and we read that, outside of this ark, all that subsisted on the earth was destroyed ... This authority ... is not human but rather divine, granted to Peter by a divine word and reaffirmed to him (Peter) and his successors ... Therefore whoever resists this power thus ordained by God, resists the ordinance of God ... Furthermore, we declare, we proclaim, we define that it is absolutely necessary for salvation that every human creature be subject to the Roman Pontiff" (Boniface VIII, *Unam Sanctam*).

[125] "Session 11," original italics. As the Pope presided personally at this session, its statement is the same as his papal bull *Cantate Domino*.

you're a baptized and faithful Protestant? As the early modern Council of Trent made clear with its unrelentingly negative statements on Protestantism,[126] that will do you no good at all.

The Catholic Church is very effective at changing its teachings, sometimes in reasonable ways, while convincing people that the new teachings are what it has taught all along.[127] The monopolistic statements we've just seen meant exactly what they said; either one is a baptized Catholic or one goes to hell. But the Catholic Church as a whole, for ethical and scriptural reasons, has in the modern era given up that strong stance. To compress a complex story, they retained the positive claim that only Church membership can save, but they posited new forms of non-standard Church membership for various groups of people. The "baptism of blood" was affirmed, in effect granting membership to a catechumen or person intending to convert and be baptized but who is martyred for their faith first; their own blood, as it were, baptizes them. There is also a "baptism of desire," which is enough for a person who is "invincibly ignorant," that is, who due to no fault of their own is without access to Catholic instruction but is disposed such that they would accept the teaching if it were presented to them. Whether these are really kinds of baptism, the driving idea is that the perfectly just God must judge people based on what they knew or should have known, and that while all have access to natural revelation—what can be known by God from the sorts of reason and experience that are shared by all peoples—not all have access to the special revelation brought by the prophets, Jesus, and the apostles (Rom. 1:18–30).

Any Christian should reject the traditional, hard-nosed Catholic position based on more than five hundred years of experience around the world. When Peter in Acts 11 reported to the Jerusalem church the surprising events of Acts 10, they exclaimed, "Then God has given even to the gentiles the repentance that leads to life" (Acts 11:17). So too should Catholic and Orthodox Christians conclude: "Then God has given even the Protestants the repentance that leads to life." Any theory on which God's grace operates only through one or both of those institutional churches has been falsified. As much as it hurts the pride of some Catholic and Orthodox Christians, they should

[126] "Session 7."

[127] For stark examples compare their present-day teachings on sex and marriage (*Catechism*, 400–15 [1601–66], 560–76 [2331–2400]) with their historical teachings (Ranke-Heinemann, *Eunuchs*).

give up their monopolistic claims on pain of denying the obvious fruits of God's spirit (Gal. 5:22–23) in the lives of non-Catholic and non-Orthodox Christians.[128] Those "fruits" are evidence of conversion, of the new life that we get through Christ. There is no institutional monopoly on salvation; there never has been. Neither Jesus nor the apostles taught any such monopoly; in the New Testament the word of God goes where it goes and has its saving effects whether or not there is the sort of church leadership structure that was considered standard by late antiquity.

How far exactly does salvation extend? If we can't simply judge by church membership, then how do we know whether someone is saved? When we know the minimal beliefs required for entry, we can simply ask a person if he believes those things. Of course, he may lie, or even be self-deceived, knowing how to parrot "the right answers" even when those things are not actually believed. But we can also observe his life to see whether the fruits of the spirit are there and that their life is not dominated by the works of the flesh. Paul tells us,

> the works of the flesh are obvious: sexual immorality, impurity, debauchery, idolatry, sorcery, enmities, strife, jealousy, anger, quarrels, dissensions, factions, envy, drunkenness, carousing, and things like these. I am warning you, as I warned you before: those who do such things will not inherit the kingdom of God. By contrast, the fruit of the Spirit is love, joy, peace, patience, kindness, generosity, faithfulness, gentleness, and self-control. (Gal. 5:19–23a)

As Jesus taught us, we know what sort a tree is by its fruit (Matt. 17:15–20).[129] Again, John tells us a useful rule of thumb, that habitual haters are unsaved, while habitual lovers are (1 John 2:9–11). Again, we can just ask someone if she has had the experience of being "born again," although it is beyond dispute that some believers never had any memorable conversion experience. For sure, there are hard to judge cases, where someone's spiritual status is known only to God and his Son. But in these ways, generally, we *can* know who is and is not saved.

---

[128] We could add obedience to Jesus in discipling and baptizing people of all nations (Matt. 28:19–20).

[129] The context concerns "false prophets" but the general principle seems applicable beyond them.

4.4.3 IMPORTANT TEACHINGS VS. ESSENTIAL TEACHINGS

In everyday life, outside of technical or theoretical contexts, "essential" usually just means "important (for some reason or other)." Any true and important claim or helpful instruction in Christian living is "essential" in that sense. But when an "essential" belief means one that is essential *to being saved*, the list of "essential" beliefs will be much shorter.

Imagine you're being interviewed for a job. The conversation has been pleasant and lively, and you're beginning to hope that an offer for employment will be forthcoming. But suddenly the interviewer's face turns serious, and she opens a drawer and pulls out a heavy, well-worn binder labeled *The Employee Handbook*. She explains, "We demand *a lot* of our employees." She pauses, looking through it, stopping somewhere in the middle. "Here," she says, "Section 9, article 4, part 1. 'No employee shall make social media posts about politics or other controversial topics.'" She closes the book and looks accusingly over her glasses at you. "You *do* that, *don't you*?"

"Well," you stammer, "yeah, I mean, I guess I got caught up in the most recent elections . . . but I understand why this company is so concerned about public relations, and I will gladly delete those posts and refrain from such posts in the future. This job is really important to me."

"Too late. I'm afraid you're in violation of *The Employee Handbook*—I can't hire you. Better luck next time. You can show yourself out."

"But I'm not an employee!"

You are correct. Until you're an employee, you can't even be expected to know what is in that handbook, much less be obligated to conform to all its demands. If you get the job, you will thereby be agreeing to conduct yourself as an employee should, and if you ignore those requirements, you may be disciplined, fined, demoted, or fired. By accepting their offer of employment, you're accepting the duty of learning and adhering to the requirements of that handbook. Hiring would be nearly impossible if one had to know in advance and be fully in compliance with those requirements.

Let's suppose for the sake of argument that the author of the "Athanasian" Creed got it right when it comes to trinitarian theology, so that the best, most correct approach is to believe, or to try to believe, some paradoxical claims. Those beliefs or commitments—for instance, that the Father is Almighty, the Son is Almighty, and the Holy Spirit is Almighty, but there is only one

Almighty, not three—are truly essential. But essential to what? At most they could be essential to your being a fully informed, adequately instructed catholic Christian. Are these commitments also essential to your making the transition from unsaved to saved? A Catholic or Orthodox Christian should say not. Suppose that a person repents of her sin, comes to church, and talks to a priest, expressing her desire to convert and be baptized. Let's suppose he tells her the paradoxical "Athanasian" sentences, and the would-be convert does not know what to make of them. She excuses herself, and as she walks home she is mulling them over, not yet either accepting or rejecting them, trying to decide what they mean. Before she gets home, she is hit by a bus and instantly killed. Is she saved? A contemporary Roman Catholic should say yes, she has received a "baptism of blood," as she died while intending to convert and be baptized.[130] But she never did believe or in any way commit to the baffling claims. Of course, not all Christians believe in such a salvific loophole, but, more importantly, any Christian of any sort can see the clear implication of many passages in the Bible that no such difficult feat of paradoxical belief (or commitment, or acceptance, etc.) is needed to go from being an unbeliever to a believer.

Of course, as Locke points out, the disciple is obligated to believe the full contents of whatever is divinely revealed.[131] The new covenant has specific conditions that must be met for entry, but of course for those in the group there is a much larger and more complex body of teaching that should be profitably studied and acted on over one's whole lifetime. A Christian deliberately going against the teachings of Jesus and his apostles is in sin. God sent them to lead and instruct us, and to go against them is to defy God. But the typical remedy is gentle and careful correction by reasonable and scriptural teaching, not denunciation, not the dropping of H-bombs. We who are in obedience must correct in gentleness and humility, taking care lest we too are tempted. (Maybe I'll go to correct this sinner and find that it is instead I who am missing the mark.) Yes, as Jesus outlines in Matthew 18:15–20, the matter can be escalated. If the person continues in their sin after you talk with them privately, the matter may have to be made public, and the assembly as a whole may even disinvite the person, as Paul says, handing them "over to Satan for the destruction of the flesh, so that the spirit may be saved in the day of the Lord" (1 Cor. 5:5).

---

[130] *Catechism*, secs. 1258–59.

[131] Locke, *Reasonableness of Christianity*, 190–95 [249–52].

4.4.4 UNITY MATTERS

The New Testament teaches functional unity as a central Christian value. According to the Fourth Gospel, toward the end of his initial ministry Jesus prayed to God for his disciples and for those who would believe their message.

> "I ask not only on behalf of these [apostles] but also on behalf of those who believe in me through their word, that they may all be one. As you, Father, are in me and I am in you, may they also be in us, so that the world may believe that you have sent me. The glory that you have given me I have given them, so that they may be one, as we are one, I in them and you in me, that they may become completely one, so that the world may know that you have sent me and have loved them even as you have loved me." (John 17:20–23)

This should touch the heart of every disciple; Jesus wants his followers to dwell together in love and unity. We should be afraid of causing strife, hate, and division between disciples of Jesus over nonessential beliefs, however important we think they are. We should be afraid of what used to be called "party-spirit," that is, of being a factionalist, a divisive person. As we saw in section 4.1.1, when the New Testament talks of "heresies," it sometimes means false teachings but more often it means sects—that is, religious groups (without any negative connotation)—and sometimes it really means factions, divided and mutually opposed groups, typically clustered around various dominant personalities (1 Cor. 11:18–19). We must do what we can to avoid the great evil of factions.

In Paul's day, a clear nonessential was his belief that a Christian is allowed to eat meat that has been sacrificed to idols. Not everyone in Paul's churches agreed. Rather than browbeating those with a tender conscience about this matter, Paul instructs both sides not to judge one another harshly.

> Welcome those who are weak in faith but not for the purpose of quarreling over opinions. Some believe in eating anything, while the weak eat only vegetables. Those who eat must not despise those who abstain, and those who abstain must not pass judgment on those who eat, for God has welcomed them. Who are you to pass judgment on slaves of another? It is before their own lord that they stand or fall. And they will be upheld, for the Lord is able to make them stand . . . For we do not live to ourselves, and we do not die to ourselves. If we live, we live to the Lord, and if we die, we die to the Lord; so then, whether we live or whether we die, we are the Lord's. For to this end Christ died and lived again, so that he might be Lord of both the dead and the living. Why do you pass judgment on your brother or sister? Or you, why do you despise your brother or sister? For

> we will all stand before the judgment seat of God. For it is written, "As I live, says the Lord, every knee shall bow to me, and every tongue shall give praise to God." So then, each one of us will be held accountable. (Rom. 14:1–4, 7–12)

But this is not all of his instruction. He then orders the church at Rome to "resolve never to put a stumbling block or hindrance in the way of a brother or sister." So even though "nothing is unclean in itself," it still may go against the conscience of some believers, and so the more knowledgeable should cede their right to eat meat in the assembly.

> Let us then pursue what makes for peace and for mutual upbuilding. Do not, for the sake of food, destroy the work of God. Everything is indeed clean, but it is wrong to make someone stumble by what you eat; it is good not to eat meat or drink wine or do anything that makes your brother or sister stumble. Hold the conviction that you have as your own before God. (Rom. 14:19–22. See also 1 Cor. 8–10.)

Paul is saying that your freedom in Christ to eat anything is important, but unity is more important. So too I suggest that you have a right as a believer to theologize, to piece together scriptural teachings into a coherent whole as best you see fit—of course, in humility—knowing that people smarter and all-around better than you have held to different schemes. Beware of judging yourself superior to anyone who doesn't hold to your theological opinions, and be ready to sacrifice having things your way, as concerns theoretical understanding, in favor of unity, especially with those in your local Christian church.

The New Testament contains many of what I call oneness slogans, which are meant to emphasize the unity of all who believe in Jesus as Messiah. Trinitarians love to emphasize the ones that mention Father, Son, and Spirit together, as if this hints that they somehow compose the one God. But really, the idea in such passages is that all Christians have one God, one Lord (the exalted man, Jesus), and one anointing or empowering from God. Instead of those triadic passages, I'll quote a oneness slogan that trinitarians often ignore, as it mentions more than three. In another of Paul's letters we read that

> there is one body and one Spirit, just as you were called to the one hope of your calling, one Lord, one faith, one baptism, one God and Father of all, who is above all and through all and in all. (Ephesians 4:4–6).

One faith: if you believe in Jesus as Messiah, you have that one faith. You may also happen to combine it with various speculations, some of which may not really be consistent with elements of that one faith. Even so, you share that one faith with many others—Catholics, Calvinists, unitarian Christians, and trinitarians alike—as well as those who are undecided regarding the choice between trinitarian and unitarian theologies. Yes, even the evangelical who thinks that Jesus is God himself and also that God is someone other than Jesus. God is merciful to us in our confusions. That's why he made the deal simple. Little is required by way of belief. More is required when it comes to repentance and obedience. And there are many truths God has revealed that are very important even though they are not essential to being a Christian.

It seems to me that, in the end, H-bombs are a legitimate weapon, but only against real opponents of the gospel—that is, those among us who oppose the minimal, saving, core message. We are not to drop H-bombs, surely, on those who, while accepting that core message, merely theorize differently than we do in trying to make sense of it all. Traditional catholic heresy-hunting is irresponsible and opposed to New Testament teaching because it always inflates what should be considered essential. We did not set the terms of the new covenant, and it's not in our power to add to them, declaring, like the "Athanasian" Creed, that no one can be saved unless they believe in (or *say* they believe in?) confused and confusing traditional speculations about Trinity and Incarnation.

One may argue that disarmament is better than a strict policy for use. Should we ban the bomb? One might argue that the language of heresy and heretics has become too poisoned by contempt, by our long history of mean, ugly, unthinking denunciations. Certainly, some people take too much pleasure in denouncing others as heretics, thereby elevating themselves as brave and noble defenders of the faith. Perhaps we could just talk about essential beliefs and false teachings that contradict those and lay aside this traditional denunciation language. We would still be forced to label some as "false teachers." In any case, if we must use these weapons, we should avoid the tragedies of friendly fire. Whether or not to lay aside the "h" words ("heresy," "heretic," "heretical") is in the end a practical question. At any rate, the New Testament makes clear that disciples will be opposed by and must oppose false prophets and false teachers.

4.5 CONCLUSION

Does someone publicly affirm that the man Jesus was and is God's Messiah, understanding more or less what that involves? If so, he believes what is essential to being saved. *Is* he saved, though? Repentance, trust, commitment, and perseverance are also required. You won't directly perceive those things, but often you can tell, by close observation, if his life over time predominantly shows the fruits of God's spirit or the works of the flesh. If you find the former, along with that profession of Christ, you are dealing with a believer. Of course, outward appearances may deceive. He may outwardly present what look like fruits of the spirit and may say the right things, all while being a false teacher, someone propounding a different gospel. Or he may be a wolf in sheep's clothing, someone who uses a congregation for his own gain, a predator and not a shepherd (John 10:11–13). There is no shortage of such people in today's churches.

But let's suppose you don't find evidence of those evils in his life, and he is confessing Christ and showing the signs of God's spirit at work in him. Does he also believe some other things you are convinced are false? That doesn't make him a heretic in the New Testament sense of a divisive person. Before you call him a heretic or a false teacher, and before you in any way blast him, you should ask yourself, in Paul's words, "Who are you to judge someone else's servant? To their own master, servants stand or fall. And they will stand, for the Lord is able to make them stand" (Rom. 14:4). Consider that God may be patiently accepting this person despite their mistaken opinions, just as he has often done with you and me.

I anticipate that some will object as follows:

> *Surely* you're requiring too little by way of belief; Muslims agree that Jesus is the Messiah, yet they do not thereby believe enough to be Christians. Any claim which implies that most or all Muslims are Christians is thereby very implausible, to put it gently.

In reply, I agree with that last sentence, but my views do not imply that Muslims are Christians. Salvation requires a belief component, which has been the focus of this chapter, and non-belief components of repentance, trust, commitment, and perseverance. Islamic teaching about Jesus is at least as wrong as it is right, and Islamic tradition tends to prevent the non-belief responses required to enter the new covenant through Christ. It is true that

Muslims, following the Qur'an, call Jesus "the Messiah",[132] but it doesn't follow from this that they believe enough to be saved.[133] Jesus in Islamic traditions is a very big topic, but at bottom, Islamic traditions cast Jesus in the mold of an Islamic prophet, one of many, although an exceptional one, as he lacked a human father and will (most think) return some day. They even call him God's "Word" and "Spirit".[134] However, based on a less-than-clear passage in the Qur'an (4:157–58), against a mountain of historical evidence, most deny his death by crucifixion[135]—and so, his resurrection by God. They also deny that God will judge all other humans through him and that he is a unique mediator between us and God. They universally hold the religious worship of Jesus to be a great sin, contrary to Philippians 2:9–11 and Revelation 5.

It is a serious error for Christians to think, like Michael Servetus, that Islamic tradition pretty much gets Jesus right.[136] In Islam the last and greatest revealer of God and his will is the prophet Muhammad; submission to God means following the teachings and example of Muhammad, and in practice this amounts to living in conformity with some version of fully-developed Islamic law. Further, Muslims traditionally hold that God's Kingdom, the "House of Islam"—the realm in which God's will is done—may and should be spread by war.[137] In contrast, Christians believe that Jesus is the last and greatest revealer of God and his will and character. Further, he—not our governments and armies—will eventually establish the fullness of God's Kingdom after he returns. One can't follow both Muhammad and Jesus, as one can't both live under Islamic law and under the new covenant established through Jesus's blood (Luke 22:20).

Islamic tradition gets some things right concerning Jesus, while on the whole distorting his job-description as God's Messiah. But the net effect of Islamic tradition is to sideline Jesus so that he is mostly of historical interest. What Islamic traditions reliably block is the commitment to Jesus as one's highest Lord under God. In that way Islam has always been and always will be an enemy to the gospel. Theologically, Islam remains an effective inoculation against any catholic form of Christianity, and militarily and culturally it permanently de-

---

[132] Parrinder, *Jesus in the Qur'an*, ch. 4

[133] See pp. 163, 167, 176 below.

[134] Parrinder, *Jesus in the Qur'an*, 45–51

[135] Akyol, *Islamic Jesus*, 152–55; Geisler and Saleeb, *Answering Islam*, 234–37, 280–85.

[136] *Islamic Jesus*, 174–76.

[137] Bostom, ed., *Legacy of Jihad.*

Christianized vast territories.[138] If Islam is around when Jesus returns, he will have to de-Islamize portions of the world, for Islamic ideas about submission to God are not the same as his.

Division is intrinsically bad when it comes to any good unit of human social life, such as a country, a group of friends, a family, or a church. Thus, blasting must be done only after careful consideration of the division that will likely result. This doesn't mean that one can never strongly oppose serious errors and false teachings. Cutting is an intrinsic evil when it comes to the human body. Nonetheless, sometimes surgery is necessary to preserve life or health; what is intrinsically bad in itself can be overall good in such circumstances. But blasting must be done with the utmost care, by the right people, at the right time, and in the right way. So too, sometimes a church must be split. But we should be very afraid of damaging any such social unit because of disagreements. Heresy-hunting should never be a sport, and blasting should be a last resort when other forms of correction fail. We should be wary of divisive people, those devoted to the sin of spreading strife, gossip, and division. Often these don the garb of traditional heresiology.

Ancient heresiology, the sort of denunciation described in section 4.1.4, doesn't survive the basic standards of modern scholarship. It essentially depends on the pseudo-science of maliciously imagining the origins of Christian (or "Christian") groups and teachings one disagrees with. Modern heresiology aims to be more accurate, but we should beware of the danger of just slapping a traditional heresy label on a doctrine, such as "subordinationism" or "modalism," and then considering the matter closed. If a teaching is false, we should be able to show either that it contradicts clear scriptural teaching or that it has no scriptural basis while being opposed by other evidence, all things considered. Whatever the claim is, we should understand it and the reasons people have for holding it as accurately as possible, and then carefully weigh any scriptural or other evidence for and against it. If we conclude that the claim is false, we should consider whether it can be corrected without blasting. As a rule of thumb, gentle, humble, and reasonable correction is better than blasting.

But sometimes blasting others within the seemingly Christian realm is justified. When exactly? It is as difficult to specify necessary and sufficient conditions for this as it is to say exactly when physical violence is justified—and

[138] Jenkins, *Lost History of Christianity.*

blasting is *like* violence. I suggest that when clergy are committing heinous crimes against the flock, such as sexual abuse or enriching themselves via false doctrine, blasting may well be justified, particularly when these crimes are being ignored, excused, or covered up. For example, those who exposed the serious wrongdoing of apologist Ravi Zacharias were well justified in doing so.[139]

But what about purely doctrinal errors? Again, the rule of thumb is gentle and reasonable correction, treating others the way we want to be treated, while being "quick to listen, slow to speak, slow to anger" (James 1:19). This rules out going off half-cocked before gathering all the relevant information, which will often require communicating directly with the person in question. Again, challenging another's doctrine should never be done to increase one's own standing, "for where there is envy and selfish ambition, there will also be disorder and wickedness of every kind" (James 3:16). As we've seen, we have apostolic examples of blasting Docetism, any teaching that states the Lord Jesus only appeared to be a real human being while instead being something else, and a false gospel according to which one can't be saved without keeping the law of Moses. A Messiah, God's Christ (anointed one), is *by definition* a human being, and so Docetism implies that Jesus is *not* the Messiah, even if its adherents apply the word "Messiah" to him. Docetism also contradicts the clear New Testament teaching that Jesus is a man (John 8:40, Rom. 5, Acts 2:22).[140] That the law must be kept for a right standing with God makes unnecessary what Jesus called "the new covenant in my blood" (Luke 22:20).

The world is full of what we can call "gospels"—religious messages of (allegedly) good news. At the heart of any religion's teaching is what some have called "a diagnosis and a cure"—a diagnosis of the fundamental problem humans face and a way to positively and permanently resolve that problem.[141] For instance, the original Buddhist teaching (based on the sutras of the Pali canon) was that we are all trapped in the cycle of "rebirth" (reincarnation) by strong desire; that was their diagnosis. And the "cure" was that by following the Buddha's teachings we can eventually escape that cycle, gaining *Nibbana*

---

[139] Shellnutt and Silliman, "Ravi Zacharias."

[140] These are not the only places in which Jesus is called a "man" (*aner* or *anthropos*), and it is also important to remember that Jesus is constantly portrayed as a real man in all four Gospels.

[141] Yandell, *Philosophy of Religion*, 17.

(Nirvana). Christians should oppose such teachings,[142] as they clash with what we think are the true diagnosis and the true cure (separation from God because of sin, and reconciliation with God through Christ, leading to eternal life in God's kingdom), and thus they prevent our fellow humans from receiving the cure they need.

False "Christian" gospels, though, do more than double damage. Not only do they distract from the true diagnosis and cure, but they also tell others that their message is the gospel of Jesus Christ. Thus, many who have heard their message and rejected it will imagine that they have heard and rejected the good news of Jesus, which prevents them from listening to the actual gospel. The false prosperity or "name-it-and-claim-it" gospel that bedevils so much of the Pentecostal realm is a good example of an eminently blastable false "Christian" gospel. Unblasted, these false teachings continue to spread, ruining people's spiritual, bodily, and economic health.

What about catholic Trinity and Incarnation speculations? You might think that catholic teaching about Jesus is straightforwardly a variety of Docetism and so should be blasted, following John's example. Why? Because this does not seem like it would be a real man: an eternal, divine Person who enters into a mysterious "hypostatic union" with "a complete human nature" (a human type of body and human type of soul that do not by themselves compose a human being). Roman Catholic sources add that the "two-natured" Christ who results from the Incarnation is "man but not a man," meaning that the word "man" can and should be said about him even though he is *not* a human person (specifically, a man), since there is already a divine Person in the story, and adding a human person would be heretical Nestorianism.[143] This, I agree, is a form of Docetism, a Christ who only appears to be but is not a real man. Should we then blast any and all people who teach what they view as orthodox/catholic Christology?

No. For one thing, most in officially trinitarian churches believe that Jesus *is* a man, a real human. They either are ignorant of or deny or misunderstand the "man but not a man" teaching. They imagine that someone can be "100% human and also 100% divine," and they understand this to imply that Jesus is a real human person. The way for unitarians to proceed here is via rational

[142] Tuggy, *Why I'm Not*.
[143] See p. 309.

argument, appealing to scriptural teachings about God, human beings, and specifically the man Jesus.[144] It is not helpful to blast those holding to what they think is an orthodox Christology on the grounds of what we think—but what they deny—is an implication of it. Rather, we must *show them how* full divinity is incompatible with being truly human and with having the limits the New Testament ascribes to Jesus during his first earthly ministry.

In sum, as we try to deal with theological and christological errors, we will do well to remember what the Lord's half-brother tells us about true wisdom:

> But the wisdom from above is first pure, then peaceable, gentle, willing to yield, full of mercy and good fruits, without a trace of partiality or hypocrisy. And the fruit of righteousness is sown in peace by those who make peace. (James 3:17)

This is not to say that there are no instances when blasting is the best policy. But we can and should do better than traditional heresiology.

---

[144] Tuggy, "Nineteen."

CHAPTER 5

What is Essential to the Gospel, According to Luke?

5.1 WHAT MUST YOU SIGN OFF ON TO MAKE THE DEAL?[1]

One who accepts the gospel is making a deal with God through Jesus, thereby entering into a new covenant. Whatever the minimum is that you have to accept and confess to get this deal, it can't later be changed, especially by the likes of you and me. We did not set the terms and can't alter them; we can only announce them and invite others to enter in. As John Locke observed in 1695,

> God alone can appoint what shall be necessarily believed by everyone he will justify . . . Nobody can add to these fundamental articles of faith, nor make any other necessary, but what God himself hath made and declared to be so.[2]

In that classic book Locke works through all four Gospels and Acts, carefully revealing what was preached as necessary to be believed to enter into the new covenant through Jesus, then moving on to what else was required beyond believing. In my view he gets these right and so does a great service to the church. I recommend the book to all present-day Christians. In this chapter, my aim is more modest; I will go through the book of Acts to discern what its author Luke considered essential to the good news—in other words, what beliefs are required for salvation through Jesus.

---

[1] This chapter began as an incomplete series of blog posts at trinities.org starting on June 6, 2017.

[2] Locke, *Reasonableness of Christianity*, 191 (sec. 250). This edition helpfully modernizes Locke's spelling, grammar, and punctuation, and is the edition I would recommend for most readers.

Many, following mainstream catholic traditions, will *say* that the deity of Christ, the Trinity, or the two natures of Christ are essential points.[3] If they are essential, then one must agree to them to be saved, to enter into the new covenant, and to be counted as a believer.

But if you look at the actions of Protestant trinitarians, specifically, how they explain the gospel to seekers, they usually *don't* convey these as essential. In the twentieth century many tens of thousands came forward and were born again at rallies held by the famous evangelist Billy Graham. What exactly were those new believers told? The person seeking peace with God is quoted John 3:16, Romans 3:23, 1 Peter 2:24, John 1:12,[4] and instructed:

> To receive Christ you need to do four things: 1. ADMIT your spiritual need. "I am a sinner." 2. REPENT and be willing to turn from your sin. 3. BELIEVE that Jesus Christ died for you on the cross. 4. RECEIVE, through prayer, Jesus Christ into your heart and life.[5]

They are quoted Revelation 3:20 and Romans 10:13[6] and instructed to pray as follows:

> Dear Lord Jesus, I know that I am a sinner and need Your forgiveness. I believe that You died for my sins. I want to turn from my sins. I now invite You to come into my heart and life. I want to trust and follow You as Lord and Savior. In Jesus' name, Amen.[7]

In this brief instruction, the prelude to many tens of thousands of conversions since the mid-twentieth century, there is no mention of either the Trinity or the Incarnation. This is no surprise if you are familiar with American evangelical theology, preaching, and piety. But these omissions seem *correct.* Assent to those difficult theological speculations is not and cannot be required to make the deal.

---

[3] Locke rightly warns us against making the entrance requirements harder than God has and points out that the good news was meant for ordinary people, and so must be believable by them (*Reasonableness of Christianity*, 193 [sec. 252]).

[4] In order: "For God so loved the world that he gave his only Son, so that everyone who believes in him may not perish but may have eternal life." "Since all have sinned and fall short of the glory of God." "He himself bore our sins in his body on the cross, so that, having died to sins, we might live for righteousness; by his wounds you have been healed." "But to all who received him, who believed in his name, he gave power to become children of God."

[5] Ward, *Billy Graham*, 7.

[6] "Listen! I [Jesus] am standing at the door, knocking; if you hear my voice and open the door, I will come in and eat with you, and you with me." "For 'everyone who calls on the name of the Lord shall be saved.' "

[7] *Billy Graham*, 8.

Some, like me, made the deal at the age of seven, not at a Billy Graham meeting but in a private meeting with my pastor. Most (officially) trinitarian Christians understand this sort of conversion to be commonplace and unproblematic. But in theological arguments, partisan passions are aroused, and in these contexts, some are eager to tighten up the requirements lest we allow that those no-Trinity or no-Incarnation heretics might actually be saved. *Beware* of those passions! We should be afraid of denouncing those whom God and his Son have accepted into the family of believers.

Suppose that the Trinity and the two natures of Jesus *are* essential to the gospel. This means that if you don't preach those things, you have failed to preach the gospel. Let's examine what Luke, the author of the Gospel of Luke and Acts of the Apostles in the New Testament, presents as model proclamations of the Christian gospel. These should reveal what Luke, a companion of the apostles, thinks is essential to the Good News. It's unlikely that he will present without comment gospel preachers who are utterly failing.

5.2 PETER'S GOSPEL ACCORDING TO ACTS 2

We'll start with Luke's account of Peter's sermon to the people of Jerusalem on the day God poured out his spirit on the first believers. First, Peter explains the odd phenomenon of their speaking in tongues; it is a miracle, not the effect of early-morning drinking! Then we have the heart of his evangelistic message:

> "Fellow Israelites, listen to what I have to say: Jesus of Nazareth, a man attested to you by God with deeds of power, wonders, and signs that God did through him among you, as you yourselves know—this man, handed over to you according to the definite plan and foreknowledge of God, you crucified and killed by the hands of those outside the law. But God raised him up, having released him from the agony of death, because it was impossible for him to be held in its power." (Acts 2:22–24)

He then cites David as prophesying the resurrection of the Messiah in Psalm 16:8–11. He continues:

> "This Jesus God raised up, and of that all of us are witnesses. Being therefore exalted at the right hand of God and having received from the Father the promise of the Holy Spirit, he has poured out this that you see and hear. For David did not ascend into the heavens, but he himself says, 'The Lord said to my Lord, "Sit at my right hand, until I make your enemies your footstool."' Therefore let the entire house of Israel know with certainty that God has made him both Lord and Messiah, this Jesus whom you crucified." (Acts 2:32–36)

Trinity? No hint of it. Incarnation? Not a word. Two natures of Jesus, that he is not only human but also divine? Nothing. Jesus as a godman? Absent. "A man attested to you by God"? Peter sounds like a unitarian here!

Is Peter blowing it? Has he by his negligence or ignorance thrown away a golden opportunity to preach the gospel of Jesus Christ? Surely, Peter is just warming up. He'll get around to those claims, right? But his message is already having its impact:

> Now when they heard this, they were cut to the heart and said to Peter and to the other apostles, "Brothers, what should we do?" Peter said to them, "Repent and be baptized every one of you in the name of Jesus Christ so that your sins may be forgiven, and you will receive the gift of the Holy Spirit. For the promise is for you, for your children, and for all who are far away, everyone whom the Lord our God calls to him." And he testified with many other arguments and exhorted them, saying, "Save yourselves from this corrupt generation." So those who welcomed his message were baptized, and that day about three thousand persons were added. (Acts 2:37–41)

Have these people jumped the gun, as it were rushing the altar call before the preacher gets to his main point? In Luke's telling, the hearers are convicted, and they repent and believe without being told anything about these alleged essentials on which Catholics and Protestants insist. Did Luke just edit out all the Trinity and deity of Christ material, referring to it as "many other arguments" (2:40)? That is very unlikely. In the context, the other arguments would seem to be other alleged fulfilled prophecies, additions to the few that Luke relates.[8] By means of this sermon summary, Luke has evidently told us what he thinks is essential to making the deal—that is, what must be believed in order to enter into the new covenant.[9]

His invitation is clear: anyone who repents of his sins and is baptized in the name of Jesus will be forgiven by God and will receive the power of God's spirit. But what must one believe or accept to make the deal? I find these claims being put forward for belief:[10]

---

[8] According to Luke the risen Jesus himself tutored some of his followers about all that had been written about him in Scripture (Luke 24:25–27, 44–49).

[9] Compare with Apollos later: Acts 18:24–28.

[10] So as to list the main points, I'm leaving out secondary, evidential points that are made to show support for the main claims, namely that God has testified to his Messiahship by deeds of power, wonders, and signs that God did through him among Jesus's Jewish contemporaries, that we believers witness to Jesus having been raised from the dead, and that various events in Jesus's life are fulfillments of ancient prophecies.

1. The man Jesus is God's Messiah.[11]
2. Jesus was crucified by the Romans.
3. Jesus's crucifixion was in accordance with God's plan.
4. God has vindicated Jesus as his true Messiah by raising him from the dead.
5. God has exalted Jesus to his right hand.
6. God has made Jesus Lord.
7. One's sins will be forgiven by God if one repents of them and is baptized into the community of Jesus's followers.
8. God has given Jesus his spirit.
9. Jesus has now poured out this spirit on believers.

At first glance, this seems rather complex, but on inspection it all rolls up under claim 1 like an old-fashioned window blind. God's Messiah is by definition a special human agent of God who, in fulfillment of prophecies, lives out various things, including all of 2–9. Claims 2–9 are not an exhaustive description of the Messiah's job; his being the king of Israel or the king of the Jews is not mentioned. But it's clear that for Peter, the Messiah is supposed to be a crucified, raised, exalted human Lord, who has now received and poured out God's spirit.

Once we realize all that is involved in the Messiah job description, the point of Peter's sermon can be boiled down to this four-word sentence: "Jesus is God's Messiah." Beyond this, Peter is spelling out things his listeners would need to know concerning the Messiah. Like the disciples before Jesus's resurrection, many of them probably think of the Messiah as only or primarily a king in David's line, a ruler of Israel who will restore its independence. Peter and Luke still think this is part of his divinely ordained destiny (Acts 1:6–7). But Peter, in preaching Jesus to be God's Messiah, emphasizes the aspects of his calling that are more immediately relevant to his hearers.

That Jesus is God's Messiah is a simple message, devoid of any fancy metaphysics or any whiff of paradox. What it means is that Jesus is a unique man whose divine calling is to live out (at least) the roles just mentioned, and these are, for the most part, easily understood. One can preach a gospel like this to a third-grader or a junior-high dropout, and by accepting these things and repenting before God, she can be saved. You can also preach it to the senile, the unintelligent, the uneducated, and probably in many cases to the mentally

[11] In this Jewish context it is assumed that the god in question is the one true god, Yahweh. This would be made explicit in a non-Jewish context. Notice how Luke swaps "God" for "the Father" in Acts 2:33. This swapping reflects his understanding that Yahweh just is the Father and vice versa, that "they" are one and the same. See pp. 95–96.

disabled. Isn't that awesome? That is truly good news! What a relief, that we can justifiably skip the agonies of the seemingly incoherent pseudo-Athanasian Creed and the alleged profundities of the Nicene Creed when sharing the gospel—*even if*, as many suppose, those creeds contain important truths.

Even knowing various subsets of these facts about the Messiah would seem to be enough for one to personally commit to Jesus, to follow him as one's human Lord under the one God. A Messiah is a prophet-plus; he is by definition a prophet, but his roles go far beyond even the greatest previous messenger or spokesperson for God. Even with a lesser prophet, to defy him when he truly prophesies is to defy the God who sent him. And to accept that prophet's message is to trust the God who inspired it. Trusting that messenger, and hence believing or accepting his message, is trusting the sender.[12] Thus, accepting Jesus to be God's Messiah, even if one is hazy on the details, is accepting him *at the very least* as a prophet, which is by definition someone who speaks by the authority of God. Having done only that, you are positioned to listen closely when you find that Jesus is making severe demands on us, that he should be our teacher.[13] The Billy Graham ministry talking points we considered in section 5.1 are a subset, an important one, of what it is for Jesus to be God's Messiah; that's why they "work"—they are a Pauline take on point 7 above. Of course, one who truly follows Jesus will come to see him as much more than a means to having one's sins forgiven.[14]

But let's follow through; in Acts Luke gives us other example sermons. Has he, in this first one, only told us part of what's essential to the gospel?

5.3 PETER'S SERMON IN SOLOMON'S PORTICO IN ACTS 3

Peter's next recorded sermon is in Acts 3. Again, the occasion is a miracle. Peter heals a crippled man "in the name of Jesus Christ of Nazareth" (Acts 3:6). This draws a crowd; it's sermon time. Let's see what this sermon suggests must be accepted to enter into this new covenant with God.

---

[12] Compare: "Do not let your hearts be troubled. Believe in God; believe also in me" (John 14:1).

[13] "Then he said to them all, 'If any wish to come after me, let them deny themselves and take up their cross daily and follow me' " (Luke 9:23). "Whoever does not carry the cross and follow me cannot be my disciple" (Luke 14:27). See also Matt. 8:22, 10:38, 16:24; Mark 8:34.

[14] See Dallas Willard's critique of "gospels of sin-management" (*Divine Conspiracy*, ch. 2).

> While he [the healed man] clung to Peter and John, all the people ran together to them in the portico called Solomon's Portico, utterly astonished. When Peter saw it, he addressed the people, "Fellow Israelites, why do you wonder at this, or why do you stare at us, as though by our own power or piety we had made him walk? The God of Abraham and Isaac and Jacob, the God of our ancestors, has glorified his servant Jesus, whom you handed over and rejected in the presence of Pilate, though he had decided to release him. But you rejected the holy and righteous one and asked to have a murderer given to you, and you killed the author of life, whom God raised from the dead. To this we are witnesses. And by faith in his name, his name itself has made this man strong, whom you see and know, and the faith that is through Jesus has given him this perfect health in the presence of all of you. And now, brothers and sisters, I know that you acted in ignorance, as did also your rulers. In this way God fulfilled what he had foretold through all the prophets, that his Messiah would suffer. Repent, therefore, and turn to God so that your sins may be wiped out, so that times of refreshing may come from the presence of the Lord and that he may send the Messiah appointed for you, that is, Jesus, who must remain in heaven until the time of universal restoration that God announced long ago through his holy prophets. Moses said, 'The Lord your God will raise up for you from your own people a prophet like me. You must listen to whatever he tells you. [Deut. 18:15] And it will be that everyone who does not listen to that prophet will be utterly rooted out of the people [Lev. 23:29].' And all the prophets, as many as have spoken, from Samuel and those after him, also predicted these days. You are the descendants of the prophets and of the covenant that God gave to your ancestors, saying to Abraham, 'And in your descendants all the families of the earth shall be blessed.' When God raised up his servant, he sent him first to you, to bless you by turning each of you from your wicked ways." (Acts 3:11–26)

As before, there is a threat of divine judgment that is specific to this generation of Jews. But regarding what must be accepted or confessed by anyone who wants to make this deal, there is little here that was not implicit in the prior message. Our (the Jews') god, *the* god, God, has raised Jesus from the dead, proving that God really was with him. Notably, he twice characterizes Jesus as God's "servant." And now he's a prophet like Moses[15] who must be obeyed.

Peter doesn't sound like a contemporary Jesus-is-God-apologist, does he?[16] Some of them would accuse someone preaching like this today of sounding

---

[15] Jesus is a (or the) fulfillment of Moses's prediction in Deut. 18:15.

[16] This is my term for someone who holds to the numerical identity of Jesus with God (Tuggy, "Podcast 124"). See also section 8.3.6.

like a Muslim. But Peter was no Muslim; he was a non-trinitarian, a unitarian Christian for whom the one god, the god of Abraham, was none other than the Father (Acts 3:13).[17] He had no conception of Jesus—as some evangelical scholars say nowadays—"belonging to the divine identity."[18] It is striking that he calls Jesus "the author of life" (3:15)—*eternal* life; in the author's view Jesus is the one who tells us how to get that.[19] Jesus as the source of our eternal life is a much bigger theme in the Gospel According to John. Jesus is this not because he's God but because God has empowered him to be the source of eternal life.[20]

What you, the hearer, must do is to repent, turn away from your sin and toward God, of course accepting Jesus as God's Messiah. This will result in your being forgiven. Part of the Messiah's job description is made more clear in this sermon: he's coming back (Acts 3:21)! He won't stay in heaven forever, for there will be a time "when he comes in his glory and the glory of the Father and of the holy angels" (Luke 9:26). But this was implicit in the first sermon, where Jesus is said to be the fulfillment of Psalm 110:1, where *the* Lord (Yahweh) says to *my* Lord: "Sit at my right hand, until I make your enemies your footstool" (Acts 2:34–35). When those enemies are subjected to him, this man, the Messiah, will literally be in charge of the earth. This will be "the time of universal restoration that God announced long ago through his holy prophets" (Acts 3:21). This is part of what it is for God to make Jesus "Lord." We know from elsewhere that this is in fulfillment of Daniel 7, where God awards "one like a human being" "dominion, and glory and kingship, that all peoples, nations, and languages, should serve him"—and this in perpetuity (Dan. 7:14–15).[21] He's

---

[17] Compare: "Blessed be the God and Father of our Lord Jesus Christ!" (1 Peter 1:3).

[18] Tuggy, "On Bauckham's Bargain." See also sections 7.3 and 9.4.2.

[19] "An expert in the law stood up to test Jesus. 'Teacher,' he said, 'what must I do to inherit eternal life?' He said to him, 'What is written in the law? What do you read there?' He answered, 'You shall love the Lord your God with all your heart and with all your soul and with all your strength and with all your mind and your neighbor as yourself.' And he said to him, 'You have given the right answer; do this, and you will live'" (Luke 10:25–28).

[20] "For just as the Father has life in himself, so he has granted the Son also to have life in himself" (John 5:26).

[21] It has recently become fashionable for conservative Protestant scholars to urge that "the one like a human being" here is "a divine figure" since he is described as "coming with the clouds of heaven." But the human author intended no such thing, as shown by his own interpretation of the vision, on which that seeming human is actually God's chosen people (Dan. 7:18). As with many other passages, evidently the New Testament authors who cite

the king of the Jews (Luke 23:38), but he's also been made the Lord to whom every knee must bow, to the glory of God, the Father (Phil. 2:9–11). What must you do? Repent. Turn to God. This time Luke doesn't mention an invitation to baptism. Again, the heart of the message is simply that Jesus is God's Messiah. In spelling out what being the Messiah involves, Peter adds a claim that wasn't explicitly said before, though it's closely related to points 5 and 6 in our list above:

10. At some future date God will send Jesus back to earth to rule it.

This too is part of what it means to assert that Jesus is God's Messiah, which is the thesis statement of each of the four New Testament Gospels.[22] The first-century apostolic crowd had a single core message, despite their different emphases, styles, and interests. Here in Acts 2–3, we've just seen Peter preaching that message twice, c. 30–33 CE. So far there are no mentions of a tripersonal God, Jesus as God in the flesh, or Jesus's two natures. Is Peter incompetent to preach the gospel? Are Luke's theology and Christology too "primitive" to include what is essential to the good news?

Or perhaps Peter is exactly what he sounds like here: a unitarian Christian who holds to what was later dismissed as a "mere man" understanding of Jesus, or, more positively, a "Spirit Christology," on which the divine in the man Jesus isn't a second nature but rather God's special empowering by his spirit, the source of Jesus's message and miraculous powers.[23] Peter doesn't seem to think that Jesus did miracles and rose from the dead by using his essential divine powers. Rather, God has empowered Jesus by his spirit, working miraculous deeds through him, constituting a divine endorsement of him, and it was God who raised him from the dead.[24] The reader of Luke's Volume 1, his Gospel,

---

this hold Jesus to be another fulfillment of the text, and none of them infers that therefore Jesus is "a divine figure" or the "divine Person" of later trinitarian thought. On that type of currently popular misinterpretation see chapter 10.

[22] Matt. 16:16; Mark 8:29; Luke 9:20; John 20:31. This thesis is not just stated once but is repeatedly driven home by each author. One can find statements of this thesis by both sympathetic and hostile characters by searching for the word "Christ" or "Messiah" in each Gospel. But as Locke points out, the Messiah is also referred to by phrases such as "the Son of God," "the Son of Man," "king of the Jews," "the king of Israel," "the consolation of Israel," "the salvation of the Lord," "that prophet that should come into the world," "He that should come," the one who was "sent from the Father," "the Son of David," and "the Just one" (Locke, *Reasonableness of Christianity*, 32 [52], 63 [101], 77 [117], 138 [183]).

[23] Newman, *Spirit Christology*.

[24] Acts 2:24, 32, 3:15, 4:10, 5:30, 10:40, 13:30, 37.

remembers how Jesus announced the start of his ministry in his hometown of Nazareth, standing up in the synagogue and reading, then saying he had fulfilled this text:

> "The spirit of the Lord is upon me, because he anointed me to proclaim good news to the poor, he has sent me to declare liberty to the captives and recovering of sight to the blind, to set at liberty those who are bruised, to proclaim the year of the Lord's favor." (Luke 4:18, REV)

For Luke (and if you trust his summary, for Peter), Jesus isn't God. Instead, he's God's special human servant, a prophet, but more than that, a Messiah, with the astounding job description we've seen—and there is more to come. Luke says Jesus is a man and does not eagerly clarify that he's also divine. So far, Luke has been consistent in what this core message is, but he has more sermon summaries in store for us. Perhaps he's saving some christological goodies for later? Is Luke starting with milk, waiting until the reader is ready for meat (Heb. 5:12–14)?

5.4 PETER'S AND JOHN'S TESTIMONY IN ACTS 4

After Peter's second Trinity-free sermon, we're told that the movement has increased to about five thousand people (Acts 4:4)! The Jewish religious authorities are alarmed and arrest Peter and John, questioning them the next day. The council demands to know: "By what power or by what name did you do this?" (4:7)

> Then Peter, filled with the holy spirit, said to them, "rulers of the People, and elders, if we this day are examined concerning a good deed done to a disabled man, by what means he was made whole, be it known to you all and to all the people of Israel that in the name of Jesus Christ of Nazareth, whom you crucified, whom God raised from among the dead, even by him does this man stand here before you whole. He is the *stone that was rejected by you builders, which has become the cornerstone.*[25] And in no one else is there salvation, for there is no other name under heaven that has been given among people by which we must be saved." (Acts 4:8–12, REV, original italics)

The leadership wasn't expecting this message and doesn't know what to say, because the healed man is standing right there! But they don't want this movement to spread—the majority of them don't believe that Jesus is the Messiah—so they call Peter and John back in and order them to desist teaching in the name of Jesus.

[25] Ps. 118:22; compare Luke 20:17, Matt. 21:42.

But Peter and John reply: Sorry, we can't obey you, because that would be disobeying God (Acts 4:13–19). "We cannot keep from speaking about what we have seen and heard" (4:20). Peter and John possess overwhelming empirical evidence for the resurrection of Jesus; they have seen, heard, and probably touched and smelled the risen Jesus (Luke 24:36–53, Acts 1:3–11, 1 John 1:1). They have also seen, felt, and heard the effects of Jesus pouring out God's spirit on the disciples, as he'd previously promised to do (Acts 2:1–6). The Jewish leadership can't see how they can legitimately punish the two, despite this impunity, so they let them go. End scene

The above is not a sermon but rather a brief testimony to Jesus in a tense, formal situation. Peter is not going for the win here (conversion), so this speech adds nothing to our list of points that must be believed to be saved. Peter, however, does here assert that Jesus is, in some sense, uniquely the way to salvation (this is closely related to point 7 in our list), and that even though most of his people reject him, God is making Jesus the foundation for his new work. But these things are said (by Luke) to teach the reader, and (by Peter) to rebuke or pronounce judgment on his fellow Jews who have rejected Jesus, and perhaps to invite them, in light of this fulfilled prophecy, to reconsider that rejection. But Luke doesn't present them here as things that must be believed to be saved.

After being released by the council, the apostles pray to the Father, calling him "Sovereign Lord, who made the heaven and the earth, the sea, and everything in them" (Acts 4:24). They cite a prophecy of the nations and their kings opposing "the Lord and . . . his Messiah" (4:26), which they see as fulfilled in their day.

> For in this city, in fact, both Herod and Pontius Pilate, with the Gentiles and the peoples of Israel, gathered together against your holy servant Jesus, whom you anointed, to do whatever your hand and your plan had predestined to take place. (Acts 4:27–28)

The believers pray for boldness and are filled with God's power, making them bold (4:29–31). They continue to do signs and wonders, and two of their own are struck dead after lying to God (5:1–16).

5.5 PETER BEFORE THE COUNCIL AGAIN IN ACTS 5

The high priest has the apostles jailed, but in the middle of the night an angel lets them out, and they go out and preach in the temple, but Luke doesn't summarize the contents of this. The temple guards arrest them. They're brought before the high priest, who demands to know why his gag order has been disobeyed (Acts 5:17–28). Now another testimony:

> But Peter and the apostles answered and said, "We must obey God rather than man. The God of our fathers raised Jesus, whom you slew by hanging him on a tree. He is the one whom God exalted to his right hand as Leader and Savior, to give repentance to Israel, and forgiveness of sins. And we are witnesses of these things, and so is the holy spirit that God has given to those who obey him." (Acts 5:29–32, REV)

The council is enraged by this; they reject the apostles' claim that Jesus is the promised Messiah. But the council is convinced to leave the matter to divine providence. They have the apostles flogged and again release them with a gag order, "not to speak in the name of Jesus" (Acts 5:33–40). Luke indicates what message the apostles are suffering for.

> As they left the council, they rejoiced that they were considered worthy to suffer dishonor for the sake of the name. And every day in the temple and at home they did not cease to teach and proclaim Jesus as the Messiah. (Acts 5:41–42)

Again, this nutshell summary of their proclamation is the same as the thesis statements of all four New Testament Gospels. Also observe that the apostles' god just is the god of the Jews, "the god of our fathers," a.k.a. "the Father" (2:33)—not Jesus and not the Trinity. They preach not that *God* died, as one hears from some preachers and theologians nowadays, but rather that the man Jesus died.[26] It is assumed that while Jesus was dead, unsurprisingly, the essentially immortal God was still alive and able to bring Jesus back to life. Implicitly, the apostles are saying that the Jewish leadership ought to accept that Jesus is God's Messiah, repent of their rejection of him, and be reconciled to God through him. Thus the leaders' fury—they are too self-righteous to hear this from people they view as outsider fanatics and nobodies.

5.6 A TRINITARIAN PASSAGE IN ACTS 5?

So far there has been no trinitarian red meat, nothing that looks like a mention, implication, or assumption of a tripersonal God, and nothing remotely resembling the deity of Christ, the incarnation of an eternal divine Person, or a godman who is both divine and human.

[26] Weatherall, "It Wasn't God"; Rom. 5.

Nonetheless, the eagle-eyed trinitarian will gather crumbs wherever he can; he may see in Peter's speech above a "trinitarian" or "triadic" passage in which, the trinitarian suggests, three divine Persons are mentioned:

> God [the Father] exalted him [Jesus, the Son] at his right hand as Leader and Savior that he might give repentance to Israel and forgiveness of sins. And we are witnesses to these things, and so is the Holy Spirit whom God has given to those who obey him. (Acts 5:31–32)

In this translation, as in most, the translators choose to render the neuter relative pronoun *ho* as the personal pronoun "whom" for God's spirit.[27] This, together with capitalizing "Holy Spirit" name-style, fits hand-in-hand with traditional catholic theologies that state this Spirit is a third divine Person in addition to the Father and the Son. This is a clear case of trinitarian translation bias,[28] but let's grant, for the sake of argument, that this translation is correct. Even if this doesn't give the trinitarian everything he'd want,[29] doesn't this text at least portray three divine Persons, and in the preferred order: Father, Son, Holy Spirit? Moreover, witnesses are those who witness, and witnessing is an activity that requires being a self. The witness experiences something and testifies to what he's seen or heard. He personally vouches for certain claims or facts. If "the Holy Spirit" *witnesses*, mustn't he be a literal someone, a self or person?

This seems a slam-dunk argument until you realize how natural and common it is to describe something that is not a self metaphorically as a "witness," as "speaking for" (that is, being evidence in favor of) some claim or fact. Later in this book Paul does exactly this. When he and Barnabas are worshiped as deities after healing a man, Paul insists they too are mere mortals and then adds,

> We bring you good news, that you should turn from these worthless things to the living God, who made the heaven and the earth and the sea and all that is in them. In past generations he allowed all peoples to follow their own ways, yet he has not left himself without a witness in doing good, giving you rains from heaven and fruitful seasons and filling you with food and your hearts with joy. (Acts 14:15b–17)

---

[27] The word can also mean "which" or "that."

[28] BeDuhn, *Truth in Translation*, 140–41. This is why elsewhere in this chapter when God's spirit is mentioned I have chosen to quote from Spirit & Truth's online Revised English Version (www.revisedenglishversion.com), which translates independently of trinitarian traditions.

[29] Tuggy, "New Testament," 105–9.

Who are the "witnesses" God has given to all nations about his own goodness? They are the adequate rains and bountiful growing seasons that result in our enjoying a cornucopia of foods. Such are not literal witnesses, but they are *like* witnesses in being important sources of evidence—in this case, for God's goodness and generosity. This is no more puzzling than "The heavens . . . telling the glory of God" (Ps. 19:1). Elsewhere Paul describes the human conscience as bearing witness, and the human spirit as a recipient of testimony (Rom. 2:15, 8:16). This last passage is most instructive:

> For all who are led by the spirit of God are sons and daughters of God. For you did not receive a spirit of slavery making you live in fear again, but you received a spirit of adoption, by which we cry out, "Abba! Father!" The spirit itself bears witness to our spirit that we are children of God. (Rom. 8:14–16, REV)

"The Holy Spirit" is referred to here as "the spirit of God." It is not supposed to be a person in addition to God any more than the spirit of a human is supposed to be someone in addition to that human.[30] God's human children are those who are led by his spirit, that is, by God's unseen power in them. They have received "a spirit of adoption," the mental orientation of a grateful adoptee, which causes them to respond to God as their loving heavenly Father. And God's spirit "bears witness to our spirit that we are his children." Here, neither the giver of the testimony—God's spirit—nor the receiver of it—the human spirit—is supposed to be a self; this is not *literal* bearing witness/testifying.

Back to our text, there seems to be no reason, other than the needs of trinitarian theology, to suppose that "the Holy Spirit" is a literal witness rather than a metaphorical one. This is one of several examples of mild personification of God's spirit in this book.[31] But we must keep the bigger picture in mind. It is

---

[30] See for example the talk of human spirits in Luke 1:47, 23:46; Acts 7:59; Rom. 1:9; 1 Cor. 5:4, 14:14, 16:18. In each text it is clear that the spirit isn't supposed to be someone in addition to the someone whose spirit it is.

[31] Most famously, Peter tells Ananias that he's lied to the Holy Spirit (Acts 5:3), that is, by lying to the apostles, who have God's spirit in them (5:4); this, it says, is also lying *to God*, the Father. Talking about being lied to—this is a mild personification of God's spirit. Others: God's spirit is said to foretell (1:16), give miraculous abilities (2:4), be tested (5:9), be opposed (7:51), speak (8:29, 10:19, 11:12, 13:2, 21:11, 28:25), transport a man (8:39), send people on a mission (13:4), approve of an idea (15:28), forbid (16:6–7), testify (20:23), and appoint overseers (20:28). When a "spirit" belongs to someone, one can describe that person's actions as being done by that spirit; these various actions, then, are really being ascribed to God and/or Jesus, whose spirit this is.

a major plot point of this book that God, through the exalted Jesus, gives his spirit to Jesus's followers, starting with the Jews, then proceeding to various Gentiles. The reader should look at every case of holy spirit reception to see if this is ever presented as the recipients becoming acquainted (or better acquainted) with a divine Person (or *any* sort of self in addition to God and Jesus).[32] I submit that Luke never does that—all the descriptions of the reception of this spirit suggest it is a power, not a person—because he understands God's spirit along Old Testament lines.[33]

Nothing in Acts 5 has added to our list of things that Luke thinks one must believe to be saved: it is still, fundamentally, that Jesus is God's Messiah.

5.7 STEPHEN'S SPEECHES IN ACTS 7

The righteous and spirit-empowered Stephen and his arrest are described in Acts 6. Acts 7 portrays a lengthy speech by him in front of a hostile council, and then a short, vision-induced speech while he is being stoned to death. What do these tell us about what is essential to the gospel? Much of this recounts key events from Genesis and Exodus.

Stephen doesn't—like Justin Martyr and many later catholics—think it was the prehuman Jesus who appeared in Old Testament theophanies. No, when God appeared to Moses at the burning bush, it was through an angel who spoke God's words (Acts 7:30–34).[34] None of Stephen's historical recap features a Jesus active before his human life (7:1–53). Stephen's speech culminates in a harsh excoriation of his own people for their habitual disobedience to the God who has so uniquely favored them (7:41–53). While they grind their teeth in murderous rage, Stephen, filled with the spirit, has a spiritual vision.

> But he, being full of holy spirit, looked up steadfastly into heaven and saw the glory of God, and Jesus standing at the right hand of God, and said, "Look! I see the heavens opened, and the Son of Man standing at the right hand of God." (Acts 7:55–56, REV)

Sound familiar (Dan. 7:14)? But they're not impressed. They stone Stephen to death as he prays to Jesus to receive his spirit (meaning, Stephen himself) and petitions either Jesus or God ("Lord") for his murderers' forgiveness (7:59–60).

---

[32] Acts 2:1–12, 8:14–24, 9:1–19, 10:34–48, 19:1–6.

[33] Jewish Bible–style spirit talk is complicated; on the uses of the Hebrew *ruach* and the Greek *pneuma*, see "Appendix 15."

[34] Justin Martyr, *Dialogue with Trypho*, 91–93 (chs. 59–60).

Stephen's prayer to Jesus, if it is a prayer,[35] is no hint from Luke that Jesus is God. The reader knows that "the God of glory," whose ancient actions Stephen has been recounting, is the Father (Acts 7:2, 55–56; Acts 2:33). Stephen sees the exalted Jesus standing at the right hand of the Father, and what he sees bears no resemblance to later trinitarian art in which three similar humanoid figures sit together side by side. The text does nothing to convey any idea of a tripersonal god, or even the idea of multiple equally divine Persons.

This speech is a prophetic confrontation, not a sermon, and so not all of the gospel is preached here. Still, the speech and Stephen's vision-inspired statements seem to presuppose some of the points we've listed, once you see that "the Righteous One" (7:52) is the Messiah.

Roman Catholic theologian Hans Küng has observed about this inspired speech during Stephen's stoning:

> In the New Testament there is probably no better story to illustrate the relationship of Father, Son and Spirit than that speech made in his own defence by Stephen the Protomartyr . . . here we have mention of God, Jesus the Son of Man, and the Holy Spirit. But Stephen does not see, say, a deity with three faces, far less three identical men, nor any triangular symbol of the kind that was similarly used in Western art. Rather:
> — The Holy Spirit is at Stephen's side, is in Stephen himself. The Spirit, the invisible power and might which comes from God, fills him completely and thus opens his eyes: "in the Spirit" he sees heaven.
> — God himself (*ho theos*—the God) remains hidden, does not have human form; only his 'glory' (Hebrew *kabod*, Greek *doxa*) is visible: God's splendour and power, the splendour of light, which emanates fully from him.
> — Jesus, finally, visible as the Son of man, stands . . . 'at the right hand of God', i.e. in throne community, with the same power and glory! Exalted as Son of God and taken up into God's eternal life, he is God's representative for us and at the same time as a human being the representative of human beings before God.[36]

---

[35] C. S. Lakin pointed out to me that some would deny that this is a case of prayer because Stephen is seeing Jesus; Stephen is simply speaking to Jesus. Others would say that prayer by definition can only be given to one who is divine. If *that* is what one means by "prayer," then one should deny that Stephen prays to Jesus here. At any rate, since Luke nowhere says or implies that Jesus is divine, it is a misreading to say that Luke is slyly hinting in this passage that Jesus is divine. Neither of Luke's New Testament books are esoteric works with an outer message for the masses and a hidden, encoded message for the elite. They wear their main thesis—that Jesus is God's Christ—on their sleeves.

[36] Küng, *Credo*, 152–53.

5.8 PHILIP IN ACTS 8

Luke tells us that Philip successfully preached in Samaria "and proclaimed the Messiah to them," that is, "proclaiming the good news about the kingdom of God and the name of Jesus Christ." The reader knows that God's kingdom will be fully realized when Jesus returns (Acts 8:5, 12; Luke 22:14–28; Acts 1:11). Then in a divine appointment with the Ethiopian eunuch (Acts 8:26–29), Philip expounds on Isaiah 53:7–8, one of the passages alluded to before, in which "God fulfilled what he had foretold through all the prophets, that his Messiah would suffer" (Acts 3:18; compare Acts 2:23). Philip, "starting with this scripture ... proclaimed to him the good news about Jesus" (8:35). Afterward, the eunuch requests and receives baptism (8:36–39). Such baptisms in Acts seem to happen very quickly, confirming the simplicity of what must be believed and confessed.[37]

5.9 PETER'S SERMON TO THE GENTILES IN ACTS 10

Through a series of miraculous events, Peter is persuaded to preach to Gentiles (Acts 10:1–33). Luke then summarizes another sermon by Peter:

> "I truly understand that God shows no partiality, but in every people anyone who fears him and practices righteousness is acceptable to him. You know the message he sent to the people of Israel, preaching peace by Jesus Christ—he is Lord of all. That message spread throughout Judea, beginning in Galilee after the baptism that John announced: how God anointed Jesus of Nazareth with the Holy Spirit and with power; how he went about doing good and healing all who were oppressed by the devil, for God was with him. We are witnesses to all that he did both in Judea and in Jerusalem. They put him to death by hanging him on a tree, but God raised him on the third day and allowed him to appear, not to all the people but to us who were chosen by God as witnesses and who ate and drank with him after he rose from the dead. He commanded us to preach to the people and to testify that he is the one ordained by God as judge of the living and the dead. All the prophets testify about him that everyone who believes in him receives forgiveness of sins through his name." (Acts 10:34–43)

---

[37] Acts 2:38–41, 8:4–8, 12, 9:18, 10:34–48, 16:14–15, 25–34, 18:7–8, 19:1–5, 22:16. We might conclude that public confession, or at least willingness to publicly confess Jesus as one's Lord, is among the nonbelief requirements for salvation (Mark 8:38, Luke 9:26, Rom. 10:9).

The first sentence here is certainly interesting in its implications.[38] But it's not part of the gospel, which is summarized immediately following. The good news here is about Jesus Christ, Jesus the Anointed One/Messiah. Some of our prior points are mentioned. Then we have what looks like a new, astounding claim:

11. God has ordained Jesus to judge all (other) humans.

This claim comes as no surprise to readers of the New Testament Gospels, and it is preached later in Acts by Paul (Matt. 25:31–46, John 5:21–30, Acts 17:31). We add this to our list as yet another part of the Messiah's job description; judging is part of what Jesus does as God's vice-regent, as our unique Lord under the unique God.

Believing those things, one is in a position to trust in Jesus, receiving divine forgiveness (Acts 10:43). Peter makes that pitch, and while he's doing it, it seems that act of trust ensues, because "the Holy Spirit fell upon all who heard the word," after which the converts are baptized (10:44–48). Hearing about all this, the Jerusalem church "praised God, saying, 'Then God has given even to the gentiles the repentance that leads to life'" (11:18).

5.10 THE GOSPEL PAUL PREACHES IN ACTS

In chapter 9 we learn that Paul (a.k.a. Saul), who had been introduced in the previous chapter as a dastardly persecutor (8:1,3), is the risen Jesus's choice "to bring [his] name before gentiles and kings and before the people of Israel" (Acts 9:15). After repenting, Paul is healed, filled with God's spirit, and is baptized. Paul's early ministry is described like this:

> For several days he was with the disciples in Damascus, and immediately he began to proclaim Jesus in the synagogues, saying, "He is the Son of God." All who heard him were amazed and said, "Is not this the man who made havoc in Jerusalem among those who invoked this name? And has he not come here for the purpose of bringing them bound before the chief priests?" Saul became increasingly more powerful and confounded the Jews who lived in Damascus by proving that Jesus was the Messiah. (Acts 9:19b–22)

The eager trinitarian reader, assuming the Athanasian premise that Jesus is a *real* son of God and, as such must have the divine essence,[39] may imagine that Paul

[38] It seems to point a Christian theologian toward what philosophers of religion have called "Inclusivism," or at least to a more permissive version of "Exclusivism" (Tuggy, "Theories of Religious Diversity").

[39] Athanasius, *Four Discourses*, 380b (2.21.59).

is preaching the deity of Christ in the synagogues. But here as elsewhere in the New Testament, the author is simply using two titles of Jesus that apply to him as God's human Messiah: "Messiah," and "the Son of God."[40] It is clear that for Luke, a ("mere") human being can truly be called "the Son of God."[41] Luke in this passage sums up Paul's preaching in two ways, seemingly varying the titles only as a matter of style.[42] If Luke had wanted to say that Paul was preaching that Jesus is God the Son, fully divine, or that he has a divine nature, he could have said such things. At any rate, when we keep in mind the whole job description of the Messiah, we can see that Luke, again in summarizing Paul's message in his early ministry, gestures at some of our points about what being Messiah involves.

Paul's ministry is the focus of Acts 13–28. In Acts 13 Paul, in Antioch in Pisidia, takes advantage of synagogue tradition to stand and speak to his fellow Jews and to the Gentile "God-fearers" who are present (Acts 13:16, 26). He adopts a very Jewish angle, starting with the Exodus of the people out of Egypt, eventually introducing king David, about whom he says, "Of this man's posterity God has brought to Israel a Savior, Jesus, as he promised" (13:23). He appeals to the testimony of the prophet John the Baptist, an authority who would presumably be accepted by many of those present (13:24–25). Paul then preaches our points 1–4, pausing to cite several fulfilled scriptural texts (13:23–37), culminating in this appeal:

> Through this man forgiveness of sins is proclaimed to you; by this Jesus everyone who believes is set free from all those sins from which you could not be freed by the law of Moses." (Acts 13:38b–39)

---

[40] That these phrases are normally co-referring is shown by their being used "in apposition," that is, as different ways to refer to the same one. Thus the high priest demands to know whether Jesus is "the Messiah, the Son of God," (Matt. 26:63), Martha confesses Jesus to be "the Messiah, the Son of God" (John 11:27), and the author of the Fourth Gospel says that his aim is to bolster belief that "Jesus is the Messiah, the Son of God" (John 20:31). Similarly, Peter confesses Jesus to be "the Messiah, the Son of the living God" (Matt. 16:16). Again, we see "Messiah" and "the Son of God" being used interchangeably, sometimes seemingly just for stylistic reasons, such as in Luke 4:41. Again, "Son of God" is used as co-referring with other titles of the Messiah, so Nathaniel says to Jesus, "You are the Son of God! You are the King of Israel," that is, the Messiah (John 1:49). See also Locke, *Reasonableness of Christianity*, 22–24 (37–39), 32–33 (52), 39 (61), 60–62 (94–98).

[41] Luke 1:32, 35; 3:38; 4:3, 9, 41; 8:28; 22:70; Acts 2:22–23, 17:31.

[42] On our practice of switching up personal names and titles simply for variety, see pp. 54–55 and my "Unfinished Business of the Reformation," 216–18.

After a brief warning, it's over. It seems Paul was angling to be invited back the next Sabbath to say more (plausibly, most or all of our other points 5–11 about Jesus's Messiahship), and they do invite him to return (Acts 13:42–44).

That following Saturday, "almost the whole city gathered to hear the word of the Lord" (13:44). (The synagogue is not mentioned; perhaps the gathering was too large to assemble there.) Luke says that Paul's Jewish opponents were aroused by jealousy, and that "they contradicted what was spoken by Paul" (13:45). Despite, and in part because of this opposition, some Gentiles are converted. Then prominent citizens are induced to drive Paul and Barnabas out of the city (13:48–50).

There is a new point addressed here, one important to both Luke and Paul: that this new covenant is greater than the one available through keeping the Law of Moses—specifically, greater in the ability to set people free from their sins (13:39). While this is an important point in preaching to Jews, it would seem that in Luke's view it is not essential to the gospel.[43] For one thing, it has not been asserted till now in the book. For another, it would seem irrelevant to preaching the gospel to the Gentiles, most of whom knew little about the laws given through Moses to the Jews. This point is meant to answer an objection to trusting in Christ by believing him to be God's Messiah: that one *already* has a perfectly good standing with God through Torah observance, rendering this proposed trust superfluous.

In Acts 14 Paul and Barnabas preach successfully in a synagogue in Iconium, such that "a great number of both Jews and Greeks became believers" (14:1)—believers, that is, in Jesus as God's Messiah. But this stimulated Jewish and Gentile opposition, and our missionaries fled, lest they be stoned to death.

Moving on to Lystra, Paul and Barnabas pass up a golden opportunity to preach a godman Jesus, had they believed in such. Paul publicly heals a man who has been lame from birth, and the Gentile crowd concludes that Barnabas is the traditional Greek deity Zeus in human form, and that Paul is his messenger deity Hermes in human form (14:8–13)[44]. As the people of the city,

[43] A corollary for Gentiles is affirmed by the wider church later (Acts 15:1–31), that those Gentiles who would follow Jesus needn't also keep the whole Law but only a few points (15:20, 29) for the sake of unity with Jewish believers who continue to keep it.

[44] The Latin poet Ovid's *Metamorphoses*, written around the year 8 CE, includes a tale in which these two traditional deities, under the Latin names Jupiter and Mercury, appear in human form to a pious elderly couple, Philemon and Baucis, who receive them with hospitality and are rewarded (*Metamorphoses*, 225–29 [Bk. 8, lines 696–817]).

led by the priest of the local Zeus temple, prepare to sacrifice to them, the missionaries Barnabas and Paul rebuke them, pleading,

> People, why are you doing this? We are mortals just like you, and we bring you good news, that you should turn from these worthless things to the living God, who made the heaven and the earth and the sea and all that is in them. (Acts 14:15)

Is Paul badly missing the point here? Imagine one of the crowd shouting back,

> Yeah, Paul, we *know* you and Barnabas are mortal human beings, but we can see that you are also gods; you are godmen, people with both a divine nature and a human nature. As divine you're immortal, but as human you're mortal.

Paul does not think that pagan "gods" are worthy of the name (1 Cor. 8:5–6). These people's idols and/or the unseen beings they represent are "worthless things"; he doesn't grant that what the pagans worship really are gods, the sorts of powerful beings portrayed in the pagan myths.

Paul knows that he and Barnabas are fragile creatures who are subject to death; he considers it sufficient to correct the pagans' misunderstanding by pointing out that he and his friend are mortals, not immortals (so, not deities). Paul assumes that God is *essentially* mortal—there is no possibility of "the living God" losing his life (Rom. 1:23; 1 Tim. 1:17, 6:13–17); this is implied by the essential quality divinity.[45] That's why pointing out one's mortality is sufficient to disprove that one is a god with the sort of divinity enjoyed by the only god, the Father.

For Paul and Barnabas the man Jesus is God's special servant, his Messiah, who has provided a new way to reconcile humans to his and our God. The gospel is that God sent his human Son as a savior, just as Paul writes in Romans 5. They never heard of a gospel in which God became human. This is why it doesn't occur to Paul and Barnabas to argue,

> *We* are not godmen but let us tell you about someone who *is* a godman! Your myths tell of deities who appeared, deceptively, in human form. But the divine Person Jesus really became human, like us in all things but sin, while remaining fully divine.

[45] In 1 Timothy 6:16 it is said that God, that is, the Father, "alone . . . has immortality." The author must be thinking of *essential* immortality. If the idea is rather contingent (non-essential) immortality, it is false that only God has that, since now Jesus does too, having been raised to immortality (1 Cor. 15:49, 50–57). Interpreting 1 Timothy 6:16 charitably, then, the author means *essential* immortality.

Instead Paul and Barnabas try to turn the subject from the false gods of mythology "to the living God," the creator, the one true god.[46] This lays the groundwork for preaching belief and trust in God's Messiah.[47]

But they don't get very far. Their Jewish opponents from the previous city catch up with them and turn the crowd against the missionaries. The mob stones Paul, leaving him for dead, although he's able to travel on with Barnabas the next day (Acts 14:19–20).[48]

From here on Luke's narrative becomes increasingly action-packed. The reader has already been given the essentials of "the word of the Lord" (Acts 15:35–36), the good news about Jesus, the gospel. Luke doesn't need to construct further sermon scenes. Thus, when the Gentile jailer cries out to Paul and Silas, in Luke's telling, he is told very little by the apostles.

> "Sirs, what must I do to be saved?" They answered, "Believe in the Lord Jesus, and you will be saved, you and your household." They spoke the word of the Lord to him and to all who were in his house . . . then he and his entire family were baptized without delay. He brought them up into the house and set food before them, and he and his entire household rejoiced that he had become a believer in God. (Acts 16:30–33)

Not much is said here about "the word of the Lord,"[49] what must be believed to trust in Jesus and be saved. But observe what seems to happen in the space of an evening: this man and his family hear the gospel, believe it, and are immediately baptized. This "word" must be fairly simple—some or all of our points 1–11, which Luke assumes the reader will mentally fill in here.

Luke is similarly brief about Paul's preaching on three consecutive Sabbaths in the synagogue at Thessalonica. There Paul

> argued with them from the scriptures, explaining and proving that it was necessary for the Messiah to suffer and to rise from the dead and saying, "This is the Messiah, Jesus whom I am proclaiming to you." (Acts 17:2b–3)

---

[46] As an idol-maker complains later in the book, "this Paul has persuaded and drawn away a considerable number of people by saying that gods made with hands are not gods" (Acts 19:26).

[47] As Paul says later, "I testified to both Jews and Greeks about repentance toward God and faith toward our Lord Jesus" (Acts 20:21).

[48] It seems that only Paul was stoned. Perhaps Barnabas ran faster?

[49] Also called "the word of God": Acts 6:7, 8:14, 11:1, 13:46, 17:13.

This is a quick gesture in the direction of 1–4, although presumably Paul said more. Again, Jewish opposition is aroused, and not finding Paul and Silas, some persecutors haul a believer named Jason before the local authorities and accuse his guests, Paul and Silas, of "acting contrary to the decrees of the emperor, saying that there is another king named Jesus" (Acts 17:7). King, yes—as in 5 and 6 in our list. And Paul may well have preached that Jesus was the future king of Israel, an aspect of the Messiah's calling not emphasized in Acts.

There are a few more occasions for preaching, such as the famous scene in Athens. Most of what Paul says there, though, is a Gentile-tailored prelude to the gospel, a plea to turn from idols and the false gods they represent to "The God who made the world and everything in it, he who is Lord of heaven and earth" (17:24). He presents the gospel too, but evidently his audience has a hard time comprehending it. When Paul preaches "about Jesus and the resurrection," they think, "He seems to be a proclaimer of foreign divinities" (17:18), that is, deities named "Jesus" and "Resurrection."[50] But they are willing to keep listening, so he speaks to them again, and gets in at least these core gospel claims:

> While God has overlooked the times of human ignorance, now he commands all people everywhere to repent, because he has fixed a day on which he will have the world judged in righteousness by a man whom he has appointed, and of this he has given assurance to all by raising him from the dead. (Acts 17:30–31)

Here Paul asserts claims 4, 7, and 11 (pp. 163, 176), together with the appeal that they should repent. Is that all? Surely Paul must have said more. We do well to remember that in New Testament times quotation marks had not been invented, so any literary presentation of a speech or sermon is assumed to be summarized. Luke has already in this book made the essentials of the gospel abundantly clear. At this point in the book, he only needs to gesture at parts of that message to get the reader to recall all of it. Thus Luke tells us about Paul's ministry in Corinth that "Paul was occupied with proclaiming the word, testifying to the Jews that the Messiah was Jesus" (18:5b)—the foundational point 1 again. Similarly, Apollos "powerfully refuted the Jews in public, showing by the scriptures that the Messiah is Jesus." (18:28)

Paul's farewell speech to the elders at Ephesus is interesting, but it is not a gospel presentation. Still, we should take note of one cause for later theological stumbling, where Paul exhorts those elders to

---

[50] Notice that Paul does not take this opportunity to say that they are partially correct, since Jesus is the god of Israel.

> keep watch over yourselves and over all the flock, of which the Holy Spirit has made you overseers, to shepherd the church of God that he obtained with the blood of his own Son. (Acts 20:28, NRSVUE)[51]

The Greek here is literally "with the blood of his own," which could be translated as "with his own blood." But the translators are surely correct here in supplying the word "Son," for it is the man Jesus, not God (that is, the Father), who has blood to spill. And the New Testament gospel is not, as one hears nowadays, that *God* died on the cross for us but rather that God sent his human Son to die for us (Rom. 5)—something God himself could not do.[52] This is why, when Jesus is crucified in the Gospels, no one wonders: "How can *God* have died?"[53] Scholars generally agree with the above translation, although this text is complicated by the fact that some ancient manuscripts have "the church of the Lord" (Jesus) rather than "of God"—in which case "with his own blood" *would* make sense.[54]

Back to Paul's adventures—on a visit to Jerusalem, he is arrested in the temple on false charges (Acts 21:27–40). He then defends himself, relating his conversion and a personal prophecy given to him by Ananias:

> "The God of our ancestors has chosen you to know his will, to see the Righteous One, and to hear his own voice, for you will be his witness to all the world of what you have seen and heard." (Acts 22:14–15)

Like the other apostles, Paul has witnessed the risen Jesus[55] and been called by him to witness to Jesus's status as God's unique Messiah, "the Righteous One." More adventures ensue, but Paul doesn't really preach the gospel again in Acts, although he does give a brief account of his message when defending himself before King Agrippa. Paul says that he proclaims

> nothing but what the prophets and Moses said would take place: that the Messiah must suffer and that, by being the first to rise from the dead, he would proclaim light both to our people and to the gentiles. (Acts 26:22b–23)

Again our author gestures at claims 1–11. Near the end of the book we find Paul under arrest in Rome but able to receive visitors, so "the local leaders of the Jews"

---

[51] As the translators of the REV note, the capitalization "Holy Spirit" seems proper here, as this is being used as a title of God.

[52] For relevant biblical texts and discussion see p. 179, note 45 and my "Podcast 145."

[53] I owe this point to Unitarian Christian Alliance podcast host Mark Cain (Tuggy, "Podcast 333").

[54] Harris, *Jesus as God*, ch. 5.

[55] Acts 9:4–6, 22:17–21, 23:11, 26:14–18.

> came to him at his lodgings in great numbers. From morning until evening he explained the matter to them, testifying to the kingdom of God and trying to convince them about Jesus both from the law of Moses and from the prophets. (Acts 29:23)

Luke ends his book, and so the reader unsatisfyingly leaves Paul, with this:

> He lived there [in Rome] two whole years at his own expense and welcomed all who came to him, proclaiming the kingdom of God and teaching about the Lord Jesus Christ with all boldness and without hindrance. (Acts 29:30–31)

The Kingdom of God will be fully enacted by the Lord Jesus (claims 6 and 10)—Luke continues to gesture at the whole message.

5.11 CONCLUSION

We asked: What, according to Luke, is essential to the gospel? What does Luke think one must believe in order to change from an unbeliever to a believer? We examined not Luke's Gospel, which is mostly about events before the whole gospel was known, but rather his Volume 2, the Acts of the Apostles.

Luke is an effective storyteller, and his story is about the advance of God's word through the communities of the Jews and Samaritans, out into the much bigger Gentile world. In telling this story, he effectively communicates what one must believe to be saved: that Jesus is God's Messiah. It turns out that being God's Messiah is far more than being destined to be a king of Israel. Acknowledging Jesus as the Messiah, the as the central figure in God's plans is a recognition of his God-appointed authority over you, as your savior (points 1–3, 7), ruler and judge (points 5–6, 10–11), and source of divine power (points 8–9).

Because of longstanding theological speculations, I've focused, like John Locke, on what must be believed or accepted to enter into a new relationship with God through his Messiah. Here God, in his perfect wisdom, has set the bar low, in contrast to the demands of the mind-breaking "Athanasian" Creed, or even "classic" early modern Protestant confessions like the Westminster Confession.[56] Locke comments,

> The writers and wranglers in religion fill it with niceties and dress it up with notions, which they make necessary and fundamental parts of it—as if there

[56] Section 2.2.

> were no way into the church but through the academy or lyceum.[57] The greatest part of mankind have not leisure for learning and logic and superfine distinctions of the schools.[58] Where the hand is used to the plow and the spade, the head is seldom elevated to sublime notions or exercised in mysterious reasoning. It is well if men of that rank . . . can comprehend plain propositions and a short reasoning about things familiar to their minds . . . Go beyond this, and you amaze the greater part of mankind and may as well talk Arabic to a poor day laborer as the notions and language that the books and disputes of religion are filled with—and as soon you will be understood.[59]

As Locke highlights throughout *The Reasonableness of Christianity*, more than belief or acceptance is required. For one thing, you must be willing not only to believe that Jesus is your human Lord but also to publicly confess him as your Lord; he demands this basic expression of loyalty in addition to your being convinced. Clearly, too, repentance is required—both sorrow over one's sins and a firm resolve to follow the path of Jesus. And there must be ongoing obedience; it is unacceptable to *say* Jesus is your master, your human Lord, while failing to obey his God-inspired commands (Luke 6:46). Locke notes that Jesus,

> being a king, we shall see by his commands what he expects from his subjects; for, if he did not expect obedience from them, his commands would be but mere mockery, and if there were no punishments for the transgressors of them, his laws would not be the laws of a king, and that authority to command and power to chastise the disobedient, but empty talk, without force and without influence.[60]

A first step in this is the initiating ritual of water baptism. But the loyal subject will not stop there; she will act as a diligent student, studying the New Testament in a community of disciples to see what Jesus requires of her. And to ultimately be saved, she will persevere in obedience, remaining in Christ.[61]

We have noticed that much in Acts concerns Jewish opposition to the nascent Jesus movement. First, the good news is preached to them and then to

---

[57] Respectively, the original places in Athens of the schools of philosophy of Plato and his star student Aristotle.

[58] Locke here means late-medieval and early modern "scholastic" traditions of academic philosophy, which he had to study when young, and came to dismiss as useless purveyors of "learned gibberish" (Locke, *Essay*, 495 [3.10.9]). In his own philosophical writing, opposing this style of philosophizing, Locke strives for clarity and tries to found human knowledge on experience.

[59] Locke, *Reasonableness of Christianity*, 193–94 (252).

[60] *Reasonableness of Christianity*, 139 (185).

[61] Matt. 13:20–21, 24:13; John 15:6; Gal. 5:4; Heb. 6:4–6, 10:26–27; 2 Pet. 2:20–22.

the Gentiles. As we saw, because most Jews then and now have expectations of a coming Messiah, that is a natural starting point for preaching the good news about Jesus to them, although there will inevitably be disputes about what the Messiah job description involves.[62] Traditional Jews enjoy another advantage when it comes to the gospel: they believe there is only one god, the creator of the universe, who loves his creation, has made men and women in his own image and likeness, and wants their trust, friendship, and obedience. In short, they have been taught about the god mentioned repeatedly in our points 1–11, the one the New Testament Jesus and his disciples pray to as "Father."

Traditionally, a lot of Jewish anti-Christian-missionary pushback has focused on catholic traditions about Trinity and Incarnation,[63] but as we've seen, those later speculations played no part in the initial spread of the gospel, and so there was no need for such pushback. The central issue now, as then, is really whether or not Jesus, as he and his apostles claimed, is God's Messiah. What will happen when the reformation of Christian traditions in light of Scripture progresses to the point where non-Christian Jews can easily consider the claims of the gospel without that later baggage? What if they closely study Acts and the rest of the New Testament until they understand why so many of their fellow Jews became believers in Jesus, even in the face of rather severe opposition from both their fellow Jews and their Gentile neighbors?

I find it refreshing that in Acts there is no trace of the shameful Jew-hating that stains so much of later Christian history.[64] Luke is frank about the opposition, but all he says is compatible with having a special place in one's heart for God's chosen people, as we see in Paul's words in Romans 9:1–5. If your human Lord is Jesus, how can you hate his extended family and their later descendants?

As Paul discovered in Athens, it's harder to explain the gospel to pagans who assume some traditional pantheon and religious practices, including the use of idols. People like this are not at first equipped to understand the proclamation that Jesus is God's Messiah. *Which* "God" is meant? Locke says

---

[62] For polemical arguments by recent non-Christian Jews against mainstream Christianity, which often center on what the Messiah is supposed to do, see Boteach, *Kosher Jesus*; Klinghoffer, *Why the Jews*; Singer, *Let's Get Biblical*, vol. 1. For Talmudic treatments of Jesus see Schäfer, *Jesus in the Talmud*.

[63] For medieval and early modern arguments see Crescas, *Refutation*; Troki, *Faith Strengthened*; Popkin, *Disputing Christianity*.

[64] Heer, *God's First Love*.

that believing that Jesus is God's Messiah presupposes the belief that there is a unique god who is invisible, eternal, omnipotent, and the creator of the cosmos.[65] I think that's basically right; they need either to acquire or to focus on the concept of a god as understood in Abrahamic monotheism, one who is not a mere deity such as populate the myths of the nations but the uncaused cause of all else, who is necessarily unique and perfect in knowledge, power, and goodness, and who cares about us so much that he even knows the number of hairs on our heads (Luke 12:7). What the risen Jesus prophesied to his apostles prior to Pentecost is still being fulfilled:

> You will receive power when the holy spirit has come upon you, and you will be my witnesses both in Jerusalem, and in all Judea, and Samaria, and to the uttermost part of the earth." (Acts 1:8, REV)

This mission will enter a new phase when it is no longer encumbered by confused and confusing catholic speculations about Trinity and Incarnation. We have yet to see the full power or the final fruits of the easily understood points 1–11, which can be summarized simply: the man Jesus is God's Messiah.

---

[65] Locke, *Reasonableness of Christianity*, 16 (25), 28 (45).

CHAPTER 6

Dealing with Apparent Contradictions in Theology

6.1 THE FOUR R'S[1]

In this chapter I will classify different ways Christians respond to apparent contradictions in theology: Redirection, Restraint, Resistance, and Resolution. These are ways of dealing with some doctrinal claim *D* that seems to imply some *P and not-P*—some claim and its denial. Thus, *D seems* to be incoherent[2]; it seems that reality cannot be as *D* says, for it implies claims that, being contradictions, can't all be true. On the face of it, then, we should not accept *D*, as we want only true beliefs when it comes to important matters like theology. But Christians respond to seeming contradictions in basically four ways, some of which authorize being content to settle for apparently incoherent beliefs.

As a first pass, the four types of response can be characterized as follows:

Redirection: God is *really* wonderful, and *D* is true, important, and practical, and many other profound theological truths depend on *D*.

Restraint: What you state as *D does* appear to be incoherent. *But* the doctrine in question needn't be understood as saying *D* . . . but I don't know what to replace *D* with.

Resistance: Yes, *D* does appear to be incoherent. Nonetheless, we may reasonably believe *D*.

---

[1] This chapter began as a series of twenty blog posts at trinities.org in 2008.

[2] Many people describe a doctrine that implies some *P and not-P* as "inconsistent." That usage is correct, but in my view the term "incoherent" is better. "Inconsistency" most often means a relation between one claim or set of claims and another. If someone labels a doctrine as "inconsistent," we need to ask, inconsistent *with what*? To say that a doctrine is "incoherent" is to say clearly that it's inconsistent *with itself*, meaning that among its claims and their implications we can find at least one claim both affirmed and denied.

Resolution: *If* the doctrine in question amounted to *D*, that doctrine would be incoherent. But on further examination, Christians needn't commit to *D* but rather to something else—call it *E*.

6.2 REDIRECTION

When confronted with an apparently incoherent doctrine, the Redirector changes the subject. She says something to direct your attention away from that doctrine, or at least away from the apparent inconsistency of certain formulations of it. The Redirector is either not arguing in defense of that doctrine at all, or she's committing a red herring fallacy (responding to an argument with some irrelevant point). Imagine this exchange:

Doubting Don: Jesus was God *and* a human? But isn't that saying that he is and isn't divine?

Redirecting Rebecca: Isn't it amazing that God loved us so much that while we were yet sinners, he sent his only Son to redeem us?

Doubting Don: Yes, that *is* amazing. But what does *that* have to do with my question? All contradictions are false. But the Incarnation doctrine looks like it implies contradictions, such as implying that Jesus is and is not omniscient.[3] It seems we shouldn't believe it, as we aim to believe only what is true.

Redirecting Rebecca: But if the divine *didn't* become human, then no human can become divine.

First, Rebecca changes the subject. When pressed, she gives (the start of) an argument for an Incarnation doctrine. But this is also a red herring, a distraction. Don has raised a worry that the Incarnation is incoherent, that the claims constituting this doctrine imply some pair of claims with the form *P and not-P*. It's pointless to mount an argument for a conjunction of claims that is incoherent because that conjunction, being incoherent, is thereby known to be false.[4] Discovering that some theory is incoherent forecloses the project of looking for evidence or argument for that theory, since we already know it to be

[3] "[Jesus said,] 'But about that day or hour no one knows, neither the angels in heaven nor the Son, but only the Father'" (Mark 13:32).

[4] A complex doctrine should be thought of as a large conjunction of claims, of the form: *A and B and C and D*. If it contains a contradiction, for example, *A and B and C and not-C and D*, then the whole doctrine consisting of those five claims will be false, since its being true requires that every individual claim is true. In the above example, it is manifestly impossible that both the third and fourth claims are true, and this implies the falsehood of the whole conjunction, the whole complex doctrine. Of course, it may still be that some of the individual claims in the doctrine are true.

false (since all contradictions are false). We should retrace our steps in order to find a more viable explanation of the texts in question. And whether what she says at the end is true or false, she simply hasn't faced the issue of whether that Incarnation doctrine is coherent (hence, *possibly* true) or incoherent (thus, necessarily false).

This seems irresponsible. God gave us critical thinking abilities so that, at least when it comes to important topics, we can maximize our true beliefs and minimize our false beliefs. Moreover, many people have faced the issue of incoherence, whatever that difficult doctrine is, whether it be Trinity, Incarnation, free will and foreknowledge, or evil and God's goodness. It's not as if Rebecca will need to explore uncharted territory. Rebecca really ought to look into it more. Granted, she may have good, practical reasons for delaying these investigations; perhaps the roof is leaking, the baby is crying, or she needs to get to work on time. It is often *practically* rational (prudent) to put off hard questions. But to resolve not to consider them even when one has the time and the ability is to cease to be concerned with theological and christological truth. Redirection, as a settled stance (rather than a temporary delaying response) toward apparently incoherent claims isn't a serious option for someone who wants to love God with all her mind (Mark 12:30).

6.3 RESTRAINT AND "IMPLICIT FAITH"

The response of Restraint is a little more reasonable. This person realizes that a certain way of understanding—for instance, the doctrine of the Trinity—seems to include or imply contradictions. The Christian walking the path of Restraint declines to endorse that way of understanding the doctrine, or any other clear formulation. "Sure, *if* it meant *D*, then the doctrine would seem incoherent . . . but *maybe* it *doesn't* mean *D*."

The Restrained believer neither affirms nor denies *D*, exercising Restraint. He declines to take a position on precisely what the doctrine in question is. He'll say he's committed to the truth of *whatever it is* that's supposed to be expressed by the traditional formulations of the doctrine. He doesn't rule out that others who are holier and/or more informed *have* understood those, so that they are not merely endorsing words but also grasping the truths those words express.

Like Redirection, Restraint is reasonable as an initial move, but it's nowhere to pitch camp. It is only a way of stalling. Stalling can be reasonable; no one has time to look into every difficulty, and we have a lot more we must do beyond developing our theology. The Restrained believer is saying that he believes, hopes, or is somehow committed to certain sentences expressing truth, but isn't aware of *what* that truth is.

Fair enough. But one should be spurred on to move past Restraint by three concerns. First, people have claimed to discern various important truths in those sentences. One should seek to find out whether or not they're correct. Second, the sentences in question could be "fool's gold," in that they really express not truths but falsehoods. One needs to rule this out to avoid forming false beliefs about important matters. Third, maybe the sentences express nothing; maybe they are unintelligible. If so, whatever their value, they won't be a means of believing, thinking, or expressing truths. Again, this needs to be ruled out. Thus, while Restraint is initially an expression of intellectual humility—one doesn't jump to dismiss a doctrine at the first sign of a problem—eventually it becomes an irresponsible stance.[5]

The medieval Catholic doctrine of "implicit faith" (Latin: *fides implicitas*) counseled Restraint for most Christians. This idea pops up frequently in early modern and present-day anti-Catholic material, and it is easy to ridicule. It was a popular teaching at both the scholarly and popular levels in late medieval Catholicism, though more recent official Catholic thought steers away from it.[6] Nonetheless, the term is still applied in apologetics contexts, though most often not to Catholic laypeople but to people who, through no fault of their own, have never been exposed to Christian teaching. But in the medieval and early modern eras, the concept was usually applied to less-educated Catholic laypeople, who were legion.

These posed an obvious problem. Suppose we agree with the "Athanasian" Creed that "whoever desires to be saved must above all things hold the Catholic faith. Unless a man keeps it in its entirety inviolate, he will assuredly perish eternally."[7] Further, one interprets "holding the Catholic faith" as *believing* all of its core doctrines, such as the Incarnation as expounded at the Council of Chalcedon in 451,[8] and the Trinity as expounded at the 1215 Fourth Lateran

---

[5] A person who exercises Restraint typically considers himself to be a believer in *D*, for example a trinitarian or a believer in Incarnation. But when one withholds on so much it is unclear that one should count as a trinitarian or a believer in Incarnation, despite one's intentions. Regarding the Trinity see my "Unfinished Business of Trinitarian," 179–80.

[6] A recent respected Cardinal and professor observes, "Wisely, in my opinion, the popes and councils have avoided talk about implicit faith, a term that is vague and ambiguous" (Dulles, "Who Can Be Saved?").

[7] *Athanasian Creed*, 17 (1–2).

[8] "Definition."

Council.[9] Consider now an illiterate Roman Catholic peasant in the year 1300—call him ditchdigger Dan. Dan has here and there heard some of the individual words in those official sources, but he really has no grasp at all of Church teaching on Incarnation or Trinity. Is Dan therefore damned, despite his faithful Mass attendance and generally submissive and favorable disposition toward the Church? Many Catholics have wanted to say no. After all, Dan can't be blamed for being born into and trapped in extreme poverty, which has deprived him of the education necessary to understand, and so to believe, Church teachings about Incarnation and Trinity.

Instead of reducing the belief requirement to a more scriptural level,[10] the doctrine of implicit faith says that Dan can, *in a sense*, "have faith in" those doctrines, after all, because he trusts in *whatever it is* that the Church teaches, and the Church teaches Trinity and Incarnation. The more learned of the Church of course do, to a significant degree, understand Trinity and Incarnation language, and so they actually believe the official doctrines. But Dan's "implicit faith" is enough for him to be saved; unlike those learned people, he doesn't have "explicit faith," but Dan's faith is good enough. We may say that Dan "implicitly believes" in, for instance, the Church's doctrine of the Trinity.

My own view is that talk of "implicit belief" isn't helpful, for what they mean by that phrase *isn't* a kind of belief. To believe is, as it were, to have one's mind in a certain shape; it's committing to reality being a certain way. If I believe, for instance, that Oswald killed Kennedy, I'm committed to that having happened. I *could not* believe that if I'd never so much as heard of Lee Harvey Oswald, or of President Kennedy, or if I didn't understand the concept of killing. To say that one need only "believe" some doctrine by "implicit faith" is really to say that *belief* in these doctrines isn't (for some folks at least) necessary for salvation. It assumes that God will accept something else from them, a sort of secondhand commitment to *whatever it is* that some others truly believe on this topic. One with "implicit faith" in some doctrine doesn't have her mind, so to speak, in the shape it would be in if she actually *believed* that doctrine. Such a pseudo-belief can't, then, guide her actions in a way that a belief does.

The famous Roman Catholic philosopher-theologian St. Thomas Aquinas (c. 1225–74) gives an objection to the implicit faith doctrine and then answers it.

[9] "Constitutions," 230–32 (1–2).

[10] Chapters 4 and 5.

> Objection 3. Further, If the simple are bound to have, not explicit but only implicit faith, their faith must be implied in the faith of the learned. But this seems unsafe, since it is possible for the learned to err. Therefore it seems that the simple should also have explicit faith; so that all are, therefore, equally bound to have explicit faith.
>
> [Now Aquinas gives a general reply before addressing Objection 3.] *On the contrary ... I answer that,* The unfolding of matters of faith is the result of Divine revelation: for matters of faith surpass natural reason. Now Divine revelation reaches those of lower degree through those who are over them ... just as the higher angels, who enlighten those who are below them, have a fuller knowledge of Divine things than the lower angels ... so too, men of higher degree, whose business it is to teach others, are under obligation to have fuller knowledge of matters of faith, and to believe them more explicitly.
>
> ... Reply to Objection 3. The simple have no faith implied in that of the learned, except in so far as the latter adhere to the Divine teaching. Hence the Apostle says (1 Corinthians 4:16): "*Be ye followers of me, as I also am of Christ.*" Hence it is not human knowledge, but the Divine truth that is the rule of faith. And if any of the learned stray from this rule, he does not harm the faith of the simple ones, who think that the learned believe rightly, unless the simple hold obstinately to their individual errors, against the faith of the universal Church, which cannot err, since Our Lord said (Luke 22:32): "*I have prayed for thee,*" Peter, "*that thy faith fail not.*"[11]

The objection here is: one should not commit to *whatever those learned guys think* because learned guys sometimes go wrong, believing falsehoods. (Every philosopher knows this is an understatement.) One ought to know *to what* one is committing.

Aquinas's answer can be explained as follows. Suppose Pedro the priest teaches *A, B, and C* to Ditchdigger Dan. Dan literally doesn't understand the meaning of claims *A, B, and C*—he's not intelligent enough and/or not educated enough—although he hears and remembers the words used to express the claims *A, B, and C*. But Dan, being a humble Catholic, decides to accept what Pedro teaches on this topic, *insofar as it truly expresses divine revelation*. Of course, Dan doesn't know to what extent *A, B, and C* express divine revelation. Let's suppose that *A* and *B* are indeed divinely revealed, but *C* is not part of divine revelation and, in fact, clashes with parts of it. Dan's intention, then, unbeknown to him, commits him only to *A and B*. But Dan will *say*, following

[11] Aquinas, *Summa Theologica*, 395–96 (2.2.Q2.A6), original italics.

Pedro, "A, B, and C." In this scenario, Dan has "implicit faith" in claims *A* and *B* (but not *C*). Aquinas is saying that because of the "insofar" clause, Ditchdigger Dan only commits *to the true parts* of what Pedro thinks.

Now, if that is what Dan is doing, you might think he can't really go wrong. Dan could commit to whatever Kim Kardashian thinks, insofar as this "adheres to divine teaching." In such a scenario, he would merely repeat what Kim says. Imagine, for the sake of argument, that she is an arch atheist and accepts nothing of the divinely revealed truths, but Dan for some reason falsely believes her to be a prophet. Because of this, he eagerly repeats her statements. On Aquinas's doctrine, this will not increase his implicit faith in divinely revealed truths, as (we're supposing) she neither believes nor teaches any. This idea of believing by "implicit faith," accepting whatever an alleged religious authority says, is very risky, as one may unknowingly commit to zero truths, or very few, while repeating language that, when understood, expresses falsehoods.

Some may think the Kardashian thought experiment is extreme and unrealistic. Consider then a rogue Catholic priest who believes and teaches fashionable New Age nonsense along with divinely revealed truths. Rogue priest Ray mounts the pulpit and teaches *A, B, C, and D*. A modern day Dan is there, absorbing the words that he doesn't really understand. He puts his trust in the teachings of Ray insofar as they reflect divine revelation. Thus, Dan will leave church and inform his friends and neighbors that "A, B, C, and D" (those words) are true, while in fact *A* and *B* are divinely revealed truths but *C* and *D* are falsehoods. This too seems very risky for Dan, in that going in, he has little idea what the percentage of divinely revealed truths will be that he will, in this indirect fashion, have "implicit faith" in. It seems risky in another way too. Not being able to separate the true from the false, Dan in this Ray scenario will unknowingly spread falsehoods. Many other people *will* understand *C* and *D*, so when they hear "C" and "D," they will hear testimony in favor of *C* and *D*.

There's something too artificial about my examples so far, as Dan doesn't understand *anything* his religious authority teaches. Generally, a religious authority will teach, in addition to alleged divine mysteries beyond human understanding, many claims that simple folk *do* understand—such as that Jesus was crucified, died, and then raised back to life by God. Implicit faith in whatever an alleged authority teaches will often be unwise, for some of what they teach *can* be understood, and some of it can be recognized as false. Imagine that rogue priest Ray is an extreme progressive, and he teaches Dan that the Church has never taught that abortion is morally wrong. Dan can very easily, by asking other people, learn that this is false. He should not discard this knowledge and adopt a stance of implicit faith in what Ray teaches. When we take someone as an epistemic exemplar, someone whose beliefs are worth our imitation, we don't merely commit abstractly to *whatever* they believe or truly believe. Rather, we listen to them and are strongly inclined to accept their testimony. We use them as a reference source. It matters a great deal, then, whether we pick Pedro or Kim, the Pope or Calvin, Jesus or Muhammad. And presumably God will hold us accountable for our choice. I don't see that Aquinas gives a good answer to his Objection 3.

But let's imagine that Dan can somehow separate the unintelligible divine mysteries from the understandable claims, and he puts implicit faith in the rogue priest Ray's teachings only with respect to the former. Suppose that Ray teaches *A, B, C, D, and E*, and that Dan understands the claims *D and E* and can think critically about them. But the compound claim *A, B, and C* Dan doesn't understand at all, although he can repeat some of the words Ray uses to express it. Let's suppose Dan has "implicit faith" in Ray's teachings *A, B, and C*, whatever those are, insofar as they express divine revelation. Unbeknownst to Dan, *B* and *C* are not part of divine revelation, although *A* is. So unbeknownst to Dan, he is committed *only* to *A*, although he faithfully parrots "A, B, and C." That is, Dan is committed to the *truth* of *A*. Presumably, the idea is that *if* Dan were to understand the meaning of claim *A*, as more learned folk do, *then* Dan would *believe A*. But since Dan *doesn't* understand the content of the claim *A*, how could he know that? How can Dan rule out that if he were to understand *A*, he would reject it, believing it to be false and not true? You may *want* to believe some claim you don't understand; however, if you *did* understand it, you would reject it.

This happens often with Catholicism today. A young person on the internet today may be drawn to Catholicism for many reasons and decide to convert before looking into all that the Church teaches. As she begins the conversion process, she's committed to whatever the Church teaches. But when she hears of their teaching on birth control[12] or other topics where they clash with her assumptions, she rejects much of it. So, too, she may discover that official Catholic sources teach the mind-breaking doctrine of divine simplicity,[13] and she may then find good reasons to reject that doctrine.[14]

---

[12] "Birth Control."
[13] "Constitutions," 230–32 (1–2).
[14] Mullins, "Simply Impossible."

Consider too that some Christian teachers have asserted that certain theological mysteries really are, when rightly understood, self-contradictory, containing some claim *P* as well as its denial *not-P*. Most people find it easy, once understood, to reject self-contradictory claims. Suppose I tell you that I have only one living sibling, yet I have a living sibling who is over six feet tall, *and* I have a living sibling who is under six feet tall—and I add that we're measuring them in the same way and at the same time. It looks as if I am asserting that I have one living brother or sister who is simultaneously over six feet tall *and not*. Most people easily and reasonably reject such claims. However, *if* the doctrine of the Trinity includes the claims that God is exactly three Persons and in the same sense God is only one Person, can't we in this case also "see" that such a doctrine must be false?

In any case, according to Aquinas himself, the whole Restraint stance, even with "implicit faith," won't do when it comes to some central and famously problematic Christian doctrines. He teaches that even the simple must "explicitly"—*not* merely "implicitly"—*believe* the Incarnation and Trinity doctrines; without this, in his view, they can't be saved.[15] This makes sense, if indeed such doctrines are divinely revealed. God reveals truths so that they may be believed by all who are able. As best I can tell, there is no provision for latching on to the true beliefs of others so that one may be counted as believing those things by proxy. This may have seemed reasonable in the Middle Ages and the early modern era, but it no longer does. The contemporary Catholic Church has been right to cease counseling implicit faith for laypeople; to do that is to punt on religious education.

6.4 RESISTANCE

The fourth "R" is Resistance. The Resister is resisting the pressure to resolve an apparent contradiction, such as changing one or both of the apparently contradictory beliefs so that no contradiction remains. Unlike the Redirector, the Resister doesn't ignore the apparent inconsistency. And unlike the Resolver (to be discussed below), he doesn't think there's a reasonable way to make the apparent contradiction go away. So the Resister makes his stand, coming up with a rationale for maintaining his apparently contradictory beliefs. These rationales vary significantly, but they have in common that they are intended to be permanent stances, at least in this life. That is, a Resistor may and should

[15] See his following two articles (Aquinas, *Summa Theologica*, 396-99 [2.2.Q11.A7–8]).

agree that Redirection and Restraint may make sense for a while, but it seems that at some point he should get around to addressing these important topics.

6.4.1 MYSTERIAN RESISTANCE

Mysterian Resistance has long been the most popular of the four Rs in Christianity, particularly among intellectuals, but among laypeople as well. Here are some examples of Mysterianism in action.

> Someone: How can the entire body of a man be present in each crumb of this wafer?[16]
>
> Mysterian: I don't know—it's a mystery.
>
> Someone: How can a man be fully divine?
>
> Mysterian: I don't know—it's a mystery.
>
> Someone: How there be one God if there are not one but three divine Persons, each of whom individually is God?
>
> Mysterian: I don't know—it's a mystery!

There will be different reactions to such exchanges. Many philosophers I know would think these are cheap, intellectually lazy answers and would be quick to suggest Rational Reconstructions of these doctrines.[17] Appeals to mystery often are mere expressions of intellectual laziness, of unwillingness to think carefully through difficult issues. Appeals to mystery are often meant merely as conversation stoppers. Sometimes "mystery" means something like a precious religious truth or thing. Many who talk of "holy mysteries" in this way are not worried about incoherence at all. But Mysterian Resistance is more intellectually serious. A sophisticated Mysterian holds that it is reasonable to believe in a mystery *despite* its problematic status. He needn't be intellectually lazy or a mystery-monger who loves paradox as such. The most thoughtful Mysterians have stories to tell about why their Resistance is reasonable after all, about why Christians must learn to live with apparent contradictions.

As far as I know, Reformed analytic theologian James Anderson's book *Paradox in Christian Theology* is the most sophisticated, well-developed, and plausible defense of the idea that Christians may rationally believe and know "mysteries" in the sense of *apparently* (but not really) contradictory doctrines.[18] Consider the following inconsistent triad of claims:

---

[16] *Catechism*, secs. 1374–77.

[17] Section 6.5.1.

[18] The rest of this section draws on material from my "Review."

C: If some claim appears after careful reflection to be incoherent, I shouldn't believe it.
O: The orthodox Christian doctrine *D* appears after careful reflection to be incoherent.
B: I should believe the orthodox Christian doctrine *D*.

If any two of those are true, the remaining one must be false. (Here the reader should pause and go through the three options.) What should the thoughtful and faithful believer do in the face of such a conundrum? Many current-day philosophical or analytic theologians habitually reject *O* (while affirming *C and B*), offering some plausible interpretation of *D* so that *D* seems to be coherent after all.[19] Anderson, along with probably many theologians and other believers outside the profession of philosophy, rejects this move, as he holds that the reinterpreted *D* always turns out to be out of line with (1) the mainstream of the historic Christian tradition, (2) the ecumenical creeds, rightly interpreted according to the intentions of their framers, and (3) the Bible itself.

A second response is to reject the Orthodox version of doctrine *D*; that is, reject *B* (keeping *C* and *O*). But theology is inherently conservative, and in keeping with this tendency, Anderson will have none of it, equating it with an abandonment of Christianity. We'll revisit this sort of Resolution by Revision in section 6.5.2.

A third response is to reject *C* (keeping *B* and *O*); this is Anderson's position, which I have elsewhere called "Positive Mysterianism."[20] He attributes adherence to *C* to "rationalism," something like a prideful preference for one's own intuitions over the clear teachings of Scripture.[21] What is surprising and refreshing is the epistemological sophistication Anderson brings to play in developing and defending his version of Mysterian Resistance.

The book proceeds as follows. A "paradox" is an apparently contradictory claim.[22] The orthodox doctrines of the Trinity and the Incarnation, according to Anderson, are paradoxes. In the second and third chapters he recounts the development of these doctrines in the fourth and fifth centuries, relentlessly

[19] This strategy, to be examined further in section 6.5.1, I call Resolution by Rational Reconstruction. For these rational reconstructions of the doctrine of the Trinity, see my "Trinity," secs. 1–3. For the many attempts at a coherent reconstruction of Incarnation, see my "Two Natures."

[20] "Trinity," sec. 4.2.

[21] Anderson, *Paradox*, 281.

[22] *Paradox*, 5–6.

swatting away attempts to render these doctrines coherent by the likes of the influential twentieth-century theologians Karl Barth and Karl Rahner, and more recent analytic theologians such as Cornelius Plantinga, Richard Swinburne, David Brown, A. P. Martinich, Michael C. Rea, Jeffrey E. Brower, Ronald Feenstra, Stephen T. Davis, and Thomas V. Morris. He argues that "those interpretations purporting to avoid both paradox and heterodoxy inevitably fail on at least one of the two counts."[23]

In the fourth chapter of his book Anderson convincingly argues against several alternatives to his Mysterian stance: theological antirealism (views on which the value of theological claims doesn't depend on their being true and not false), anti-deductivism (urging that the laws of logic can't be applied to some theological matters), dialetheism (views on which there can be true contradictions),[24] doctrinal revisionism,[25] what he calls semantic minimalism (claiming that the content of the doctrine in question is too vague to be even apparently contradictory), and the physics-inspired epistemological theory of "complementarity."[26]

The long fifth chapter starts with a helpful exposition of Alvin Plantinga's proper functionalist theory of knowledge. Anderson locates an ambiguity in the role of the Bible in Plantinga's epistemology of Christian belief and suggests some fixes.[27] He points out that in *Warranted Christian Belief,* Plantinga is only trying to offer a model of how Christians might be warranted in believing what Plantinga calls "the main lines of the Christian story."[28] These do not include Trinity and Incarnation; contrary to Anderson, Plantinga is committed to Resolving by Rational Reinterpretation; he holds that there are orthodox and apparently consistent versions of the Trinity and Incarnation doctrines.[29] Moreover, Plantinga's "extended A/C" (Aquinas-Calvin) model of how it is that Christians can *know* what they believe covers

[23] Anderson, *Paradox*, 105.

[24] I discuss this sort of Resistance in section 6.4.2.

[25] That is, the second response to the inconsistent triad above, which we'll explore in section 6.5.2.

[26] I won't attempt a summary of this; see *Paradox*, 137–52.

[27] *Paradox*, 181–89.

[28] *Paradox*, 189–90. For the full exposition of Plantinga's ideas regarding how Christians can know the contents of Christian teaching, see his *Knowledge and Christian Belief*; *Warranted Christian Belief*. In a more recent book chapter Anderson has also developed his defense instead using the epistemic framework of phenomenal conservatism (Anderson, "Seeming").

[29] *Paradox*, 215.

only beliefs based on the explicit contents of the Bible and not creedal doctrines that are (in Anderson's view) based on the explicit and implicit biblical teachings.[30] Anderson aims to fill this gap.

Anderson thus extends Plantinga's theory, in his fifth and sixth chapters, to cover how Christian beliefs may, if Christianity is true, be warranted, both for sophisticates and for ordinary believers. Following Plantinga, by "warrant" he means whatever it is that is required for a true belief to be known by the one with the belief. While this extension involves some Reformed assumptions about Scripture and tradition, Anderson claims they are not obviously essential to the project's success. Basically, if Christianity is true, it's plausible to think that a believer could be warranted in taking the Bible to be a reliable communication from God. And Christian beliefs may be directly or indirectly based on the Bible.

But, comes the objection, if a doctrine appears to be incoherent, shouldn't that trump its claim to be part of a divine revelation, since incoherence is strong evidence of falsity? Even if Chrissy Christian's belief in the Trinity were warranted, wouldn't the realization that the doctrine seems incoherent give Chrissy a "defeater" for her trinitarian belief? Anderson takes the bull by the horns here, deploying the whole machinery of undercutting vs. rebutting defeaters, defeater-defeaters, and defeater-insulators.[31] He argues that a warranted belief in divine incomprehensibility will prevent one's beliefs

---

[30] Anderson, *Paradox*, 190–91, 209.

[31] In recent epistemological literature, a "defeater" is a belief that, once you acquire it, you are no longer rational, warranted, or justified in believing something else—the new belief "defeats," that is, takes away the rationality (or whatever) of that other belief. A stock example is that you seem to see cows in a field two hundred meters away, leading you to believe that. But then someone tells you that many farmers in this area have been putting up fake cardboard-cutout cows in order to make their farms look more prosperous. Now, believing that, you have acquired a "defeater" for your belief that there are real cows in that field; it is no longer reasonable for you to believe that. This would be an "undercutting" defeater, as it doesn't also justify a belief that there are no cows in that field. A similar but "rebutting" defeater would be your finding out that there have been no cows in this region for years, only cardboard cutouts. This new information would not only render your belief that *there are real cows over there* unjustified, but it would also justify a belief that it is false that there are cows there. If you then came to find out that this particular farmer has recently restocked his farm with actual cows, that would be a "defeater-defeater," and it would again be reasonable for you to believe, based on your visual experience, that there are cows about two hundred meters away in this man's field. If you had known this all along, that would have been a "defeater insulator" which would have prevented your being convinced that no one in this region has had actual cows for some years.

regarding the Trinity and Incarnation from being defeated by one's belief that they seem incoherent.[32] (More on this crucial point to follow.)

In his sixth chapter Anderson gives the heart of his account of our knowledge of "mysteries," what he calls his RAPT (Rational Affirmation of Paradoxical Theology) model. He argues that we should take apparent contradictions in orthodox Christian theology to be MACRUE's (Merely Apparent Contradictions Resulting from Unarticulated Equivocation). When we can't find adequate terms to express some claim, we're sometimes driven to assert what *appears* to be a contradiction, such as "I'm concerned about my wife's operation, and I'm *not* concerned about my wife's operation."[33] This is a MACRUE, but we can understand how it may express true (and therefore coherent) claims, despite appearances. The equivocal term here is "concerned"; he is concerned in that he cares about what happens to his wife, but he's not concerned in the sense of being worried about the outcome, as he knows the surgeon to be highly competent.[34] Thus understood, what at first glance appears incoherent is in fact coherent after all. In this case, as Anderson points out, we can grasp both meanings of "concerned" that constitute the equivocation.

But theological cases are more worrisome. One paradox he examines is "God is one divine being and God is three divine beings."[35] None of those terms appears equivocal, and yet at least one must be, if that statement could possibly be true. Anderson tries putting subscript numbers on the various terms (for example, "God is one $divine_1$ being and God is three $divine_2$ beings"), but that seems to be an arbitrary save—and worse—it seems empty, the epitome of a merely formal or verbal solution to a very real difficulty.

Anderson argues that this move isn't arbitrary because if God is incomprehensible, meaning that he can't be *fully* known, then we should *expect*

[32] Anderson, *Paradox*, 250–56.

[33] *Paradox*, 222.

[34] *Paradox*, 223.

[35] *Paradox*, 226. These two claims are *not* themselves a contradiction as they don't have the form *P and not-P* (the affirmation and denial of the same assertion). But as Anderson points out in a footnote, each seems to imply another statement that is the denial of the other original statement. If God is one divine being, it follows that this is false: God is three divine beings. And if God is three divine beings, it is false that God is one divine being. Because these implications seem clear and undeniable, to most people the statement that "God is one divine being and God is three divine beings" seems impossible almost as strongly as a logical contradiction like "God is one divine being and it is not the case that God is one divine being." In both cases it is self-evident that the whole claim can't be true but must be false.

apparent contradictions to arise in our thinking and speaking about him.[36] Moreover, all of this, Anderson argues, fits well with a doctrine of analogy, which says that any terms that apply to God do so only in a sense that is analogous to how we use those terms of creatures. Assuming that, we can see that the disambiguated terms needn't be devoid of meaning. Rather, they each have a meaning that partially but not completely overlaps how we use those terms in ordinary, non-theological contexts.

In sum, Anderson's view is that if Christianity were true, we would expect that Christians would reasonably believe in and know about mysteries, where a mystery is "a metaphysical state of affairs the revelation of which appears implicitly contradictory to us on account of present limitations in our cognitive apparatus and thus resists systematic description in a perspicuously consistent manner."[37] In Anderson's preferred terminology, facts are "mysterious" in the primary sense, and doctrines are "mysterious" derivatively, insofar as they are about these sorts of facts.[38] Notice that Anderson avoids the hard-to-justify claim that a mystery is permanently beyond human capacities. The seventh chapter tangles, somewhat less convincingly, with other objections to his Mysterian position on the Trinity and the Incarnation, and the eighth chapter briefly summarizes his project and suggests a few implications for biblical interpretation and apologetics.

By way of critique, Anderson's Mysterian project involves the following invalid argument:

1. If God exists, then he's incomprehensible.
2. Therefore, if God exists, then it's likely that humans, in thinking about God along the lines of God's self-revelation in the Bible, will be forced into apparently contradictory thoughts and statements.

The problem is that 2 doesn't follow from 1, because Anderson's doctrine of "divine incomprehensibility" is merely the uncontroversial claim that "although God can be known in part, he cannot be known fully and exhaustively."[39] That is a very modest, uncontroversial claim, one which any Christian will accept.

Contrary to Anderson, I would say that given our limited information, the probability of God putting us in a paradoxical theological situation is

[36] Anderson, *Paradox*, 237–43. I challenge this claim in the next paragraphs and in my "On Positive Mysterianism."

[37] *Paradox*, 245, original italics.

[38] *Paradox*, 246.

[39] *Paradox*, 237.

inscrutable—that is, such that we can't assign any probability to it, whether low, high, or middling—not, as Anderson says, more probable than not. Here is an analogy. A child may not understand the sexual aspect of her parents' relationship, but it doesn't follow that she'll probably run into paradoxes in thinking about her parents. Whether she does or not depends on her cognitive capacities, on precisely what information her parents choose to reveal, and perhaps on her own free choices concerning how she reflects on her parents' relationship. It only follows from divine incomprehensibility that we can't rule in or out in advance that we'll never run into paradoxes in theology. Non-Mysterians, it seems to me, can happily admit this and proceed in their non-Mysterian ways.

But if we lack adequate grounds to *expect* theological paradoxes, then the clear and stable appearance of contradiction seems to provide an undefeated defeater for the warrant or justification of our paradoxical theological claims.[40] In other words, we're left with the fact that the doctrine in question seems to imply at least one contradiction, and this is strong evidence that the doctrine in question is false. In the face of this evidence, it seems that if it ever was reasonable to believe that doctrine, it no longer is.[41] Without a stronger doctrine of incomprehensibility, there's no way to rule out that our cherished paradoxes have been created by our misguided theological speculations or wrongheaded scriptural exegesis rather than being thrust on us by transcendent facts together with our epistemic limits. In sum, it isn't clear that the Mysterian response to my inconsistent triad above (p. 197) fares better than the other two.

If you defend a problematic doctrine as a Mystery, you're asserting that it to some degree lacks what we can call "understandable" content, that is to say, propositions (thoughts, claims) that positively seem coherent to you. A claim

---

[40] See Anderson, *Paradox*, 252. In a reply to my more extensive published critique, Anderson has retreated from the claim that given God's greatness we can expect MACRUE's, to the position that God's greatness together with our limitations provide the best explanation of apparent contradictions in theology (Tuggy, "On Positive Mysterianism"; Anderson, "On the Rationality"). But how do we rule out the explanation that we've gone wrong somewhere in our theologizing, so that the apparent contradiction is due to that?

[41] At this point a Mysterian Resister may object, "But we have *really strong* grounds for believing in the paradoxical doctrine, enough to outweigh the evidence of non-truth provided by the apparent incoherence." Elsewhere I engage with this reply at length. In brief, that may be so, but a firm, steady, apparent contradiction is *really strong* evidence of falsity, so that it will never be outweighed by counter-evidence (Tuggy, "On Positive Mysterianism"; "Two Natures," sec. 6). See also Anderson's reply, which contains some important changes to his position (Anderson, "On the Rationality").

may fail to be understandable for two different reasons. The Positive Mysterian Resistor holds that a doctrine is a mystery and in a sense fails to be understandable because it has "too much" content, in that the content of the doctrine *seems* to include or imply some pair of claims of the form *P and not-P*. I emphasize "seems" here because the Positive Mysterian thinks his mysterious doctrine is true and assumes (justifiably, in my view) that no contradiction is true.[42] Hence, any true set of claims must be coherent (self-consistent) and in the end will not imply any pair of claims of the form *P and not-P*. For a theologian like Anderson, then, doctrines like the Trinity lack "understandable" (that is, apparently consistent) content, since their content (firmly and continuously, not dimly and fleetingly) *seems* incoherent. I believe that an undeveloped form of Positive Mysterianism is popular among contemporary theologians. There is a widespread assumption that in theology apparent contradictions are no big deal, since God is so beyond our understanding. It is highly unusual for such a theologian to possess, as Anderson does, a sophisticated backstory about how this situation comes about and how it is reasonable to maintain apparently incoherent beliefs.

While I've occasionally found a medieval or ancient theologian mentioning some sacred mystery as apparently contradictory, it seems to me that Positive Mysterianism only became popular in the early modern era. Starting in the sixteenth century, Socinians and other unitarians often objected that Catholic dogmas like the Trinity, transubstantiation, and the Incarnation were not only unbiblical but incoherent as well. As such, they were self-refuting; once a contradiction is discovered, we have found strong evidence for the falsity of that doctrine. This was a general Protestant tactic for objecting to Roman Catholic doctrines. However, many Protestants, especially Calvinists, needed this sort of mystery-defense given their extreme views on divine providence. I suspect, then, that these factors contributed to the popularity of Positive Mysterian Resistance in modern times up to the present.

But there is another way to say that a doctrine fails to be "understandable" in the above sense; it may be so because we don't grasp the meaning of some or all of its constituent claims or because we barely grasp the meaning of them. I call this Negative Mysterianism Resistance. Concerning the Trinity, it seems to me that this is the dominant form of Mysterian Resistance from the time of the

[42] In section 6.4.2 I will discuss a type of Resistance on which contradictions *can* be true in addition to their being false.

church "fathers" to the early modern era. To exaggerate a little, ancient trinitarian theologians think that our concepts can barely be stretched enough to be put to use in discourse about the divine. We can use multiple analogies to talk about God, but in the end they're all bad analogies.[43] They held the Trinity to be mysterious because of a lack of content.

Typically, neither sort of Mysterian is merely confessing that *at the moment* the doctrine in question seems problematic *to him*. Usually, they are making a stronger claim than Anderson does, that given God's greatness and human limitations (at least, in this present life), the doctrine in question can only be a mystery (in either or both senses). But on the face of it, this is an unjustifiable claim: how, short of divine revelation, could one know (or justifiably believe) that no human could better grasp the content of the dogma in question so as to be reasonably sure whether or not it is coherent? In suggesting that no human can do that in this life, am I locating myself at the very pinnacle of what humans are currently capable of understanding? If so, how could I *justifiably* do that? Rather than make such a claim, it seems better for them just to say that we're stuck with mysteries for some reason or other; maybe this can't be explained.

Enthusiastic Mysterians of either sort tend to be complacent traditionalists about Bible interpretation—that is, people who are pretty sure that their Christian group (whether this is Catholicism, Reformed Christianity, Eastern Orthodoxy, or small-c catholic tradition) has understood the Bible (generally) correctly. There is a reason for this. If you're trying to reason your way toward the correct interpretation of some passage rather than rest on the laurels of longstanding and distinguished precedent, then it looks like a showstopper if your proposed interpretation seems self-contradictory (Positive Mysterianism) or nearly unintelligible (Negative Mysterianism). Such interpretations seem uncharitable to the human authors of these texts. Should we really attribute such confusions to them, in the case of positive mysteries, or suppose they're saying things that can barely, if at all, be understood, if they're teaching negative mysteries?

Conversely, if one thinks of oneself as standing in the stream of a Great Tradition, who cares if one's interpretation of Scripture seems to be either a positive or a negative mystery? Such difficulties, one supposes, must have been known and accepted by the many Great Men, such as Gregory of Nazianzus, Augustine, Thomas Aquinas, and John Calvin, who preceded us in this Great

---

[43] See my summary of Augustine's thoughts on the Trinity in "History," sec. 3.3.2.

Tradition, and evidently *they* were unworried. So why should we today be worried about unavoidable theological mysteries?

But any Protestant should remember that God has allowed mainstream Christian groups to go very wrong on important matters for long periods of time. And human experience generally shows that both individuals and groups can be very right on some topics while being very wrong on others. These thoughts ought to wake us from our complacency and make us willing to acknowledge apparent contradictions for what they are: clear signposts of falsehood, counseling us, as it were, to reverse our course and then travel in some other direction. It is not humility that causes us to ignore their counsel.

6.4.2 DIALETHEIST RESISTANCE

This sort of defense has been virtually unexplored by Christian theologians and philosophers until this current century.[44] The reason is that historically, nearly all western philosophers, and so nearly all Christian theologians, assumed that all contradictions are false and not true. But that assumption has been challenged by some recent logicians who have argued that some contradictions are true.[45]

To see where proponents of Dialetheist Resistance are coming from, let's consider the ancient liar paradox. A man walks up to you and announces, "This sentence is false." If what he said is true, then it is false. But suppose that his statement is, as he says, false. If it's false that his sentence is false, *and* if every claim is either true or false, then it must be true! One might conclude that what he said was neither true nor false, since no claim can be both. But some have argued instead that we should think that the Liar's statement is *both* true *and* false.

This last solution was once held by the Christian logician and philosopher Jc Beall.[46] But nowadays his point in bringing up this paradox is that we can't rule out in advance that some statements may be both true and false, so we can't rule out in advance that there are what he calls "contradictions" in reality that is, existing things about which there are true contradictions

[44] For a few much less developed attempts, see Anderson, *Paradox*, 117–26.

[45] Priest, Berto, and Weber, "Dialetheism."

[46] Beall, *Spandrels of Truth*, 1–17. Beall no longer holds that logic itself forces us to conclude that unusual sentences like the liar's are both true and false; he now denies that logic, rightly understood, includes the law of excluded middle, which says that it is an axiom that for any *P*, either *P or not-P* (Beall, *Spandrels of Truth*, 3; Beall, *Contradictory Christ*, 8, note 5).

(statements of the form *P and not-P*).[47] Beall argues that, while it would seem unreasonable to admit too many contradictions or to admit them too readily, nonetheless, according to catholic traditions, Christ *seems* to be a contradiction. We must either explain away this appearance or embrace it, and Beall argues at length that we should embrace it, even if Christ should end up being "the unique contradictory being in reality."[48]

Beall argues that this approach is superior to what I call Rational Reconstructions, which suffer from various problems, including often distorting the meaning of the doctrine one is trying to defend.[49] It's not possible to summarize here Beall's objections to all of these, but I can tell you that many of his criticisms are on target, and that proponents of such theories would do well to pay attention to his arguments. Beall argues that his approach of ceasing to try to "consistentize" Christ, instead embracing him as a contradiction (a being about which there are true contradictions), enjoys seven theoretical virtues over rival approaches: simplicity, avoiding arbitrary changes in the meanings of traditional Incarnation sentences, metaphysical neutrality, properly "balancing" Christ's divinity and humanity, "preserving the mystery" of the "hypostatic union," and making clear the need for "faith" rather than "full belief."[50]

Beall ably defends this approach against many objections. More traditional logics endorse an axiom often called a "principle of explosion," according to which any contradiction would, if true, imply any claim whatever. Assuming such a logic, if Christ is immutable and not, this implies that your mother is a ham sandwich, that 1 + 1 = 3, that purple hates long division, and that both atheism and theism are true. But, argues Beall, we should not accept such a logic but rather a "subclassical" logic on which there are no such implications.[51]

---

[47] Roman Catholic analytic theologian Timothy Pawl points out that some alleged contradictions in this sense will be observable things. But then it's not easy to imagine what it would be like to encounter such. For this concern and Beall's response, see Beall, *Contradictory Christ*, 96–101.

[48] *Contradictory Christ*, 9.

[49] *Contradictory Christ*, ch. 5.

[50] *Contradictory Christ*, ch. 3.

[51] *Contradictory Christ*, 34, 79–81.

If you object that such a Christology runs afoul of an undeniable logical principle called the principle of non-contradiction,[52] Beall will point out that his preferred logic—and he's hardly unique in this respect among contemporary logicians—doesn't feature any such principle.[53]

From where Beall stands as a logician, it seems that opposition to true contradictions must arise from naïve, outdated assumptions about logic.[54] I disagree; in my view, it is part of our God-given common sense that there are no contradictions in Beall's sense—real things such that statements of the form *P and not-P* are true of them. If I say that I have a brother who was *and* was not (in the same sense) born at a particular time and place, people will not—once they see that I'm not merely speaking paradoxically but rather asserting an actual contradiction—waste their time in trying to find out if I really do have a brother like that. We naturally and reasonably relegate guys like that—like square circles and married bachelors—to the realm of fiction.

This point seems obvious when it comes to other people's contradictory religious views. If a Buddhist should try to persuade you that Nirvana is and is not real (in the same way and at the same time), you would not be inclined to listen to her argue this very long, as you are convinced that contradictions are all fictional. "*If* there *is* any such thing or place as Nirvana," you'll tell her, "it can't be quite as you're saying." If you are arguing with a Mormon missionary and make the point that Joseph Smith was a liar, and the missionary grants that this is true but adds that it is *also* false that he was a liar, and so consequently it is also true that he was truthful and trustworthy in his statements, I suggest that you will not be impressed. You will, reasonably, be disinclined to believe that the would-be prophet Joseph Smith is a contradiction.

How is the case of Christ different from these? In his case we encounter a Great Intellectual Tradition that takes seriously that Jesus is a godman, a single Person with both a divine nature and a human nature, which goes back at least to an august assembly of bishops that met in the year 451 in Chalcedon.[55] Enormous

[52] See Gottlieb, "Aristotle on Non-Contradiction," sec. 1 for various formulations of PNC (the Principle of Non-Contradiction). She observes that principles such as my IDI (section p. 267) presuppose the truth of some version of PNC. For some recent attacks on and defenses of versions of PNC see Priest, Beall, and Armour-Garb, *Law of Non-Contradiction.*

[53] Beall, *Contradictory Christ*, 79, note 24.

[54] *Contradictory Christ*, 107.

[55] For the interesting story of this council, see Jenkins, *Jesus Wars*; Davis, *First Seven Ecumenical Councils*, ch. 5. For the difficulty of interpreting its statement about Christ, see my "Two Natures," sec. 2.

intellectual energy has been spent trying to show that these claims are coherent, so that they may in good conscience be defended as true (only—so, not also false). Beall holds that this tradition is correct in claiming that Jesus is a godman but mistaken in assuming the need to defend the coherence of such a Christology. It is overall better, he argues, to accept the appearance of contradiction here at face value, so that a bunch of claims about Christ will be both true and false. This defense can also be extended, in a particular way, to the doctrine of the Trinity.[56]

As clever and carefully argued as Beall's proposals are, they are gifts that practically no Christian wants. There are many reasons for this, among them our built-in conviction that there are no real things that are contradictions in his sense. Another is the embarrassment many experienced apologists, theologians, or pastors would face given such a huge about-face. Would-be defenders of the faith learn at their mother's knee to lead with something like this when discussing the Trinity with an unbeliever: "We're not saying that God is exactly one *A* and exactly three *A's*. That would be a contradiction. We're saying that God is one *A* and three *B's*. Where's the contradiction?"[57] Moving from this common defense to Beall's ultra-sophisticated Dialetheist Resistance would not only be a drastic and, for many, embarrassing public change, but they would also be handing a huge stick to critics of Incarnation and Trinity doctrines (be they atheist, agnostic, Jewish, Islamic, or unitarian Christian) that such critics would relentlessly and mercilessly beat them with. (Headline: "Major Christian apologist admits the Trinity is contradictory!" Or: "Theologian admits Incarnation is false!") To many on both sides of the questions, such a defense would be perceived as a loss.

Beyond this, it seems to me that Christian traditions simply don't countenance the teaching of Christian doctrines as true *and false*. Rather, we take ourselves to be proclaiming important truths (which are not also false). We read that "grace and truth came through Jesus Christ," who tells us that "you will know the truth, and the truth will make you free" (John 1:17, 8:32). Our human Lord has told us "the truth" that he "heard from God," and he prays to God, saying "your word is truth" (John 8:40, 17:17). In the Fourth Gospel, Jesus says that he came into the world "to testify to the truth" (John 18:37). It's hard to

---

[56] Beall, *Contradictory Christ*, ch. 6; Beall, *Divine Contradiction*; Molto, *Review*. For a summary of this see my "Trinity," sec. 4.3.

[57] On this point see Tuggy, "Standard Opening Move." For examples of this in the wild, see Barnett, "What Is the Trinity?"; Copan, "Is the Trinity," 210–11; Esposito, "Is the Trinity"; White, *Forgotten Trinity*, 24.

imagine any New Testament author—or any pastor, priest, missionary, or Sunday school teacher—adding that *also* some of what Christianity teaches is false—but not to worry, as those claims are also true. Is the Christian *generally* to be "speaking the truth in love" (Eph. 4:15), but on the topic of Christ the godman, or that and the Trinity, we are *also* in love speaking falsehoods (ones that are also true)? It's hard to imagine widespread, positive responses to Beall's brand of Resistance rather than rejection or uncomprehending stares.[58]

As Catholic theologian Philip-Neri Reese argues, Beall's brand of Resistance puts one in a very odd position concerning the history of theology. The catholic and conciliar traditions have long been trying to consistentize Christ, to formulate a non-contradictory Christology. (And arguably the same is true with respect to the Trinity.) According to Beall, this whole project was wrong-headed all along. But it is these wrong-headed theologians who provide the standard divine-and-human Christology that Beall means to be defending as reasonable. Reese observes that

> *all* the arguments that laid the ground for, directly contributed to, and subsequently defended conciliar teaching presupposed that the correct Christology requires consistency . . . This puts the contradictory Chalcedonian [like Beall] in an awkward position vis-à-vis history. Where the consistent Chalcedonian is free to say that, in the months just prior to the Council of Chalcedon, Cyril and Leo had good reasons to hold the doctrines that the council would shortly define . . . the contradictory Chalcedonian has to say that, in the months just prior . . . neither Cyril nor Leo had *any* good reasons to hold those doctrines—for they were both equally and deeply committed to the erroneous idea that consistency is requisite for Christology. Moreover, once Chalcedon had defined its doctrines, Cyril and Leo almost certainly did not begin to believe those doctrines simply because they had faith in the council . . . they took the council to have confirmed the general lines of argument that they themselves had put forward prior to the council . . . the contradictory Chalcedonian . . . would have to say that Cyril and Leo *were never right to believe* what Chalcedon taught, since their misguided lines of argument were their sole reasons for belief.[59]

Further,

> the contradictory Chalcedonian needs "the early councils were *methodologically* misguided" to be true and "the early councils were *doctrinally* misguided" to be

[58] See for example the hostile responses of Catholic theologian Karen Kilby ("Divine Contradiction").

[59] Reese, "Contradictory Christology," 8–9.

> false. But . . . the truth and falsity of the two . . . *are* tied together. For it is absurd to think that we, in 2023, are justified in believing that there are two natures and one person of Christ, but Leo, in 450, was not.[60]

A related problem is that on Beall's account of logic, common argument forms such as *modus ponens* and *modus tollens*[61] are invalid, and these were widely deployed in the ancient theological debates.[62] In Beall's view, such forms of argument may have a theory-specific validity rather than a purely logical validity.[63] But none of the ancients saw any need for a notion of theology-specific validity and simply deployed what Beall says are logically *in*valid arguments (ones such that even if all the premises are true, it still may be that the conclusion is false).

For many reasons, then, this sort of Resistance is a hard sell. Nonetheless, the believer in Incarnation or Trinity may be justifiably pessimistic about existing solutions.[64] Will she really embrace truths that are also false in her attempt to defend these doctrines as reasonable? One wonders: Will she do *anything* other than reconsider whether her traditional catholic interpretations are, all things considered, the best ways to understand Scripture?[65]

6.5 RESOLUTION: RATIONAL REINTERPRETATION VS. REVISING

The Resolver holds that the apparent contradiction implied by some doctrine *D* can be made to disappear upon further investigation. She doesn't (like the Redirector) change the subject, nor does she claim ignorance of the doctrine's meaning (as with Restraint). Nor does she, like the Resister, try to show that there's nothing wrong in just accepting the apparent (or apparent *and real*) contradictions.

But *how* does the Resolver get rid of the apparent contradiction? Take the Incarnation doctrine: Jesus is both human and divine, which seems to imply

---

[60] Reese, "Contradictory Christology," 9.

[61] *Modus ponens*: *P*, if *P* then *Q*, therefore *Q*. *Modus tollens*: if *P* then *Q*, *not-Q*, therefore *not-P*. Traditionally it has been held that all arguments of either sort for are valid (in other words, that the premises, if true, really would require the truth of the conclusion).

[62] McCall, "Trinity," 702–5.

[63] Beall, "Replies to Critics," 728–30; *Divine Contradiction*, ch. 2.

[64] While he has not yet made the purchase, one Protestant analytic theologian seems willing to entertain Beall's proposals regarding the Trinity, given the dire state of Trinity theories when it comes to coherence (McCall, "Trinity," 699–701).

[65] Tuggy, "New Testament." For the sorts of scriptural assumptions I'm referring to see sections 2.3–5.

being created and not. The Revising Resolver simply denies part of the doctrine in question—either that Jesus is divine or that he's human. Problem solved, apparent contradiction resolved! But many will consider this change too radical, a cure worse than the disease. Let's consider Resolving first in the form of Rational Reinterpretation.

6.5.1 RESOLVING BY RATIONAL REINTERPRETATION

This way of responding to apparently contradictory doctrines should have an official seal of endorsement from the Society of Christian Philosophers and the Evangelical Philosophical Society, for it is the preferred way for recent Christian philosophers and analytic theologians to address apparent contradictions in theology. If all you have is a hammer, everything looks like a nail. These scholars have been given powerful tools for analyzing arguments and making fine distinctions to avoid implying contradictions, and they rightly see that these tools can be deployed in defense of traditional Christian claims. But sometimes more than such clever defenses are called for—sometimes one needs to reconsider one's commitments to those claims that seem to imply one or more contradictions.

The basic pattern of Resolving by Rational Reinterpretation is yes, *at first glance D* looks incoherent. But why not understand the doctrine in question as *E*? The set of claims *E* seems coherent and, moreover, pretty defensible. A famous example is the "two minds" approach to the Incarnation doctrine. According to catholic Incarnation traditions, Christ has both a divine nature and a "complete human nature," body and soul. Yet there is only one person, one someone here, not two or three. This one is the Son, the second eternally and fully divine Person of the Trinity. This doctrine bristles with problems, and Christian philosopher Tom Morris gamely takes them on one by one in his book.[66] His central move is to say that Jesus's having two natures amounts to (1) his having two minds—a divine mind and a human mind—with the first having complete access to the second, whereas the second has limited access to the contents of the first, (2) and his having one set of causal and cognitive powers. This version of the Incarnation doctrine, whatever its final merits, at least, at first glance, seems coherent. (Or, at least it doesn't immediately seem incoherent.) Problem solved?

[66] Morris, *Logic of God Incarnate.*

One problem with Resolution through Rational Reinterpretation is that often only a metaphysician could love the newfangled (but precise and arguably coherent) version of the doctrine in question, because it involves controversial metaphysical claims that ordinary Christians don't understand. And many highly educated people who *do* understand these metaphysical claims reject them. There have been recently suggested Rational Reconstructions of the doctrine of the Trinity that require the metaphysical possibility of time travel,[67] the idea that there's something analogous to matter in God,[68] the controversial claim that there are only numerical sameness relations relative to a sortal term,[69] or the dubious suggestion that somehow three Persons would supervene on a soul if that soul possessed three general cognitive faculties.[70] Another assumes the possibility of "group minds."[71] Since I have degrees in philosophy and am former philosophy professor, I understand these suggestions (and I reject all of them as impossible) but some Christian PhDs and their students accept various of them as plausible. But if a "solution" to the seeming incoherence of a doctrine divides the experts and baffles the laity, what use is it to the church as a whole?

A second concern is that many believers think this new version of the doctrine isn't the original doctrine at all but rather a knock-off, a counterfeit. If that is so, the would-be defense amounts to mere subject changing. "You're worried that *D* may not be coherent? Well, *E is* coherent!" To this we should say, "That's interesting, but what about *D*? *Who cares* if *E* is coherent? What, if anything, might that tell me about *D*?"[72] For example, analytic theologians have suggested that the divine nature should be thought of as "constituting" each of the three divine Persons, not unlike the way a certain portion of marble may simultaneously constitute both a pillar and a statue of a woman, as we see in the ancient Parthenon in Athens.[73] In a published critique I have objected that this would-be version of the doctrine of the Trinity can't be that, as it does not posit any tripersonal God—an indispensable claim for any *trinitarian* theology.[74]

---

[67] Leftow, "A Latin Trinity."

[68] Brower and Rea, "Material Constitution"; "Understanding the Trinity."

[69] Section 11.2.

[70] Moreland and Craig, *Philosophical Foundations*, 588–94; Craig, "Tri-Personal," 52–54; Tuggy, "Changing the Subject," 159–60.

[71] This is discussed but not defended in Leftow, "Anti Social Trinitarianism," 221–27.

[72] Branson, "Ahistoricity in Analytic Theology."

[73] "Material Constitution"; "Understanding the Trinity."

[74] Tuggy, "Constitution Trinitarianism." On this Trinity theory the word "Trinity" is a

The idea is generally that *E* is supposed to be *an acceptable version of D*, or, at least, *we can't rule out that E* is *really* what they meant to be saying all along, when they propounded *D*. Or at least for some reason or other *D* can now be legitimately interpreted as meaning *E*. But does Christian tradition, rightly understood, really allow for these sorts of "discoveries"?

For their part, Roman Catholic tradition rules them out. According to the First Vatican Council of 1869–70,

> that meaning of the sacred dogmas is ever to be maintained which has once been declared by holy mother church, and there must never be any abandonment of this sense under the pretext or in the name of a more profound understanding. May understanding, knowledge and wisdom increase as ages and centuries roll along, and greatly and vigorously flourish, in each and all, in the individual and the whole church: but this only in its own proper kind, that is to say, in the same doctrine, the same sense, and the same understanding.[75]

> If anyone says that it is possible that at some time, given the advancement of knowledge, a sense may be assigned to the dogmas propounded by the Church which is different from that which the Church has understood and understands: let him be anathema.[76]

Notice that they don't say the new way of understanding the doctrine in question must be incompatible with the old way. Rather, it is bad enough that they differ. And these Rational Reconstructions are always different, being more precise than what certain bishops or theologians in the second, fourth, fifth, thirteenth, or sixteenth century wrote. Further, attempts to show that certain historical theologians or councils *really* meant this newfangled claim are generally unconvincing. The authoritative pronouncements above prohibit Roman Catholics from defending any traditional doctrines from charges of incoherence using Rational Reconstruction.

Other Christians are freer. But we should note the assumption—I would say a *demonstrably false* assumption—of these pronouncements that catholic tradition has meant one thing all along by, for instance, the traditional Trinity language. As I see it, Trinity proponents have never had just one set of claims in mind, which is why competing interpretations of "the doctrine of the Trinity"

---

plural referring term referring to each of the three divine Persons; see sections 1.10.1 and 3.7.2. These are non-identical but are "to be counted as" one god; the theory is a version of relative-identity accounts of the Trinity (chapter 11).

[75] "[Decrees of] the First Vatican Council," 809 (Session 3, ch. 4).

[76] "[Decrees of] the First Vatican Council," 811 (Session 3, canon 4).

have repeatedly surfaced in church history.[77] Indeed, before there was any doctrine of the Trinity, it was immediately clear after the 325 council at Nicaea that bishops who had voted in its language about God and his Son did so while holding clashing interpretations of that language.[78]

That is one problem that conservative believers and theologians have with any given Rational Reinterpretation: its newness. If you think the doctrine was divinely revealed at some past time, then there's little positive theoretical work for clever folks nowadays to do. How can this new claim *E* be part of "the faith that was once delivered to the saints" (Jude 3, ESV)? But many Christian thinkers, and friends of Rational Reconstruction generally, imagine that God led the church into the correct language and, at least conceptually, in the right direction, perhaps leading people to employ vague mental images so that things might be sorted out and made more precise later.

Others will admit the possibility of theological progress in these latter days but will reject all or at least most Rational Reconstructions as unorthodox. Rational Reconstructions are intended to be orthodox and advertise themselves as such (or at least, as not *obviously un*orthodox). But many object that the newfangled version of the doctrine, despite its inventors' orthodox intentions, is a version of some historical heresy, such as modalism, tritheism, Monophysitism, Nestorianism, and so on. Merely intending that one's theory is orthodox does not ensure that it is. The road to heresy is paved with good intentions.

Others object that the Reconstruction leaves out part of what the Bible teaches. In his book analytic theologian James Anderson repeatedly uses this hammer on recent attempts at Rational Reinterpretation. He argues that one can have orthodoxy (accurately representing all Bible teaching on the topic) or evident coherence but not both.[79]

Finally, some object that Rational Reconstruction wrongheadedly "removes the mystery" of the doctrine. This is an objection given by people committed to the rival strategy of Resistance. But there's an interesting little dance that people often do when offering a Rational Reconstruction. They say they *don't* intend to remove the mystery from *D*, or at least not *all of* it.

[77] For the plethora of competing present-day Trinity theories, see my "Metaphysics and Logic"; "Trinity." For a controversy in England that revealed a plethora of competing Trinity theories in the last decade of the seventeenth century, see Dixon, *Nice and Hot Disputes*.

[78] Hanson, *Search*, 163–235.

[79] Anderson, *Paradox*, 31–59, 80–106.

This is partly an admission that there are still serious difficulties left, even if their new theory is on track (that is, *E* suffers from fewer problems than *D*). They also often hint or outright say they don't *believe* their own Rational Reconstruction at all, or don't consider it to be the only way or the obviously best way to understand that doctrine. Nor, generally, do they insist that all Christians should believe *E*. What's going on in these cases?

The answer is defensive apologetics, as it were, merely deflecting bullets. They have in mind an opponent of (small-c catholic, orthodox, or "historic") Christianity who holds that *D* is obviously, perhaps even demonstrably, contradictory. They're responding like this:

1. We can't rule out that *D* ought to be understood as *E*.
2. *E* might strike some people as weird or unfamiliar, but
3. *E* isn't *obviously* incoherent, *and*
4. *E* isn't *demonstrably* incoherent.[80]

Notice that they're not telling us what the doctrine *D* means or the best way to understand *D*. They're not even, necessarily, revealing what they think this great and true doctrine *D* is. Rather, they're showing that the traditional formulas that are taken to express *D* can be understood in at least one seemingly coherent way—*E*—which way they have carefully, with a philosopher's skill and precision, laid out, perhaps for the first time.

There are a couple of unsatisfying things about this genre of apologetic works. For one thing, they're often merely defensive.[81] But a mere defense doesn't give the inquiring mind anywhere to rest; they're not suggesting that *D really* means *E* so that we should now think that *E*. If you only have this shield in the face of someone claiming to prove that *D* is incoherent—well, *maybe* it means *E*, and it seems that *E* is coherent—still, you're left wondering what to think about *D*!

In apologetics literature the opponents of doctrine *D* are largely imaginary or uninteresting, or they wouldn't (and shouldn't) be satisfied with the above style of argument. Sometimes atheists are mentioned, but atheists generally don't think much about Trinity or Incarnation doctrines. (Why should they? They don't even believe in God, and they certainly don't accept the Bible or later

[80] That is, there's no knockdown argument that *E* is incoherent, an argument such that any sane, unbiased, and informed adult human will recognize as obviously valid and sound.

[81] They are not always merely defensive; sometimes the author holds forth his newfangled *E* as something Christians ought to believe.

Christian traditions as instruments of divine revelation.) Other supposed opponents are "cultists," imagined "rationalists," or nebulous "skeptics." Lumping together allegedly unorthodox doctrines with "cults" is a common modern rhetorical strategy.[82] But how relevant is it to the truth or falsity of a theological or christological claim if some high-control group agrees with it? There is no reason to think that all high-control-group-endorsed claims are false. This rhetoric is designed to rally one's own social group against disliked outsiders, but it doesn't help us to separate the false from the true.

The aforementioned "rationalist" is an imaginary bogeyman who appears in some apologetic and theological works; he proudly refuses to submit his mind to divine revelation and so consequently rejects the Trinity or the Incarnation, or whatever doctrine is in view. This generic term is probably meant to cover three kinds of people who engage in theology: the extremely revisionary liberal or progressive theologian, the unitarian Christian, and the deist (who believes in a divine creator but not in any divine revelation). But the first and last simply don't believe that the Bible is (or is a reliable means of) divine revelation. Thus, they aren't concerned with doctrines allegedly based on those sources and pay little attention to *D*. There has never been a sizable deist movement; deists are not very relevant to Christian arguments about revelation-based doctrines, although their arguments against divine relation should be addressed.

While many unitarian Christians argue that Trinity and Incarnation doctrines are incoherent, arguably at least as worrisome are their biblical objections. They find biblical support not for God as the Trinity or for Jesus as a godman, but rather for the one God as the Father alone and Jesus as his human Son. They prioritize clear New Testament teachings over the pronouncements of ancient catholic councils, the Catholic Church's alleged teaching authority, and Protestant creeds. Thus, their objections aren't only or even primarily "rationalistic" (that is, reason-based or philosophy-based); they are exegetical, methodological, and theological. The standard apologetics defensive judo I've been describing doesn't and can't help with those sorts of difficulties. Someone who thinks the Bible supports neither *D* nor *E* but rather some rival view will not care at all about the coherence of *E*.

Perhaps the most significant limitation of Resolution by Rational Reconstruction is that it is no great victory if some doctrine fails to be *obviously* or *demonstrably* incoherent. Some doctrine may not be *that* poorly

[82] Chandler, "Cult-Rhetoric."

off, but, nonetheless there is little to no reason to believe it, or some reason to believe it but more to disbelieve it.

Again, a claim may seem incoherent to me—it may be that every time I carefully consider it, it seems incoherent—but I may not be able to demonstrate to all comers via a knockdown argument that it is incoherent. In a case like this, still, it seems I ought not believe it, since I can see that it bears a strong mark of falsehood—apparent incoherence. If I'm trying to let Scripture form my views, and Scripture doesn't clearly send us in the direction of this doctrine, it makes sense that, as a student of Scripture, I should leave it aside.

In sum, arguments that some new theory *E* is not *demonstrably* incoherent are generally pretty effective because they aim so low. Still, they are not terribly helpful to the serious Christian trying to decide what to think of doctrine *D*. Oftentimes, we find that *E* amounts to little more than a logically possible (and often implausible and unlikely) contender for understanding *D*.

6.5.2 RESOLUTION BY REVISION

Sometimes a problematic doctrine doesn't need fixing or for us to find some excuse to embrace it despite or even because of its problems. Sometimes the best response is to change our views on that topic so that they better fit the available evidence. When it comes to apparently contradictory claims in theology, there's more than one way to resolve the apparent inconsistency. But as I mentioned, the more popular way nowadays among Christian philosophers and analytic theologians is Rational Reinterpretation. *Why* are they so locked into this approach?

I believe it is because too often they assume that the Bible actually forces one to accept some apparently incoherent doctrine *D*. Sometimes they have simply never questioned this, and others tell themselves to respect a sort of intellectual division of labor, thinking,

> *My* field includes theoretical explanations, conceptual analysis, and the construction and evaluation of arguments. I'm not qualified to determine what the Bible does and doesn't teach—that's the job of biblical scholars. And I don't determine what is good or bad Christian theology—that's the job of professional theologians. I will stay in my lane, working with what the biblical scholarship guild tells me the Bible teaches and what the systematic theology guild tells me are the essential Christian doctrines. What's left for me to do, then, is to provide helpful Rational Reinterpretations of problematic traditional doctrines.

This is an irresponsible stance. For one thing, the books of the Bible were written for ordinary people to understand, and so we don't always need to defer to the experts when it comes to interpreting them. And as to the experts—for instance, PhDs in biblical studies—they don't speak with one voice, nor are they without theological commitments of their own. Further, philosophy-trained Christians *are* qualified to evaluate the arguments of these other PhDs, which can sometimes be very poor, and those of us trained in the history of philosophy have the advantage of being accustomed to "getting into the heads" of historical authors, people very different from us with different presuppositions, concerns, and terminology. This directly helps in interpreting the views of the New Testament authors.

Again, in sections 2.6 and 2.7 I argued that different approaches to interpreting Scripture should be understood as offering competing explanations of what the authors were thinking and that philosophers can be experts in comparing rival explanations to see which is the best overall. Neither the biblical studies guild nor the theology guild does a very good job of enabling its members to become proficient in the style of argument called inference to the best explanation.[83] Finally, if the above compartmentalizing stance were correct for a Christian philosopher, then such a philosopher should have entirely refrained from participating in the Reformation. But that shows the stance to be unreasonably conservative. Reformers like Luther showed that large areas of Catholic doctrine and practice were unsupported by and contrary to scriptural teachings. The proper response is to fearfully and humbly but courageously, as a disciple of Jesus, reconsider one's commitment to those. Doubling down on ever-more-clever defenses in such cases is wrongheaded, just as was merely pointing to the then-current consensus of biblical scholars and theologians in the sixteenth century who overwhelmingly supported Roman Catholic traditions. Sometimes theological repentance is called for.

Unlike Redirectors, Revisers don't change the subject. Unlike Resisters, they don't claim we should just "live with the tension." Unlike practitioners of Restraint, they don't think we should keep putting off the issue. Like Resolvers through Rational Reinterpretation, they have a solution, one that involves changing one's views so that they no longer imply any contradiction. But they don't think tricky, new, more careful formulations of the traditional doctrine are what is called for. Rather, changes of belief are called for. Revisers are often

[83] Section 2.7.

accused of arrogance, lack of respect for tradition, biblical ignorance, idolatry of human reason, or not being Christians at all. But in many cases all they are trying to do is reform traditional teachings that clash with, and are not supported by, clear biblical teachings. They are trying to be good "Bereans" (Acts 17:11) who carefully listen to the voices of tradition but then carefully examine Scripture to see if it really teaches what those voices say.

Open theists are revisers about divine foreknowledge (understood as unchanging and unincreasable).[84] Many Christian philosophers revise traditional theology by denying medieval doctrines of divine simplicity and divine timelessness as un- and anti-biblical.[85] The famous philosopher of religion John Hick was a reviser about Incarnation and about traditional Christian stances regarding other religions.[86] The early modern Socinians revised their views on the Incarnation, the Trinity, and other doctrines.[87] Luther and those who followed him revised many medieval Catholic doctrines, which they saw as contrary to Scripture and/or reason (they emphasized the former).[88]

I divide Revisers into two groups: Reforming Revisers, and Reinventing Revisers. The former are trying to bring accepted Christian doctrines into better accord with some authority on which they are supposed to be founded, and from which they have, despite themselves, sadly strayed, such as the Bible, reason, the apostolic tradition, or the "church fathers." In contrast, Reinventing Revisers think that Christian theology is something that ought to be remade by each generation, especially now, because of some important developments in other areas of human knowledge, usually "Science," or "a modern, scientific worldview," or a "critical" and historic perspective on Scripture. They either de-emphasize core, non-negotiable Christian beliefs or deny that there are any such. Revisionary theologians such as Hick are Reinventers. Luther and the Socinians were Reforming Revisers.

Revision comes at a price; the Reviser is often considered a heretic within his base community—the one he urges should change—because he denies something they affirm as essential. This is a main difference between the Rational Reinterpreter and the Reviser: the former is trying to be (or at least

---

[84] Pinnock et al., *Openness of God*; Boyd, *God of the Possible*; Hasker, *God*; Tuggy, "Three Roads."

[85] Mullins, "Simply Impossible"; Mullins, *The End*.

[86] Hick, *Metaphor of God Incarnate*.

[87] Wilbur, *History of Unitarianism*, vol. 2, chs. 20–32.

[88] Kolb, "Lutheran Theology."

to *sound*) orthodox with respect to their starting tradition, while the latter is not. Say what you will, generally Revisers are willing to pay the price for their convictions. Because of this heresy issue, offended traditionalists don't see a lot of difference between a Hick-type reviser and a Luther-type one—in their view a heretic is a heretic.

I would argue that in general, Revision should be considered a last resort, or at minimum something one considers only after trying out the various Rational Reinterpretations and perhaps some sort of Resistance. We ought to assume that our forerunners were on the right track until the evidence compels us to deny this. Further, Reforming Revision is preferred to Reinventing Revision, as the latter is more radical and a greater departure from tradition. As with medicine and musical arrangements, the rule of thumb should be "less is more." But facts are facts, and sometimes they may even compel us to revise or reinvent.

6.6 CONCLUSION AND ADVICE TO TRINITARIANS

My own theological journey through the R's may perhaps be instructive. Being raised within the American evangelical mainstream, I assumed that some Trinity theory or other must be right, since the Bible clearly implies that there is one God—the Trinity—and exactly three divine Persons somehow "in" that God.[89] When I was a committed and somewhat thoughtful teenage Christian, I believed that Jesus, as the Son of God, must be divine, and since there's only one god, one who is divine, Jesus must be God himself. Yet when I read Scripture, I could see that the man Jesus was one character and that his and our god is someone else: the Father. I didn't have any way to think of these doctrines as coherent, so on rare occasions when I saw such beliefs challenged, I practiced Redirection, and as I grew older, Restraint.

As a high school and college student, I engaged in Positive and Negative Mysterian Resistance, which I expressed by saying things like, "Any God we can understand wouldn't be the one true God," and "We wouldn't expect the infinite God to make sense to our finite minds." By the time I was a PhD student I was fairly well trained in analytic philosophy, and having long been interested in apologetics, I was sympathetic to Resolving by Rational Reinterpretation. I began carefully working my way through competing newfangled interpretations

[89] That is, I was convinced that Bible clearly implies claims 1–7 on p. 75.

of the doctrine of the Trinity to see which, if any, should be accepted.[90] I assumed any biblically faithful Christian was, as such, committed to God being the Trinity, and that any non-trinitarians must be pseudo-Christian, Bible-denying cultists, radical theological liberals, or modernistic, speculative Resolvers by Reinvention.

But when I was a graduate student and then a young professor, I became aware of the minority report of unitarian Christians since the Reformation. These people held, in many cases, the same views about the Bible as their trinitarian brethren; indeed, many of them had been trinitarians but became convinced that the Bible doesn't support any triune-God doctrine. Many of them left a good testimony regarding their lives and reputations, showing fear of and love for God and love for their neighbors. I read debates between them and their trinitarian contemporaries, and it seemed the unitarian Christians always had the stronger case.

This led me to revisit questions of New Testament interpretation. I went through every popular trinitarian and deity-of-Christ proof text, discovering, one by one, that some non-trinitarian interpretation was suggested by facts in the same paragraph, in the same book, by other writings of the same author, or by other ideas current at the time. Any support that I thought the Bible gave to Trinity speculations slowly but steadily melted away.

I came to see that the fundamental problem is not that Trinity theories seem incoherent—some do and some don't—but rather that the Bible, rightly understood, doesn't support any triune-God doctrine. Both the terminology and the concepts needed for any Trinity theory are absent from Christian Scripture, and moreover, any Trinity theology conflicts with clear New Testament teaching.[91] It was clear to me that Scripture teaches that the one god is the Father, not the Trinity.

The remaining issues of whether Jesus literally existed before his human career and whether the Holy Spirit is a literal divine Person were more difficult. Ever conservative, I stuck with traditional views on these topics as long as I could. But with more years of study, I came to firm convictions about these matters, rejecting them both on scriptural and other grounds.[92]

[90] I published my first peer-reviewed paper ("Unfinished Business of Trinitarian") on this topic when I was still working through these, becoming increasingly frustrated with them.

[91] Chapter 3.

[92] Tuggy, "Podcast 235"; "New Testament," 105–6.

I was now a unitarian Christian, my faith and Christian life intact and indeed strengthened by my new, firmer grasp of New Testament teachings. Resolving by Reforming Revision preserved my trust in God and my spiritual life; while my trust in post-biblical traditions as taught by catholic councils and Great Theologians lessened, my trust in God and my trust in the teachings of the New Testament were strengthened.

Traditional scare tactics like the saying "Try to understand the Trinity and you'll lose your mind; try to deny it and you'll lose your soul"[93] are destructive and without any biblical or any other justification. To the contrary: if you're a child of God—the God who instructed us to love him with all our mind (Matt. 22:37), and stated that "perfect love casts out fear" (1 John 4:18)—you need not fear humbly using your God-given powers of critical thinking to sort through competing interpretations of divine revelation—revelation from one who is competent to communicate even to little creatures like us. We should assume that this revelation is clear enough on its own and that some of the difficulties we now face are due to the interference of competing human speculations.[94]

A key aspect of human cognitive biases is selective attention. We choose to pay attention to facts we think support our cherished theory, and we deliberately ignore facts that don't fit well with it. Trinitarian traditions teach Christians to wield what I call "the canon within the canon," a small subset of texts they believe can be explained only by "the deity of Christ" and/or "the doctrine of the Trinity," whatever those amount to. About arguments, trinitarians are taught to pay attention to apologists and theologians who heroically defend these great, historically affirmed truths, or at least something faintly resembling them.[95] *Their* arguments are to be heard, rehearsed, and regurgitated. But the arguments of the other side? What arguments? The other side "doesn't get it"; they are outsiders, enemies of God who surely do not regard Scripture like we do. They are spiritually blind, and there is no point in listening to them or carefully engaging with their arguments. Any so-called "arguments" they come up with will be deceitful, uninformed, question-begging, or not

---

[93] Sanders, "Lose My Wits."

[94] Tuggy, *What is the Trinity*, ch. 1.

[95] It is striking how in much recent evangelical scholarship, traditional catholic Incarnation and Trinity language has been set aside in favor of unclear neologisms such as "divine identity" (Tuggy, "On Bauckham's Bargain"). I discuss and criticize this phenomenon of what I call "fauxthodoxy" in my "Podcast 393" and in sections 7.3 and 9.4.2.

helpful for some other reason(s).[96] In this way, today's trinitarians celebrate what feels to them like victory in their self-created echo chamber. Having heard only one side of the case, that case *seems* very strong indeed!

But this is not the way of sober truth-seeking. "The first to speak in court sounds right—until the cross-examination begins" (Prov. 18:17, NLT). In the discipline of philosophy we're taught to seek out the strongest defenders of opposing theories and to "steel man" others' arguments rather than "straw-manning" them—that is, wrestling with what seem to be the best forms of those arguments, not the weakest versions. I was shocked when I realized that late twentieth century and early twenty-first century academic theology and biblical studies have deliberately forgotten the unitarian Christian minority reports, both ancient and modern. At most the modern ones are superficially treated as a brief, "rationalistic" aberration, their arguments and scriptural interpretations almost entirely ignored. This is very convenient, given the strength of the unitarian Christians' arguments!

It has been observed that many things unitarian interpreters say about various passages of Scripture have also been said by *trinitarian* scholars engaging in historical-critical biblical interpretation.[97] This shows, for many passages, that unitarians' interpretations, whether correct or not, are not mere arbitrary, theology-motivated misreadings. Trinitarian scholars should take care not to dismiss these rival interpretations without a full and fair hearing. That means reading and understanding work scholarly work produced by unitarian Christians, past and present, not merely recycling excuses not to weigh them carefully.

Today's trinitarian apologists are coached to fall back very quickly to the lazy accusation that unitarian Christians are "merely assuming unitarianism," rather than arguing for it. Of course, *any* reader approaches Scripture assuming that various claims are true or false. But their point is that, allegedly, unitarian Christians adopt the scriptural interpretations that they do only or mainly because they uncritically *assume* that God can't be tripersonal or at least multipersonal.

[96] Philosophers call this sort of *ad hominem* (against the man) fallacy "poisoning the well"; the point is that these people are not worth arguing with, so one should not waste one's time arguing with them. This contemptuous attitude goes back to the brawling polemicist Athanasius, bishop of Alexandria (295–373).

[97] Wilson, *Unitarian Principles Confirmed*; Wilson, *Scripture Proofs*; Kapusta, *Scripturae Contra Trinitatem.*

To the contrary, many of us do argue for the points at issue, and there are ways of making a case for unitarian Christian views on God and his Son that demonstrably do not commit the fallacy of begging the question—merely assuming the very points at issue.[98] Anyone can examine these arguments and so learn that the common "assuming unitarianism" accusation is unfair and uninformed. Today's trinitarian apologists are only now beginning to grapple with these powerful non-question-begging arguments.[99]

My advice to the thoughtful and humble trinitarian is to patiently and critically hear out both sides of the case in trinitarian-unitarian disputes.[100] You are of course free to appeal to your favorite Trinity or Incarnation proof-texts, but you also need to understand why some Bible-believing people, even well-trained scholars, don't interpret those as you do. They appeal to features of the whole Bible—what is and is not there—to support their interpretations, trying to use the clear passages to illuminate the more obscure ones. You need to understand the paradigm shift experienced by studious Christians who have changed from trinitarian to unitarian. Many of them also argue that various historical facts support their views over trinitarian ones. You must get to the bottom of why they think what they do. Only then will you be equipped to make the case that your brand of trinitarian interpretation better explains what is and isn't in Scripture than its unitarian rivals.

If your own theological and christological views were *not* the best explanations of the relevant scriptural passages, wouldn't you want to know? And if unitarian Christian views are, as catholic traditions allege, leading people to hell, you should want to help them. You cannot help them merely by accusing them of assuming unitarianism and repeating your controversial interpretations. When you are ready to argue from a fully informed standpoint, you will find that there is no shortage of unitarian Christians who will respectfully and reasonably engage with you about these important matters of common interest.

---

[98] Ware Jr., *Outline of the Testimony*; Tuggy, "Unfinished Business of the Reformation"; Tuggy, "Podcast 334"; Tuggy and White, "Debate"; Tuggy, "New Testament."

[99] Some of the arguments of some recent unitarian Christian books are engaged with in Bowman Jr. and Komoszewski, *Incarnate Christ*. The engagement, though, is not very deep or wide, since the authors decided to argue against a broad range of other views on Christ.

[100] Five good places to start are Date and Tuggy, *Is Jesus Human*; McIntosh, *One God*; Smith and White, "Does the Bible Teach?", Tuggy and White, "Debate"; Wilson, "Jesus Is Yahweh?"

CHAPTER 7

How to Be a Monotheistic Trinitarian

7.1 TRINITARIANS AND TAWHID[1]

Some recent authors celebrate that the Bible is thoroughly trinitarian, that all Christians have always been trinitarian, and that the Christian life involves trinitarian belief.[2] Here the word "trinitarian" is being used in the widest sense, meaning, believing in the Father, Son, and Holy Spirit spoken of the New Testament. In this sense, truly, any Christian is a "trinitarian," and this always been so.[3]

But this is not the time for a thoughtful Christian merely to celebrate trinitarian doctrine. The second biggest religion in the world, currently claiming around 26% of the human race,[4] is not only non-trinitarian but is actively anti-trinitarian. Islam proclaims exactly one God and has always criticized Christians for preaching monotheism while also implying polytheism. This religion has since the seventh century proven itself an effective inoculation against traditional, catholic Christian beliefs, and so has created a high barrier to Christian evangelization. With modern travel, publishing, and the long arm of YouTube, Muslims aggressively argue that they, and not Christians, are the true sons of Abraham, the true monotheists. Islam has always been book-oriented and has strong traditions of theology and apologetics. Moreover, many informed Muslims are convinced that here they are on stronger ground; their clarity trumps trinitarian obfuscation, and their consistent monotheism trumps trinitarian polytheism. And while in ages past only a few Muslim scholars had

[1] An early version of this chapter was presented at a conference at Fuller Seminary in January 2014.

[2] For example: George, *Is the Father*, 55.

[3] Section 1.10.1.

[4] Galen, "Share of Global Population."

detailed knowledge of the Bible and Christian theology, today the gates are thrown open and any hobbyist debater or internet apologist can, after a little study, pit Christian sources against traditional Christian theologies.

Part of their case against Christianity is based on a simple line of reasoning rooted in common sense. It goes something like this:

1. A claim that strongly and steadily *seems* incoherent (that is, seems to imply one or more logical contradictions), unless it can be more accurately restated in a seemingly coherent way, probably *is* incoherent.
2. Incoherent claims are false, not true.
3. Trinitarian theology strongly and steadily seems incoherent and can't be restated in a seemingly coherent way.
4. Therefore, probably, trinitarian theology is false, not true. (1-3)

Premises 1 and 2 are parts of common sense. Denying one or both in order to save some theological speculation is wrongheaded. But what basis do they have for premise 3? Their basis is common sense together with a fair first glance at both the Bible and at catholic traditions. I shall argue that Christians can and should deny premise 3 but let us first ask what grounds the Muslim thinks she has for believing 3.

She knows that the New Testament affirms monotheism as clearly and strongly as the Old Testament[5], and that monotheism is a part of any trinitarian confession. But she also knows, like all people, what a god is supposed to be. The concept of a god is a the concept of a being capable of having a first-person point of view, which is great in knowledge and power, having even supernatural powers, powers to act despite how the natural world normally runs.[6] And she knows that Yahweh, the god of monotheistic, Abrahamic religion is supposed to be a god, but greater than any of the alleged deities crowding the pantheons of polytheistic religions. Unlike them, this God never was a human, and essentially has unsurpassably great knowledge, power, and goodness. He is of necessity unique, and he singlehandedly made the cosmos.[7] If Christians say

---

[5] Mark 12:29, 1 Cor. 8:6, John 17:1–3, Rom. 3:30, Gal. 3:20, Eph. 4:6, 1 Tim. 2:5, James 2:19, Acts 14:15, 1 Thess. 1:9, Deut. 6:4.

[6] For more on the analysis of the concept *god* and how it relates to the monotheistic (and other) meanings of "God," see my "On Counting Gods." For more on the Old Testament doctrine of monotheism, see my "Divine Deception."

[7] See, for example, the attributes of God in Islamic theology as expounded by Farah, *Islam*, 108–12. A reader of a previous draft of this chapter objected that some Islamic theologians don't consider Allah to be a god. In reply, while it is true that in the throes of

there are three who are unsurpassably great creators of the cosmos, the Muslim will quite reasonably infer that those are three monotheistic gods—which, of course, makes no sense, because Christians agree that of necessity there can be at most one such god. As a recent Christian writer notes, to Muslims, the Trinity seems to amount to "three discernible gods with separate personalities ... Christians are branded polytheists (*mushrikun*) because of the belief that Jesus is God."[8]

Christian apologists often skip over the metaphysical agonies of trinitarian theorizing,[9] instead arguing that trinitarian theology is directly and obviously implied by the Bible.[10] Employing various traditional biblical proof texts, some trinitarians argue that the Father is God and that the Son is God, where "is God" in each case expresses numerical identity, a relation that can only obtain between a thing and itself. It follows that the Father and the Son are numerically identical. (It is self-evident that for any a, b, and c, if $a = c$, and $b = c$, then $a = b$.)[11] And yet it is a core part of trinitarian orthodoxy that the Father and Son are *not* numerically identical but are numerically distinct from one another. Understood in this way, trinitarian theology is incoherent, and so is self-refuting.[12]

Other trinitarians, intending to avoid incoherence, deny that "the Father is God" and "the Son is God" are statements of numerical identity. Instead, they urge, "is God" in each case means no more or less than "has the divine essence." But such a trinitarian must face the following argument.

---

philosophical speculation, some Islamic thinkers will posit that God is "beyond existence and non-existence, [so] that only negative properties should be applied to him" (Leaman, *Introduction to Classical*, 4), still, on the face of it the central Islamic and Quranic confession that "there is no god except God" implies that God is a god, since he's the only god. In the Qur'an see 2:163; 5:73–76, 116; 6:19; 16:22, 51; 17:42; 23:91–92; 36:23; 38:5; 39:6; 43:45; 59:22–24; 112:1–4. Perhaps most to the point is this compressed Quranic argument: "Nor is there any god beside Him—if there were, each god would have taken his creation aside and tried to overcome the others. May God be exalted above what they describe!" (*Qur'an*, 218 [23:91].) The conclusion here is that though it is conceivable, it is not possible that there be more than one god. Of necessity, then, there is only one god, Allāh (*the* god). This implies that Allah is a god.

[8] van Gorder, *No God but God*, 114.

[9] Tuggy, "Trinity."

[10] Section 2.3.

[11] Things identical to the same thing must also be identical with one another. For more on the concept of numerical identity see sections 3.2 and 8.3–4.

[12] Tuggy, "Trinity," sec. 1.4.

1. The Father has the divine essence. (premise)
2. The Son has the divine essence. (premise)
3. The Father ≠ the Son (The Father and the Son are numerically distinct, that is, not numerically one). (premise)
4. To have the divine essence is to be a god. (premise)
5. The Father is a god. (1, 4)
6. The Son is a god. (2, 4)
7. There are (at least) two gods. (3, 5, 6)

This sort of trinitarian explicitly endorses the first three premise. The fourth premise is true by definition; an essence is supposed to be a property (or set of properties) that is necessary and sufficient for being a thing of a certain kind. When the essence in question is divinity or deity, the kind is: god. It follows that the Father is a god (5), and the Son is a god (6). They are either the same god or they are two different gods. But they can't be the same god because they're numerically distinct from one another (3). Thus, there must be (at least) two gods, the Father and the Son. This conflicts with what any Christian is committed to, that there is only one god.

Some trinitarians deny the first two premises on the grounds that the only god is the Trinity, so each divine Person must be something less than a god, and so can't have the highest sort of divinity, the kind that entails being a god.[13] But these are in effect trying to defend mainstream Christian tradition by denying key claims affirmed by it, namely, the Nicene claim that the Father and Son share the divine essence. That they have some lesser sort of divinity, a sort that doesn't imply being a god would traditionally be denounced as "Arian" heresy.

A few others deny the validity of the argument. Specifically, they deny that 3, 5, and 6 entail 7. They suggest instead that the Father and Son can be the same god even though they are numerically distinct from one another.[14] But this flies in the face of what seems to be a self-evident principle, which is that for any things *a* and *b*, they are the same *F* (some sort of thing) only if three things are true: (1) *a* is an *F*, (2) *b* is an *F*, and (3) $a = b$ (that is, *a* and *b* are numerically identical, one and the same thing). For instance, if Peter and Cephas are the same apostle, Peter is an apostle, Cephas is an apostle, and Peter = Cephas. To say that Peter and Cephas are the same apostle is to make those three claims. In the case at hand, if the Father and the Son are the same god, then the Father is a god, the Son is a god, and the Father = the Son.

[13] Moreland and Craig, *Philosophical Foundations*, 588–94.

[14] In chapter 11 I develop a new, biblical argument against relative identity trinitarianism.

What about denying premise 3? The problem with this is that according to any Christian, the Father and Son have simultaneously differed, and it is self-evident that numerically identical things can't ever simultaneously qualitatively differ (because they're *really* just one thing). If any *x* and *y* have qualitatively differed, it follows that *x* is not *y* and *y* is not *x*, that is, *x* and *y* are truly two.[15] Again, this is common sense, and something agreed to by nearly all analytic trinitarian theologians.[16]

Going back to our first, main argument (p. 226), premise 3—that trinitarian theology seems incoherent—will strongly seem true to the thoughtful Muslim. She sees trinitarians either implying that there is more than one god while saying there is only one or claiming that the Father and Son are the same god even while thinking them to have simultaneously differed or saying that each has the divine essence but neither of them is a god.

The objection that if Jesus is a god (divine being) then he can't be the same god as God (a.k.a. the Father) has been effectively pressed by recent Islamic apologists, but it goes back to the Qur'an itself, which doesn't countenance Jesus and the Father being one god but instead assumes that Christians consider Jesus to be an additional god.[17]

Some will object that Christians have no obligation to meet Islamic criteria for genuine monotheism. But the value of self-consistency and the concept of deity above are not Islamic but are common to human minds. The main argument above is not dependent in any way upon distinctively Islamic ideas about divine unity, or on the authority of the Qur'an or of any of the traditional Hadith collections.

Will theologians pause their trinitarian celebrations and "revivals" long enough to find a good answer to this argument? It would seem that a Christian should want a convincing and principled answer. Everyday people from historically Christian communities convert to Islam, and often they cite as a reason for their conversion that Islam is clearly and self-consistently monotheistic while Christianity is not. Christians must be able to explain to Muslims and those considering Islam why premise 3 in the main argument is

---

[15] Sections 8.3 and 8.4.

[16] See the theories surveyed in my "Trinity." An exception would be the extreme viewpoint of Catholic philosopher Peter Geach, on which un-relativized or absolute identity statements are without meaning. On this see "Trinity," sec. 2.1.1 or sections 8.3.4 and 11.2 below.

[17] "God says, 'Jesus, son of Mary, did you say to people, "Take me and my mother as two gods alongside God?"'" (*Qur'an*, 79 [5:116]).

false, appealing to a trinitarian Christian theology that seems self-consistently monotheistic.[18]

It won't do to reply: "*We say* our trinitarian theology is monotheistic."[19] The Muslim objector knows that. But she also knows there's a difference between asserting monotheism and *self-consistently* asserting monotheism, asserting monotheism without *also* implying something inconsistent with it. She grants that Christians assert it but is waiting to be shown, not told, that they assert it self-consistently. She thinks, with some reason, that Christians are self-inconsistent here. And it will only be special pleading if Christians reply that they *are* self-consistent monotheists. Nor can they merely point out that we call both Father and Son by the title of "God." She will point out, using Christian scriptures, that it doesn't follow that they are the same god.[20]

7.2 THE DEAD END OF NICENE SPECULATION

It's a central part of catholic Christianity's narrative about herself that the Christian doctrine of God was finally clearly and explicitly worked out at Constantinople in 381, or between the 325 Council of Nicaea and that 381 council. Therefore, these are the first place one would look for an official, mainstream solution to the worry that trinitarian theology implies polytheism. What we usually call "the Nicene Creed" today is actually a creed produced by the 381 Council of Constantinople,[21] hence the name also used, the "Nicene-Constantinopolitan Creed."

But this famous creed only exacerbates concerns about mainstream Christian theologies and monotheism. It starts, "We believe in one God the Father all-powerful, maker of heaven and of earth, and of all things both seen and unseen." So far, so good. This is monotheism to be sure, a theology on which

---

[18] The problem with a strong and steady appearance of incoherence is that such claims also appear, on balance, to be false, even when we have significant evidence for them. Thus, in my view, we ought not use the traditional strategy of christening our seemingly incoherent claims as "holy mysteries" and urging that their seeming incoherence is a virtue. On the rationality of believing apparent contradictions, see the arguments of my "On Positive Mysterianism," my "Two Natures," secs. 5–6, and section 6.4.1 above.

[19] For a clear case of this see Bird, *Evangelical Theology*, 115.

[20] John 10:22–39. For exposition of this passage see section 9.5. On being called "God" in the New Testament see sections 1.1–5.

[21] For the differences between the 325 and the 381 creeds see Hanson, *Search*, 815–20. For the difficult historical evidence pointing to two creeds from the council in 381, see Kinzig, *History*, chs. 7–9.

the only god and the Father are one and the same, and he is the one creator. But then it continues, "And in one Lord Jesus Christ, the only-begotten Son of God, begotten from the Father before all ages, light from light, true God from true God."[22] Both the Son and the Father here are called "true God," and it is clear that they are numerically distinct from one another, since the first mysteriously derives from the second. (The informed reader knows this is a gesture at the doctrine that the Father "eternally generates" the Son.) One presumes then, as each is a "true God" and not merely a so-called "God," that each is a god. Thus, the creed seems to teach at least two gods, immediately after asserting only one.

But the great innovation of the 325 creed, which was repeated in the 381 creed, was its new term *homoousios*, its claim that the Father and Son are or share the same *ousia*.[23] Surely the answer lies here, in this term—*this* will show how Father and Son are the same god, and not two different gods, right?

It depends. When it is said that Father and Son are one and the same *ousia*, or the same respecting *ousia*, or one in *ousia*, what does *ousia* mean? Sometimes in philosophy *ousia* means a being, an entity, a reality. Are Father and Son, in the New Testament, the same being? Surely not, for they are there assumed to have simultaneously differed. We all know that a single being can't, either at one time, or in eternity, differ *from itself*. It is self-evident that identicals (being one and the same thing) can't simultaneously differ, and so don't ever differ. But the Son died, and the essentially immortal Father did not.[24] The Son was exalted to the Father's right hand, but the Father was not so exalted (Acts 7:55). They are, then, two, not one and the same. Thus, the terms "Father" and "Son" in Christian discourse should not be thought of as co-referring.[25]

---

[22] "Exposition," 24.

[23] Historian R. P. C. Hanson observes about the key term *homoousios* (same in or one in *ousia*—essence, or being, or substance) that its meaning was unclear, and "nobody could pretend that it was Scriptural, and much the most satisfactory explanation of why it was put [in the 325 Nicene creed] is that it was certainly a word . . . which serious and wholehearted Arians could not stomach" (*Search*, 167). It seems to have been chosen not because it expressed some new insight but rather because of the ecclesial effects of adopting it, as it would drive out the party the majority of catholic bishops at that meeting wanted to drive out, the Egyptian presbyter Arius and his friends.

[24] Mark 15:37; Rom. 1:23; 1 Tim. 1:17, 6:16.

[25] The start of every Pauline epistle reveals the assumption of a distinction between Jesus and God; greetings and blessings are sent from both. As John says, "our fellowship is with the Father *and* with his Son Jesus Christ" (1 John 1:3, emphasis added). Presumably, in none of these greetings is the author speaking redundantly. See pp. 44–46.

Perhaps if *ousia* means "being" then the claim is not that the Father is a being, the Son is a being, and they are, moreover, the same being. Perhaps the claim is instead that there is but one being between the two of them, that they *share* one "being." Perhaps the idea is that the Father is himself a being, but the Son is merely a way the Father exists or lives. Or, conceivably, the reverse. Or perhaps both Father and Son are mere modes, ways of existing of a certain being, namely, the one God. It is plausible that in addition to beings, there are mere modes of those beings, ways they are, whether essential or not. For example, evangelical apologists have given the example that "Muhammad was simultaneously a prophet, a husband, and a leader."[26] Prophet-Muhammad is just Muhammad acting in his (alleged) capacity as a prophet, not another man in addition to Muhammad. Whatever Husband-Muhammad does is just what Muhammad does; Husband-Muhammad is just a way Muhammad is; it is Muhammad, standing in at least one marital relationship. Back to the case of God, each of these three views is conceivable: that the Father is merely a mode of the Son, that the Son is merely a mode of the Father, or that both are merely modes of the one God. On any of these three readings, consistent monotheism is safeguarded. Each reduces the number of apparent gods to one, namely, the Father, the Son, or the God of whom both Father and Son are modes. But this, I shall argue, is not an acceptable way to be a monotheistic trinitarian.

Why? Because all three of these interpretations of the creed's claim go strongly against the grain of the New Testament. In its pages, the Father and Son enjoy a hierarchical friendship. The Son prays to, serves, cooperates with, and submits to the Father, and the Father sends, empowers, guides, publicly affirms, and vindicates the Son by raising and exalting him. The Father works through the Son, who only does what he sees his Father doing.[27] Each has a will, and sometimes those wills differ. But the Son freely submits his will to his Father's; "yet not my will, but yours be done" (Luke 22:42). Only beings, not mere modes of beings, can be friends. Only beings have wills. Only intelligent beings perform intentional actions, such as sending one's unique Son on a mission of salvation or obeying God's will even to the point of death (Phil. 2:8). Moreover, the exalted Son, still a human being, now operates as a mediator between the rest of humanity and his Father. This presupposes that both he and his Father are two beings, indeed, two selves (intelligent beings, intelligent

[26] Geisler and Saleeb, *Answering Islam*, 276.

[27] Mark 1:35; John 14:10, 5:19–20; Matt. 17:35.

agents). Again, it is obvious that a human being (a human self) is not a mode of anything else but is rather a being (entity, individual reality, existing thing) in his or her own right.

When first introduced, *homoousios*, to many, smelled of these modalistic interpretations, and they feared that something like these interpretations was intended.[28] And Nicene theology has yet to get out from under their shadow, despite their manifestly poor fit with the New Testament.[29] As we've seen, such interpretations conflict with the Bible. And a leading recent historian judges that none of these interpretations could have been the original intent of the creed makers in 325. R. P. C. Hanson observes,

> We can be pretty sure that *homoousios* was not intended to express the numerical identity of the Father and the Son. If the fathers of Nicaea had meant this ... why could they not have said so?[30]

Let us move on, then, in search of a consistently monotheistic reading of these creeds. *Ousia* can also mean a shareable essence, a complex, defining property that is had by all members of some kind. (We encountered this concept in our second argument above.) This sort of *ousia* is what philosophers call a universal. Thus, classical philosophy considered *human nature* to be an essence, one equally and wholly present in both you and me. On this reading, Father and Son both have present in them, or exemplified in them, the universal *ousia* we call *divinity*, or *the divine nature*, the property of being a god. As we've seen, the problem is that two beings, each with the essence *divinity*, implies two gods, just as two beings each with the essence *humanity* are, on the theory of essences at hand, two humans.[31]

---

[28] The word may have previously been used, in the third century, for a modalistic monarchian or "Sabellian" theology on which in some sense the Father and Son are not distinct (Hanson, *Search*, 190–202).

[29] In this connection consider the present-day evangelical slogans that "Jesus is God," or "the deity of Christ," which many ordinary Christians seem to understand as meaning that the Son and the Father are numerically one, that is, that Jesus is God himself (Tuggy, "Podcast 124"). And at the level of academic trinitarian theology, we have the ever popular one-self or "Latin" views of the Trinity (on which see my "Trinity," sec. 1).

[30] Hanson, *Search*, 202. This is reinforced by the fact that earlier theologians such as Justin and Origen found it easy to express that Father and Son are, in Justin's words, "distinct in number," "two in number," and "distinct in real number" (*Dialogue with Trypho*, 85 [56.11], 194 [128.4, 129.1]. Compare: 94 [60.3], 191–92 [ch. 127]. What can be affirmed can be denied. Origen's views on the Father and Son will be discussed below.

[31] A theologian influential in the period leading up to 381 flailed unsuccessfully against

This problem is so seemingly insurmountable that a number of serious Christian thinkers have redefined monotheism to get around it. Thus, analytic theologian Richard Swinburne suggests that in affirming just one god, and so implicitly denying polytheism, the ancient councils "were denying that there were three independent divine beings, any of which could act independently of each other."[32] In other words, they meant "monotheism" to be consistent with multiple gods, so long as those gods were essentially unable to exist or act apart from one another. But to the contrary, all ancient catholic creeds of note profess belief in "one God, the Father," that is, in one monotheistic god, one perfect and unique creator.

But some philosophers don't believe in universals (abstract, shareable properties). Instead, they believe in *particular* properties. They would deny, for example, any need to posit the existence of a universal property *humanity* that is present in all humans. They instead believe in such properties as your humanity and my humanity.[33] Each human, it is thought, must have his own property of humanity. Such properties are by definition not shareable; a particular property is such that numerically distinct (non-identical) beings can't both have it. (This seems right; it seems like nonsense to say that, for instance, a brother and a sister share *an individual* property of being five and a half feet tall.) This position is thought to have various advantages over belief in universal properties (or belief in *only* universal properties). If this is how we understand *ousia* in the creed, then the claim is that Father and Son share one individual, essential property, *divinity*.

Here again, monotheism is preserved. If Father and Son share that sort of *ousia*, it is logically implied that they are one and the same being, so they must be one and the same god.[34] But this comes at too high a cost. Their being one *ousia* in this sense straightforwardly implies that they are one *ousia* in our first sense above. That is, it implies that they are numerically identical, one and the

---

this problem. Though his attempts are widely read in seminaries nowadays, his stature in the catholic tradition seems to largely prevent the perception of his obvious theoretical failure (Gregory of Nyssa, "Answer to Ablabius"). For critical discussion see my "History," sec. 3.3.1; Hasker, *Metaphysics*, 26–39.

[32] Swinburne, *The Christian God*, 180. Hasker's strategy is similar (*Metaphysics*, 177-84). See also section 3.7.2.

[33] Then again, some metaphysicians believe in *both* universal and particular properties. For more on how theories of properties relate to the Trinity and monotheism, see my "Hasker's Quests."

[34] An *individual* essence is by definition unshareable.

same being (thing, reality, entity). If that were so, it'd be impossible for them to ever differ.[35] But we know, based on divine revelation, that they actually have differed from one another.

Some present-day philosophers would say that being one in *ousia* could mean being one in matter, that is, being composed of the same stuff. Consider a coin made of pure gold. The portion of matter composing it would, it seems, survive even if the coin were melted, smashed, shredded, or spun into gold thread. But not so for the coin; melting, etc. would destroy it. If you believe, then, that both the portion of gold and the coin it now composes are beings, they can't be the same being, since it's possible for the first to exist while the second doesn't exist. (Oddly, these two things, the coin and the quantity of gold, will occupy the same spaces at the same time.) Some present-day metaphysicians urge, for philosophical reasons, that such beings as that portion of gold and the coin it now composes are "to be counted as one," for they are "numerically the same" even though they are not identical but rather distinct beings.[36]

But this suggestion faces three difficult challenges. First, it is doubtful that the creed-makers meant to assert Father and Son to be composed of the same stuff—some sort of matter, presumably, or something analogous to matter.[37] Second, the above metaphysical analysis of things like the quantity of gold and the gold coin is controversial. Many metaphysicians consider it a better response to deny the existence of either the coin or the quantity of gold, or both, believing only in the particles therein, arranged coin-wise. The very concept of "numerical sameness without identity" is controversial. (If some *a* and some *b* are *not* numerically identical, then they are numerically distinct, non-identical. But then, *why* should *a* and *b* be counted as one, as being "numerically the same"?) Finally, will a core Christian doctrine presuppose a metaphysical thesis about composition that very few humans understand, and of those, probably a majority reject? Is this the way of divine revelation?[38]

We've been discussing *ousia* as something that a being such as God has. But proponents of the traditional Platonic and catholic theory of divine simplicity will argue that this is a grave mistake. They would urge that God *just is* his

---

[35] Sections 8.3–4.

[36] See my "Trinity," section 2.1.3 and the sources cited there.

[37] See, for example, the testimony of Eusebius (an attendee of the 325 Council of Nicaea) and the judgment of Hanson (*Search*, 165, 183–84).

[38] For these and other difficulties for this new Constitution theory of the Trinity, see my "Constitution Trinitarianism." See also section 6.5.1.

essence, so he is numerically the same with his divinity.[39] A metaphysical concern here is that unless God just is his essence, he'll have to "participate in" or bear some relation to the universal *divinity*, and this, it is feared, would render God dependent, composite, and changeable. There is a reason it was Platonists who originated this doctrine; the core concern depends upon a doctrine of universals, on which for anything to have a property is for it to "imitate," "participate in," "exemplify," "instantiate," or at any rate, to bear *some* unique relation to the appropriate universal. This concern seems to evaporate if you think that having a property amounts to intrinsically being a certain way. Suppose God is wise and loving, and that we deny that he "is" both (that he is numerically identical with each), that his wisdom just is his love and vice versa. These features are plausibly two aspects of God, ones that God could not fail to have. This sort of "composition" or multiplicity doesn't seem to imply that God depends on anything else, that is, on any being other than himself, or that he's composite in any undesirable sense, or that he's changeable or a creature.[40]

As concerns monotheism, the doctrine of divine simplicity would seem to only cause trouble similar to what we've just seen. The thrust of divine simplicity is that God is numerically identical with anything you might think of as being "in" him, since God can't have complexity of any sort whatever. But mainstream theology says that the Father is a divine Person in God, and that the Son is a divine Person in God. If the traditional doctrine of divine simplicity is true, these claims would entail that God just is the Father, and that God just is the Son. But then, it would follow that the Father just is the Son, and vice-versa.[41] We're back, it would seem, to our first bad option above, on which the Father and Son are one and the same *ousia* in the sense of one and the same thing (reality, entity).[42]

Perhaps there are other ways to interpret the word *ousia* in the Nicene claim that Father and Son are *homoousios*. Christian philosophers continue to philosophize on this topic, generally starting from the "Athanasian" Creed."[43]

---

[39] Vallicella, "Divine Simplicity."

[40] For a full case against divine simplicity see Mullins, "Simply Impossible"; Mullins, "Divine Simplicity"; Mullins and Bird, "Modal Collapse."

[41] This logically follows because identity is a symmetric and transitive relation. See sections 8.3.1 and 8.4 and p. 97, note 9.

[42] As Hasker observes, "a strong [that is, a traditional] doctrine of simplicity ... is incompatible with *any* objectively existing Trinity" (*Metaphysics*, 39).

[43] A seminal source for this approach is Cartwright, "Logical Problem." See also my "Unfinished Business of Trinitarian."

Sometimes this work aims to find an interpretation of traditional claims that all Christians can understand enough to actually believe. But in many cases, the goal is the lesser one of showing that traditional Trinity claims can't be demonstrated to be incoherent, that is, *proven* inconsistent by an *obviously* valid deductive argument from premises all of which any trinitarian must *by definition* grant. The problem with this lesser goal is twofold. First, some who argue against traditional Trinity doctrines will grant that it can't be in the above sense demonstrated to be incoherent; their reasons for rejecting them lie elsewhere, generally in the convictions that no such doctrine is either taught or implied in the Bible, that no such doctrine best explains what is and what is not said in those sources,[44] and that the theology of the New Testament is contrary to any traditional Trinity theory.[45] Second, even if the doctrines can't be *demonstrated* to be incoherent, there may still be strong reasons for thinking they *are* incoherent—reasons that fall short of the high standard of demonstration. For example, consider the claims that (1) the Father just is (is identical to) the one God, (2) the Son just is the one God, and (3) all that the New Testament teaches about the Father and Son is true. These claims contradict; they can't all be true, for the New Testament teaches that the Father and Son have qualitatively differed.[46] But these three claims are not *demonstrably* contradictory, for (3) is not true by definition and can, without contradiction, be denied by someone who is trinitarian and affirms (1) and (2).

We've seen a pattern so far. When any clear interpretation of the key Nicene term *ousia* is given, the result is either inconsistent monotheism or a form of consistent monotheism that misfits the New Testament. The catholic streams of Christianity have, so to speak, wagered everything on this unclear and still-disputed creedal claim, so there's a temptation to insist that there must be some interpretation or other of that claim that is suitable, perhaps one that no human currently understands. But this won't move anyone who doesn't already hold to Nicene, catholic orthodoxy. Nor should it. Such an insistence would be textbook case of the fallacy of special pleading or begging the question.

---

[44] Thus, the argument strategy of Islamic scholar Timothy Winter, "Trinity is Incoherent." This is also a common unitarian Christian stance, for example, Clarke, *Scripture Doctrine*, xiii–iv. For what I claim is an overwhelming case of this sort see my "New Testament."

[45] Chapter 3.

[46] I again assume the self-evident truth that identicals (that is to say, a thing *and itself*) can't at one time differ; see section 8.3.2 below.

7.3 UPDATING NICENE TERMINOLOGY

Some would object that it's wrongheaded to become obsessed with an ancient Greek word. Can't we express what the ancient bishops were getting at, that is, the gist of it, without employing their language or relying on their philosophical assumptions? I suggest that the prospects for this are not good, as recent creative solutions drive into the same ditches we've just seen.

British biblical scholar Richard Bauckham suggests that a more Jewish way of thinking about the one God employs the concept of personal identity. Rather than speculating on the divine essence or nature, he suggests, Jews thought about God as the one who created and governs the cosmos. The one God Yahweh, then, is the only one who does those mighty deeds. And in Bauckham's view, the Bible says that *Jesus* does those things.[47] Thus, it follows that Jesus is the one God himself; Jesus has the "personal identity" of God and so is one and the same person or self—and one and the same being—as God. Here, we're back to the collapse of the Father and Son into numerically one being, just as with the first interpretation of *ousia* discussed above (p. 231), with the absurd implication that one being has, at one time, differed from itself.

But Bauckham's new lingo also includes the dark saying that Jesus is "included in the divine identity," seemingly, that Jesus is *a proper part of* the one self who God is. It's none too clear what is meant by this, and so it is unclear whether catholic tradition or anything in the Bible would support it.[48] It is probably a gesture towards the "social trinitarian" tradition, or three-self Trinity theories, which I have argued against elsewhere.[49] For now, I'll just say that this doesn't seem an improvement on Nicene language.

Theologian Keith Ward tries in a different way to improve on Nicene language. He prefers to say that God non-contingently acts as Creator, Redeemer, and Comforter, and speaks of "God as transcendent abyss, God as particular yet unbounded intelligence, and God as the immanent creative energy of being . . . three distinct ways of being God," with the named ways being intrinsic and essential to God, and not mere ways that God appears.[50] This seems but another version of the idea that the Persons of the Trinity are mere modes of God, ways God is, and so not the sorts of beings who may love

---

[47] Bauckham, *Jesus,* 7–13, 154–57, 172–81, 182–236.

[48] For a sustained attempt to coherently interpret Bauckham and criticisms of his proposal, see my "On Bauckham's Bargain"; "Podcast 213"; "Podcast 214"; "Podcast 393."

[49] See my "Unfinished Business of Trinitarian" and my "Divine Deception."

[50] Ward, *God: A Guide*, 236. Compare: Ward, *Christianity*, 90.

one another, cooperate, and stand in I-Thou (self to self, interpersonal) relationships to one another and to you and me.

In a later discussion Ward posits the biblical Father, Son, and Spirit as ways that God appears to humans, which is contrary to catholic traditions.[51] He then suggests that this "economic Trinity" is

> Rooted in a threefoldness of subjectivity, creativity, and unitive love . . . That in turn is rooted in a deeper "immanent" threefoldness of primal origin, expressed thought, and beatific love.[52]

Whatever the merits of such speculations, this language is clearly not restating in different words what ancient councils and "church fathers" taught. Rather, something new—and on the face of it something unsupportable by anything in Scripture—is being put forward.[53] Like other Reinventing Revisions,[54] such claims suffer from the disadvantage of being neither traditional nor biblical.

7.4 TRINITARIAN ORIGENS: BACK TO PRE-NICENE THEOLOGIES

When at the start of this chapter I defined the term "trinitarian" very broadly, perhaps you worried that it's an abuse of language to call someone a "trinitarian" who merely believes in the existence of what the New Testament calls the Father, the Son, and the Holy Spirit. After all, one who does that, may or may not also believe in a tripersonal God, in a God that "is" three equally divine "Persons."

But my broad usage of the word "trinitarian" has ancient roots; it derives from the original uses of the terms we translate as "Trinity." When the Greek *trias* and the Latin *trinitas* were introduced in the late second century, these were used as plural referring terms, referring to a triad, a triple, a threesome of entities (beings, realities) who so to speak lie behind this cosmos that somehow came from them.[55] But this Christian triad was *not* the Christian God, the one God of Jesus, David, Moses, and Abraham. Rather, the Christian God was *one member of* this triad, its founding member. We can see this in the theology of

---

[51] Ward, *Christ and the Cosmos*, 256–62. Mainstream tradition assumes that the one God would be Father, Son, and Spirit even if creation never occurred.

[52] *Christ and the Cosmos*, 256.

[53] For other criticisms see my "Some Objections."

[54] Section 6.5.2.

[55] In this it seems they were influenced by the Platonist cosmologies of their era, which typically featured three transcendent realities, one of which was the ultimate reality (Guthrie, *Numenius of Apamea*, 115–26; Alcinous, *Handbook of Platonism*, 17–19 [sec. 10]; Dillon, *Middle Platonism*, 280–85, 312–17, 366–72).

Tertullian, the first on record as using the Latin word *trinitas*. The one God, for him, is the Father, not the Trinity, even though God shares some of his divine material ("spirit") with his Son just before the creation of the cosmos.[56]

The point is even clearer in the greatest Christian scholar in antiquity. Origen (d. c. 253) was an inhumanly prolific writer and a pioneer of textual criticism, apologetics, theology, and Christian philosophy. One of his most important surviving works is his eight-book *Against Celsus*, probably written around 246–48. Celsus was a pagan philosopher, or at least an aficionado of classical philosophies, a cultural and religious conservative, who had written in the second half of the 100s a book attacking Christianity called *The True Word*. Decades later (it is unclear why), Origen wrote a massive refutation of this, quoting substantial portions of it.[57] Here's an exchange from Origen's book:[58]

> [Celsus writes:] If these men [Christians] worshipped no other God but one, perhaps they would have a valid argument against the others. But in fact they worship to an extravagant degree this man who appeared recently [Jesus], and yet think it is not inconsistent with monotheism if they worship His [God's] servant [Jesus].
>
> [Origen responds:] I should say to this that if Celsus had considered the saying, "I and my Father are one" [John 10:30], and the prayer uttered by the Son of God in the words, "As I and thou are one" [John 17:21–22], he would not have imagined that we worship another besides the supreme God. "For the Father," he says, "is in me, and I am in the Father" [John 14:10–11].[59]

What is Origen's argument here? One might jump to the conclusion that Origen thinks the Father and Son to be one god. Thus, his point would be that in worshiping the Son, the Christians worship the same god they worship when they worship the Father. But that is not Origen's point. He continues:

---

[56] Tuggy, "History," sec. 3.1.2; Tuggy, "Tertullian the Unitarian"; Lamson, *Church*, 128–36; Biddle, "Testimonies," 14–18. See also pp. 245–46, note 77. Unfortunately theological sources continue to misrepresent Tertullian as an early believer in a tripersonal god, for example: Bird, *Evangelical Theology*, 138; Olson and Hall, *Trinity*, 29–31.

[57] These are the only portions of any of Celsus's writings that survive.

[58] Recently David Litwa has trimmed out and retranslated these quotations from Celsus's book, about 70% of which he reckons has been quoted by Origen (Celsus, *The True Teaching*). But I shall quote the exchanges between Origen and Celsus as they appear in Chadwick's translation of *Against Celsus*, noting any important differences between his at Litwa's translation of the Celsus excerpts in footnotes.

[59] Origen, *Against Celsus*, 460 (8.12). In this and the following quotations I've omitted the translator's italics that he uses when he believes Origen to be quoting Celsus's words.

> If, however, anyone is perturbed by these words lest we should be going over to the view of those who deny that there are two existences (*hypostases*), Father and Son, let him pay attention to the text, "And all those who believed were of one heart and soul" [Acts 4:32], that he may see the meaning of "I am my Father are one." Accordingly we worship but one God, the Father and the Son, and we still have a valid argument against the others.[60]

Origen goes on to make clear that there are two whom Christians worship:

> we worship the Father of the truth and the Son who is the truth; they are two distinct existences, but one in mental unity, in agreement, and in identity of will . . . we worship the one God and His one Son, His Logos and image, with the best supplications and petitions that we can offer, bringing our prayers to the God of the universe through the mediation of his only-begotten Son. We bring them to him [the Son] first, asking him who is a propitiation for our sins to act as a high-priest, and to bear our prayers and sacrifices and intercessions to the supreme God. [Heb. 2:17, 4:14] . . . And Celsus cannot show that there is any *discord* in our belief about the Son of God. Indeed, we worship the Father by admiring His Son who is Logos, Wisdom, Truth, Righteousness, and all that we have learnt the Son of God to be.[61]

Origen adds in another place that the Son now holds "the second place of honour after the God of the universe, the position given to him on account of the great deeds which he did in heaven and on earth."[62]

But Celsus has another objection:

> [Celsus:] If you [Christians] taught them that Jesus is not his [God's] Son, but that God is the father of all, and that we really ought to worship him [God] alone, they [Christians] would no longer be willing to listen to you unless you included Jesus as well, who is the author of their sedition. Indeed, when they call him Son of God, it is not because they are paying very great reverence to God, but because they are exalting Jesus greatly.
>
> [Origen answers:] We have learnt who the Son of God is, even that he is "an effulgence of his glory and the express image of his person" [Heb. 1:3] . . .

---

[60]Origen, *Against Celsus*, 460 (8.12). This translator's trinitarian bias may be reflected in his placement of the comma: he has "one God, the Father and the Son" instead of "one God, the Father, and the Son." But it is the latter that best fits a careful reading of Origen's extant writings. However, Origen does argue that despite their numerical distinctness, God and the Logos/divine Son can be *called* "one God" (Origen, *Dialogue*, 58–60 [1–3]).

[61]*Against Celsus* 460–61 (8.12). Elsewhere he calls them "two lights," citing Ps. 35:10, and says the Father is greater (Origen, *Commentary on John*, 134 [2.151–52]).

[62]*Against Celsus* 443 (7.57). Compare with Rev. 5.

and we know that Jesus is the Son come from God and that God is his Father. There is nothing in the doctrine which is not fitting or appropriate to God, that He should cause the existence of an only-begotten Son of this nature . . . We affirm that this person is Son of God—yes, of God to whom, if we may follow Celsus' words, we pay very great reverence; and we know His Son who has been greatly exalted by the Father.

But we may grant that some of those among the multitude of believers take a divergent view, and because of their rashness suppose that the Saviour is the greatest and supreme God. But we at least do not take that view, since we believe him who said: "The Father who sent me is greater than I [John 14:28]." Consequently we would not make Him whom we now call Father subject to the Son of God, as Celsus falsely accuses us of doing . . . the Son is not mightier than the Father, but subordinate . . . We affirm that the Saviour . . . is Lord of all that has been subjected to him . . . but not that he is also lord of the God and Father who is mightier than he . . . It is not our purpose to worship any merely assumed God, but to worship the Creator of this universe and of all else which is not sensible or visible.[63]

Like other second and third century theologians, Origen does call the Son "God," and he does so often, in striking contrast to the New Testament.[64] But unlike many later theologians, he's careful to explain his use of terms. He thinks this Son is eternal, and that he is divine in a derived way. But he never says that the Son's divinity makes him the same god as his Father. Hear his explanation of his own God-terminology in his commentary on the Fourth Gospel:

[The word] God, with the article [Greek: *ho theos*], is very God, wherefore also the Savior says in his prayer to the Father, "That they may know you, the only true God." [John 17:3] On the other hand, everything besides the very God, which is made God by participation in his divinity, would more properly not be said to be "the God," but "God" [that is, not *ho theos*, but *theos*, also translatable as "a god"].[65] To be sure, his "firstborn of every creature" [that is, the Son, Col. 1:15], inasmuch as he was the first to be with God and has drawn divinity into himself, is more honored than the other gods beside him [that is, Christians] (of whom God is God as it is said, "The God of gods, the Lord has spoken, and he has called the earth." [Ps. 49:1] It was by his [the Son's]

---

[63] Origen, *Against Celsus,* 461–63 (8.14–15).

[64] On the few cases where the New Testament arguably uses *theos* in reference to Jesus, see section 1.4 above.

[65] Reader beware: Origen's claim here does not match with actual New Testament usage of *ho theos* and *theos*, which both normally refer to the Father (Harris, *Jesus as God*, 36–50).

> ministry that they became gods, for he drew from God that they might be deified, sharing ungrudgingly also with them according to his goodness.
>
> The God [that is, the Father], therefore, is the true God. The others are gods formed according to him as images of the prototype. But again, the archetypal image of the many images is the Word with the God, who was "in the beginning [John 1:1]." By being "with the God" he continues always to be "God." But he would not have this if he were not with God, and he would not remain God if he did not continue in unceasing contemplation of the depth of the Father.[66]

Origen's language is not like that of Muslims, nor like that of later catholic Christians who reserve the term "God" for the one god or the fully divine "Persons" somehow "in" that god. Earlier in this book Origen says, citing biblical texts, that "There are certain gods of whom God is god,"[67] and elsewhere he says that "we do not hesitate to speak in one sense of two gods, and in another sense of one god."[68] His looser god-talk certainly fits his Hellenistic milieu, but it is not radically different than the Bible, which uses god terminology for humans, Satan, idols, the alleged gods of polytheistic religions, and angels.[69]

Finally, let's look at Origen's *On First Principles*. In a passage discussing his view that the Holy Spirit is eternal, he says that

> the Holy Spirit would never have himself been in the unity of the Trinity, that is, along with God, the unchangeable Father, and with his Son, unless he had always been the Holy Spirit.[70]

Conditioned by Nicene concerns, we might think Origen is assuming the Spirit to be equally divine with the Father, and to be one god with him. But Origen later writes that

> the God and Father, holding all things together, is superior to every being, giving to each, from his own, to be whatever it is; the Son, being less than the Father, is superior to rational creatures alone, for he is second to the Father; and the Holy Spirit is still less, dwelling with the holy ones alone. So that in this way the power of the Father is greater than the Son and the Holy Spirit,

---

[66] Origen, *Commentary on John*, 98–99 (2.17–18). Italics are supplied by the translator; the material in brackets has been added by me. Elsewhere he describes the Son as "a second God" and as "a God like God the Father of the universe" (Origen, *Against Celsus* 296 [5.39], 377 [6.61], 73 [2.9]).

[67] *Commentary on John*, 76 (1.12).

[68] Origen, *Dialogue*, 58 (sec. 2), modified.

[69] See section 1.5 and Schoenheit et al., *One God*, 486–87.

[70] Origen, *On First Principles*, trans. Behr, 1:73 (1.3.4).

> and that of the Son is greater than the Holy Spirit, and again, the power of the Holy Spirit differs greatly from other holy beings.[71]

The Son and Spirit here are beings other than God, beings in addition to him, and they are lesser beings, depending on God for their existence, while he depends on nothing.[72] Nor, as we've just seen, are the Son and Spirit equal to one another. In an uncorrupted, mature work Origen teaches

> that the Holy Spirit is the most honored of all things made through the Word, and that he is [first] in rank of all the things which have been made by the Father through Christ.[73]

In sum, for Origen there is a Trinity, but it is not a god. Rather, the one true god, the Father, the ultimate source of all else, is the founding member of that triad (group of three beings). The Son and Spirit are divine in lesser ways, since they eternally emanate from and "participate in" God.[74] Of the two, the

[71] Origen, *On First Principles*, trans. Behr, 2:598 (text no. 6). In my view this Greek passage, which survives only as a quotation in a letter from the year 543 by the emperor Justinian to Menam, was "corrected" by the Latin translator Rufinus (d. 410), who upon seeing non-Nicene ideas in Origen's work leaped to the conclusion that it must have been corrupted by heretics, and so undertook to "correct" those passages. For Rufinus's own testimonies about this, see his *Epilogue*; *Preface*; *Apology*, 440-42 (1.12–15). The most recent English translator, John Behr, relegates this passage to an appendix, whereas an earlier translator, using the 1913 critical text of Paul Koetschau, inserts this passage into section 1.3.5 (*On First Principles*, trans. Butterworth, 33–34). Behr complains that Koetschau was too speculative and arbitrary in his reconstructions of this text, and is concerned to defend, despite Rufinus's admissions, Rufinus's fundamental reliability as a translator. (See Behr's Introduction to volume 1 of his edition, xx–xxviii.) The reader of any edition of *On First Principles* should be aware that not all of Rufinus's corruptions can be corrected, as we lack a complete text of the book in its original Greek. A number of suspicious passages that sound orthodox by late fourth century standards are found particularly in Rufinus's Latin version of Book IV, which unfortunately has been reprinted more than once in recent years as representative of Origen's views on the God, the Logos, and the Holy Spirit.

[72] That these are his considered views is confirmed by his claim in a commentary that Father, Son, and Spirit are "three hypostases," that is, beings (entities, realities, things) because they differ from one another, only the Father being "unbegotten" (Origen, *Commentary on John*, 114, [2.75]).

[73] *Commentary on John*, 114 (2.75). For Origen being the greatest creature is compatible with being "a god" who has a degree of divinity from God (via the Logos/Son).

[74] The Son and Spirit "participate in" God in a manner similar to how, for example, humans "participate in" the Platonic universal *humanity*. The Father is divine underived, whereas the Son is a god because of his participation in the Father's *divinity*, and lesser gods (such as the Holy Spirit, redeemed humans, and the heavenly bodies) are deified by means of the Son. In sum, "*The* God [that is, the Father], therefore, is the true God. The others are

Son is greater than the Spirit. God, that is, the Father, is greater even than both Son and Spirit, and there's no way to construe this, as so many recent theologians do with the New Testament, as being a mere matter of function, that is, as functional subordination without any difference in kind or degree of divinity or greatness. This is why Origen was wholly unworried by considerations like our second argument in section 7.1 (p. 2228); he would have denied premise 2 or premise 4 in that argument, as he denied that the Son is divine in the same way the Father is.

Were Tertullian and Origen "trinitarians"? Yes, in the sense explained above: they believed in the reality of the Father, Son, and Holy Spirit spoken of in the New Testament. Did they believe that the one most high God is tripersonal, that God somehow "is" three eternal and equally divine "Persons"? No. They were not, then, "trinitarians" in the more specific, post-fourth-century sense, the sense which has been mandatory for catholic Christians since 381.

Were Origen and Tertullian monotheists? One may worry that they have too many gods, since they call both Father and Son "God." But they are clear that the term "God" is equivocal. Tertullian's explanation is similar in spirit to Origen's.[75] We can loosely paraphrase Tertullian's explanation as follows. Suppose the company I work for is owned by one man who demands to be called "Boss." But when he's not around, I say "Yes, Boss" to my immediate supervisor. When the owner comes around, out of respect I switch to using "Boss" to refer to him, and I now call my supervisor "Sir." This practice could potentially confuse, but as my coworker, you would quickly understand what I was doing, especially if I directly explained my usage of "Boss" and "Sir." Similarly, Tertullian says that when he mentions the Father and Son together, he calls them, respectively, "God" and "Lord," but in contexts where the Son alone is in view, he calls the Son "God."[76] This because he holds the Father to be greater than the Son.[77] Like Origen,

gods formed according to him as images of the prototype" (Origen, *Commentary on John*, 99 [2.18]). Any of these is properly called "god," in contrast to idols, which are "said to be gods, but which are in no way gods" (*Commentary on John*, 101 [2.27]).

[75] Tertullian, *Against Praxeas*, trans. Souter, 57–61 (ch. 13).

[76] Compare: 1 Cor. 8:6, on which see below section 9.5.

[77] Speaking of the special type of matter called "spirit" that Tertullian believes to compose God, he says, "For the Father is all being, but the Son is a tributary of the whole and a portion, as He Himself declares [in John 14:28]: "Because the Father is greater than I" (Tertullian, *Against Praxeas*, trans. Souter, 46 [ch. 9]; compare: 65 [ch. 14]). He also holds the Son to have come into existence when it was time to create the cosmos, so

Tertullian would have denied premise 2 or premise 4 in our second argument above (p. 228), that is, "The Son has the divine essence." In their view the Son does not have the divine essence in the same sense that the Father does, so that the Son (really, the Logos) must have all the essential divine attributes. Instead, he gets a lesser degree of divinity from God the Father.

Monotheism is the claim that there is exactly one god. It is not the thesis, nor does it imply, that exactly one being may be properly addressed as "God" or truly described as "a god."[78] Most monotheistic religions allow there to be, in addition to the one God, any number of lesser beings that may still be truly called "divine" or "gods." In the Bible angels, and occasionally even humans, are called *elohim* (gods), the same word that, when used in contexts referring to the unique god, Yahweh, is translated as "God." But Tertullian and Origen are no less monotheistic than the most enthusiastic Islamic supporter of *tawhid* (monotheism), despite their more generous use of god-terminology, and despite their speculations regarding the Son either at the time or creation (Tertullian) or eternally (Origen) somehow emanating out of or being caused by the one true God. Such an origin doesn't make him equally divine as, or the same god as his Father. It doesn't make the Son a monotheistic god at all; for

---

that God might create indirectly, by means of him (Tertullian, *Against Praxeas*, trans. Souter, 38–42 [chs. 5–7], 50–54 [ch. 11]; Tertullian, *Against Hermogenes*, 487 [ch. 18], 502 [45]). On the sometimes tricky matter of interpreting Tertullian's views see Tuggy, "Tertullian"; Date and Tuggy, *Is Jesus Human*, 123–26, 142–45, 153–56. Origen holds that the Father's knowledge is greater than the Son's; in another passage evidently corrupted by Rufinus, he says (in Jerome's Latin translation) "the careful reader will want to know whether the Father is known by himself in the same way he is known by the Son; and knowing what is written [in John], *The Father who sent me is greater than I,* he will affirm it to be true in every respect, so that he will say that even in his knowledge the Father is greater than the Son, being more perfectly and more clearly known by himself than by the Son" (Origen, *On First Principles*, trans. Behr, 2:621 [passage 29.d]. Compare: Origen, *Exhortation to Martyrdom*, 412 [29].) It seems that Rufinus also corrupted another famous passage, which in his version says that "nothing in the Trinity can be called greater or less," as in another Greek fragment seemingly cut out by Rufinus but preserved by Justinian, Origen says that "in the case of the Saviour . . . he is *the image of the goodness of God* [Wis. 7:26], but not goodness itself. And perhaps also the Son is good, but yet not good simply, and that just as *he is the image of the invisible God* [Col. 1:15] and, in this respect, God, but not the one of whom Christ himself says [in John 17:3] *that they may know you the only true God,* so also he is *the image of the goodness,* but not, as the Father, invariably good" (*On First Principles*, trans. Behr, 2:597 [passage 4], original emphases). Elsewhere Origen insists that "the Father who sent" Jesus "is alone good and greater than the one who was sent" (Origen, *Commentary on John*, 224 [6.20]).

[78] On monotheism vs. monotheosism see section 1.3.

them, that god, the god of Israel, is none other than the Father himself, and no one else is that sort of god.

Christian-Muslim disagreements remain.[79] The Muslim insists it is sinful "association" to worship any being other than the one true God.[80] She would insist that *true* monotheism requires monolatry, that is, having only one object of worship. In reply, as a matter of terminology, we should insist that "monotheism" concerns merely the existence of exactly one god, and that one could well be a monotheist (a believer in one supreme being) and yet worship no one at all, or only lesser beings. We should distinguish between belief and practice; some monotheists are polyolaters, believers in one true God who nonetheless mostly worship certain lower deities, fearing that (at least in normal circumstances) only they are truly accessible to human petitioners, whereas the Supreme Being can't be bothered.[81] Again, some monotheists worship both God and lesser deities, supposing the latter give them better access to the former.

In any case, Origen has a ready-made answer to the Muslim: worship given to the Son doesn't rest in him, as it were, but passes on till it reaches the Father. Worshiping the Son is a means of worshiping the one God.[82] When you honor the one sent, in the way the sender intended, you thereby honor the sender (Mark 9:37). Nor do Christians, Origen argues, confuse the sender with the sent. We recognize the Father as the one true God, he urges, citing the New Testament. It simply can't be sinful association to worship the Son alongside the Father when it was the Father himself who raised the Son up to such an exalted position, holding him up and out to us as an object of worship. As Larry Hurtado observes,

> the early Christians' fundamental answer to the question "How dare you worship this figure?" at the earliest moment, would be, "Because God says so—because God requires it. And to refuse reverence to Jesus is to disobey God."[83]

---

[79] See pp. 152–54 for some other christological and practical clashes between Christianity and Islam.

[80] *Qur'an*, 55 (4:48), 62 (4:116), 261 (31:13), 299 (39:65–66).

[81] This belief is common to many indigenous religious traditions (Hiebert and Shaw, *Understanding Folk Religion*, 51–54).

[82] See pp. 241–42. For a fuller unitarian Christian defense of worshiping or religiously honoring Jesus see my "Who Should Christians Worship."

[83] This is my transcription of a portion of a public talk in 2011 by Hurtado at the School of Divinity, Edinburgh University. The audio of this is posted at Wasserman, "Evangelical." Comments and more transcription are in my post "Larry Hurtado." See also my "Hurtado."

Going beyond Tertullian and Origen, it is the New Testament that shows us how to be monotheistic trinitarians. It rules out the modalistic strategy of supposing the Father, Son, and Spirit to be serially God, one after the other. And it rules out our reducing all of the "Persons" of the Trinity even to essential and eternally concurrent modes of God, because the loving interpersonal relationship of the Father and Son is an inescapable theme of every New Testament Gospel. Any heavy negative theology seems ruled out by the Bible,[84] and appeals to mystery to paper over theological contradictions are wholly absent from its pages.[85] Also absent is the Nicene suggestion that somehow the Father, Son, and Spirit are one God *because* they are one in *ousia*.

The New Testament asserts monotheism as firmly as the Old Testament. Yahweh is the only god—that is, the only unsurpassably and uniquely great creator of the cosmos, the only god. The man Jesus is God's Messiah, Son, and servant (Acts 3:13, 26; 4:27, 30). There is no term anywhere in the Bible that was originally meant by its author to refer to a tripersonal deity.[86] More importantly, such a conception is nowhere assumed or implied in any biblical book. As A. T. Hanson wrote over three decades ago, about trinitarian doctrine in the later catholic sense of a tripersonal god (the Trinity) somehow containing three equally divine Persons,

> No responsible New Testament scholar would claim that the doctrine of the Trinity was taught by Jesus, or preached by the earliest Christians, or consciously held by any writer in the New Testament.[87]

---

[84] That is, biblical language about God is contrary to the notion that we can only say what God is not, rather than what God is. For example, it is a clear biblical teaching that God is kind and merciful (Ps. 103); we are not confined to thinking that God is not un-kind and not un-merciful.

[85] Tuggy, *What is the Trinity*, ch. 8. Two classic early modern unitarian sources on this are Nye, *Impartial Account*; Toulmin, *Meaning*.

[86] See section 1.5. After exhaustively surveying the New Testament usage of *ho theos*, the leading Catholic theologian Karl Rahner concludes that "Nowhere in the New Testament is there to be found a text with *ho theos* which has unquestionably to be referred to the Trinitarian God as a whole existing in three Persons" ("*Theos*," 143). Similarly, Harris finds no use of god-terms for the Trinity as a whole anywhere in the New Testament (*Jesus*, 48–50), and he observes that "When *(ho) theos* [(the) god] is used, we are to assume that the NT writers have *ho pater* [the Father] in mind unless the context makes this sense of *(ho) theos* impossible" (47). Other scholars have come to the same conclusions; see the summaries and sources in Zarley, *Restitution of Jesus Christ*, ch. 1.

[87] Hanson, *Image*, 87. Compare with a similar admission in Bird, *Evangelical Theology*, 112. Bird suggests, though, that a Trinity doctrine is the best explanation of scriptural data.

Nor should we think that the New Testament authors *un*consciously identified God with the Trinity. Every author in the New Testament everywhere assumes, and sometimes asserts, that the one true God is the one Jesus called his Father, his God and our God (John 20:17).[88] This rules out the one god being the whole Trinity. The Father, we hear in a prayer of Jesus, is "the only true God" (John 17:1–3), which echoes the statement of Jeremiah that "Yahweh, there is no one like you . . . Yahweh is the true God . . . The gods who did not make the heavens and the earth will vanish from the earth and from under these heavens" (Jer. 10:6, 10, 11 NJB).[89]

The New Testament holds forth the exalted Jesus as an object of worship alongside his and our god and teaches that worship given to Jesus glorifies both him and the god who exalted him (Rev. 5, Phil. 2:11). On this point Origen was neither innovating nor speculating. Origen was not averse to innovation and even very bold speculation. Nonetheless, in the core of his theology, he's faithful to the New Testament identification of the one God with the Father. He is, to a degree, a biblical trinitarian. But he's also, we have seen, a unitarian, a Christian who identifies the one God with the Father alone. He is not, to be sure, a Socinian, an anti-trinitarian, or a rationalist (whatever that means). Those terms are anachronistic, as Origen had never heard of Socinus, had creedal Trinity doctrine to react against, and though he can be called a Christian Platonist, he was nothing like a deist in the modern sense. The defining thesis of "unitarianism," used descriptively, is simply that the one God just is (is identical to) only a certain perfect self, namely, the Father. The term is used in this sense, for example, when Judaic and Islamic theologies are described as "unitarian."[90]

This thesis is clearly affirmed by Origen and Tertullian, and by most other prominent catholic pre-Nicene theologians, even while they speculated as to how this one God caused there to be lesser deities, either eternally or long ago.[91] It is

---

[88] See chapters 8–9, chapter 3, and Tuggy, "New Testament"; "Unfinished Business of the Reformation"; "Divine Deception."

[89] There is a confusion promulgated by Christian apologists about John 17:3, that Jesus there predicates the term *only-true-God* of the Father but does not thereby rule out that the term applies to himself too. This misunderstands the logical structure of what Jesus presupposes there, which involves quantification and not merely predication. See section 9.2.

[90] For my attempts at descriptive, non-controversial definitions of "unitarian" and "Christian unitarian" see my "Defining the Concept of a Unitarian"; "Defining the Concept of a Christian Unitarian."

[91] These speculations, which we now call "Logos theology," on which the Son is to a degree

fascinating, and for many, inconvenient, that these two leading intellectual champions of early catholic Christianity held the one God to be the Father alone. The lesson is that the tripersonal-God vs. unipersonal-God dispute is one matter, and theories about the "divinity" or "deity" of Christ (and of the Holy Spirit) are another.[92] They should not be confused, for the second preceded the first by something like two centuries. It is only some time after Nicaea, in the years leading up to the 381 Council of Constantinople, that we find clear affirmations of the one God as a tripersonal deity consisting in some sense of equally divine "Persons."

This, then, is the ancient, pre-Nicene way to a monotheistic trinitarian: to identify the one God with the Father alone. As best I can tell, and I've looked hard, it is the only good way, the only way that is both self-consistent and faithful to the Bible. And conveniently, it enables a Christian to not only deny premise 3 in the Muslim's argument (in section 7.1, p. 226) but also to persuade the Muslim that she too should deny that premise. There is, for all we can tell, nothing incoherent about the claim that the one God just is the Father of Jesus, *even if* we add that in a lesser sense, Jesus and the Spirit are divine, can be called "gods," and already existed (whether timelessly or in time) when creation occurred. Any "trinitarian revival" that hearkens back to the fourth century doesn't go far enough. Let us go back to the second, and indeed, to the first, for that is when we received "the faith that was once for all delivered to the saints" (Jude 3, ESV).

divine, literally preexists his miraculous conception, and helped to create the cosmos, were controversial in the second and early third centuries. They gave rise to charges of innovation and polytheism both from ordinary Christians and from other catholic theologians, including the Dynamic Monarchians and the Modalistic Monarchians. On this see Tertullian, *Against Praxeas*, trans. Souter, 31–33 (ch. 3); Heine, "Christology of Callistus."

[92] Origen and Tertullian are mistaken in thinking that the holy spirit (or the spirit of God) of the New Testament is supposed to be a self/person in addition to the Father and the Son (Finnegan, "Unitarian View"; Smith, *Systematic Theology*, chs. 28–32; Tuggy, "New Testament," 105–6; Tuggy, "Podcast 25"; Tuggy, "Podcast 26"; Huffer, *Systematic Theology*, 89–93).

CHAPTER 8

A Crash Course in Logic, Similarity, and Identity

8.1 LOGIC AND LANGUAGES [1]

The main character in the whole Bible is God. But the main focus of the New Testament books is the man Jesus, the Son of God. How are these related? That is the subject of this and the next chapter. In this chapter I'll explain the logical and metaphysical concepts that analytic philosophers have found so helpful in understanding certain claims and arguments even about God. In the next chapter we'll apply what we've learned to interpreting the New Testament on the topics of God and Jesus.

Logic is a formal science closely related to mathematics. *A* logic, a particular system of logic, is an artificial language, a precise set of symbols with rules about how to put them together and how to form valid arguments with the resulting sentences. Why construct such artificial languages, when we already have so many natural languages, such as English, Hindi, and German? These natural languages suffer from numerous ambiguities; by translating our claims into an artificial, more precise language—a logic—we can remove these ambiguities, which empowers us to critically evaluate both individual claims and arguments constructed from those claims. Such translations help us to get beneath the grammar of the original sentences to better understand the structure of what is being said. With a better understanding of what is being said, we are now able to seek evidence for or against these claims and to evaluate arguments featuring them as sound or unsound. In short, logical

[1] This chapter and the next are based on my screencast lecture "God and his Son" and on my experience teaching university courses in logic, critical thinking, and metaphysics.

analysis—translating the claims of a natural language into an artificial, logical language—is a first step in a whole process of reflective evaluation of a text.

Mainstream Christian traditions have produced significant confusion about God and his Son. Some Christians think Jesus is God himself, although when reading the New Testament, it seems to them that God is someone and Jesus is someone else. Others think of Jesus as part of God, one third of him. Or perhaps he's not so much a part of God as he is a member of the group of divine Persons that, somehow, is God. Others hold that Jesus is a different Person than his Father but that the two are nonetheless the same god. Are any of these the New Testament perspective? I shall argue that they are not.

8.2 A CRASH COURSE IN LOGIC

First, we need to gather our tools and put them on the table, the tools of logic, as taught around the world nowadays in classes with titles like Logic or Introduction to Deductive Logic. Logic in this sense is subject-neutral; it can be applied to any subject matter humans can think, speak, or write about. The reader is encouraged to slowly and patiently work through this section; my promise is that this technology will enable one to better understand what the apostles John and Paul say about God and Jesus. Logic is a vast subject, and like all areas of philosophy, it encompasses a lot of disagreement. But in this chapter I will apply what has been a standard approach for more than a hundred years.

This language is called "predicate logic" because it employs letters to stand for predicates, terms that we apply to things. The predicate is what is being said about the subject. By convention, we use capital letters for predicates. We use lowercase letters for singular referring terms, name-like words that refer to exactly one thing. Thus, if *c* names Constantine, and *E*_ means "_ is an emperor," then *Ec* translates the English sentence "Constantine is an emperor." The sentence "Hirohito is an emperor" would be translated as *Eh*, using *h* as a name for the man Hirohito.

Here's another tool, what logicians call the material conditional, represented by the symbol $\supset$.[2] The sentence $Eh \supset Ec$ translates "Hirohito is an emperor only if Constantine is an emperor" or, equivalently, "If Hirohito is an emperor, then Constantine is an emperor."[3] If we add the predicate *P*_ meaning "_ is powerful,"

[2] Some textbooks use $\rightarrow$ instead of $\supset$ for the material conditional.

[3] When I say that one sentence is equivalent to another, I mean that they will be true or

we can translate "If Constantine is an emperor, then he is powerful" as $Ec \supset Pc$. This sentence doesn't say that Constantine *is* an emperor, or that he *is* powerful; it merely asserts a connection between the two statuses. That is, *if* he's an emperor, *then* he's powerful. It's one variety of what logicians call a conditional sentence. Such a statement is commonly used in arguments like this:

English sentence	*Logic Sentence*
1. If Constantine is an emperor, then he's powerful.	1. $Ec \supset Pc$
2. Constantine is an emperor.	2. Ec
3. Therefore, Constantine is powerful.	3. Pc

This is a valid argument. That is, 1 and 2 imply 3. If the first two statements are true, then the third one must be true as well; it is impossible that 1 and 2 are true but 3 is false. Put differently, one who is committed to the truth of both 1 and 2 is also committed, whether she knows it or not, to the truth of 3.

Many valid arguments fail to be convincing because they have one or more false premises. Consider the following argument:

English sentence	*Logic Sentence*
1. If Dale is an emperor, then he's powerful.	1. $Ed \supset Pd$
2. Dale is an emperor.	2. Ed
3. Therefore, Dale is powerful.	3. Pd

Premise 2 is false; Dale is *not* an emperor. Still, the argument *is* valid. *If* both 1 and 2 were true, *then* 3 would be true as well; that's all it means to say that an argument is valid. Although not everyone is familiar with this technical meaning of the term "valid," practically everyone is able to recognize simple arguments like this as valid.[4] When we understand the meanings of 1, 2, and 3, we can "see" that 1 and 2 logically imply 3.

Some statements are not about one named individual, or about a couple of them, but about all things. And sometimes we want to say that there is at least one thing of a certain kind, or even exactly one thing of some kind. Sentences like this involve what logicians call "quantification." Standard logics use two quantifiers, represented by the symbols $\forall$ (for the universal quantifier) and $\exists$ (for the existential quantifier). These are used with variables (by common convention, x, y, or z), together with at least one predicate. Thus "Everything

---

false in all the same circumstances. In other words, if one is true, then the other will be true, and if one is false, then the other will be false.

[4] For more help with the logical concepts of validity and soundness, see "Validity and Soundness."

is powerful" would be translated $\forall x Px$.[5] That is: for anything whatever, call it x, x is powerful. This sentence is false, as the x here ranges over realities such as mice, protons, and pebbles, and these are not powerful. "Something is powerful" would be translated $\exists x Px$; that is, there is some x such that x is powerful. This is true, since presidents, kings, and God *are* powerful. It is true that something—that is, *at least* one thing—is powerful.

More often, we don't make statements about all things whatever but rather about all things *of some kind*, such as the class of emperors. We might say, for example, "All emperors are powerful," or equivalently, "Every emperor is powerful." Either of these is translated as $\forall x\ (Ex \supset Px)$: for any x whatever, if x is an emperor, then x is powerful. "All dogs are friendly" is $\forall x\ (Dx \supset Fx)$: for any x whatever, if x is a dog, then x is friendly. (Sadly, this is false.)

With these tools in hand, plus the negation symbol $\neg$ for "it is not the case that," we can consider this argument (written in three ways, just to be clear). The left column has sentences in normal English, the translation of these into logic is in the middle column, and the right column shows how you would woodenly read out the logic sentences in the middle column.

English	*Logic*	*Logic-English*
1. All emperors are powerful.	1. $\forall x\ (Ex \supset Px)$	1. For any x, if x is an emperor, then x is powerful.
2. Rufus is not powerful.	2. $\neg Pr$	2. It is not the case that Rufus is powerful.
3. Therefore, if Rufus is an emperor, then he is powerful.	3. $Er \supset Pr$	3. Therefore, if Rufus is an emperor, then Rufus is powerful.[6]
4. Therefore, Rufus is not an emperor.	4. $\neg Er$	4. Therefore, it is not the case that Rufus is an emperor.

This is a valid argument; if one commits to the truth of 1 and 2, one has already committed to 3 and 4. Premise 1 implies 3, and the conjunction of 2 and 3 implies the conclusion 4.

Let's consider an argument in which a premise employs the existential quantifier $\exists$. It will help to add the symbol $\wedge$ for "and"; this is used to conjoin

[5] Some sources, instead of using the symbol $\forall$ simply enclose the universally quantified variable in parentheses: (x). In this style the sentence $\forall x Px$ would be written as $(x)Px$.

[6] If what is in parentheses of premise 1 applies to all things whatever ever, it applies to Rufus in particular. Thus, 1 implies 3. Logic textbooks usually call this rule of inference "Universal Instantiation."

single claims into a compound claim. These two are often used to translate a sentence that asserts there is at least one thing that matches two criteria. For instance, the sentence "There is a powerful emperor" becomes $\exists x \ (Ex \land Px)$. "There is an x such that x is an emperor and x is powerful." This means that there is *at least* one powerful emperor; the sentence will be true if there is exactly one or seven, and it will be false only when there are no powerful emperors.[7]

We need one more tool: the concept of numerical identity. Consider the former president of the United States of America, George W. Bush. He has gone by many names, including "President Bush," "Dubya" (a Texan pronunciation of the letter "W"), "George Bush Jr.," and even "The Shrub," because he's the son of the late George H. W. Bush, also a former president.

Consider the names "Dubya" and "George W. Bush." Imagine that your foreign friend, newly arrived in the USA, thought that Dubya died in 1995, whereas George W. Bush was president of the USA in 2003. You would explain to her that no, Dubya and Bush are one and the same; they are related to each other just as your friend is related to herself and as you are related to yourself. Dubya *just is* Bush and vice versa; they are numerically one. Using d for "Dubya" and b for "George W. Bush," in logic, we would write $d = b$. This reads: "Dubya just is Bush" or "Dubya and Bush are numerically one thing" or "Dubya and Bush are numerically identical." If you're counting men, ex-presidents, Texans, or hobbyist painters, and you count both of those, you've overcounted. The terms d and b in our logic sentence, and all the proper names in this paragraph, are co-referring terms, referring to one and the same thing.

These tools help us understand claims that such and such is *the only* thing of some kind. We've seen how to represent "Constantine is an emperor," or "Constantine is emperor": Ec. But what if we wanted to translate "Constantine is *the only* emperor"? It would be a mistake to coin the predicate $O\_$ for "_ is the only emperor," giving us Oc. The reason this is a mistake is that it hides the logical structure of the statements being made. Any logic textbook will tell us instead to translate "Constantine is the only emperor" using either the universal quantifier $\forall$ or the existential quantifier $\exists$.

[7] Philosopher John Hawthorne points out that understanding a sentence like this requires the concept of numerical identity, as the sentence implies that there is at least one emperor, and there is at least one powerful thing, *and* at least one of the emperors is identical with one of the powerful things ("Identity," 100).

English	*Logic*	*Logic-English*
Constantine is the only emperor.	$Ec \wedge \forall x\ (Ex \supset x = c)$	Constantine is an emperor, and for any *x*, *x* is an emperor only if *x* just is (is identical with) Constantine.
or	*or*	*or*
Constantine is the one emperor.	$Ec \wedge \neg\exists x\ (Ex \wedge x \neq c)$	Constantine is an emperor, and it is not the case that there's some *x* such that *x* is an emperor and *x* is not identical with Constantine.

Both translations in the second and third columns are correct for either of the logically equivalent English sentences in the first column. The translations are logically equivalent as well; that is, the sentences are true in all the same possible circumstances and false in all the same possible circumstances. In other words, they can't differ with respect to truth and falsity; in that sense, they mean the same thing. For purposes of analysis, you can use whichever one seems more intuitive to you. I have a slight preference for the second translation, but you may prefer the first.

Both translations reveal an important fact that would be obscured if we mistranslated the sentence "Constantine is the only emperor" as *Oc*. This is the fact that *two* claims are being made: first, Constantine is an emperor, *and* second, no one else is. (Note the "and" symbol ∧ in each translation.) Either correct translation above brings out that there are multiple ways the claim could be false. It'd be false, first of all, if Constantine *isn't* an emperor, but second, (even if he *is* an emperor) the statement would be false if someone else is too, that is, if he's not unique in this respect since there exists one or more additional emperors. (It'd be false too, of course, if *both* parts were false: if Constantine weren't an emperor and there were emperors who are not him.) In contrast, there's only one way "Constantine is an emperor" could be false: if the world is such that he does not hold such an office.

Notice that both translations into logic require the symbol =. In the next two sections we're going to go deep into this concept of numerical identity or being the same thing as, which will pay off in many ways when it comes to navigating the scriptural portraits of Jesus and God.

8.3 REASONING ABOUT SAMENESS

It is important to get a firm grip on the concept of numerical identity because some trinitarians affirm, while others deny, that Jesus and God are related in precisely that way. In other words, when some trinitarians say that "Jesus is God," the "is" indicates numerical identity, as in the true sentence "Dubya is George W. Bush." But other trinitarians argue that these are misinterpreting the tradition, since "Jesus is God" should be understood as meaning "Jesus is divine," which features an "is" of predication (description), not an "is" of identity. Is either group correct? Or are they both mistaken? What does Scripture really teach about Jesus and God? What does it mean to numerically identify one thing with another?

8.3.1 NUMERICAL VS. QUALITATIVE IDENTITY OR SAMENESS

The point of the sci-fi scenarios in this section is to help you to see some important differences between qualitative sameness or identity and quantitative sameness or identity. In the imaginative world of the Star Trek shows and movies, crew members often travel from their ship to a planet using a transporter machine aboard their spaceship. A transporter is supposed to copy the entire pattern of one's body, destroy that body, and then somehow create a copy of that pattern, a new body, down on the planet. This is supposed to be a method of transporting a person from the ship down to the planet and then back, when a crew member says over the radio, "Beam me up."

Let's call the person who stepped into the transporter device on the ship *a* and the one who appears on the planet *b*. Is it true that $a = b$, that *a* and *b* are numerically one? Remember, we're stipulating that, given how this machine works, *b* will be intrinsically just like *a*; *b* is a perfect copy of (the now-destroyed) *a*. Another way to put our question is, did this device just move a man from the ship down to the planet? If so, it must be true that $a = b$ (moving is not replacing but involves one and the same thing first being here, then being there).

But it would seem that *a* is *not* identical to *b*. We know that *b* just began to exist a few moments ago, when it was "printed out" by the transporter, when the data taken from *a* on the ship was used to somehow assemble a living human (*b*) on the planet's surface. In contrast to *b*, *a*, we think, began at some time in the pregnancy of *a*'s mother. Again, *a* has been annihilated, destroyed by the transporter, whereas *b* never has been annihilated. If you're ever given the opportunity to travel via such a machine, you should turn it down, as this "travel" would in fact be your own demise, followed by the creation of a duplicate of you![8]

[8] This reasoning assumes that you are a certain animal or some physical object. If a human

Sometimes the Star Trek writers have some fun with the plot device of a transporter malfunction. Person *a* steps into the transporter, is copied and annihilated, and then, by some malfunction, the transporter prints off *two* copies of *a*, call them *b* and *c*. If Captain Picard is the *a* who enters the transporter, are we supposed to think that *b* is him or that *c* is him? Are we to think that *both* are him? To understand how to approach this question, we first need to make some observations about the concept of numerical identity or sameness (=). Along the way, we'll compare and contrast it with the concept of qualitative similarity.

First, identity is a two-place relation; identity sentences require two singular referring terms or names: _ = _. In this, identity is like the relation *best friends*. It makes no sense to say that "Bob is best friends"; we must supply two names to employ that concept, for example, "Bob and Fred are best friends."[9] The relation of qualitative similarity is like this too. It makes no sense to say, "Susan is similar." Similar *to what*?

Second, numerical identity is necessarily a one-to-one relation. Many relations, like *bigger than* can be one to one ("France is bigger than Jamaica"), but they can also be one to many ("China is bigger than any of these: Ecuador, Mexico, Nigeria," or "Sally is friends with Tiffany, Amber, and Olivia"). But identity can *only* be one to one. It will always be false to say that some thing *a* is identical with *b* and also identical with some *other* thing *c*.[10] If you're *truly* saying that *a* and *b* "are the same" where *a* is one thing and *b* is another, you must be saying not that $a = b$ but rather that *a* and *b* are qualitatively similar.[11]

---

person is a soul, or has a soul as her only essential part, then what happens to one who "rides" on the transporter would depend on what happens to her soul. But why would we think that the soul somehow then enters the new body on the planet rather than either being destroyed or continuing to exist disembodied?

[9] By convention, usually two-place relations are written with a predicate first, followed by the two singular referring terms. Thus "Bob and Fred are best friends" would be written as $F(b,f)$, using *F* for the predicate "best friends." A sentence asserting numerical identity could be written this way too, where "*a* and *b* are identical" would be $I(a,b)$. But it is common to write an identity statement instead as $a = b$, and I've followed that practice here. And instead of $\neg I(a,b)$ (it is not the case that *a* and *b* are identical) I will write $a \neq b$.

[10] That is, for any *a*, *b*, and *c*, these three claims can never be true: $a = b$, $a = c$, $b \neq c$.

[11] Qualitative similarity/sameness comes in both degrees and kinds. Human identical twins may be very similar, for instance, with respect to their outward appearances, while being in some cases less similar, say, in their habits or character traits. In contrast, numerical sameness is all-or-nothing (there are no degrees of it), and it's not aspect relative. Whereas

Qualitative similarity can be one to one ("Jim is like his twin Joe"), or it can obtain between any number of things. You, as a human being, are similar in various ways to every other human being.

Third, some relations can be reflexive or not, such as the *hitter to hitee* relation. You can hit yourself, or you can hit your brother. If you are a and your brother is b, and H is the relation between a hitter and their hitee, these can both be true: $H(a,a)$, $H(a,b)$. Again, it can be true that a is qualitatively similar to b, and trivially, any a will be maximally similar to itself. In contrast, the identity relation can *only* be reflexive; it is a relation that obtains only between a thing *and itself*. For any a that exists, it will be true $a = a$. Of course, any statement like $a = a$ will be trivial, uninteresting. But we do sometimes discover true identity statements like $a = b$. A famous example, much discussed by philosophers, is the morning star and the evening star. They were, it was thought, two heavenly bodies, one observed in the morning and the other in the evening. But once astronomy advanced enough, it was realized that "both" are simply the planet Venus being observed at different times. Using m for the morning star and e for the evening star, it was discovered that $m = e$. And using v for the planet Venus, it was also discovered that that $m = v$ and $e = v$. This was a very interesting discovery, not a trivial truth.

Fourth, whenever it is true that $a = b$, then in the realm of discourse at hand a and b are co-referring terms, picking out the same item in reality.[12] In our previous example, they realized that their astronomical terms m, e, and v (the Morning Star, the Evening Star, and the planet Venus) were co-referring.[13] Generally, statements of similarity employ terms that are *not* co-referring; the exceptions are the trivial cases in which we observe that something is qualitatively similar to itself.

Fifth, as with *similar to*, identity is symmetrical. If a is similar to b, it follows that also b is similar to a. Just so, if $a = b$, then it will also be true that $b = a$. In contrast, some relations, like *parent of*, are asymmetrical. If it is true that a is a parent of b, it doesn't follow that b is a parent of a—in fact, that second claim must be false if the first is true. So too with a is bigger than b.

---

you may be like your sister in respect of habits but unlike her in respect of appearance, when it comes to numerical sameness it is simply a fact that you and your sister are not numerically the same, and it makes no sense to say the two of you are *numerically* distinct in some way but not in some other way—there are no such ways.

[12] A statement like $a = b$ is not itself about the *terms* "a" and "b" but rather and a (a.k.a. b), whatever that is in the world.

[13] In other realms of discourse those terms may refer to other things. A pagan talking about religion who says "Venus" believes that he's referring to a goddess, and a Christian discussing "the morning star" may be talking about Christ (Rev. 22:16).

Sixth, as with *bigger than*, identity is transitive. If a is bigger than b and b is bigger than c, it follows that a is bigger than c. Just so, if $a = b$ and $b = c$, it follows that $a = c$. Is similarity transitive? The answer is far from straightforward because similarity comes in degrees and is relative to aspects or qualities. Again, we can ask if and to what degree this thing and that thing are similar in certain respects, or we can ask if and to what degree this and that are *overall* similar.[14] Philosophers have argued that if the similarity in question is maximal in degree and concerns a well-defined group of qualities, it will be transitive. If we stipulate that by "similar" we mean *similar in all qualitative, intrinsic respects*, then if a is similar to b, and b is similar to c, it follows that a is similar to c. But many similarity relations that we appeal to in ordinary life are non-transitive. Suppose you're examining paint samples at the hardware store. You hold up a sample of dark blue and one of medium blue and judge them to be very similar. You hold up the medium blue sample next to a light blue one and judge them to be very similar. But when you compare the dark blue sample to the light blue sample, you do not think they are very similar.

Finally, _ = _ implies that there can be no differences between "the first thing" and "the second thing"—since *really* these are one and the same thing. Sometimes philosophers state this abstractly by saying that identity forces absolute indiscernibility (no qualitative differences at all), and they call this the Indiscernibility of Identicals. But there are some complications here that we need to think through carefully.

8.3.2 THE IMPOSSIBILITY OF DIFFERING IDENTICALS (IDI)

How should we express our intuition that numerical identity requires absolute qualitative sameness? There is a vast philosophical literature on what is often called the "Indiscernibility of Identicals" or "Leibniz's Law," in part, because some such principle is often used in metaphysical disputes.[15] Unfortunately,

---

[14] But overall similarity seems to depend on the interests and purposes of the one judging. In a classic article philosopher Nelson Goodman writes, "Consider baggage at an airport check-in station. The spectator may notice shape, size, color, material, and even make of luggage; the pilot is more concerned with weight, and the passenger with destination and ownership. Which pieces of baggage are more alike than others depends not only upon the properties they share, but upon who makes the comparison, and when" ("Seven Strictures," 445). Here is another contrast with numerical identity. Asking whether a and b are numerically one is asking whether a and b are one and the same entity in the world, which doesn't depend on anyone's interests, concerns, or aims.

[15] Magidor, "Arguments."

there is a widespread confusion found in many publications, even ones intended for students.[16] For some, "Leibniz's Law" is understood as a principle not about things in world but rather words, specifically, about substituting singular referring terms in a sentence. It is the principle that whenever you start with a true sentence and then replace a singular referring term in it with another, co-referring term (making no other changes), then the resulting sentence will be true too. It's easy to think of sentences and terms this works for. Given that we know that Samuel Clemens = Mark Twain, consider these two similar sentences.

1. Samuel Clemens was once a riverboat captain.
2. Mark Twain was once a riverboat captain.[17]

Claim 1 is true. The only difference between 1 and 2 is that in 2 we have swapped in the co-referring name "Mark Twain" for "Samuel Clemens." This change, as promised, results in a sentence that is also true: 2.

But consider this example featuring the pro wrestler and actor most known for playing Fezzik in the beloved 1987 film *The Princess Bride*. We know that André the Giant = André René Roussimoff.

1. André the Giant is so-called because of his size.
2. André René Roussimoff is so-called because of his size.

Claim 1 is true, and the only difference between 1 and 2 is that we've swapped one co-referring term (his wrestling name) with another (his legal name). But 2 is false. This example shows that the suggested substitution principle is false. But that principle was about sentences and co-referring terms, not about the impossibility of identical things being qualitatively different—and it is the latter we're interested in.

A common formulation of the Indiscernibility of Identicals is: For any x and any y, if x and y are the same object, then x and y have the same properties.

[16] Among the sources that notice and correct this confusion are Cartwright, "Identity"; Forbes, "Frege's Problem," 1; Hardegree, *Introduction*, sec. 8.5; Inan, "Defense"; Hawthorne, "Identity," 109–10; Maunu, "Indiscernibility"; Noonan and Curtis, "Identity," sec. 2; Williamson, "Vagueness," 286–87.

[17] Claim 2 is true even if his riverboat captain career wholly preceded his use of the pen name "Mark Twain." We often refer to people using a name, title, or description that they only acquired later than the time in question. For instance, we truly say that "President Richard Nixon was born in 1913"—even though he was not president in 1913.

More precisely: $\forall x \forall y (x = y \supset \forall F (Fx \equiv Fy))$.[18] But philosophers have many different ideas about how to understand properties (a.k.a. qualities, features). Are they universal or particular? Abstract or concrete? Are properties in some sense components or ingredients of what has them? Can they be instantiated or exemplified? Would a property exist even if nothing actually had it? Are they sets of things? Do all predicates we say of objects express or refer to properties, or is it only a small subset of them that do? Does property possession explain similarity? Do properties depend on their owners for their existence, or are their owners composed of those properties? Do properties include things like *being-identical-with-Isaac-Newton*? Perhaps it is better to bypass the great diversity of property theories by formulating the Indiscernibility of Identicals in a way that doesn't refer to properties.

Another way to express the Indiscernibility of Identicals is this: for any x and y, if $x = y$, then whatever is true of x is true of y and vice versa. But what *are* truths? Are they abstract objects,[19] namely propositions?[20] Not all philosophers believe in those.[21] Or are truths fundamentally thoughts in a mind or sentences in a language? But the principle we're trying to state is about things and how they are, not about thinking, writing, or speaking. Although we're searching for a true general principle, it may be better to avoid mentioning truths in formulating it.

Here, I suggest, is a better way. Everyone has the concept of similarity. The similarity of this sheet of printer paper and that sheet is a fact. Similarity comes in kinds or aspects and degrees. And let's clarify that we mean objective, mind-independent similarity rather than merely apparent similarity, which might be grounded in some perceptual distortion. Any lack of similarity is a qualitative difference. Difference too comes in aspects and degrees. Let's define a predicate *D_, _* as meaning that the specified things differ in any way to any degree. If some a and some b are maximally similar, this will be true:

---

[18] The predicate *F_* means "_ has the property *F*." $\forall F$ expresses "For any property whatsoever, call it F." The symbol $\equiv$ (in some sources $\leftrightarrow$) is what logicians call a "biconditional." The sentence $Fa \equiv Fb$ is logically equivalent to $(Fa \supset Fb) \wedge (Fb \supset Fa)$. If a is F then b is F, and if b is F, then a is F. That is to say, if one is true, the other is true, and if one is false, the other is false too—their truth values never differ.

[19] Falguera et al., "Abstract Objects."

[20] McGrath and Frank, "Propositions."

[21] Cowling and Giberman, "Nominalism in Metaphysics."

$\neg D(a,b)$ (it's not the case that *a* and *b* differ).[22] On the other hand, if it is true that $D(a,b)$, reality is such that in some way(s) and to some degree(s) *a* and *b* differ, or, we could say, fail to be similar or resemble. This formula sidesteps the plethora of property theories and different views about what are the fundamental bearers of truth. The suggestion is that something like this is what we're looking for: "for any *x* and *y*, if $x = y$ then *x* and *y* don't differ," in the artificial logical language we've been using, $\forall x\ \forall y\ (x = y \supset \neg D(x,y))$.

But there's another complication. What is the tense of the verb "differ" there? We have it in the present tense, but our principle is not *only* about what is currently so. It should apply to things that don't exist but that used to; for instance, we can say that Palmyra = Tadmur.[23] And referring to that amazing regime that will only fully come to exist after Jesus returns, we can say that the kingdom of God = the kingdom of heaven. Philosophers usually read verbs in logical principles, such as "differs" and "is" in the formulations that employed concepts of properties or truths, as timeless; abstracting away from any consideration of time, they're supposed to tell us not what is at some time(s) but rather from what some call a "God's eye" perspective, as if one could climb up on a hill and look down upon the whole timeline at once—past, present, and future. From that perspective, so to speak, we imagine that we can see a man's whole life, from cradle to grave.

There is a problem for our principle here. Let *y* be five-year-old John, and *m* be middle-aged, fifty-five-year-old John. We all believe, and John's genuine memories imply, that $y = m$. He remembers that when he was five, he did not like spicy foods. He doesn't only remember that *some five-year-old boy* didn't like spicy foods; he remembers that *he* didn't. It's just part of the content of John's genuine memory that this boy and John are one and the same. In contrast to that boy, fifty-five-year-old John *does* like spicy foods, and that's a difference between *y* and *m*, so how can they be one and the same thing? Our principle states a necessary condition for being numerically identical: failing to differ. This and that can't be identical *unless* they fail to differ. But the boy and the man in our thought experiment differ: the latter likes spicy foods, but the former does not. And of course there are *many* other differences between

---

[22] I am arguing that it can't be true that $a = b$ unless $\neg D(a,b)$. The latter is a necessary condition for the truth of the former. I take no position about whether $\neg D(a,b)$ implies $a = b$ (the Identity of Indiscernibles). This is a far more controversial thesis, and I don't see that we need any such principle.

[23] "Palmyra" and "Tadmur" are the Greek and the Aramaic names for the same city.

that boy and that man. Something has gone wrong! Our "timeless" principle seems to imply that nothing can change in even the smallest way. What look like changes would instead be replacements, if the timeless principle is true![24]

But no one with common sense, and least of all Christians, should deny the reality of change (1 Cor. 15:51–52). We know by experience that change is real. I was hungry before, but I'm not hungry now. I was over there, but now I'm over here. We *know* that change happens, so we know that one and the same thing *can* be different ways at different times; in that sense, typical changes are "survivable" and even imply the survival of the changed thing.[25]

We also know that a thing can't *at one time* differ from itself. The banana can't today both be and not be wholly yellow. You can't simultaneously be wholly in your chair, and also not at all in your chair since you're across the room. And it can't be that at one time you are thinking about pizza and at that same time you are not thinking about pizza. If someone told you, with a straight face, that right now she's thinking about pizza and also she's *not* thinking about pizza, you would be strongly inclined to interpret her charitably, as meaning that *now* she's thinking about pizza, but *now* (a moment later) she's not, or that she means in one sense she's now thinking about pizza but in another she's not. You would hardly consider the interpretation that she means that right now, *in the same sense*, she is and is not thinking about pizza. If after extensive questioning you determined that this is indeed what she meant, then you would take her to be suffering from some cognitive malfunction, so that she can't see the obvious, which is that if it's true that she's thinking of pizza now, then it is false that she's *not* thinking of pizza now, and

---

[24] Our standard idea of change is that at time 1 a thing is a certain way, and then at time 2 *that same thing* is not that way. Most or all changes, we think, presuppose that the changed thing exists through the change, existing both before and after it. (See the following footnote.) Suppose I tell you that I have a magical power of bending spoons with my mind. But unbeknown to you, I already have a bent spoon in my pocket. When you're distracted, by sleight of hand, I change spoons and then show you the bent one. (Now I'm hiding the unbent one in my pocket.) Obviously, I have not bent any spoon. To bend a spoon would be for one and the same spoon to first be unbent and then bent. I have only fooled you, via surreptitious substitution, into thinking that such a change occurred.

[25] Certain other changes—or apparent changes—are not survivable. If you throw a paper airplane into the fire, it will be destroyed by that fire. Coming into existence (creation or generation) and going out of existence (annihilation) are non-standard changes in that, with the former, the thing in question had no before state, while in the latter the thing has no after state—or perhaps generation and annihilation should not be thought of as kinds of changes.

if it's true that she's *not* thinking of pizza now, then it is false that she's thinking of pizza now. Which is it? It can't be both! Someone who is and is not thinking of pizza, at the same time and in the same way—things like this we firmly banish to the realm of fiction.

We know, then, that it is impossible for anything to ever differ from itself. When a statement like $a = b$ is true, that is just to say that a and b are numerically the same thing (one thing we're referring to in two different ways, using "a" and using "b"). But then, when it is true that $a = b$, it must also be true that $\neg D(a, b)$—that a and b don't in any way or to any degree differ, that *at that time* they're maximally similar. (*Of course* "they" are, since "they" are just one thing!)

Why are we now talking about impossibility? It would be simpler to set aside any concepts relating to what can or can't be and say that if $a = b$, then all of these must be false: a and b have differed, a and b differ, and a and b will differ. That covers all of the past, present, and future? Isn't that enough?

Interestingly, it is not! The mere possibility of a and b ever differing implies that they are not one and the same, that $a \neq b$. And a and b being one and the same implies the impossibility of their ever differing. Here's a thought experiment that may help you to see this. Suppose that God created a special pair of angels, Ned and Ted. The way he's made them, they're always doing and experiencing the same things at the same times. Let's stipulate that spirits like angels exist in space. Ned and Ted, then, exist at all the same places at the same times; they completely overlap when it comes to space and time. In fact, they are so alike that only God knows them to be two. Everyone else thinks that Ned and Ted are the same angel, whom God addresses using those two names. For reasons known only to himself, God has made Ned and Ted so that they in fact will never differ. But they could, in principle. God might have created one just before the other, or he might have decided that their lives should diverge after a million years, or he might have made them independent like other angels. That they could in principle differ implies that Ned ≠ Ted.

Again, imagine there's some sort of physical particle such that pairs of them naturally double up like Ted and Ned, occupying all the same places at the same times and not actually differing in any way. But for some reason, if such a pair is involved in a fire, the overlapping particles diverge. Imagine these pairs that seem like single particles are sprinkled through the natural world, including in the trunks of trees. Whether or not any given pair actually ever diverge depends, in part, on the free choices of humans, whether we end up here or there, whether or not we end up making a campfire or whatever out of the wood that includes them. Such a pair would not *become* two when they diverge; that they *can* diverge shows that they were two all along.[26]

We only need one more concept to better formulate the Indiscernibility of Identicals: the concept of a time. We all have and use this concept. A time might be a mere location on the timeline, an extensionless dividing point between earlier and later times, akin to a point on a geometric line. Or more commonly, a time is *any portion of* time: a second, a day, a year. We can even refer to all of the times up till now, or all of time from this moment ever after, or *all* of time—past, present, and future. We all think that (take your picks) claims are true, or situations obtain, or events happen, or things exist at various times, whether these are points, finite portions, infinite portions, or all of time. Thus we all understand what it means to say that some a and some b differ at a time.[27] Here then is the principle we've been looking for:

---

[26] Some will resist this, imagining that one thing might become two things. Certainly, we might have some whole (c) composed (let's keep it simple) of two parts—call them a and b, at time 1. At time 2 c is split, so that now a is over here and b is over there—they no longer compose c. This is not c becoming both a and b. Here is the proof. In this scenario, $a \neq b$, since a is over here and b is over there. But it's being suggested that also, $c = a$ and $c = b$—this is what it would be for c to survive as a and for c to survive as b. From $c = a$ it follows by the symmetry of = that $a = c$. Now we have $a = c$ and $c = b$. By the transitivity of = it follows that $a = b$. But this contradicts $a \neq b$ (which is required by, after the split, a being only over here while b is only over there). This is a proof that the initial suggestion, that c survives the split both as a and as b, implies a contradiction and so must be false.

[27] Some people think that claims can be true, situations can obtain, events can happen, or things can exist timelessly, not at any time at all. They say these things are "in eternity" or "outside of time" as if time were a location that something could be outside of. For instance, Catholic theologians hold that God exists timelessly (Ott, *Fundamentals*, 36–37). I'm inclined to think, because of my views on God and time, that it's not possible for anything, even God, to be timeless (Mullins, "Divine Timemaker"), and I believe it has been proven that Scripture provides no support for claims that God exists timelessly, and that Scripture straightforwardly portrays God acting in time and teaches that God has always existed, exists right now, and always will exist (Mullins, *End of the Timeless God*). But if the reader believes that it's possible for something to exist or to be true timelessly, he is free, whenever I mention differing at a time, to change it to differing at a time *or* at a quasi-time such as timeless eternity. In my principles below, simply redefine the predicate $T\_$ as meaning _ is a time *or* a quasi-time.

The Impossibility of Differing Identicals (IDI)

Logic	*Logic-English*	*English*
$\Box \forall x \forall y (x = y \supset \neg \Diamond \exists z (Tz \land D(x,y,z)))$	Necessarily, for any x and any y, if x just is y, then it's not possible that there is some z that is a time at which x and y differ.	It is a necessary truth that if this *just is* that, then it's not possible for this and that to ever differ.

When you understand this principle, you can see that it is as obviously true as the impossibility of an apple existing and not existing at the same time. That's the point—don't let the complexity of the formula fool you. This principle is logically equivalent to:

The Distinctness of Possible Differents (DPD)

Logic	*Logic-English*	*English*
$\Box \forall x \forall y (\Diamond \exists z (Tz \land D(x,y,z) \supset x \neq y))$	Necessarily, for any x and any y, if it's possible that there is a z such that z is a time at which x and y differ, then x is numerically distinct from y.	It is a necessary truth that, if this and that are such that it's possible that there's a time at which they qualitatively differ, then this and that are numerically distinct.

The modal concepts of metaphysical necessity ($\Box$) and possibility ($\Diamond$) are, in a sense, inter-definable. Some sentence P is necessarily true just in case it is not possible that $\neg P$. (In symbols, $\Box P \equiv \neg \Diamond \neg P$.) And a sentence P is possibly true just in case it is not necessary that $\neg P$ ($\Diamond P \equiv \neg \Box \neg P$). These statements of necessity and possibility are not relative to anyone's powers, even God's. What is necessary must exist or be true *no matter what*. And what is possible *may* be in the sense that it's not necessary that it's not.

In recent analytic philosophy it has become popular to explain these concepts in terms of "possible worlds." (In my view there are no such things,[28] but speaking this way helps people to grasp the relevant concepts.) We imagine that in addition to the actual past, present, and future, there are an infinity of non-actual, merely possible total histories of everything ("worlds"). We imagine that God surveyed this infinity and picked one total history ("world") to be the one actual one. The possible worlds he passed over remain merely possible.

[28] See footnote 74 on p. 307.

With these fictions in hand we can explain in another way the concepts of metaphysical necessity, possibility, impossibility, and contingency, as well as the idea of a truth or a thing being actual. The definitions have to do with how many possible worlds there are in which the statement is true or the thing exists. What is necessary exists or is true in *all* possible worlds. What is possible exists or is true in *at least one* possible world (whether the actual world or some other). What is actual exists or is true *in the actual world*, and so is by definition possible (since by being so in the actual world, it is so in *at least one* possible world). What is metaphysically impossible exists or is true in *no* possible world. What is contingent exists or is true *in the actual world*, but there is also *at least one* possible world where it is not. To help you to grasp these concepts, on the following page there is a chart with *mostly* uncontroversial examples.[29]

The top half of the table concerns things—let's consider them left to right. A necessary thing absolutely must exist; it's not possible that it should not exist. An impossible thing absolutely can't exist. What is actual exists and must therefore also be possible (the sort of thing which in principle can exist—not an impossible thing). Consistent with being actual, a thing might also be necessary, and of course a necessary thing therefore must be both possible and actual. A contingent thing is actual but not necessary. It must, as contingent and actual, be possible, but it is the sort of thing which, in principle, might not have existed. A merely possible thing (one which is neither necessary nor impossible nor actual nor contingent) does not in fact exist, though it could have existed. About truths (bottom half of the table), necessary truths absolutely must be true and can't be false. What I've here called "impossible truths" (usually called necessary falsehoods) absolutely must be false and can't be true. A necessary truth must also be an actual truth, but some actual truths are contingent and so not necessary. Finally, a merely possible truth in fact is not true, although it might have been.

While philosophers disagree about some of the things in the various boxes here, the five concepts at the top have been well-explored by analytic philosophers in about the last eighty years. The subject in metaphysics is called modality, and logicians have developed a number of modal logics, ones which include symbols like $\Box$ and $\Diamond$.

[29] I include numbers, sets, and universals in the category of necessarily existing things since many philosophers, logicians, and mathematicians believe in such things. But I am not convinced that we should believe in any abstract objects, and I'm inclined to think that God is the only necessarily existing thing. For arguments for this view see Craig, *God Over All*; *God and Abstract Objects*.

	Necessary (so, Actual & Possible)	**Impossible** (Necessary that not)	**Actual** (so, Possible)	**Contingent**[30] (so, Actual & Possible)	**Merely Possible**[31]
things	*God*	a square circle	you	you	the sibling you never had
	abstract objects such as numbers and sets	a man who is and is not human	God	the United States of America	your first great-great-great-grandchild
	universal qualities	an angel who created himself	the United States of America	any wholly physical object	Batman
truths	God exists.	There is no god.	The earth exists.	You exist.	There are unicorns.
	1 + 1 = 2.	There's a cube that's also a sphere.	There are human beings.	The American revolution happened.	Men landed on the moon in 1775.
	If a 2D polygon is a triangle, then it has 3 sides.	It is morally permissible to torture innocent babies just for fun.	The Allies won World War II.	There are physical objects.	The Axis won World War II.

We can add to the necessary truths our principles above, IDI and DPD (p. 267). We can add to the impossible things some *a* and *b* that are numerically identical yet differ (or just *could* differ) at some time, and the existence of a time at which numerically identical things (really: a thing and itself) differ.

[30] What is actual may also be necessary, but what is contingent is by definition not necessary, since it is possible that it is not.

[31] That is, metaphysically possible and not also any of: necessary, actual, contingent. What is *merely* possible, so to speak, only exists or is true in *other* possible worlds, and not in the actual world.

8.3.3 REASONING ABOUT IDENTITY, QUALITATIVE SAMENESS, AND QUALITATIVE DIFFERENCE

If you know that some *a* just is *b* ($a = b$), then by IDI (p. 267) you know that it's impossible that *a* and *b* should simultaneously differ, even in the slightest way. It follows that *a* and *b* never have differed, don't differ now, and will never differ. At any time at which *a* and *b* exist, "they" (really, it) will be maximally similar, lacking any qualitative difference. Thus, if *a* is objectively a certain way at time 1, it follows that *b* is that same way at time 1 (and vice-versa). In short, the numerical identity of *a* and *b* forces their maximal qualitative sameness (lack of any qualitative difference) at any time *a* and *b* exist.

Call this a "cost" of identifications. For example, if you identify Jesus with God, and you think that God is tripersonal, then you have already committed to Jesus being tripersonal. More generally, you've committed to thinking that however God objectively is at a time, Jesus must be that same way at that time. Strangely, it is common for Christian apologists to argue for the numerical identity of Jesus and God without realizing such costs.[32] For instance, after the start of Jesus's public ministry it was true that God sent his human Son to save the world. If Jesus = God, then it would also be true that Jesus sent *his* human Son to save the world. That would be big news, that Jesus had a human Son! These implausible similarities implied by identifying God with Jesus should prompt us to think twice about such identity claims.

Suppose that you know a bunch of things about God—that he is perfect in love, that he's the only creator, and that he is uncreated. You have, as it were, a mental file folder of data on God.[33] And based on your reading of the Old Testament, you know a bunch of things about Yahweh, and you have a mental file folder of information on him, including: he made amazing promises to Abraham, he sent the prophet Moses to bring a covenant law to his chosen people, and he is great in kindness and mercy. Since God = Yahweh (which implies Yahweh = God), you should simply combine those two mental files into one. Whatever you know about one, you also know about the other. Thus you know that *Yahweh* is perfect in love and is the uncreated creator, and you know that *God* made promises to Abraham, sent Moses with the Law, and is great in kindness and mercy. Again, you know that Jesus was born to Mary, and that

---

[32] Tuggy, "Apologetics Blind-Spot."

[33] I learned this helpful metaphor from Morris, *Understanding Identity Statements*, ch. 3. But I don't agree with his unique position on how to understand identity statements.

Jesus = the Christ. Therefore, the Christ was born to Mary. Jesus died on a cross. Therefore, the Christ died on a cross. The Christ was specially empowered by God. Therefore, Jesus was so empowered.

Suppose you find out that at some time *a* and *b* qualitatively differ (in any way and to any degree, whether significant or insignificant). By definition whatever *actually* is so is also *possibly* so.[34] By DPD (p. 267), you infer that $a \neq b$. This is how juries exonerate the accused. Suppose our evidence shows that the killer was in Salt Lake City, Utah, on May 12, 2024. But the accused was in New York City, and there only, for all of May 12, 2024. The jury reasons: The killer was in Salt Lake City on that date, but the accused was not in Salt Lake City on that date, so it is not the case that the killer and the accused are one and the same, that is, $k \neq a$. The killer and the accused, it seems, differed in that spatial property, *being-in-Salt-Lake-City-on-May-12-2024*. Therefore, they are two, not one and the same man. This is airtight reasoning; so long as they are correct about the locations of these two men on that date, they can't go wrong in their inference that they are two different men. Generally speaking, *dis*proving identity claims is easy; simply find a real or possible simultaneous difference between them, any sort of objective, non-mind-dependent difference. On the other hand, there is no simple way of *proving* identity. Finding qualitative similarities, even many important ones, is not enough to establish that this *just is* that.[35]

Even if we can't find any difference between *a* and *b,* it doesn't follow that $a = b$. Suppose that far away there are two stars, which are, on a cosmic scale, rather close together. On earth, you're out at night with your cheap telescope, and when you point it at these stars, you seem to see only one; the resolution of your equipment doesn't show the space between them. They appear to you as a single star that alternates between red and blue. In fact, one star is blue (only) and the other is red (only). But the constantly-changing atmospheric conditions let through one color, then the other, then the first again, in a cycle. Perhaps you've heard at your local astronomy club that some think that at this location in the night sky there are really two stars—call them Reddy and Bluey. But you set out to disprove this (true!) hypothesis of two close-together stars. You reason as follows:

[34] In the lingo of possible worlds, since one of the possible worlds is the actual world, whatever is so in the actual world is so in at least one possible world.

[35] See the Obama and Obana example on p. 292.

1. If Reddy and Bluey were one and the same, there would be no differences between them.
2. Using my trusty telescope, I can detect no differences between Reddy and Bluey. (To me it *seems* this is just one star, now called "Reddy" as it puts out red light, and then called "Bluey" while it is putting out blue light.)
3. Therefore, Reddy and Blue are one and the same.

But you've only proven yourself to be a poor astronomer. Just because you can't presently detect any differences between some *a* and some *b*, it doesn't follow that there are no differences between them. In this example Reddy is over here, and Bluey is over there; it's just that you're so far away, and your vision even with the telescope is so poor, that they appear to you to be in the same place. In this scenario both 1 and 2 are true. But it does not follow that 3 is true. Thus, the argument is invalid. The lesson is if you can't find or detect any difference between *a* and *b*, it doesn't follow that they're one and the same. But *dis*proving identity, as we've seen, is often very easy, as it requires finding only one actual (or even merely possible) difference.

Even though there's no simple procedure for knowing that $a = b$, often we know that this and that are numerically identical. A new reader of the Bible may not realize that Abram = Abraham, or that Saul = Paul, or that Cephas = Peter, but all of those, according to the texts in question, are true. With more reading and a better grasp of the whole story, she will eventually "see" the identities in question, reducing the number of characters she finds in those texts by collapsing together this character and that (such as Abram and Abraham). On the other hand, if she thought on first reading Matthew 11:7–14[36] that the prophet Elijah and John the Baptist are one and the same, presumably more careful reading would lead her to withdraw that mistaken inference. And if for some reason she thought that Peter and John were one and the same, after more study she should recognize the authors presupposing them to be two.[37] Finding this, she ought to change her mind about the texts' views on Peter and John, that they are supposed to be two, not one and the same.

A much-discussed recent example of a merely possible difference proving numerical distinctness (non-identity) concerns a statue and what that statue is made of or constituted by. Suppose you take fifty kilograms of pure gold and

---

[36] "As John's disciples were leaving, Jesus began to speak to the crowd about John … 'Truly I tell you, among those born of women there has not risen anyone greater than John the Baptist … if you are willing to accept it, he is the Elijah who was to come.'"

[37] Matt. 10:2, 17:1; Mark 5:37, 13:3; Luke 8:51, 22:8.

lovingly shape it into a realistic bust of the famous twentieth century theologian Karl Barth. Call the fifty-kilo lump of gold g and call the finished statue b. Is it true that $g = b$? It seems not; when you started your art project, g existed but b did not. That actual difference (existence at that time) proves that $g \neq b$. But let's consider a weirder but still possible scenario. Imagine that God created this statue (and so this lump of gold) at the moment he created the heavens and the earth and that they have existed ever since. In this scenario there has never been any observable difference between g and b. But even in this scenario we would still know that gold is malleable; someone could take a sledgehammer to this bust until it is flattened out like a large pancake. This would destroy the statue b (we would no longer have a bust of Karl Barth) but not g, the lump of gold which can have many shapes and needn't have any particular shape, so long as it remains a lump. So it seems possible that g exists while b does not. This mere possibility of simultaneous, objective difference proves that $g \neq b$.[38]

8.3.4 WHAT IS "RELATIVE" IDENTITY?

We've spoken so far about simply being numerically the same, or numerically one, or being numerically the same thing. But we often ask whether or not, say, Abram and Abraham are *the same man*, or whether the morning star and the evening star are *the same heavenly body*, or whether Zeus and Jupiter, in the view of some ancient person(s), are supposed to be *the same god*. One might think that for any kind of thing, call it K, there is a unique relation of *being the same K as*. Instead of just numerical sameness (*being-the-same-thing-as*), we would instead have an enormous number of sameness relations. For starters: *being-the-same-human-as*, *being-the-same-planet-as*, *being-the-same-god-as*, *being-the-same-ham-sandwich-as*, *being-the-same-tree-as*, and so on.

But a majority of recent philosophers have thought that this proliferation of sameness relations is unnecessary and wrongheaded. This is because it seems that we can analyze any statement of the form *a is the same K as b* as the

[38] As far as I know, all recent metaphysicians who believe in things like statues and lumps of gold accept this sort of argument as showing them to be numerically distinct. However, some philosophers point out some surprising implications of such spatio-temporally co-located things and so deny the existence of one or both of them. For instance, in our example, if g and b are real and numerically distinct, and each one of them weighs fifty kilograms, we would expect them together to weigh one hundred kilograms. But if we put them on a scale, the scale will read only fifty kilograms.

conjunction of three assertions: a is a K, b is a K, and $a = b$. In the book of Genesis, Abram and Abraham are the same man. The truth of that requires that Abram is a man, that Abraham is a man, and that Abram = Abraham. Those three claims, according to the book, are true. Again, in the Old Testament, Yahweh and El Shaddai (sometimes translated as "God Almighty") are supposed to be the same god.[39] There are fundamentally three ways this could fail to be true: if (1) Yahweh were not a god, (2) if El Shaddai were not a god, or (3) Yahweh and El Shaddai were numerically distinct ($y \neq e$). So too, it would be false that they're the same god if any two, or all three of those claims were false. But since according to the texts, Yahweh is a god, and El Shaddai is a god, and the one just is the other (so that that name and that title are normally co-referring), it is true that Yahweh and El Shaddai are the same god. Again, if a and b are different *K's*, this will be true only if (1) a is a K, (2) b is a K, and a ≠ b. If any one or more of those conditions fail, a and b will *not* be different *K's*.

Given these conceptual analyses, it will be impossible for any a and b whatever to be the same F but different *G's*, where F and G are different kind-terms. Why? If a and b are the same F, this implies that $a = b$, but if a and b are different *G's*, this implies that $a \neq b$. For example, it could not be true that Peter and Cephas are the same man but different apostles, or that Abram and Abraham are the same prophet but different husbands.

Desperate to find some way to show it to be possible for the Father and Son to be the same god while being different Persons, some trinitarians have urged that there is no contradiction in supposing some a and b to be the same F but different *G's*, but they've never been able to give any plausible non-theological examples of such things, and the clear conceptual analyses just discussed count against their claims. The Father and Son being the same god would imply Father = Son, and their being different Persons would imply Father ≠ Son. However, both of those implications cannot be true, since it is obviously impossible for any a and b to be both numerically identical and not. Any such claim is a necessary falsehood (column 2, p. 269). It follows that the Father and Son could not be the same god while being different divine Persons.[40]

---

39 The term is introduced in Gen. 17:1; notice there that it is supposed to co-refer with the name "Yahweh."

40 On relative-identity Trinity theories, see chapter 11 and my "Trinity," sec. 2.1.

8.3.5 LIKE FATHER, LIKE SON

Bible readers can't help but notice features that God and Jesus share: both are called in various places "Lord" and "God," both are objects of prayer and worship in the New Testament, and both are said to fulfill certain prophetic passages.[41] Indeed, as we've seen, they're *so* similar that Jesus says if you know him, you know what God is like.[42] Doesn't all of this reflect that for these authors, Jesus and God are one and the same?

Absolutely not. Remember, a and b can be similar in *billions* of ways, can even be hard for people to tell apart, and yet it can still be true that $a \neq b$, that they are distinct, not one and the same. We know a and b are distinct when a and b have ever objectively differed (or even just *could* differ) in but the smallest way. Do these authors think God and Jesus to have differed? They surely do. In their view God sent his unique Son, but we read nothing of Jesus sending his unique Son. In their view, Jesus died on the cross, but God has never died. In their view, Jesus is now exalted to God's right hand, but God is not exalted to his own right hand. Jesus is the mediator between God and all other humans, but God is not such a mediator. And Jesus himself tells us that God knew something that Jesus, at least at that time, did not know. So any Bible-reading Christian thinks there are many God-Jesus differences. Even the trinitarian must agree to this: God is tripersonal, yet Jesus is not tripersonal. It follows that God and Jesus are not one and the same ($g \neq j$).

Remember, identicals can't simultaneously differ in any objective way—as they're really one and the same thing. Thus, if God and Jesus were one and the same, it would be true that, being God, Jesus has sent Jesus's only Son into the world, and being Jesus, God himself died on the cross. And Jesus, being God, did, like God, know the day and the hour of his future return, contrary to his own clear assertion. And God, being Jesus, will have exalted himself to his own right hand (whatever that could mean!), and nonsensically God himself, since he just is Jesus, will be the mediator between himself and us.[43]

---

[41] See, for example, Phil. 2:10–11 and Is. 45:23. On the exegetical error I call the "fulfillment fallacy," see chapter 10.

[42] "Whoever has seen me has seen the Father" (John 14:9).

[43] This is nonsense because conceptually, if someone is mediating between two or more parties, he can't himself be one of the parties who need mediation. Of course, it is possible that a mediator be a member of a group that is one of the parties, and our mediator Jesus is a member of the human race. The New Testament never says, implies, or assumes that to perform his mediating function Jesus must also be a member of the group of divine Persons.

All of this is to say that numerically identifying God and Jesus makes nonsense out of the New Testament. No Christian, whether trinitarian or unitarian, should want these to be true: $g = j$, $j = g$. Indeed, trinitarians who have a firm grip on the logic of identity *deny* that claim; they understand "Jesus is God" to mean not $j = g$ but rather that Jesus has divinity as an essential quality.[44]

8.3.6 "ONLY GOD" ARGUMENTS COLLAPSE TOGETHER JESUS AND GOD

That disastrous collapsing together of the two main characters of the New Testament must be avoided. Yet carelessly made trinitarian arguments often have this identity claim as their conclusion; these are what I call "only God" arguments. For instance, inspired by some of Jesus's critics (!) in Mark 2, many trinitarian apologists argue like this:

1. Only God can forgive sins.
2. Jesus can forgive sins.
3. Therefore, Jesus is God.[45]

Many a trinitarian offers arguments of this form (you can replace "can forgive sins" with: "can answer prayer," "should receive worship,"[46] or "can truly be called 'God' ").[47] Unfortunately they don't understand the unintended strength of the conclusion 3. This last step *must* be an identity claim; it's not merely attributing divinity or a divine nature to Jesus, or saying that Jesus is somehow within God, that he is a divine Person in God, or that he "belongs to the divine identity," whatever that may mean. To see this, we need to reveal the underlying structure of premise 1, using the tools we learned in section 8.2.

English	*Logic*	*Logic-English*
1. Only God can forgive sins.	1. $\forall x\, (Fx \supset x = g)$	1. For any x, x can forgive sins only if x just is God.
2. Jesus can forgive sins.	2. Fj	2. Jesus can forgive sins.
3. Therefore, Jesus is God.	3. $j = g$	3. Therefore, Jesus just is God.

Notice that premise 1 is a conditional statement. *If* anything whatever triggers the antecedent, the "if" part, by being able to forgive, *then* it logically follows

[44] This is the position of all three of my trinitarian opponents in McIntosh, *One God*.
[45] James Anderson seems to ascribe this argument to the author of Mark (*Why Should*, 181).
[46] Bowman Jr. and Komoszewski, *Incarnate Christ*, 121.
[47] *Incarnate Christ*, 466–67.

that the thing in question is numerically identical with God himself ($= g$). In this argument Jesus is the trigger (premise 2), and thus by 1 and 2, it follows that Jesus *just is* God. Since the numerical identity relation is symmetric, it follows that God = Jesus. And since identity requires there to be no objective differences, whatever is objectively true of one will be true of the other as well—a christological and theological disaster.

The unitarian in all these cases has an easy, Scripture-motivated reply: premise 1 is false. God can, according to Scripture, authorize a human being to forgive sins (Matt. 9:1–8, John 20:23), empower a man to hear and answer prayers,[48] make it appropriate for us to worship a man in a way that gives glory to God (Rev. 5; Phil. 2:9–11; Matt. 28:9, 17),[49] and inspire writings in which Jesus is called "God."[50] It is easy for the unitarian Christian to provide scriptural grounds for thinking that "only God" arguments are all unsound, as each has a false first premise.

Trinitarians should abandon all such only God arguments; not only are they unsound, but if they were to be sound, the doctrine of the Trinity would be false. How? According to any Trinity doctrine Jesus is not tripersonal but is instead a single divine Person. Add to such a doctrine that Jesus and God are one and the same, and it follows that God too is a single divine Person. But trinitarians deny exactly that. Before we move on, here is an argument showing that any Trinity theory plus Jesus = God implies a contradiction.

English	*Logic*	*Justification*
1. God is tripersonal.	1. Tg	Core thesis of any trinitarian theology.
2. Jesus is not tripersonal.	2. $\neg Tj$	Implied by any trinitarian theology; God the Trinity is tripersonal, but no individual divine Person is tripersonal.
3. Jesus is God.	3. $j = g$	The conclusion of one or more "only God" arguments.
4. God is not tripersonal.	4. $\neg Tg$	Follows from 2 and 3 by IDI (p. 267).

Notice that 1 are 4 are of the form $P \wedge \neg P$ (*P and not-P*). That is the point. Any contradiction is false, and any conjunction of claims that imply a contradiction is false. Anyone seeking a Trinity doctrine that doesn't refute itself in this way must deny 3 and refrain from making any arguments that imply 3.

---

[48] Rom. 10:9–13; John 14:13–14; Acts 7:59, 9:5; 1 Cor. 16:22; 2 Cor. 12:8; Rev. 22:20. See also Wierwille, "Can We 'Pray' to Jesus."

[49] See also my "Who Should Christians Worship"; "Podcast 227."

[50] Sections 1.4–5.

8.4 SIXTEEN PRINCIPLES ABOUT NUMERICAL AND QUALITATIVE SAMENESS

Let's pause to review what we've learned. Here is a chart listing the principles we surveyed, with a sample theological or christological application or two in the right-hand column.

General Principle	A Sample Theological or Christological Application
Principle # 1 Qualitative vs. Numerical Sameness/Identity: Qualitative sameness is one relation and numerical sameness is another.	Even though Son and Father are so similar that if you've seen the Son you've seen the Father (John 14:9), it is a further question whether they are numerically one or two.
Principle #2 One to One: Numerical identity is a one-to-one relation.	It is confused to think that God could be numerically one with this: the Father plus the Son. Or this: the Father plus the Son plus the Spirit.
Principle #3 Necessary Reflexivity: Numerical identity is a relation that can obtain only between a thing and itself (never between one thing and another.)	The Father = the Father, and the Son = the Son, but since the Father is one person and the Son is another, it is false that Father = Son.
Principle #4 Symmetry: Numerical identity is symmetric; if $a = b$ then $b = a$.[51]	If the Son = God, then God = the Son. If the God = the Trinity, then the Trinity = God. If God = the Father, then the Father = God.
Principle #5 Transitivity: Numerical identity is transitive. If $a = b$ and $b = c$, then $a = c$.	If the Father = God, and God = the Son, then the Father = the Son. If Jesus = the Son of God, and the Son of God = the Christ, then Jesus = the Christ.

[51] Sometimes scholars who are not trained in logic will express an assertion of numerical identity (of the form $a = b$) as "All of *a* is all of *b*" (White, *Forgotten Trinity*, 49). And sometimes they will recognize the symmetry of = by noting that if "*a* is *b*" in this sense it will also be true that "*b* is *a*."

Principle #6 Things Identical with the Same Thing Are Identical with One Another. If $a = b$, and $c = b$, then $a = c$.	If the Father = God and the Son = God, then the Father = the Son. If the Father = the Creator, and the Son = the Creator, then the Father = the Son.
Principle #7 Co-referring Terms: Whenever some identity statement $a = b$ is true, "a" and "b" are co-referring terms—that is, two ways we can refer to the same thing.[52]	Since God = the Father, "God" and "the Father" are (normally) co-referring terms. Since Jesus = Christ, "Jesus" and "Christ" are (normally) co-referring.
Principle #8 Change Is Real: Some things are one way at an earlier time and a different way at a later time. Thus if some a is F at time 1 and some b is not F at time 2, it does *not* follow that $a \neq b$.	Suppose that now the risen and exalted Jesus *does* know the day and hour of his future return. It wouldn't follow that he is not the man who once said[53] that he did not know those things.
Principle #9 Consistency of Reality: It is impossible for anything to simultaneously and objectively be and not be some way (or to have and simultaneously lack the same objective quality or property).	None of these are true: Today Jesus knows and does not know the hour of his future return. God now exists; also, now God doesn't exist. God is a Trinity and God is not a Trinity.
Principle #10 No Real Contradictions: There are no real things such that one or more contradictory statements (of the form $P \wedge \neg P$) are simultaneously true of them.	This Jesus is not real: a man who died on the cross but who did not die on the cross (because as divine, he is essentially immortal). This God is not real: he is one, but he is not one (because he is three).

[52] Notice the difference in subject matter: $a = b$ is about a and about b (which are really the same thing)—*not* about words or terms. But to say that "a" and "b" are co-referring terms is a point about *the terms* "a" and "b." For example, Jesus = the Son of God is a point about our human Lord. But to say that "Jesus" and "the Son of God" are co-referring terms is to make a point about those words. It is necessary to point this out because sometimes even philosophers confuse the two, for instance, thinking that the claim $a = b$ is directly about the term "a" and the term "b."

[53] Matt. 24:36, Mark 13:32.

Principle #11 The Impossibility of Differing Identicals (IDI): Necessarily, if $a = b$, then it's not possible for a and b to simultaneously differ.	If God were tripersonal, and Jesus were numerically one with God, then Jesus would also be tripersonal. If the Father were the Trinity, then the Father would be tripersonal.
Principle #12 The Distinctness of Possible Differents (DPD): If it's possible that a and b should simultaneously differ, then a and b are numerically distinct.	It is possible that at a certain time Jesus is praying to God but God is not praying to God. Therefore, Jesus and God are numerically distinct (not numerically identical).
Principle #13 Similar Doesn't Imply Identical: We can't know that $a = b$ simply by finding many similarities between a and b.	We know that both God and Jesus love us and that both have done amazing things to bring about a new covenant between God and humans. But it doesn't follow that God = Jesus or that Jesus = God.
Principle #14 If Same Thing of Some Kind, Then Same Thing: Being the same thing of some sort implies being numerically the same (identical). (If a and b are the same F, then $a = b$.)	If Jesus and the Father are the same god, then Jesus = the Father. If Jesus and the Son of God are the same person, then Jesus = the Son of God. If Paul and Saul are the same man, then Paul = Saul.
Principle #15 If Different Things of a Kind, Then Different Things: Being different things of some sort implies being numerically distinct (non-identical). (If a and b are different F's, then $a \neq b$.)	If the Father and the Son are different divine Persons, then Father ≠ Son. If the Logos and Jesus are different natures, then the Logos ≠ Jesus.
Principle #16 Identity Not Kind-Relative: It's impossible to be the same F (thing of a certain kind) while being different G's (numerically distinct things of some other kind).	It's impossible for the Father and Son to be the same god while being different divine Persons. It's impossible that Abram and Abraham are the same prophet while being different husbands.

8.4.1 LOGIC IS SUBJECT-NEUTRAL

Deductive logic has to do with the meanings of sentences and with what implies what. Whether or not a deductive argument is valid is wholly a matter of its structure. The subject matter of an argument is not relevant to whether or not it has that right kind of structure. Since ancient times logicians have taught us to recognize certain schemas for valid arguments; you might think of them as recipes for creating valid arguments. The point of these is that they reveal certain patterns that always form valid arguments, no matter what assertion-making sentences you replace the letters with. Since the nineteenth century, the simple arguments in the chart below have been among the standard examples.[54] The capital letters here represent whole, claim-asserting, indicative sentences, such as "The sky is blue," "God exists," "The weather in England is great," "There are an odd number of roughly head-sized rocks on the surface of Mars," or "Jesus died for our sins."

1. P 2. Q 3. $P \wedge Q$	1. P *or* Q 2. $\neg P$ 3. Q
1. $P \supset Q$ 2. P 3. Q	1. $P \supset Q$ 2. $\neg Q$ 3. $\neg P$
1. $P \equiv Q$ 2. P 3. Q	1. $P \equiv Q$ 2. $\neg P$ 3. $\neg Q$

In each case 1 and 2 are premises and 3 is the argument's conclusion. Take the first schema (upper left), and substitute for P "Believers in Christ will be raised from the dead" and substitute for Q "Believers in Christ will be made immortal." *If* each of those claims are true, *then* $P \wedge Q$ must be true as well, that "Believers in Christ will be raised from the dead and believers in Christ will be made immortal."

The reader should pause here and try substituting her own sentences for P and for Q in the above schemas. The replacement sentences may be on any

[54] These are not all the valid argument forms; there is no finite number of those! In earlier times most logicians' examples would have been of Aristotelian categorical syllogisms such as: All *As* are *Bs*, All *Bs* are *Cs*, therefore, All *As* are *Cs*. Or: No *A* is a *B*. Every *C* is an *A*. Therefore, No *C* is a *B*. In analyses of categorical syllogisms the capital letters stand not for sentences or predicates or features but rather for groups or classes of things.

topic—the subject needn't be theology or Christology. In each case, the result will be a valid argument, one in which 1 together with 2 logically imply 3. (Of course, depending on which sentences you pick, it may or may not be true that both 1 and 2 are true.) Logically valid arguments like these will be logically valid whether the subject is basket weaving, history, biology, or theology; when you understand the meaning of 1 and 2, and you see that *if* they're both true, *then* so is 3.

Is this "subjecting God to human logic"? No. All of this has nothing at all to do with pride, unbelief, doubt, demanding that God conform to our expectations, or refusing to believe what we can't explain or what we can't fully understand. The point is simply that all human statements are within the subject matter of logic, even when we're speaking about the Almighty. And the logical analyses we've been looking at don't only apply to human statements; they apply just as well to God's own statements, even to statements about himself.

Through the prophet Moses God said to his chosen people, "I want you to refrain from idol worship" (Exod. 20:4–5). He also told them, "I want you to refrain from working on the first day of the week" (Exod. 20:8–11). The ancient Israelites could and surely did reason, validly, as follows:

1. God wants us to refrain from idol worship.
2. God wants us to refrain from working on the Sabbath.
3. Therefore, God wants us to refrain from idol worship *and* God wants us to refrain from working on the Sabbath.

There are implication relations between declarative sentences. Logic helps us to understand these in a systematic way. Those who denigrate logic show thereby that they are disinterested in and/or hostile to clear thinking, often because they want the unthinking obedience of those subject to their control. Those who love truth love logic, which helps us to go from truth to truth.

The same subject neutrality holds for more complex schemas like the arguments we looked at before, expressed in predicate logic with either universal quantification $(\forall)$ or existential quantification $(\exists)$. Here are two schemas that you can easily recognize as valid:

1. $\forall x\,(Fx \supset Gx)$ 2. Fa 3. Ga	1. $\neg\exists x\,(Fx \wedge Gx)$ 2. Fa 3. $\neg Ga$

Here's an argument with the same structure as the left-hand one at the bottom of the previous page:

1. For any x, if x is a man then x is a human being. (More simply: any man is a human being.)
2. Joe is a man.
3. Joe is a human being.

And here's an argument with the right-hand structure.

1. It's not the case that there is some x such that x is smart and x is a pug dog. (More simply: There are no smart pugs.)
2. Petunia is a pug dog.
3. Petunia is not smart.

You can replace the predicates (*F_*, *G_*) with whatever you want and the individual name *a* with whatever you want. As long as the same replacements were used through the whole argument, you'll have constructed a valid argument. Whether the resulting arguments are also sound is another question; my most recent example would start a fight among certain dog owners. The point is that, as with our simpler examples above, the analyses will be the same whether our subject is emperors, fried chicken dinners, geometry, or God.

Even though, as we saw, the standard analyses of "only" statements use the symbol =, and merely understanding a sentence like $\exists x\ (Fx \land Gx)$ requires understanding the concept of numerical identity (since it implies that at least one thing that is *F just is* a thing that is *G*), some logicians deny that the concept of numerical identical is part of logic.[55] They would say that the concepts of qualitative and numerical identity, as well as the modal concepts we explored in section 8.3.2 (necessity and possibility, etc.), are not within the subject of logic but rather the field of metaphysics, the fundamental branch of philosophy that deals with what is (as opposed to how things appear) and with what fundamental sorts of realities there are.

I don't see why such boundary disputes are important. In this chapter I have focused on concepts that we all possess and truths that ordinary adults can know. The common sense God has blessed you with includes both logical and metaphysical truths, and in thinking about God and his Son you should employ all the tools at your disposal. There is no reason to think that the principles we've explored in this section pertain only to the created realm, and someone who

[55] Beall, *Divine Contradiction*, 43–52.

suggests that is most likely engaging in special pleading in the attempt to prevent critical thinking about their own incoherent speculations. Using these principles when thinking about God and his Son is not "putting God in a box." Nothing here presupposes that we can fully understand, comprehend, or explain God, or that God is a creature or finite. The only assumptions we're making in deploying the above principles is that (1) we can refer to God and to God's Son using singular referring terms such as "God" and "Yahweh" and "Jesus" and "the Son," and (2) we can apply some of our concepts (and so, some of our predicates that express those concepts) to God and to his Son.[56] For instance, our concept *Messiah* applies to Jesus, and our concept *god* applies to God. God can be as transcendent ("beyond us") as you please—that won't exempt our thinking, writing, and speaking about him from the sixteen principles in section 8.4.

8.4.2 OBJECTIONS AND REPLIES

Objection: "But why didn't I ever learn these things in seminary, or in reading the works of theologians and biblical scholars?"

Reply: Because seminaries are deficient when it comes to teaching logic, critical thinking, and basic principles of metaphysics. Many theologians and biblical scholars are confused about the truths we've been exploring in this chapter. And recently, some leading scholars who are unable to think clearly about the concept of numerical identity have made a mess of all talk of "identity" when it comes to God and his Son, and their students and readers inherit the same confusions.[57] Some theologians have been trained in theological movements influenced by branches of philosophy that don't value clarity of expression and well-constructed arguments, such as recent continental philosophy, post-modernism, and Neoplatonism. Some wings of theology habitually denigrate "human reason" so as to protect their own outrageous claims—claims to which there are obvious objections. But there is a whole book in the Bible extolling wisdom, human and divine (Proverbs), and in following Jesus we must love God with our minds (Matt. 22:37, Mark 12:30, Luke 10:27). We can and must do better than recent theologians and biblical scholars have done when it comes to understanding identity claims and evaluating arguments employing such claims.

---

[56] This is true even if, as some have thought, human predicates apply to God only in a special, "analogical" sense. But against that implausible claim see Williams, "Doctrine of Univocity."

[57] Section 9.4.

Objection: "You sneaky snake! You've concocted a philosophy of qualitative and numerical sameness custom-tailored to support unitarian theology and to refute trinitarian theology."

Reply: No, I have not. Principles 1–16 in section 8.4 are truths I learned by studying and teaching logic and metaphysics. They are widely accepted by people trained in analytic philosophy, including trinitarian Christians. I first encountered principles 1–6 and 10 and versions of 11 and 12 in a course at the evangelical Biola University taught by the presumably trinitarian professor J. P. Moreland.[58] Were I to change my mind and become trinitarian again, I wouldn't change my mind about any of 1–16. Further, some carefully constructed Trinity theories are consistent with all of them.[59] Given that, it is silly to imagine that the sixteen principles are some sort of unitarian Trojan horse designed to defeat any trinitarian theology. They are what they seem when applied to other subjects: helpful and rather obvious general truths. But yes, clear, sober thinking when it comes to qualitative and numerical identity does narrow one's range of options when it comes to Trinity theories.

Objection: "But why should I think those principles are true?"

Reply: Good question! We know principles 1–7 simply by understanding the concepts in question: qualitative similarity, numerical identity (being the same thing as), and linguistic reference to some item in reality.

We know 8 by experience, especially of ourselves. In my view 9 is self-evident to humans, what Alvin Plantinga calls "properly basic" (something we know but not on the basis of other things we know)[60] because the capacity and propensity to have this intuition are built into our minds; this is how every elementary school child knows that you're joking when you say that you have a cat that *is* and at the same time *is not* striped all over. Whenever you ponder the existence

---

[58] He is the co-author of Moreland and Craig, *Philosophical Foundations*, but I understand that Craig and not Moreland authored the Trinity chapter. Moreland is also the author of an excellent introduction to logic and critical thinking for Christians (*Love Your God*). I also recommend Craig's book on logic for children (*Learning Logic*).

[59] Tuggy, "Trinity," secs. 1.5, 2.3–6, 3.1, 3.4, 4.1–2.

[60] Plantinga, *Warranted Christian Belief*, 175–80; *Warrant*, 183–85; *Knowledge*, 35–37. Just because a belief is properly basic to humans, it doesn't follow that all humans have that belief. For one thing, babies and perhaps some mentally handicapped humans will lack it. For another, people can suppress and even lose these intuitions when they are driven to defend some theory incompatible with them. When it comes to Principles 9 and 10, one analytic theologian has recently denied both in order to defend his version of catholic Incarnation and Trinity theories, according to which there are true contradictions (Beall, *Contradictory Christ*; Beall, *Divine Contradiction*).

of something the description of which is contradictory, such as a figure that is and isn't a triangle, it strongly seems to you that there can be no such thing. You don't feel obligated to go looking to see whether or not there actually are any such things.

Principles 10 and 11 follow from 9, and 12 follows from 11. We know 13 from the experiences we have of things that are similar in many ways yet are two, such as this golf ball and that golf ball, taken from the same pack.

We know 14 and 15 by understanding that statements of the form "*a* and *b* are the same *F*" are really conjunctions of three claims, namely: *a* is an *F*, and *b* is an *F*, and $a = b$. Principle 16 follows from the conjunction of 14 and 15.

All in all, our sixteen principles seem understandable and knowable by the typical human adult of sound mind. It is true that some philosophers have denied some of them because they clash with a pet theory—even principle 8 (p. 279). But it doesn't follow from such denials that the rest of us don't know principles 1–16. I do, and I hope that after adequate reflection you do as well.

8.5 CONCLUSION

From the beginning Christian theologians have made use of the intellectual tools available to them, in particular, the tools of logic.[61] Why shouldn't they, since they are concerned with separating the true from the false? We must think, and we ought to think as well as we can. Logic sharpens our understanding both of individual sentences and of the arguments built from them. Neither logic nor philosophy generally are infected with pagan germs, so that a believer is sullied by any contact with them. They are just useful human fields of study that the disciple can use as she loves God with all her mind. And as we'll see in chapter 9, they can even help us to think clearly as we interpret the New Testament.

---

[61] As Thomas Gaston points out, this applies even to ancient biblical unitarians (Dynamic Monarchians) (*Dynamic Monarchianism*, 73–77).

CHAPTER 9

The One God and His Son: the Logic of the New Testament

9.1 DOES JESUS IN JOHN 10 IMPLY THAT HE IS GOD HIMSELF?

With the tools of chapter 8 in hand, having gained some hard-won clarity about numerical identity and similarity, we are now equipped to carefully reexamine various New Testament passages that have been claimed to imply or assume the numerical identity of Jesus and God. Many readers have thought that Jesus claimed to be God himself in this famous passage in the Fourth Gospel.

> At that time the festival of the Dedication took place in Jerusalem. It was winter, and Jesus was walking in the temple, in the portico of Solomon. So the Jews gathered around him and said to him, "How long will you keep us in suspense? If you are the Messiah, tell us plainly."
>
> Jesus answered, "I have told you, and you do not believe. The works that I do in my Father's name testify to me; but you do not believe, because you do not belong to my sheep. My sheep hear my voice. I know them, and they follow me. I give them eternal life, and they will never perish. No one will snatch them out of my hand. What my Father has given me is greater than all else, and no one can snatch it out of the Father's hand. The Father and I are one." The Jews took up stones again to stone him. Jesus replied, "I have shown you many good works from the Father. For which of these are you going to stone me?"
>
> The Jews answered, "It is not for a good work that we are going to stone you, but for blasphemy, because you, though only a human being, are making yourself God."
>
> Jesus answered, "Is it not written in your law, 'I said, you are gods'? If those to whom the word of God came were called 'gods'—and the scripture cannot be annulled—can you say that the one whom the Father has sanctified and sent into the world is blaspheming because I said, 'I am God's Son'? If I am not doing

> the works of my Father, then do not believe me. But if I do them, even though you do not believe me, believe the works, so that you may know and understand that the Father is in me and I am in the Father." Then they tried to arrest him again, but he escaped from their hands. (John 10:22–39)

His opponents say they want to stone him for blasphemy because, in their view (this translation says) he is "making himself God." Many understand their complaint here to be that Jesus is identifying himself with God. Seeing the sudden vehemence of his opponents' response here, they argue, "See? *They* understood his radical claim to be God."

But as we've seen in chapter 8, this would be to claim by clear implication that he and God could never differ in the slightest way. It is *very* unlikely that Jesus's opponents thought he was collapsing together God and himself. Notice the beginning of the conversation: they demand to know whether he's claiming to be God's Messiah, meaning a man called, sent, and empowered for a special mission by God. And he's just claimed to be doing amazing things "in my Father's name," that is, by the authority of someone else. Do Jesus's enemies here think he's claiming to have sent *himself*, and to be acting in *his own* name? No, a messiah is by definition someone other than the god whose anointed one he is. A claim of numerical identity with God, by a would-be messiah, would be perceived as the statement of an insane person. But there's no reason to think that his opponents here thought Jesus to be insane, and their anger suggests that they did not think that. The better translation seems to be "make yourself a god."[1] Jesus's opponents would have been familiar with pagans claiming that their dead emperors had become deities. When Jesus said "The Father and I are one"—that is, the same in some way—they thought Jesus was claiming likeness to God in the form of some degree or kind of divinity, in their view a blasphemous claim. But *was* Jesus claiming that? I think the author is very clear about what conclusions the reader is and is not to draw from this passage.

We must not ignore Jesus's brilliant and forceful argument in reply to their accusation of blasphemy.[2] He argues that if lesser people than him may be called

---

[1] This translation choice is made by the trinitarian New English Bible and by the unitarian Revised English Version. I believe that most translations here reflect the trinitarian's desire for Jesus to be saying something that sounds like what a trinitarian would say.

[2] The common trinitarian misreading of this passage also ignores that all through the middle of this Gospel, "the Jews" (the Jewish leaders who publicly opposed Jesus) are presented as spiritually blind people who foolishly misunderstand Jesus's teachings. For an in-depth exploration of this theme, see Dustin Smith's *The Biblical Unitarian Podcast*, "Podcast 204" and following episodes through 222.

"gods," then it can't be blasphemous for the greater Jesus to accept the lesser title "Son of God." I would paraphrase his argument as follows.[3]

> As you (my opponents) understand Scripture, human recipients of God's word may, without disrespect to God, be called "gods." But I, God's specially commissioned agent, am greater than such people. The title "god" is a higher title than "God's Son." Therefore, it is not disrespectful to God for me to be called "God's Son."

With the first statement Jesus shrewdly argues from an assumption of his opponents.[4] The second sentence is a clear implication of many New Testament texts.[5] The third is true by definition; it is so obvious that Jesus feels no need to state it. Still, one may argue for it. "King" is a loftier title than "Prince," and "Champion" is a loftier title than "friend of a Champion." Likewise, a god is a mighty being, but a *son of* a god is someone else somehow related to such a mighty being, and somehow subordinate to him, as a human son is to his father. The first two sentences imply that there would be nothing wrong with applying the title "god" to Jesus. But Jesus corrects their understanding; he's claiming to be God's *Son.*

We must not lose sight of the whole conversation. Jesus's opponents demand a plain statement from him that he's the Messiah (a.k.a. "Son of God"), but Jesus insists that he's already made it plain by his actions. They are blind to this evidence, not having been called by God and given as followers to Jesus (v. 29). He ends with the provocative "I and the Father are one," which sets them off, but the more reasonable reader can see that in the context he's asserting that they are one in purpose and mission, unified in action, in saving and preserving the "the sheep." This is a clear theme later in the book.

---

[3] For a more complete analysis see my "Jesus's Argument."

[4] He refers here to Psalm 82:6: "I say, 'You are gods, children of the Most High, all of you; nevertheless, you shall die like mortals, and fall like any prince.'" As understood by many of Jesus's contemporaries, the "gods" here are certain human beings. In my view, following many recent commentators, they were mistaken in this; see pp. 303–4. Yet the point is correct that in New Testament times, there was an established use of *theos* for certain humans (section 1.5). In another famous text, God says to Moses, "See, I have made thee a god to Pharaoh" (Exod. 7:1, KJV). Most modern translations correctly capture the meaning by translating this as something like, "See, I have made you like God to Pharaoh" (NRSVUE). In Psalm 45:6–7, quoted in Hebrews 1:8–9 in reference to Jesus, an ancient king is addressed as "God," at least if most translations are correct (section 1.4.5).

[5] In the New Testament no angel or mere prophet should be worshiped, but the exalted Jesus should be (Heb. 1:6, Rev. 5), and only Jesus will serve as God's judge of humankind (Rom. 2:16, Acts 10:42, 1 Cor. 6:2).

> Philip said to him, "Lord, show us the Father, and we will be satisfied."
>
> Jesus said to him, "Have I been with you all this time, Philip, and you still do not know me? Whoever has seen me has seen the Father. How can you say, 'Show us the Father'? Do you not believe that I am in the Father and the Father is in me? The words that I say to you I do not speak on my own, but *the Father who dwells in me does his works*. Believe me that *I am in the Father and the Father is in me*, but if you do not, then believe because of *the works* themselves. Very truly, I tell you, the one who believes in me *will also do the works that I do* and, in fact, will do greater works than these, because I am going to the Father . . . I will not leave you orphaned; I am coming to you. In a little while the world will no longer see me, but you will see me; because I live, you also will live. On that day you will know that I am in my Father, and you in me, and I in you. They who have my commandments and keep them are those who love me, and those who love me will be loved by my Father, and I will love them and reveal myself to them."
>
> Judas (not Iscariot) said to him, "Lord, how is it that you will reveal yourself to us and not to the world?"
>
> Jesus answered him, "Those who love me will keep my word, and my Father will love them, and *we will come to them and make our home with them*. Whoever does not love me does not *keep my words*, and the word that you hear is not mine but is from the Father who sent me. (John 14:8–13, 18–24, emphases added)

Here Jesus says that he and God are "in" each other, living and acting together,[6] and that similarly God will be "in" Jesus's followers, doing even greater things through them, and that God and Jesus will dwell within the obedient disciple. All of this presupposes that Jesus and God are numerically distinct. For Jesus and God to be cooperating, working "in" each other, they must be two actors.

Returning to our text, Jesus has shown that he's *nowhere near* a sin of blasphemy, and his enemies must agree on the basis of their own principles, *if* they will admit that he is the Messiah. Even if they deny that he's the Messiah, if they will only admit that he's a prophet, they must, on their own principles, allow that he might be called "a god" without committing blasphemy. He has roundly defeated them while reasserting his claim to be the Messiah (God's Son) and correcting their misunderstanding that he was claiming to be either God himself or some sort of lesser god.

---

[6] In the text Jesus mentions God acting through him. Elsewhere he mentions himself acting, we could say, through or in God: "Very truly, I tell you, the Son can do nothing on his own but only what he sees the Father doing, for whatever the Father does, the Son does likewise" (John 5:19).

After correcting them about which title he is claiming, he turns to the theme of evidence. They should believe in him because of what he does. To paraphrase: "Don't trust what I'm saying; trust what I've done."[7] They have not just his own testimony but weighty evidence consisting of public miracles—for example, the healing described in John 9. Jesus and God are "in" each other, that is, working together.[8] But as the passage ends, it is clear that Jesus's opponents are not going to be moved by that evidence. They reject his claim to be Messiah and seek to arrest him.

To focus on his opponents' allegation that he's "making himself God" is to cherry-pick an isolated statement that at first glance supports the confusion that Jesus is God himself. But the passage in its entirety doesn't support that claim and implicitly refutes it, as it portrays Jesus and God as differing in multiple ways, such as anointer and anointee, God and his Messiah, initiator and cooperator, the unique god and the son of that god—and even the smallest difference implies them to be two.

Although a number of other passages in this book are commonly misread as implying that Jesus and God are numerically one, we must deploy two anchors when interpreting the Gospel of John. One is its clear thesis statement, which seems to be part of the book's original ending, where the author highlights his main point, "that Jesus is the Messiah, the Son of God" (John 20:31).[9] From the title alone it is clear that the *Son of* God is not God himself but someone else, someone closely related to God; no father is his own son. This point is reinforced by his equivalent title, "Messiah," or "Christ," which means "anointed one." Anointed by whom? Not by himself but by God. That clear thesis statement is one anchor. Another anchor is the self-evident truth that any difference implies distinctness, together with the many God-Jesus differences presupposed in this Gospel.[10]

---

[7] "The works that I do in my Father's name testify to me" (John 10:25). Compare: "If I testify about myself, my testimony is not true. There is another who testifies on my behalf, and I know that his testimony to me is true . . . I have a testimony greater than John's. The works that the Father has given me to complete, the very works that I am doing, testify on my behalf that the Father has sent me. And the Father who sent me has himself testified on my behalf" (John 5:31–37). Notice that these statements assume that God is someone and Jesus is someone else.

[8] See the passage quoted on p. 290 and John 10:38, 17:21.

[9] Notice that the author here uses "the Messiah" and "the Son of God" in apposition, as two ways to refer to the same one.

[10] We'll return again to this text in section 9.2.2, where we'll see some recent authors misreading this text in order to support their misreading of John 17:1–3.

I suspect that many laypeople identify Jesus and God simply because a few passages call Jesus "God." Here's a non-theological example to help us to see where their reasoning goes wrong. Imagine that in addition to former president Barack Obama, there's a very similar man named Barry Obana, the mayor of a small town. Both have been chief executives of a political entity, both are married, both have two daughters, and both are black Americans with one Caucasian parent. Because of these similarities, Barry Obana's friends teasingly call him "Barack Obama." Suppose that, hearing this teasing, someone argued,

1. Barack Obama is called "Barack Obama."
2. Barry Obana is called "Barack Obama."
3. Therefore, Barack Obama just is Barry Obana (they are numerically one).[11]

This argument is invalid; 3 doesn't follow from 1 together with 2. The people in our scenario would know that 1 and 2 were true, and they would also know that 3 is false. How? They would know that Obama and Obana have differed, and they know that a man can't (at one time) differ from himself. For example, they may know that on a certain date, Obama was in Washington, DC, while on that same day Obana was in the small town where he was mayor. And they know that Barack is married to Michelle, whereas Barry is married to Nichele. They know, then, that Obama and Obana are truly two; they are not numerically one.

This argument is just as clearly invalid.

1. God is called "God."
2. Jesus is called "God."
3. Therefore, Jesus just is God (they are numerically one).[12]

Premise 1 is granted by all. Premise 2 is plausible; arguably at least a few times in the New Testament, Jesus is addressed or referred to as "God."[13] But 3 doesn't follow from 1 and 2—it is possible for 1 and 2 to be true while 3 is false.[14] The lesson is that being called by the same name or title does not imply being numerically the same, even when the things are also qualitatively similar in numerous other ways.

---

[11] In logic we can translate the argument using b for Barack Obama, r for Barry Obana, and C for the predicate *being called "Barack Obama."* It would be: 1. Cb, 2. Cr, 3. $b = r$.

[12] Notice that this argument has the same structure as the previous one. Using g for God, j for Jesus, and C for the predicate being called "God," we would have: 1. Cg, 2. Cj, 3. $g=j$.

[13] Section 1.4.

[14] And it is more than possible; we know it to be actual. How? We know that 3 is false because we know that Jesus and God have simultaneously differed from each other.

But there's a similar argument with a more complicated first premise that *is* valid. To aid in understanding, we'll state it in three ways.

English	*Logic*	*Logic-English*
1. Whatever's called "God" is God.	1. $\forall x\,(Cx \supset x = g)$	1. For any *x*, if *x* is called "God," then *x* just is God.
2. Therefore, if Jesus is called "God" then Jesus is numerically identical with God.	2. $Cj \supset j = g$	2. Therefore, if Jesus is called "God," then Jesus just is God.
3. Jesus is called "God."	3. Cj	3. Jesus is called "God."
4. Therefore, Jesus is God.	4. $j = g$	4. Therefore, Jesus and God are numerically identical.

This argument is valid; 1 implies 2, and 2 together with 3 implies 4. And let us grant the truth of 3. Thus, *if* 1 is also true, we have a sound argument, a valid argument with only true premises, which shows us that the final conclusion is true too. But *is* 1 true?

If we believe the Gospel According to John or the lexicon authors,[15] premise 1 is false, and so the argument, though it is valid, is unsound and gives us no reason to believe its conclusion 4.

9.2 WHO IS THE ONE TRUE GOD?

The critical-thinking tools we've been exploring are helpful for avoiding and answering the ill-advised claims and unsound arguments some trinitarians foist on the public. But they also have many positive uses, helping us to grasp the meanings and implications of some important New Testament texts.

John chapter 17 comes at the end of a long farewell discourse of Jesus to his disciples. The chapter starts with Jesus praying.

> After Jesus had spoken these words, he looked up to heaven and said, "Father, the hour has come; glorify your Son so that the Son may glorify you, since you have given him authority over all people, to give eternal life to all whom you have given him. And this is eternal life, that they may know you, the only true God, and Jesus Christ whom you have sent." (John 17:1–3)

---

[15] Section 1.4

Jesus is here anticipating his own glorification.[16] This is an important passage for understanding the relationship between Jesus and God in the New Testament. It's clear to whom Jesus is speaking: the Father. Jesus asserts here that eternal life consists in knowing the Father and himself. But he takes the opportunity to express the difference between them. After mentioning the Father, "you" (*se*), he then refers to him via a phrase in a subordinate clause. Grammarians describe this phrase as being used "in apposition"; it gives additional information about the one just referred to by referring to him in a different way. It would have been enough to simply use the word "God" here: "And this is eternal life, that they may know you, God, and Jesus Christ whom you have sent." After all, as we've seen, "God" in a New Testament context is nearly always the Father and means this unless something about the context rules out him as the referent.[17] More generally, in a monotheistic, first-century Jewish context, "God" normally refers to the only true god, Yahweh. Thus, there would have been no significant ambiguity in "you, God." Why then were three additional words added: "the only true" (*ton monon alēthinon*)? Their only functions seem to be to make the Father's unique status both explicit and emphatic.[18] If the Father is *the only* true god, then no one else is—that's what "only" means!

"All" and "only" statements often presuppose some limited domain. The sentence "Only Jill has blue eyes" may be true when the presupposed domain is the children in a certain kindergarten class. And "*Everyone* loves Ms. Kind" will be true if all the kids in that class love her. Exploiting this fact about human languages, some have argued that "the only true god"[19] here is meant only to exclude the false gods or so-called "gods" of the nations and not anyone else, so not the Son or the Holy Spirit.[20]

---

[16] This is mentioned in verse 5 as eternally foreknown by God.

[17] Section 1.4. Summarizing his findings about the uses of *theos* in the New Testament, Harris writes, "When *(ho) theos* [(the) god] is used, we are to assume that the NT writers have *ho pater* [the Father] in mind unless the context makes this sense of *(ho) theos* impossible" (*Jesus as God*, 47).

[18] Chang and Chan, *Only Perfect Man*, 33.

[19] In this sentence, contrary to English Bible translations, I have the word "god" lowercased because it's being used as a common noun in the assertion that the Father is the only god, the only being of that kind.

[20] Basil of Caesarea, *Letter 8*, 117 (sec. 3); Gregory of Nazianzus, *Oration 30*, 104 (4.13/30.13); Bowman Jr. and Komoszewski, *Incarnate Christ*, 441–42.

But expressions of monotheism don't presuppose any limited domain; the only god is supposed to be unique (full stop)—unique *in all of reality*—not unique among some limited class of beings. It's no good to insist that "the only true god" isn't meant to exclude the Son when this god and his Son are contrasted in this very passage. Eternal life consists in knowing this one *and* (*kai*) that one. As John writes elsewhere, "Truly our fellowship is with the Father *and* with his Son Jesus Christ."[21]

This is and has always been a favorite passage of unitarian Christians because Jesus here assumes the identity of his Father with the only god. If the Father is *the only* true god, then no one else is—not Jesus, and not the Trinity (assuming there is such a thing).[22] That there is only one true god would shock no one in the first-century Jewish context of both Jesus's life and this Gospel; this is a Jewish assumption that Jesus, his opponents, and all the New Testament authors share. But here we're told *who* this one God is: the Father. If the Father just is God, then God just is the Father; as we've seen, identity is a symmetric relation.

What Jesus is presupposing here is, in its logical form, like the sentence we translated into logic in section 8.2:

English	*Logic*	*Logic-English*
Constantine is the only emperor.	$Ec \land \forall x\ (Ex \supset x{=}c)$	Constantine is an emperor, and for any x, x is emperor only if x is identical with Constantine.
or	*or*	*or*
Constantine is the one emperor.	$Ec \land \neg\exists x\ (Ex \land x \neq c)$	Constantine is an emperor, and it is not the case that there's some x such that it is an emperor and is not identical with Constantine.

Someone in Constantine's court may have flattered him by saying, "You, *Dominus* (Lord), are the only emperor." In so doing, the flatterer would be presupposing the sentence above, which is a conjunction of two propositions: that Constantine is an emperor and that no one else is. These are parallel to the convictions presupposed by Jesus in his prayer. These are revealed by a logical analysis of what Jesus presupposes in John 17:1–3:

[21] 1 John 1:3, emphasis added.
[22] See section 9.3 and chapter 3.

English	*Logic*	*Logic-English*
The Father is the only true god.	$Tf \land \forall x\ (Tx \supset x = f)$	The Father is true-god, and for any x, x is true-god only if x just is (is identical with) the Father.
or	*or*	*or*
The Father is the one true god.	$Tf \land \neg\exists x\ (Tx \land x \neq f)$	The Father is true-god, and it is not the case that there exists some x such that x is true-god and x is not identical with the Father.[23]

Many a unitarian Christian has been amazed that when they were trinitarian they could not see the significance of what Jesus says here. For instance,

> I marvel at the fact, yet am also saddened by it, that as a trinitarian, I could not see the clear meaning of many of Jesus' words ... Jesus is simply saying "You, Father, are the only true God," a statement that rules out everyone else, including Jesus himself, as being God. How then could we have failed to grasp this short and clear statement?[24]

9.2.1 ANOTHER TRUE GOD

This was not a problematic text for most Christians until partisans of the Nicene creed began in the 340s to assert its new language as the very definition of orthodoxy.[25] They had called the Son and Father, respectively, "true God from true God."[26] This flatly contradicts what Jesus assumes in John 17:3, that the Father is the only true god. No, if the Nicenes are right, then he's one of two![27] Starting with Athanasius, mainstream theologians have been driven to either avoid or distort the meaning of this text.

---

[23] The only differences between these two examples are that in the second the predicate is the compound term *true-god*, and that in the first presumably Constantine's flatterer is speaking with reference to some limited domain, lest his claim be made false by another emperor, for instance, in Mongolia.

[24] Chang and Chan, *Only Perfect Man*, 32–33.

[25] Hanson, *Search*, ch. 10.

[26] "Profession," 5.

[27] The ontological status of the Holy Spirit was not addressed by the 325 Nicene Creed. Oddly enough, the trinitarian innovators at the 381 council stopped short of calling the Holy Spirit "true God," even though they seem to presuppose that he is as divine as are the Father and the Son ("Exposition of the 150 Fathers," 24).

9.2.2 MODERN TRINITARIANS AGAINST JOHN 17:1–3

In modern times simple avoidance is the most popular strategy; reading most trinitarian commentaries on the Gospel According to John, one would never know that this text has ever been controversial or problematic for trinitarian theology. But one could fill a book with the lame ways trinitarian interpreters have twisted and distorted this passage, trying to make it consistent either with there being more than one true-god or with the only true-god being the Trinity. In this brief section I'll only cover some recent abuses.

Some trinitarians who battle against the clear meaning of this text realize that if the only god just is the Father, this clashes with their trinitarian theology, on which the only god just is the Trinity. They reason like this:

English	*Logic*
1. God is the Trinity.	1. $g = t$
2. The Trinity is not the Father.	2. $t \neq f$
3. Therefore, the Father is not God.	3. $f \neq g$

Premise 1 is required by post-381 catholic orthodoxy; a trinitarian is committed to 1. Premise 2 is true if there is such a thing as the Trinity. The Trinity can't be the Father, for it is, by hypothesis, tripersonal, and the Father is not tripersonal. Differing, they must be two, not one. Premise 1 says that God and the Trinity are one and the same, and 2 says that the Trinity and the Father are *not* one and the same. But then this God that just is the Trinity (per premise 1) will have to be distinct from the Father, since the Trinity is so distinct (per premise 2). This is valid reasoning; 3 follows from 1 and 2. But the conclusion 3 is inconsistent with the text we're examining. The name "God" most properly belongs to the only true god, the only one with the status true-god, and this, according to our text, is the Father. In this way the text assumes the truth of $f = g$, that the Father and God are one and the same, the very claim 3 denies, so the trinitarian must fight against its clear meaning. Further, no New Testament text teaches premise 1.

One way to do this is through anachronism. Apologist Chris Date presumes to speak for all trinitarians about this passage, saying, "We think 'God' here refers to the one and only divine being in which we think the three divine persons subsist."[28] But as we've seen, there is no such usage of *theos* in the New Testament.[29]

---

[28] Tuggy and Date, *Is Jesus Human*, 88. Here Date follows White, *Forgotten Trinity*, 90.

[29] The word *theos* never refers to the divine being or essence, where this is supposed to be something other than the Father. See section 1.5.

Another strategy is to misread this passage as merely attributing the quality *only-true-god-ness* to the Father.[30] This, it is argued, doesn't exclude others from having that same quality. It is true that generally, ascribing some quality F to a thing doesn't imply that nothing else also has F.

But this misunderstands what the text presupposes, and logic helps to bring this out. The claim that the Father is true-god, that he has that quality, is translated into logic as Tf (where "$T\_$" means that _ has the quality true-god). This is a single claim. But the proposition that the Father is *the only* true God, the only one enjoying the quality true-god, as we've seen, consists of two claims, not one, so it is translated as $Tf \wedge \forall x\ (Tx \supset x = f)$. That is: the Father is true-god, and for any x, it is true-god only if it is identical with the Father. The second half of the sentence, after the "and" symbol ($\wedge$) captures the force of the "only."[31] The trinitarian apologist can't or won't see that there are two claims here; "the Father is the only true God" is a compound claim, with two halves: the Father has the status true-God *and* nothing else has that status. It is simply a mistake to detect only one claim in what is a conjunction of two claims.

Some of these present-day apologists misuse logic as well, alleging that the above reading commits the fallacy of denying the antecedent.[32] This universally acknowledged fallacy (type of invalid argument) has the following structure, where P and Q stand in for claims or propositions (that is, what is expressed by an indicative sentence):

1. $P \supset Q$
2. $\neg P$
3. Therefore, $\neg Q$

---

[30] Slick, "John 17:3"; White, *Forgotten Trinity*, 90–92. Compare with Hilary of Poitiers, *Trinity*, 354–55 (9.33–34).

[31] Some sources us a dot • instead of the symbol $\wedge$ for "and." As we saw above, we can equally well translate this sentence using the existential quantifier: $Tf \wedge \neg\exists x\ (Tx \wedge x \neq f)$. That is, the Father is true-god, and there isn't anything that is both true-god and distinct from (not numerically identical with) the Father.

[32] "Apologists Bible Commentary," n. 1. The author alleges this fallacy but then gives an argument that is not of that exact form: "If one is the Father, one is the only true God," [the Son is not the Father, therefore the Son is not the only true God]. This argument *is* invalid, but it is not an example of that fallacy, as the first premise is a universally quantified claim about anything whatever. It would be analyzed as $\forall x\ (x = f \supset Ox)$—for any x whatever, x just is the Father only if x has the quality *only-true-god*. In my analysis on the next page I've written what the author meant to give, an argument that is a case of the denying the antecedent fallacy.

This is a fallacious argument; any argument of this form is invalid, such as:

1. If Jan lives in New York, then she lives in America.
2. It's not the case that Jan lives in New York.
3. Therefore, it's not the case that Jan lives in America.

Here, then, is the fallacy alleged regarding our text:

English	*Logic*	*Logic-English*
1. If Jesus were the Father he would be the only true God.	1. $j = f \supset Oj$	1. Jesus is identical with the Father only if Jesus is only-true-god.
2. Jesus is not the Father.	2. $j \neq f$	2. It's not the case that Jesus is identical with the Father.
3. Therefore, Jesus is not the only true God.	3. $\neg Oj$	3. Therefore, it is not the case that Jesus is only-true-god.

This is a fallacy of denying the antecedent, but this is not the argument the soundness of which Jesus presupposes in this passage. That argument is as follows:

English	*Logic*	*Logic-English*
1. The Father is the only true god.	1. $Tf \wedge \forall x\ (Tx \supset x = f)$	1. The Father is true-god, and for any x, if x is true-god, then x is identical with the Father.
2. Whatever is true-god is the Father.	2. $\forall x\ (Tx \supset x = f)$	2. For any x, if x is true-god, then x is identical with the Father.[33]
3. Jesus is true god only if he just is the Father.	3. $Tj \supset j = f$	3. If Jesus is true-god, then he is identical with the Father.[34]
4. Jesus and the Father are distinct.	4. $j \neq f$	4. It is not the case that Jesus just is the Father.
5. Therefore, Jesus not true god.	5. $\neg Tj$	5. It is not the case that Jesus is true-god.[35]

---

[33] Claim 2 follows from 1 because a conjunction implies each of its conjuncts. That is, from $P \wedge Q$ one can infer P, and from $P \wedge Q$ one can infer Q.

[34] See p. 254, footnote 6 for how claim 3 follows from claim 2.

[35] Claims 3 and 4 imply 5 by the valid form of argument traditionally called *modus tollens*. The form is: 1. $P \supset Q$, 2. $\neg Q$, 3. $\neg P$.

This argument *is* valid. Trinitarians affirm 4 (the distinctness of the Father and the Son), so to escape this valid argument's final conclusion 5, they *need* to deny premise 1. But 1, as we've seen, is precisely what Jesus is presupposing in his prayer in John 17:1–3. Hence the Scripture-twisting when it comes to this text.

In an earlier treatment Bowman and Komoszewski lamely assert that "Jesus' statement in John 17:3 distinguishes himself from the Father (to whom he is speaking in prayer), but grammatically it does not *deny* that Jesus is also the true God."[36] It is true that Jesus in this text doesn't *deny* that he is true god. However, as we've seen, he is *presupposing* that it is false that he is true God, since he is distinct from the Father, and the Father is *the only* true god. It's not enough to urge, as they go on to do, that Jesus is called "God" in other passages, as that is consistent with only the Father having the status true god.

In a later treatment they try a lot harder to dispose of the threat of this text. Their first move is to assert that what this text says is fully consistent with "the doctrine of the Trinity," which "*affirms* that the Father is the only true God."[37] There is something to what they're saying here, but as apologists often do, they're working under the false assumption that trinitarians mean just one set of claims by "the doctrine of the Trinity." Some trinitarians do identify the Father—and, incoherently, also the Son and the Spirit (each of which is numerically distinct from the Father)—with God.[38] But others, seeing the incoherence of saying that three distinct things are each identical with the same thing, construe statements like "The Father is God" as predications of divinity, that is, as ascribing the quality of being fully divine—not $f = g$ but rather Df (the Father is divine).[39] Not realizing that as trinitarians they are committed to the identity of the only god with the Trinity, Bowman and Komoszewski instead reason, "If there is only one true God, and the Father is really God, then the Father must be *that* God—that is, the only true God."[40] This is valid reasoning.[41]

But do our authors here *really* want to assert that each of the "Persons" of the Trinity "is God" in this sense, where that Person and God are numerically one? This is ill-advised, since the trinitarian should say that the one god and the

---

[36] Bowman Jr. and Komoszewski, *Putting Jesus*, 353, note 21.

[37] Bowman Jr. and Komoszewski, *Incarnate Christ*, 384.

[38] See Principle #6 in section 8.4, p. 279.

[39] For example: Moreland and Craig, *Philosophical Foundations*, 589; Hasker, "Knowing God," 21–26; Craig, "Tri-Personal," 52–53.

[40] *Incarnate Christ*, 384.

[41] I omit the proof of this, as it is long and uses an inference rule I haven't explained in this chapter (Existential Instantiation), on which see Howard-Snyder et al., *Power of Logic*, 505–7.

Trinity are one and the same (the one god just is the triune god), and the Trinity (and so in their view God) can't be numerically identical to any single Person.[42] Just as bad, any trinitarian is committed to $f \neq s$, $s \neq h$, and $f \neq h$, the distinctions of each Person from each of the others. But then we have construed "the doctrine of the Trinity" as the obviously false claim that each of *three different things* is *numerically the same with* one thing, God.[43] Alas, a close look at their book reveals that Bowman and Komoszewski understand "the doctrine of the Trinity" to be exactly that.[44]

But let's look at the further arguments they make about this passage. First, they urge that the location of "only" in the word order makes all the difference. There is an important, if subtle, difference between saying that *only the Father is the true God* (to the exclusion of the Son) and saying that *the Father is the only true God.* John 17:3 says the latter, not the former.[45]

Logically speaking, "Only the Father is the true God" and "The Father is the only true God" both get analyzed as: $Tf \wedge \forall x\ (Tx \supset x = f)$.[46] They have no grounds for their complaint about the New English Bible translation "to know thee who alone art truly God."[47] These authors are urging a distinction without a relevant difference. But their idea seems to be that the latter rendering, "The Father is the only true god" is consistent with someone else also being true god, so that anyone who thinks this rules out the Son's being true-god is merely assuming that the one true god is unipersonal.[48] But as

---

[42] Moreland and Craig, *Philosophical Foundations*, 589. For why any Christian should rule out such an identity claim, see sections 8.3.3 and 8.3.6.

[43] For a formal proof the incoherence of this, see my "Trinity," sec. 1.4.

[44] In the passage just quoted they affirm $f = g$. It is clear too that they affirm the anti-modalist trinitarian creedal commitment that $f \neq s$, $s \neq h$, $f \neq h$. In their many long discussions of the Son's deity/divinity, they often seem to confine themselves to the claim that Ds (the Son has the quality of being divine), but sometimes, by their deployment of "only God" arguments (section 8.3.6), they also imply $s = g$, and presumably so too for the Spirit (Bowman Jr. and Komoszewski, *Incarnate Christ*, 76, 377, 381, 500, 526, 731–33, 758, 761, 763).

[45] *Incarnate Christ*, 385. The same move is made by Craig, "Tri-Personal," 45, note 32.

[46] Perhaps some people may hear "Only the Father is the true God" as meaning "Only the Father is identical with God." On such a reading "the true God" would be taken as an expression referring to God, and the analysis would be: $f = g \wedge \forall x\ (x = g \supset x = f)$. This is true but trivial; if the Father *just is* God, then *of course* anything identical with God will have to be identical with the Father.

[47] *Incarnate Christ*, 385. There are not any significant differences between major English translations when it comes to this text, on which see https://biblehub.com/john/17-3.htm.

[48] *Incarnate Christ*, 385.

we've seen, "The Father is *the only* true god" *does* rule out that anyone else has that status.

A silly variant of this move is to urge that for the text to mean what our analysis says, it would need an extra "only."[49] So for our analysis to be correct, it would have to say not "you, [are] the only true God," but rather, "*only* you [are] the only true God." That this is silly is shown by our Constantine example given earlier. His flattering courtier only needs to say, "You, *Dominus*, are the only emperor," to assert Constantine's uniqueness in respect of being an emperor. He does not need to say, "*Only* you, *Dominus*, are the only emperor"—the first word would be redundant; with or without that extra "only," the flatterer is asserting two claims: $Ec \land \neg\exists x\ (Ex \land x \neq c)$, Constantine is emperor and no one else is.

Back to Bowman and Komoszewski, they observe that Jesus is displaying humility here, which in their view befits his incarnate state in which he "had become part of the creation" and so became subject to God.[50] But Jesus's humility is irrelevant; Jesus's assumption is what it is, even humbly expressed.

Finally, Bowman and Komoszewski try to turn the tables on their critics, arguing that it is the non-trinitarian for whom this passage presents a problem. To do this they present a rather complicated argument.[51] I'm not going to reproduce it here since it is not clearly valid and so doesn't serve its purpose. I think their point is better put as follows:

1. Jesus is a god.
2. Jesus is not a false god.[52]
3. Every god is either a true god or a false god.
4. Therefore, Jesus is a true god. (1–3)
5. There is only one true god.
6. Therefore, Jesus is that one true god. (4, 5)

---

[49] "He did not say that *only* the Father is the only true God" (Thompson, "Revisiting").

[50] Bowman Jr. and Komoszewski, *Incarnate Christ*, 380, 385–86. It's hard to see how one could "become part of the creation" without becoming a created thing. (Isn't every part of God's creation itself a created thing?) But an orthodox Incarnation doctrine by definition insists that in becoming incarnate, God the Son didn't lose his divinity, and divinity implies being uncreated.

[51] *Incarnate Christ*, 386.

[52] In support of 1 and 2 they refer to John 1:1, 18, 20:28; Rom. 9:5; Titus 2:13; Heb. 1:8; 2 Peter 1:1; 1 John 5:20 (*Incarnate Christ*, 386). This reflects their false assumption that in the New Testament only a god can be referred to as *theos*. About 2, no text explicitly denies that Jesus is a false god. I think the reason is that it never occurs to the New Testament authors that someone might think Jesus to be one of the false gods, the alleged deities of the Gentiles. After all, he is God's "Son, born of a woman" (Gal. 4:4)—a man.

The argument is valid,[53] and I grant the truth of 2, 3, and 5. The soundness of the argument depends on the truth of 1. Unfortunately, 1 is false. Even if a few texts apply the word *theos* to Jesus,[54] the New Testament authors don't think he's any kind of god, either a true or a false one, because in their view he is the unique human *Son of* the only god—an assumption reflected in this very context: "Father," Jesus prays, "glorify your Son," that is, the man who is praying (John 17:1). Bowman and Komoszewski seem to assume that anyone who is correctly referred to as *theos* in the New Testament is thereby assumed to be a god—either a real ("true") or a fake ("false") one. But as we've seen that assumption is false according to both Scripture and the state-of-the-art New Testament Greek lexicon.[55] Further, the argument foolishly collapses together (identifies) Jesus and the only god, implying the impossibility of them differing in any way. But Jesus is *the Son of* that god, and that god is *not* his own son.

Bowman and Komoszewski then spend a whole chapter (21) arguing that the word "god" in the New Testament can't be applied to Jesus in the sense of a being who is inferior to God but who is nonetheless a divine being.[56] But as we've seen, there doesn't need to be a meaning of "god" like that which applies to Jesus. There is another sense brought up by Jesus himself in John 10: people who are called *theoi* (gods) because they have received God's word. Being a "god" in this sense doesn't require having a divine essence or literally being a deity, and it certainly is true that this book teaches Jesus to have received God's word, even while it teaches him to be greater than any past prophets or teachers.[57]

The authors discuss the passage we investigated in section 9.1, noting that the dominant view today is that John 10 reflects the interpretation (documented in later Jewish literature) that the "gods" were the Israelites when they received the law.[58] Against this consensus they say that "Jesus' argument can be understood without settling this question" of the referent of "gods" in Psalm 82:6.[59] I agree; as

---

[53] I skip giving a full, formally valid argument here, as it would be long and would employ inference rules beyond what we've seen in this chapter. But the reader should be able, on reflection, to "see" that 1–3 imply 4 and that 4 and 5 imply 6.

[54] Section 1.4.

[55] Sections 1.3, 1.5.

[56] Bowman Jr. and Komoszewski, *Incarnate Christ*, 389.

[57] John 1:14–18, 8:52–54, 10:36, 14:24, 17:14.

[58] *Incarnate Christ*, 404. In favor of this idea, the passage does use the term "gods" as interchangeable in meaning with "children of the Most High." Another Jewish interpretation has been that it is specifically the judges who are being condemned in this Psalm (Levine and Brettler, *Jewish Annotated*, 200).

[59] *Incarnate Christ*, 404.

I've said, Jesus's argument only depends on what his Jewish opponents believe about Psalm 82. In *their* view certain humans, those to whom the word of God came, are without blasphemy called *theoi*. Therefore, *according to his opponents'* view, it can't be blasphemous that Jesus is claiming the *lesser* title of God's *Son*, especially since God has sanctified Jesus and sent him into the world, making him more special than those "gods." This understanding of Jesus's argument is consistent with the prevailing scholarly view that the psalm originally depicted a judgment God passed on unseen beings—be they deities, angels, or members of the divine council.[60]

But Bowman and Komoszewski argue for a minority interpretation on which Jesus is claiming these "gods" in Psalm 82 are a negative type of himself:

> Whatever those gods were, Scripture did not call them "gods" for no purpose. What those so-called gods failed to be, Jesus really was . . . They failed to live up to the titles of "gods" and "sons of the Most High" . . . Jesus really was "the Son of God" . . . Thus, Jesus' argument was not, "They were rightly called gods, and so am I," but rather, "Their failure as 'gods' is stated in Scripture to point forward to me coming from the Father as his real Son . . . If Jesus was not claiming deity, it would have been easy enough to have said something like, "I'm not God; I'm just one of his many sons. He never did."[61]

Of course Jesus never claimed to be *one of* God's many sons—his claim in this Gospel in to be *the unique* Son of God.[62] The minority interpretation overlooks that Jesus's opponents—as they often do in this Gospel—misconstrue his words.[63] While defending himself against the accusation of blasphemy, Jesus simultaneously corrects their misunderstanding: he is claiming to be God's Son, not a god or God himself. That this correction was perceived is shown by the fact that at his trials his enemies do not accuse him of any such claims.[64] Had

---

[60] This seems to be required by verse 6: "I say, 'You are gods, children of the Most High, all of you; nevertheless, you shall die like mortals and fall like any prince.'" For this sort of interpretation, see Berlin and Brettler, *Jewish Study Bible*, 1375; Heiser and Stricklin, *John 10*; Heiser, "Plural Elohim"; Heiser, "Jesus' Quotation"; Heiser, *Unseen Realm*; McClellan, "Gods-Complaint." Bowman and Komoszewski argue, I think needlessly, against this interpretation (*Incarnate Christ*, 401–4). In my view they are overlooking a semantic shift here in the term "god" from the concept of a mere deity to the concept of a god, that is, a necessarily unique, perfect, and ultimate deity (Tuggy, "On Counting Gods"; "Divine Deception," 188–91).

[61] *Incarnate Christ*, 405–6.

[62] John 1:49, 3:18, 5:25, 11:4, 11:27, 19:7, 20:31.

[63] Carter, *John*, 67–73, 114–16.

[64] John 18:12–19:16; this is confirmed by the other Gospel accounts: Matt. 26:57–27:26, Mark 14:53–15:15, Luke 22:66–23:25.

Jesus set himself up for such an accusation, his enemies surely would have hurled it. But he had pointedly and publicly corrected such misunderstandings, so his enemies knew they would not be able to get away with that false accusation.

There is nothing new under the sun. R. P. C. Hanson observes, "This is one of the texts most strongly exploited by the Arians."[65] It is often referred to in that great product of sixteenth and seventeenth century Socinian scholarship, the *Racovian Catechism*,[66] and we find the best early American unitarian scholars appealing to it as well.[67] Why? Because its meaning is both clear and clearly contrary to any Trinity theory. The sorts of interpretive shenanigans we've looked at began only after the new Nicene creedal language of Son and Father as "true God from true God" emerged.[68] Before that, its clear assertion that only the Father has the status true god was simply accepted by mainstream theologians.[69] Some traditions contradict rather than building on Scripture.

---

[65] Hanson, *Search*, 836.

[66] Crellius et al., *Racovian Catechism*, 24, 33–34, 57, 79–80, 290.

[67] Norton, *Statement of Reasons*, 198–99; Ware Jr., *Outline*, 7.

[68] It is telling that Athanasius only wrestles with this text in one place in his extant works—he feels the weakness of his case, that this text on the face of it favors his opponents (*Four Discourses*, 398 [3.24.9]). A little later, the influential Latin author Augustine is a surprisingly bold distorter. Augustine, *Trinity*, 211–12 (4.3.10); Augustine, *Tractates*, 258–59 (105.3); Augustine, *Answer to Maximinus*, 290–91 (2.15.4).

[69] There are no quotations of or obvious references to John 17:3 anywhere in the "apostolic fathers," the second-century apologists, or the New Testament Apocrypha. It seems to have been put on the map of theological disputing by Irenaeus, who seems to refer to it in his endeavors to refute heretics who held the creator and the god of the Jews to be a lesser god than the highest god who was taught by Jesus (Irenaeus, *Against the Heresies 2*, 37 [2.11.1]; *Against the Heresies 3*, 40 [3.6.4]; *Against the Heresies 4–5*, 15 [4.1.1]). Origen and Cyprian cite it without distortion (Origen, *Against Celsus*, 153 [3.37]; Origen, *Commentary on John*, 98–99 [2.12–18]; Cyprian, *Iubaianus*, 207 [17.1]; Cyprian, *Demetrian*, 92 [ch. 23]; Cyprian, *Lord's Prayer*, 455a [ch. 28]; Cyprian, *Testimonies*, 516a [Bk. 2 Test. 1]). Novatian cites it once without distortion against modalists who identify the Father and Son (Novatian, *Trinity*, trans. DeSimone, 91–92 [26.17]), but earlier in the book, arguing against those with a "mere man" Christology (Dynamic Monarchians, people who we would today call biblical unitarians), he makes the ridiculous claim that in this text "If He [Jesus] did not wish Himself to be considered also God [or a god, or a "god," Latin: *deus*], why did He add: 'and Jesus Christ, whom Thou hast sent,' unless He wished to be acknowledged also as God [or: a god, or a "god," Latin: *deus*]. He would have added: 'and the man Jesus Christ, whom Thou hast sent.' As a matter of fact, He did not add anything; nor did Christ teach us in this present passage that He was only man; He associated himself with God. He wanted us to understand that He was, on account of this association, also God [or: a god, or a "god," Latin: *deus*]—as he truly is" (*Trinity*, trans. DeSimone, 62–63 [16.4]). But he goes on to affirm that the Father is the only true God (63 [16.5]), and it is clear from the end of his book (chs. 30–31) that this is his considered position. On his subordinationism see Lloyd, *Novatian's Theology*.

9.3 THE ONE GOD, A.K.A. THE FATHER

In this section we'll briefly review some texts showing the New Testament authors' assumption that the one god and the Father are one and the same and that he is distinct from Jesus.

9.3.1 MY GOD AND YOUR GOD

In John 20, a distraught Mary Magdalene is looking for the body of Jesus, but instead she encounters the risen Jesus.

> But Mary stood weeping outside the tomb. As she wept, she bent over to look into the tomb; and she saw two angels in white, sitting where the body of Jesus had been lying, one at the head and the other at the feet. They said to her, "Woman, why are you weeping?" She said to them, "They have taken away my Lord, and I do not know where they have laid him." When she had said this, she turned around and saw Jesus standing there, but she did not know that it was Jesus. Jesus said to her, "Woman, why are you weeping? Whom are you looking for?" Supposing him to be the gardener, she said to him, "Sir, if you have carried him away, tell me where you have laid him, and I will take him away." Jesus said to her, "Mary!" She turned and said to him in Hebrew, "Rabbouni!" (which means Teacher). Jesus said to her, "Do not hold on to me, because I have not yet ascended to the Father. But go to my brothers and say to them, 'I am ascending to my Father and your Father, to my God and your God.'" Mary Magdalene went and announced to the disciples, "I have seen the Lord"; and she told them that he had said these things to her. (John 20:11–18)

In his last sentence Jesus assumes there is one who has the following four features: (1) his father, (2) his disciples' father, (3) his god, and (4) his disciples' god. Clearly this one isn't Jesus himself but rather someone else to whom Jesus will ascend. As we've seen, this same one can't be the Trinity. In the first-century Jewish context (of Jesus's life and/or the composition of the Fourth Gospel), it is obvious that this one who is Jesus's father, the disciples' father, Jesus's god, and the disciples' god is *the only* god, the only true god mentioned in chapter seventeen, Yahweh, a.k.a. God, God the Father.[70] Yahweh, then, is not the Trinity; it is false that the only god is the triune god imagined by catholic orthodoxy since the late 300s. Moreover, the one true god is assumed to be necessarily godless (such that it is not possible in

---

[70] "But the LORD is the true God; he is the living God and the everlasting King" (Jer. 10:10). Compare: Isa. 44:6, John 6:27.

principle for him to be under any god). Therefore, this god can't be Jesus, who here counts himself together with us in being *subject to* this god.[71]

9.3.2 GOD IS NECESSARILY GODLESS

The one true god in the Bible is assumed to be necessarily unique (without any true peers), and since he is supposed to be the free creator of everything else, all the possible total situations can be divided into two groups: those in which God freely creates, and those in which God does not choose to create, so that only he exists.[72] If only God exists, then God can't be under anyone else. And if God creates, any others will be his creatures and will thereby be subject to his authority. Therefore, whether or not God creates, he is not under any other; those being all the possibilities, we can say that *necessarily*, no matter what, God is not under any other. He is godless, so to speak, in all possible worlds.

From another angle, necessarily, God is the only god. Just conceptually, the *god-over* relation is irreflexive; it makes no sense to say that one and the same god is the god over himself.[73] Since there can't be another god, necessarily, God is not under any god.

Ancient Israelites and the earliest Christians probably lacked any firm grasp of the modal concepts I just employed, as well as the imaginative device of "all possible worlds" (all metaphysically possible situations).[74] In their language, they describe God, the only god, as above, over, or in charge of any other "gods," whether these are lesser unseen beings (what I call mere deities)[75] or merely

---

[71] I agree with trinitarians that this does not imply that Jesus's relationship with God is exactly like ours (Bowman Jr. and Komoszewski, *Incarnate Christ*, 381–82).

[72] Yes, "he"; there is no incoherence, as some medieval and recent speculative, philosophical arguments have alleged, in the idea of a perfect God existing as a single someone (Tuggy, "Antiunitarian Arguments").

[73] People talk about the joys of "being your own boss," but that is not to be taken literally. "To be one's own boss" is precisely to have a job *without having a boss*. Similarly, God is necessarily "his own boss" or "his own god," but that is just to say that he is necessarily bossless and godless.

[74] Many analytic philosophers in recent times believe these "possible worlds" to be real but abstract, namely maximal consistent propositions or states of affairs. Against these, I think it is confused to believe in these "ersatz worlds" (so-called worlds that are *not* total ways-things-could-be but that are only supposed to represent such). For me, talk of possible worlds is only a heuristic device that is useful in discussing what can't be, what must be, what could be but is not, and what actually is but could fail to be. For this type of approach to understanding modality and "possible worlds" see Lycan, "Metaphysics of Possibilia"; Lycan, "Concepts"; Pruss, "Actual"; Kalhat, "Primitive Modality."

[75] Tuggy, "On Counting Gods."

mythical beings, or some mix, such as real, unseen beings who are the subjects of a lot of fictional stories. "For Yahweh is a great God, a king greater than all the gods" (Ps. 95:3, NJB). "Yahweh is great, our Lord is above all gods" (Ps. 135:5, NJB). "Give thanks to the God of gods" (Ps. 136:2, NJB). Notice too that God has no backstory, no mythological origin. He is not the son of some older god; he doesn't have a wife; he didn't need to fight his way to his current top position. Their assumption, I suggest, is that as the only god, he is *necessarily* in the top position, the god over any others there may be. This is why they felt no need to explain how he got there. In principle, God must be godless and top-level in authority and power.

9.3.3 CAN GOD INCARNATE HAVE A GOD?

This seems rather obvious, and from a biblical perspective it is, but it is denied by trinitarian apologists. They can't deny the clear New Testament teaching that the Father is the god over Jesus.[76] So they insist that *somehow*, by being incarnate, God—or more precisely, God the Son—is under a god, namely, the Father. Apologist Chris Date argues that

> Jesus' affirmations of monotheism, and his identification of his Father as the only true God, are precisely what one would expect if one divine person of a triune God became incarnate. One would not expect him to behave like an atheist and refuse to subject himself to God, for ... [the] God of Israel is the God of all flesh ... and any enfleshed (incarnate) divine person must therefore ... obey, worship, and pray to his God.[77]

God is necessarily the god over any "flesh," yes, over any human beings there may be. But most trinitarians assume that the one self or person in the Incarnate Christ is the eternal, divine Son. And by our reasoning above, by his being the necessarily uncreated, free creator, and moreover the only god, it is impossible for him to be under a god. Put differently, his top-level authority, and so his godlessness, seems to be implied by his full divinity, or his being a fully divine Person. For his part, Date holds the Father and the Son to be the same god and so embraces the nonsensical statement that one and the same god is literally the god over himself, or that God in one of his Persons is the god over God in another of his Persons.[78]

---

[76] See section 11.4 for discussion and biblical references.

[77] Date and Tuggy, *Is Jesus Human*, 88.

[78] *Is Jesus Human*, 90.

James White adopts the same hopeless position and adds that "as the God-Man, He prayed to the one true God, just as we would expect."[79] But the tradition insists that in becoming, in some sense, "human," the eternal, divine Son does not thereby cease to be fully divine. So as still God (or a Person "in" God who is fully divine) we would expect him *not* to pray to anyone, since we would expect such a one to be godless, not under any god. Similarly Bowman and Komoszewski argue,

> According to the doctrine of incarnation, Jesus Christ was and is truly human—he really became a man . . . [Thus, the] Father really is *the God of Jesus Christ* . . . in becoming a human being, the Son, though he was himself God by nature, had humbled himself to become part of the creation.[80]

If only things were so straightforward! The fully developed catholic tradition insists that Christ's human nature is *not* a human being, and that, properly speaking, the divine Son becomes "man" (that term is predicable of him because of his mysterious union with a body and soul that, because of that union *don't* compose a human person) but not "*a* man," not a human person. He's an eternal divine Person who is "human" in the special sense just defined—*not* a human person. Thus a Catholic book on Incarnation explains that, at the councils,

> the Church taught officially and infallibly that the divine and human natures in Jesus Christ are united in one Person—and that Person is the Logos or the Second Person of the Blessed Trinity . . . the child Mary gave birth to in Bethlehem is not a human person; he is a divine Person . . . who has taken to himself a human nature in the womb of Mary.[81]

Protestant theologians often commit to this as well, and they will say that the "assumed" human body and soul, the "complete human nature" that the divine Son somehow unites with, is in itself "anhypostatic" (that is, not a self/person/intelligent agent) but that it in some sense becomes personal or at least is *called* that because of its mysterious union with the second divine Person, which they call its being "enhypostatic."[82]

Second, many trinitarians have held that an essential divine attribute is being timeless; *if* this is right, then the divine Son cannot in the Incarnation have (as

---

[79] White, *Forgotten Trinity*, 91.

[80] Bowman Jr. and Komoszewski, *Incarnate Christ*, 380.

[81] Baker, *Jesus Christ*, 31. For the official Roman Catholic teaching see *Catechism*, secs. 456–83, esp. 464–70.

[82] Crisp, *Divinity and Humanity*, ch. 3; Crisp, *Word Enfleshed*, ch. 5. For the many agonies of Incarnation speculations see my "Two Natures."

they said) *become* anything or have objectively changed in any way.[83] Third, it is a straightforward contradiction to say, as Bowman and Komoszewski do, that someone who is essentially fully divine, and thus is necessarily uncreated, and who thereby necessarily exists (exists "in all possible worlds," or just, exists no matter what) should become a part of God's creation, that is, one who directly or indirectly exists because of God's free choice to create, which implies existing not necessarily but rather contingently (see pp. 268–69).[84]

9.4 "EARLY HIGH CHRISTOLOGY" AND IDENTITY CONFUSIONS

Basic critical thinking skills for claims involving numerical identity are enough to undermine a whole realm of recently fashionable speculations about "early high Christology." These speculations—essentially late twentieth and early twenty-first century trinitarian pushback against modern Bible scholarship—need to be understood in their historical context.

9.4.1 THE MODERN CRISIS FOR TRINITARIAN EXEGESIS

Traditional trinitarian biblical interpretation made many dodgy moves in the attempt to derive fourth-century and later ideas from the New Testament.[85] For example, Psalm 45:1 (LXX): "My heart has belched forth a good Word"[86] was interpreted as teaching the eternal generation of the Logos (Word, the divine Son) by the Father,[87] and Proverbs 8, about Lady Wisdom (an obvious personification of a divine attribute), was read as about the prehuman Jesus and/or the divine Son or Logos.[88]

In the modern era the prevailing view has been that biblical books should be understood in their historical contexts—according to the times and places in

---

[83] But what the trinitarian should do here is to jettison the assumption that divinity implies timelessness, as this has no biblical support and clashes with biblical teaching about God (Mullins, *End of the Timeless God*). This requires denying what has been recently marketed as "classical" theism—a price some trinitarians are willing to pay but others are not.

[84] For an evangelical defense of Incarnation that agrees with the catholic tradition that his assumed human nature is impersonal, the one self/person in the Incarnation being the divine Son, and which assumes the impossibility of any change in a divine Person, see Geisler and Watkins, "Incarnation and Logic."

[85] Hanson, *Search*, 825–49.

[86] In the Greek Septuagint (LXX) translation of the Old Testament the numbering of this verse is 44:2.

[87] Augustine, *Psalm 45*, 302 (sec. 4).

[88] *Search*, 832.

which they were written; we should not project later ideas back into the texts. For instance, we should resist the claim that the doctrine of the Trinity is taught or even hinted at by the first-person plural in Genesis 1:26.[89] As a result, as evangelical theologian Fred Sanders observes,

> the doctrine of the Trinity stands today at a point of crisis with regard to its ability to demonstrate its exegetical foundation ... one by one, many of those venerable old arguments have been removed from the realm of plausibility. The steady march of grammatical-historical exegesis has tended in the direction of depleting Trinitarianism's access to its traditional equipment ... a prominent feature of the current era is the growing unpersuasiveness and untenability of the traditional proof texts that were used to establish and demonstrate the doctrine ... The presupposition has become widespread that the doctrine of the Trinity is a local phenomenon in the realm of systematic theology, with no provenance in the territory of New Testament scholarship.[90]

Here Sanders says out loud what is presupposed within the guild of biblical scholarship but routinely hidden from the laity.[91] By the final decades of the twentieth century, a broad swath of biblical and historical scholarship acknowledged a significant gap between the demands of fourth century and later catholic orthodoxy and the ideas actually found in the Bible. These scholars also recognized substantial innovations in the early development of mainstream Christian theology and Christology.

Simultaneously, the academy saw strong currents of religious pluralism—broadly, the idea that in some sense all religions are equally valid.[92] In this context, Jesus might be considered a great spiritual teacher but merely one among many. At the same time, there was a post–World War II resurgence of evangelical Christianity, especially in America, which assumed the basic correctness of catholic views on God and Christ, even while often ignoring much of the conciliar and patristic traditions.

The conditions were ripe for a conservative revolt in the biblical scholarship and history of Christian thought guilds. This took the form of what has been dubbed the "early high Christology club"—not an actual club, but a group of

---

[89] For starters, note the singular main verb in verse 27.

[90] Sanders, *The Triune God*, 162–63.

[91] This admission contrasts with Sanders's confident cheerleading of "the doctrine of the Trinity" as an obviously biblical doctrine in his popular writing and speaking, for example, Sanders, *Deep Things*, 40–41.

[92] Tuggy, "Theories."

scholars emerging in the 1970s–90s, intent on defending traditional catholic beliefs in the Trinity and Incarnation and rejecting any pluralistic reduction of Jesus to a mere "great spiritual teacher."

They largely abandoned direct defenses of any Trinity doctrine, instead making their stand on the catholic idea that Jesus is a god-man—one Person with both a divine and a human nature. However, they recognized that such language is not found in the biblical books, and so it would be anachronistic to read such a Christology there. Thus, they invented proxy language—various stand-ins for the orthodox formulas. These substitutes invariably involve confusion about numerical identity. In the next three subsections we'll briefly examine the work of the most influential club members.

9.4.2 BAUCKHAM'S "DIVINE IDENTITY" NEOLOGISMS

The most influential early high Christology scholar is Richard Bauckham. He considers traditional orthodox language outdated and overly dependent on classical philosophical categories. He replaces it with murky talk of "divine identity"—who God is. He argues that Old Testament thinking about God is not ontological (in the Greek philosophical sense) but characterizes "divine identity" in terms of actions only God performs.

Bauckham borrows the term "identity" from modern philosophical discussions of personal identity—what it is to be a certain person at a time or through times. As we've seen, being the same person—or the same anything—means being numerically the same thing. If Donald Trump and "The Donald" are the same person, then Donald Trump just is The Donald—they are one and the same. But Bauckham misunderstands this. He simultaneously suggests that Jesus just is God and that Jesus is, per Trinitarian speculations, some but not all of what is "in" God. But it is impossible that both claims are true. If there is in some sense more to God than the Son, then the Son and God can't be one and the same, since on all accounts there is *not* more *to the Son* than the Son.

In an influential short book[93] that was later republished within a longer book,[94] Bauckham says, "God used no one else to carry out his work of creation, but accomplished it alone,"[95] which implies that anyone who was involved in

---

[93] Bauckham, *God Crucified*.
[94] Bauckham, *Jesus*, ch. 1.
[95] *Jesus*, 29.

creating is numerically one with God himself.[96] Bauckham, following catholic traditions, sees a few texts as implying that Jesus was at work in the Genesis creation. It follows that Jesus and God must be one and the same.[97] Yet as we've seen, this won't serve trinitarian purposes, since the triune God must qualitatively differ from any one of the Persons in the triune God. So Bauckham more often concludes that somehow Jesus is "included in the divine identity," as is the Father, whatever that may mean.[98]

"Identity" here means personal identity, that is, what it is to be a certain someone/person/self. It's unclear what it means to say that this someone and that other someone are "in" an identity. Bauckham argues that the identity of the one God is understood in the Bible in this way: he is the only creator, the only one who is sovereign over the cosmos, and the only one who has a covenant relationship with Israel.[99] It follows that anyone who has any one of those characteristics *just is* the one God.[100] Bauckham doesn't seem to understand that numerical identity forces absolute indiscernibility, or that numerical identity is transitive—which is why he's just restating in his own language the problematic trinitarian claims that each of the Father and the Son just is God, yet they are distinct from each other.[101]

9.4.3 WRIGHT CONFUSES TOGETHER GOD AND JESUS AND DOESN'T

Identity confusions are as evident in the work of probably the second most influential member of the early high Christology club, Anglican bishop N. T. Wright. His work foregrounds the idea that when the chosen people went into captivity, God in some sense departed from them, but prophets then promised that Yahweh would return to them.[102] As he points out, in the New Testament the ministry of Jesus is considered to be a visitation of God or an encounter with God, of course, working in and through his human Messiah. But like other club

[96] This is an "only God" argument, as discussed in section 8.3.6

[97] The implicit argument is: For any x, if x was involved in the Genesis creation, then $x = \text{God}$. Jesus was involved in the Genesis creation. Therefore, Jesus = God. In my view Scripture asserts the truth of the first premise but implicitly denies the second premise.

[98] Bauckham, *Jesus*, 29, 55–56, 101, 213.

[99] *Jesus*, 7–13, 86–87.

[100] Section 8.3.6.

[101] He never clearly responds to this inconsistent triad of claims: the Father just is God, the Son just is God, and it is not the case that the Father just is the Son ($f = g$, $s = g$, $f \neq s$). For a more thorough critique see my "On Bauckham's Bargain."

[102] For accessible presentations see Wright's *Challenge of Jesus*, ch. 5; *How God*, ch. 5.

members Wright argues that something like an orthodox, fully divine Christology is present in the New Testament. Yet Wright seems uncomfortable with the Chalcedonian "one Person with two natures" formulations and with common apologetic approaches to defending "the deity of Christ."[103] Instead, in numerous books, articles, and videos, Wright offers his own language, which he seems to present as at least as good if not better than any traditional catholic language about Christ. It is that God has returned to his people "in and as" Jesus. With this phrase Wright is simply having it both ways regarding the relationship between God and Jesus. If someone visits us "in" (by means of) another, that presupposes that the first and second ones are numerically distinct.[104] But if someone visits us "as" another, that is, in the guise of another, then really there is just one someone there. Wright's claim implies that Jesus and God are numerically distinct and that they are one and the same—and so it must be false.

As we've seen, that God and Jesus are numerically distinct follows from their qualitatively differing in but the smallest way. As a New Testament scholar, even a translator of the whole New Testament,[105] Wright well knows that many simultaneous God-Jesus differences are assumed there, such as God having a human Son while Jesus lacks any human son, or God never having died although Jesus has died. But like traditional catholic apologists and other "early high Christology" thinkers, Wright repeatedly says that Jesus does things that only God himself can do. In a remarkable passage Wright says,

> I propose, as a matter of history, that Jesus of Nazareth was conscious of a vocation: a vocation given him by the one he knew as "father," to enact in himself what, in Israel's scriptures, God had promised to accomplish all by himself.[106]

---

[103] Wright contrasts his approach with "the somewhat shrill and unfocused normal 'apologetic' arguments for 'proving Jesus's divinity'" (*How God*, 101). Wright also thinks that his account better reveals the Gospels' Christology than catholic creedal traditions: "The gospels . . . deconstruct the old either/or of Jesus as *either* a human being *or* a divine being (which the creeds, and particularly the Chalcedonian formula, held together, but always with the appearance of a kind of confidence trick). The gospels offer us not so much a different kind of human, but a different kind of God: a God who, having made humans in his own image, will most naturally express himself in and as that image-bearing creature" (Wright, *How God*, 104).

[104] As Steven Nemes shows, in general, if at some time a does something by means of or through b, there is something a does and something else that b does (Nemes, "Early High Christology"). By IDI (p. 267) this implies $a \neq b$.

[105] Wright, *Kingdom New Testament.*

[106] Wright, *Jesus and the Victory*, 653.

Wright's thesis, then, is that Jesus was called by someone else, God, to be the Messiah, and that being the Messiah involves doing what only God himself can do. Let *S* stand for being a someone, a self. Wright at first implies that Jesus and God are different selves—*j* and *g* are two *S*'s. But then he implies that *j* and *g* are the same *S*. As we've seen, the first implies $j \neq g$ and the second implies $j = g$.[107] Unfortunately, Wright is peddling learned-sounding nonsense about Jesus and God: the implicit assertion and denial of their numerical identity. The same incoherent implications are found in the work of Wright's collaborator, the evangelical Anglican Bible scholar and theologian Michael Bird.[108]

9.4.4 HURTADO: "BINITARIAN" WORSHIP . . . AND THEOLOGY?

The late Larry Hurtado was another enthusiastic member of the club. Pushing back against claims of early twentieth-century scholarship that the worship of Jesus must have developed somewhat later than the New Testament, Hurtado argued that the evidence shows that right from the beginning Christians worshiped and prayed to Jesus, or more precisely, that they gave "cultic" (public, communal, religious) worship, rather than (only) individual devotion. In an early publication he concluded abstractly that "the early Christian mutation in Jewish monotheism was a religious devotion which took a certain binitarian shape."[109]

In a follow-up work that has been much cited by trinitarian apologists, he went further, concluding that there was

> a literal reshaping of the monotheism inherited from the Jewish/biblical tradition, initially taking things in a binitarian direction, though a trinitarian model subsequently became dominant.[110]

Thus there was not only a "'binitarian' pattern of devotional practices" but also a view of God "as 'one' and yet somehow comprising 'the Father' and Jesus . . . [a] novel endeavor to incorporate plurality within the one God."[111]

---

[107] Section 8.3.4.

[108] Bird, *Evangelical Theology*, 523–31; Bird, "Did Jesus," 57–61; Bird, *Jesus Among*, 388, 392; Ehrman, Bird, and Stewart, *When Did Jesus*, 89. However, as I read him, in his latest work Bird more often seems to be thinking of God and Jesus as closely "identified," meaning *somehow* closely associated together while being numerically distinct (*Jesus Among*, 384–411).

[109] Hurtado, *One God, One Lord*, 129.

[110] Hurtado, *Lord Jesus Christ*, 651. Hurtado expresses himself exuberantly here; no reshaping of monotheism will ever be a *literal* reshaping.

[111] *Lord Jesus Christ*, 651.

In Hurtado's view, then, not only the devotion but the theology too was "binitarian"—that is, involved multiple divine Persons in the one God. If a "binitarian" theology says there are *at least* two Persons in God, then it's compatible with later trinitarian views, but if it is the claim that there are *exactly two* divine Persons, then binitarian theology rules out trinitarian theology. Hurtado, as best I can tell, never clarifies which he thinks they held. But it's clear that the early Hurtado saw himself as *somehow* aiding the cause of orthodox, Nicene theology, so we should charitably interpret him has meaning *at least* two, not exactly two.[112]

But in his magnum opus[113] and in later works, he also argues that Christ was worshiped not because he was a divine Person but rather because the early Christians believed that God's exaltation of him required this sort of honor, which in fact glorifies the God who so elevated him.[114] In a later publication he states unclearly that "I have argued that devotion to Jesus as in some real and unique sense partaking in divine attributes and powers erupted very quickly and quite early" in Christian history,[115] a statement that any trinitarian or unitarian Christian could accept. Yet while disavowing the attribution of orthodox trinitarianism to the New Testament as a historical anachronism,[116] and seemingly recognizing the New Testament assumption that Yahweh = God = the Father,[117] he also teases that "the NT already reflects a certain 'triadic' shape to the early Christian experience of 'God'" and that a "triadic-shaped discourse surely . . . reflects the shape of the religious experiences" of the early Christians.[118]

The theological payoff of all of this is as clear as mud. What might such experience "shapes," whatever those may be, have to do with theology? What *is* "triadic-shaped" discourse? Does that have something to do with God being tripersonal, or not? What is the nature of Jesus's "partaking of divine attributes and powers" that Hurtado is suggesting? Is all of this merely a Rorschach inkblot that the reader can interpret according to her theological inclinations?

[112] Hurtado, *At the Origins*, 102, 118.

[113] Hurtado, *Lord Jesus Christ*.

[114] *Lord Jesus Christ*, 151–52; Hurtado, *How on Earth*, 30, 53, 137; Hurtado, *Honoring the Son*, 13, 66–67; Hurtado, *God*, 64, 108; Hurtado, "Did Jesus Demand."

[115] Hurtado, *God*, 99.

[116] *God*, 100, 102, 109.

[117] *God*, 33, 46, 111.

[118] *God*, 45, 101.

As I read him, Hurtado was increasingly more interested in history rather than in theology or Christology. Many a reader has thought that a main takeaway from Hurtado's work was that the New Testament shows that Jesus was worshiped, and since only God should be worshiped, clearly they were assuming that Jesus and God were one and the same.[119] Or, for those whose Trinity theory denies that any divine "Person" is identical with God, their takeaway is this: Jesus is properly worshiped, and only someone who is a fully divine Person should be worshiped, therefore Jesus is a fully divine Person.[120]

But as we've seen, Hurtado himself doesn't attribute either line of thinking to biblical authors and it is unclear what the theological payoff is supposed to be from his historical discoveries about the worship of Christ. When publicly asked if Jesus thought he was God, Hurtado said, "Hell no!"[121] In his last publication he doesn't seem to go any further than positing a "dyadic devotional pattern" in early Christianity—that is, honoring "the risen Jesus as a recipient along with the one God."[122] As a unitarian Christian, I say "Amen" to that, as it is taught in Philippians 2:10–11 and in Revelation 5.[123]

9.5 ONE GOD AND ONE LORD: 1 CORINTHIANS 8:4–6

This confused and confusing recent tradition of early high Christology has birthed and spread a new misreading of a text long favored by unitarians. Some of Paul's converts had evidently asked him if it was permissible for them to dine on meat that had been sacrificed to pagan deities. Part of Paul's answer is as follows:

> Hence, as to the eating of food offered to idols, we know that "no idol in the world really exists," and that "there is no God but one." Indeed, even though there may be so-called gods in heaven or on earth—as in fact there are many gods and many lords— yet for us there is one God, the Father, from whom are all things and for whom we exist, and one Lord, Jesus Christ, through whom are all things and through whom we exist. (1 Cor. 8:4–6)

---

[119] The line of thinking is as follows. Jesus is properly worshiped. But only God is properly worshiped. Therefore, Jesus and God are one and the same. See section 8.3.6.

[120] Hasker, *Metaphysics*, 178–83.

[121] I have seen this video of a roundtable discussion with Hurtado, Bart Ehrman, Michael Bird, and others, but it seems that the host seminary has taken it down. Hurtado does not disavow this statement in Buzzard, "Anthony Buzzard Hosts," at 1:03:04.

[122] Hurtado, *Honoring the Son*, 65.

[123] Tuggy, "Podcast 227;" "Who Should Christians Worship?"

"One God, the Father." Isn't this one of many passages that confirm that Paul is a unitarian (a Christian who holds to the numerical identity of God with the Father)[124] and so is committed to the falsity of any theology according to which the one God is the Trinity?

But a new interpretation has recently emerged and has been widely accepted among scholarly evangelical authors in the hope that it somehow supports a traditional deity of Christ teaching and perhaps even a doctrine of the Trinity. According to this new interpretation, in the above passage Paul is reformulating a longstanding, scriptural, Jewish theological statement.

9.5.1 WHAT PAUL MEANS

Before we get to that, let's make some observations about this passage. First, note the assertion of biblical monotheism against pagan religions. Second, we are told who this one God is: the Father. The phrases "one God" and "the Father" are used in apposition; the meaning is that "for us [Christians], there is one God, [namely,] the Father." This expresses Paul's assumption that the only god and the Father are numerically identical.

That is what unitarian Christians think, that the one God is one and the same with the Father (and so not with anyone or anything else). Paul here passes by the opportunity to say that for us the one god is the Father, the Son, and the Spirit. No, he states clearly that the unique god is the Father. This is why modern unitarian Christian writings commonly appeal to this as a clear New Testament text supporting unitarian theology.[125] In nineteenth century unitarian-trinitarian disputes, this text is never appealed to by trinitarians, and so unitarians don't bother to argue against any trinitarian interpretation of it.[126]

One nineteenth-century unitarian author comments:

> The Trinitarian ought never to cite this passage in support of his system; for it expresses the distinguishing doctrine of Unitarianism in the most explicit and comprehensive language. "There is NONE OTHER GOD BUT ONE," says the Unitarian Paul: "To us there is ONE GOD THE FATHER; and one Lord, Jesus Christ."[127]

---

[124] Tuggy, "Podcast 253."

[125] A small sample: Christie, *Dissertations*, 42–43; Crellius et al., *Racovian Catechism*, 29, 34, 57; Chang and Chan, *Only Perfect Man*, 36–37, 40.

[126] Wallace, *Plain Statement*; Yates, *Vindication of Unitarianism*; Wilson, *Unitarian Principles Confirmed*.

[127] Wilson, *Scripture Proofs*, 235, original capital letters.

We can observe about this passage that Paul implies that Father and Son are numerically distinct by his "and" (*kai*) and because he asserts them to differ somehow in verse 6; the Father is the one "from whom" while the Son is the one "through whom." If we assume, as many readers do, that his subject is the Genesis creation,[128] Paul's claim is that the Father is the ultimate source of the cosmos, and the Son is the agent through whom the Father created—thus *a* source but *not* the ultimate one. This fits hand in glove with the ancient subordinationist unitarian views that scholars call Logos theologies, which seem to have been initiated by Justin Martyr in the mid-second century. Originally a motivation of these was the Platonic assumption that somehow it is impossible for God to create directly, given his transcendence and remoteness from the material world. Oddly, some trinitarians today read the alleged Christ-creator passages in this way, where the Father is the ultimate source who indirectly creates through the eternal Son; only the second as it were "gets his hands dirty." This clashes with the fully developed trinitarian view as expressed by the 681 council, that the Persons of the Trinity have only one divine power between them,[129] and so it can never be that one Person is doing something and another is not, or is instead doing something else. But that's precisely what would be required for the Father to create through or by means of the Son—one Person performing an action while another Person performs a different action.[130]

But given the clear scriptural teaching that God (a.k.a. Yahweh, the Father) created on his own,[131] it is more likely that Paul's topic is the new creation, the recent reordering of the cosmos through Jesus Christ. The "all things"(*ta panta*) may be either believers themselves or the various blessings of the new covenant. Either way a qualitative difference is presupposed; Paul assumes, as he does throughout his letters, that the Father (a.k.a. God) and the Son of God are numerically two beings.[132] This passage seems to commit Paul to the soundness of the following argument.

---

[128] In my view this common assumption is mistaken; see my "Podcast 259."

[129] Williams, "Discovery."

[130] Nemes, "Early High Christology."

[131] Isa. 44:24b, 45:12; Ps. 33:6, 148:5; Gen. 1.

[132] See, for example, the dual greetings that come near the start of every Pauline letter, sent from both God (often "God the Father") *and* from Jesus.

English	*Logic*	*Logic-English*	*Justification*
1. The Father is the only god.	1. $Gf \wedge \forall x\,(Gx \supset x = f)$	1. The Father is a god and for any *x*, *x* is a god only if *x* just is the Father.	1 Cor. 8:6a; John 17:1–3, etc.
2. If anything is a god, then it just is the Father.	2. $\forall x\,(Gx \supset x = f)$	2. For any *x*, *x* is a god only if *x* just is the Father.	Implied by 1.[133]
3. The Father and Son differ.	3. $D\,(f, s)$	3. The differing relation obtains between the Father and the Son.	1 Cor 8:6b: "from" vs. "through," etc.
4. Identicals don't differ.	4. $\forall x \forall y\,(x = y \supset \neg D(x,y))$	4. For any *x* and any y, if *x* just is *y*, then *x* and *y* do not objectively differ.	Implied by IDI, p. 267.[134]
5. Therefore, Father and Son are not identical.	5. $f \neq s$	5. It is not the case that the Father is numerically identical with the Son.	Implied by 3 and 4.
6. Therefore, the Son is not a god.	6. $\neg Gs$	6. Therefore, it is not the case that the Son is a god.	Implied by 2 and 5.

[133] If a compound assertion (such as step 1) is true, then one-half of it must be true as well (the half that forms step 2). This is why 1 implies 2; the form of this valid inference is $P \wedge Q$, therefore Q.

[134] The Impossibility of Differing Identicals is: $\Box \forall x\, \forall y\, (x = y \supset \neg \Diamond \exists z\, (Tz \wedge D(x,y,z)))$. That is: Necessarily, if this just is that, then it's not possible that there's a time at which this and that objectively qualitatively differ. Since the differing of identicals at some time is absolutely impossible, premise 4 in this argument must be true, which says that if this and that are numerically identical, then they don't (now) differ. The Son but not the Father has been the one "through whom"—but then, they must be two (3 and 4 imply 5).

This argument draws out the clear implications of what Paul says. We're entitled to appeal to 4 in interpreting Paul, as 4 is something all normal adult humans know; it's a part of common sense, and so we can bring this assumption to our reading of any author. About the final conclusion 6, if the Son is not a god, then he's not the same god as the Father. But this is just an obvious implication of the Father being the only god. Paul, then, does not think that Jesus is "included in the divine identity" if that means that Jesus is God himself. Jesus is, for Paul, someone else, and so is neither the same someone nor the same being/thing nor the same god as the Father. Paul is certainly not identifying God and Jesus when he calls Jesus the "one Lord."

Why then does Paul call Jesus the "one Lord"? Joseph Fitzmeyer observes:

> [Paul admits here] that he is aware of the beliefs of . . . Greeks, Romans, and others in many "gods" (e.g. . . . Zeus, Apollo, Athena . . .) and their respect for many "heroes" called *kyrioi* [Lords] (apotheosized [divinized] humans such as Heracles, Asclepius, various Roman emperors, who were accorded the title *divus* [god]), as well as of the sacrifices offered in honor of such beings.[135]

The point is that there were two tiers of deities in popular Roman religion—this is the distinction some scholars make between "high" gods and mere or "lower" gods in polytheistic religions. It is plausible that Paul is exploiting this distinction here. "For us" Christians, he says, there is only one *god*, the Father, *and* there is only one *lord*, Jesus. (In contrast, the pagans believe there to be many gods and many lords.) The unique lord here is thus understood to be subject to the one god, as Paul clearly teaches elsewhere.[136] The point is not that Christ is a second tier deity, but simply that, in contrast to the pagans, we Christians recognize one top-level authority (God, the only god), and one second-level authority under him, the man Jesus, as he says elsewhere, God's "Son, born of a woman" (Gal. 4:4).

Whether or not Paul is exploiting that pagan distinction, it is clear that he uses "Lord" and "one Lord" in reference to Christ (1) in distinction from the one God,[137] and (2) this use of the title "Lord" is consistent the referent with being

---

[135] Fitzmyer, *First Corinthians*, 341. Compare: Clarke, *Scripture Doctrine*, 4 (1.1.8); Perriman, *In the Form*, 39.

[136] "God is the head of Christ" (1 Cor. 11:3). "Blessed be the God and Father of our Lord Jesus Christ . . . the God of our Lord Jesus Christ, the Father of glory" (Eph. 1:3, 17). See also 1 Cor. 15:20–28.

[137] 1 Cor. 8:6, Eph. 4:5–6.

under a god, the one God, the Father.[138] While "Lord" is ambiguous in the Pauline letters, sometimes referring to God and sometimes to Jesus, it is indisputable that, as applied to Jesus, it is a "lower" title than when it is applied to God.[139]

The interpreter should also remember the entirely practical nature of 1 Corinthians 8. Paul is not engaging in systematic theology here, and he gives no signal that he's doing anything to separate Christian theology from Jewish theology, that he's prying open the Jews' overly narrow, stingy, or rigid monotheism, so as to (in some sense) allow another "Person" into the one god. This passage is part of a bigger whole, the practical point of which is that yes, the Corinthian Christians may eat food sacrificed to idols so long as they don't damage the conscience of any fellow believer (v. 7–13).[140] Given this wholly practical—not theoretical—context, we should think that Paul is here mentioning a truism in passing, that Christians have a unique god and a unique human lord,[141] not making some surprising theological point. Here Jesus is called "Lord," but it hardly follows from that that he is a Person in the triune God, that he is fully divine, or that he is the one God himself.[142] But recent "early high Christology" scholars claim there is some *obvious* "high" (divine) christological point in this passage.

9.5.2 SHEMA SPLITTING?

The interpretive mischief began with James Dunn's influential study on early Christology, the first edition of which was published in 1980.[143] Dunn writes that Paul here "splits the *Shema*."[144] The Shema, the longstanding prayer and confession of mainstream Judaism is "Hear, O Israel: The Lord is our God, the Lord alone" (Deut. 6:4). Whereas in the Shema it is Yahweh who is the unique "God" and "Lord," here the "one God" is the Father, and the "one Lord" is Jesus. And whereas in the Old Testament Yahweh alone creates, in Dunn's view here God in some sense creates "through" the Son. It's not wholly clear quite what the "high Christology" payoff of this might be.[145] The general trend of Dunn's

---

[138] Eph. 1:3, 17; compare: 1 Cor. 3:23, 11:3, 15:24–28.

[139] Section 1.6.

[140] At least, that is Paul's initial answer. The larger passage, chapters 8–10, is harder to interpret, on which see Wright, *Climax*, ch. 6.

[141] Compare: Eph. 4:4–6.

[142] Barrett, *Commentary*, 193. See also section 1.6.

[143] Dunn, *Christology*.

[144] *Christology*, 180.

[145] *Christology*, 180–83.

book is to refrain from projecting later, fully divine Christology onto New Testament texts, much to the annoyance of Dunn's evangelical critics. Others adopting this reading have been less restrained in their conclusions.

Interpreters following Dunn in this new Shema-splitting interpretation make much of the fact that many of the words in the Greek Septuagint translation of Deuteronomy 6:4 occur also in 1 Corinthians 8:6. They take it as obvious that Paul is both referring to and modifying that traditional confession.

But it's not even clear that Paul is referring directly to the Shema. As New Testament scholar Andrew Perriman observes,

> It . . . appears to be on the basis of the presence of many gods *and many lords* in the pagan world that he constructs the two part confession regarding the "one God, the Father," and the "one Lord, Jesus Christ."[146]

Further, notes Perriman,

> "Lord" [Hebrew: Yahweh] occurs twice in the Shema but is absent here. This seems odd if Paul has intended to divide the Shema between "one God, the Father" and "one Lord, Jesus Christ"—all the more so if this is or echoes a familiar confessional statement, as is widely supposed.[147]

Again, Paul speaks here of one God *and* of one Lord; he uses the word "one" (*heis*) twice, which is

> pointedly *unlike* the Shema with its single *heis*. The effect is not to fuse two identities in one but to . . . create two distinct affirmations, anticipated in the previous acknowledgement of many gods and many lords: not only is God the Father one but the Lord, Jesus Christ, also is one—two separate unities. McGrath makes the point well: " . . . Paul does not say here that there is one God who is both Father and Son; he says rather that there is one God and also one Lord."[148]

There is evidence that Dunn at first thought this text implied a fully divine Jesus but that he later changed his mind. Andrew Perriman reports that at an academic conference in 2011,

> Dunn remarked that he used to favour the view that in 1 Corinthians 8:6 Paul incorporates Jesus as Lord into the *shema*, effectively identifying Jesus with God or making him equal to God . . . He has since changed his mind. He thinks now that while the first part of Paul's statement is a reference to the *shema* and, therefore, a classic affirmation of Jewish monotheism, the second part—"for us

146 Perriman, *In the Form*, 39, original italics.

147 *In the Form*, 38–39.

148 *In the Form*, 39–40, quoting McGrath, *Only True God*, 39.

there is . . . one Lord, Jesus Christ"—brings into focus Psalm 110:1: "The Lord says to my Lord: "Sit at my right hand, until I make your enemies your footstool."[149]

In later books Dunn makes it clear that he doesn't collapse together (numerically identify) Jesus and God on the basis of this or any other biblical texts.[150] But the damage had already been done; this misreading has steadily spread through evangelical Bible scholarship.

Abstract statements that Paul has "split" or reconfigured the Shema or that he's "inserted Jesus" into it are harmless enough. So what? The unitarian Christian well knows that the New Testament confession is of one God—that is, the Father—*and* of one human Lord under him, his Messiah Jesus.[151] Besides, as Dunn points out, although Paul surely has in mind the Jewish confession of Yahweh as the only God, this may be only in v. 4 ("there is no God but one") and in the first part of v. 6 ("for us there is one God, the Father"), not all of verses 4–6, including the Jesus part.[152] Many authors imagine that "inserting Jesus into the Shema" means inserting him as a fully divine Person into the multipersonal God, as in trinitarian theology. But Paul can't have meant that, any more than Thomas Jefferson could have said something about the Internet.

In the early 1990s N. T. Wright argued that this famous text presupposes "the highest possible Christology"[153] and he considers this so obvious that he

---

[149] Perriman, "Jimmy Dunn." Perriman then remarks, "This seems to me very plausible. The consistent story elsewhere in Paul is that Jesus is given lordship—given the name *kyrios*—as a result of his faithful obedience in suffering, and that this status will have future consequences with regard to the nations and to the final enemy death (cf. Rom. 1:3-4; 1 Cor. 15:24–28; Phil. 2:6–11). So in 1 Corinthians 8:6 Paul is not saying that Jesus must be assimilated into an essential Jewish monotheism. Rather he is setting out the fundamental 'Christian' response to the challenge of the dominant pagan culture: for us as heirs of Jewish monotheism there is one God, but this one God has given authority over the enemies of his people to the one who suffered, died and was raised from the dead. It is *through* him—not *from* him, as Dunn stressed—that these communities of new creation now exist. So I would say that the two-part confession reflects the fact that this *new creation* has come into existence under conditions of *eschatological conflict*."

[150] Dunn, *Theology of Paul*, 253–55; Dunn, *Did the First*, 108–10, 142–44. However, in one late work Dunn uncharitably suggests that even though Paul habitually distinguishes between God and Jesus, sometimes in his exuberance he thinks of them as one and the same (Dunn, *Jesus*, 134).

[151] Rom. 1:7, 15:6; 1 Cor. 1:3; 1 Thess. 1:1; 2 Thess. 2:1–2; Eph. 4:5–6; John 20:28.

[152] *Did the First*, 109.

[153] Wright, *Climax*, 132.

wonders how previous interpreters could have missed it.[154] Comparing the Septuagint Greek translation of Deuteronomy 6:4 with Paul's Greek here, he says Paul takes the Shema and redefines "it christologically, producing what we can only call a sort of christological monotheism."[155] He never quite spells out just what this abstract phrase "christological monotheism" means, although he characterizes it as an "unprecedented bifurcation within monotheism,"[156] which the reader will assume means the idea of multiple "Persons" somehow in God—which, again, is an anachronism when it comes to reading Paul's first-century letters. Wright seems to assume that Jesus "being the creator's obedient agent," "the creator's mediating agent"[157] (which is how he reads v. 6), requires "the highest possible Christology."[158] But to the contrary, the "highest possible Christology" would be the *identification* of Jesus with the one God; there can be none higher than the one God, so identification with him is the pinnacle of all possible christologies. But then Jesus would be *the* creator, not an agent through whom the creator works, and it would be implied that Jesus and God can't differ in any way, a claim ruled out by the New Testament.

Wright's discussion is exuberant, hasty, and unclear. Had he been more aware of the unitarian Christian minority report in theology and biblical scholarship, he may have tried harder to argue for a clear interpretation. As we saw above, he's now settled on the hopeless position that Jesus and God are and are not one and the same. About this text he remains overconfident.[159]

After Wright, the gifted and prolific biblical scholar Richard Bauckham took up the early high Christology mantle and has done more than anyone else to popularize this still newish scholarly movement. He projects his hazy "divine identity" ideas onto the whole New Testament, and so here in this passage he thinks that Paul "incorporates Jesus Christ into the unique divine identity,"[160] whatever that means.

---

[154] Wright, *Climax*, 132, 193.

[155] *Climax*, 129.

[156] *Climax*, 130.

[157] *Climax*, 131.

[158] *Climax*, 132.

[159] This text, he says, "encapsulates . . . everything that later generations and centuries would struggle to say about Jesus and God. From here on, we must say that if trinitarian theology had not existed it would be necessary to invent it. That is, in fact, effectively what the first generation of Christians did, worshipping Jesus within the framework of Jewish monotheism" (Wright, *Challenge of Jesus*, 107).

[160] Bauckham, *Jesus*, 211. See also 26–30, 210–18.

There's a stridency in Bauckham's discussion of this text that betrays the weakness of his arguments. He makes much of the fact that Paul here uses most of the words in the first part of the Greek version of the Shema text,[161] but of course this is wholly consistent with unitarian readings of this text. He then argues,

> If he were understood as *adding* the one Lord to the one God of whom the Shema speaks, then, from the perspective of Jewish monotheism, he would certainly be producing, not Christological monotheism, but outright ditheism ... The only possible way to understand Paul as maintaining monotheism is to understand him to be including Jesus in the unique identity of the one God affirmed in the Shema.[162]

But other scholars disagree.[163] And James McGrath rightly observes that Bauckham's interpretation "remains at the level of assertion."[164] In other words, Bauckham has not even tried to argue for his controversial spin on this passage.

Bauckham continues,

> Paul is not adding to the one God of the Shema a 'Lord' the Shema does not mention. He is identifying Jesus as the 'Lord' (YHWH) whom the Shema affirms to be one ... Thus ... the unique identity of the one God consists of the one God, the Father, and the one Lord, his Messiah (who is implicitly regarded as the Son of the Father) ... Paul rewrites the Shema to include both God and Jesus in the unique divine identity. [The Jewish view about creation, which Paul assumes, is that it is] unthinkable that any being other than God could even assist God (Is. 44:24; Sir. 42:21; *4 Ezra* 3:4; 6:6; Josephus, *C. Ap.* 2.192; Philo. *Opif.* 23) ... No more unequivocal way of including Jesus in the unique divine identity is conceivable within the framework of Second Temple Jewish monotheism.[165]

These are strong claims! Unfortunately there is a failure of clear thinking about identity here. Bauckham asserts that Paul is *identifying* Jesus and God; contra Wright (and Bauckham is right about this) God in the Bible creates *on his own*, so

---

[161] Bauckham, *Jesus*, 212.

[162] *Jesus*, 212–13.

[163] Dunn, *Did the First*, 109.

[164] McGrath, "Review." New Testament scholar Andrew Perriman observes that "What we have in 1 Corinthians 8:6 is not a *bifurcation* of the *Shema* but a *convergence*: Paul *brings together* the Jewish monotheistic confession and the apocalyptic narrative about Jesus, who suffered, died, was raised, and was given authority to rule at the right hand of God" (Perriman, "Is Jesus").

[165] *Jesus*, 213.

anyone who is involved in the Genesis creation *just is* God himself.[166] But if Bauckham is right, God and Jesus can't be one and the same; they must be distinct, since God is in some sense or other composed of the Father and the Son. If there is more to God than the Son, then God and the Son qualitatively differ, and so by the DPD (p. 267) they must be two. Bauckham is uncharitably and implausibly attributing to Paul the confusion that Jesus and God are *and are not* one and the same. In the search for a charitable and plausible interpretation of Paul's theology and Christology, Bauckham's suggestions are a non-starter.

Unfortunately, Bauckham's "divine identity" language is repeated in dozens if not hundreds of recent articles and books by otherwise competent scholars.[167] The sad truth seems to be that graduate programs in theology and biblical studies do a poor job in educating their students in the sort of critical thinking we explored in chapter 8. Many of these scholars have inherited not only Bauckham's confused and confusing neologisms but also his overconfidence. Thus, New Testament scholar Gordon Fee, after a Bauckhamite treatment of our text, concludes that it "could well serve as the basic text from which all Pauline christological discussion should flow."[168]

But this is upside-down; this is among the *less* clear Pauline texts because of the compressed statements in v. 6. Translated literally, these are:

> For us one God, the Father,
> from whom all things and we for him,
> and one Lord Jesus Christ,
> through whom all things and we through him.[169]

Is this about the Genesis creation? The new creation? Both? Interpreters are divided. And yet the identity of the one God with the Father, and his numerical distinctness from Jesus, are about as clear as they could be. The unitarian Christians are right; on the face of it this passage favors their theology. It's a problem for trinitarian theologies,[170] not a supporting text. The "inserting Jesus into the Shema" idea is a *very* recent interpretive twist. This should automatically make it suspect. I can't find this take on this passage in any author before James Dunn in 1980. Are we to think that no one detected what Paul is

[166] That is: for any x whatever, x creates only if $x = \text{God}$. See pp. 255–56.

[167] On 1 Cor. 8:4–6 see Fee, *Pauline Christology*, 88–94; Bowman Jr. and Komoszewski, *Incarnate Christ*, 496–504, 608–12.

[168] *Pauline Christology*, 94.

[169] *Incarnate Christ*, 608.

[170] It reflects Paul's commitment to the truth of premise 2 in the argument on p. 94.

doing here before the twentieth century? That seems *very* unlikely. Despite the overconfident assertions of some recent scholars, we should deny that Paul is making any new or post-Jewish or trinitarian theological claim in this passage about eating food that has been sacrificed to idols.

9.6 Conclusion

Is Jesus in *some* sense(s) "divine"? Yes, since the adjective "divine" can mean something importantly associated with God, such as the church or the scriptures. Who would deny that Jesus is "divine" in such a sense? After all, Jesus is God's unique Messiah and Son. And many things about Jesus are God-like; he has "a divinity of commission, of doctrine, and of character."[171] At the same time, the New Testament consistently

> represents him as a different being from God, dependent upon him for his wisdom, authority, and power; and inferior to him, as the being sent is inferior to him who sends; as the son is inferior to the Father; the creature to the Creator.[172]

Scripture implies Jesus to be a creature by its constant portrayals and descriptions of him as a real human person, a "man" (*aner, anthropos*).[173] In Scripture a human being is by definition a creature of God the Creator.

Did Jesus exist prior to being a human? Did he help create the world? However we answer these questions, the New Testament is clear: Jesus and his god are two, not one and the same. We know this because all the New Testament authors assume and imply simultaneous God-Jesus differences. Nor do we ever see these authors making misguided "only God" arguments that imply the numerical sameness of God and Jesus.[174] That error belongs to a later time. According to Scripture, quite explicitly, the only god is yours and Jesus's—the Father.[175]

In these books Jesus is not God himself, not the one true god, but is someone else, someone who has a submissive, faithful, unique personal relationship with the one true god. He trusts in God, prays to him, and faithfully serves him as a Jew under the Mosaic covenant. In the New Testament Jesus is not the Christian god but rather the unique human Son,

---

[171] Ripley, *Divinity of Jesus*, 4.

[172] *Divinity of Jesus*, 5.

[173] Jesus said to his opponents, "but now you are trying to kill me, a man who has told you the truth that I heard from God" (John 8:40).

[174] Section 8.3.6.

[175] Section 11.4.

servant, and Messiah of that god—all of this is explicitly taught.[176] In contrast to today's confused usage, in Scripture "Jesus" is not the proper name of the Christian god. According to the Gospels, in Jesus's theology the one god is none other than the Father himself. Dare we call Jesus "Lord" while disagreeing with his theology?[177] Dare we, his disciples, judge our greatest human teacher to be a confused, "primitive" theologian? Have the so-called "ecumenical" councils from 325–787 and/or later theological speculations empowered us to see past *his* confusions?

If you accept the points made in this chapter, you adhere to a unitarian interpretation of the New Testament. Thus, if you're a Christian, you're a unitarian Christian, someone who believes in the Messiah Jesus, but who identifies the one true god as the one Jesus, Paul, and John called "Father," "God the Father," and simply "God." You may believe in a "Trinity" or triad of sorts, but this won't be a triune God somehow consisting of equally divine Persons—an idea never stated, implied, or assumed in the New Testament. Rather, your triad will be like that of many pre-Nicene "fathers," consisting of this group: God, God's Son, and God's spirit or Spirit.[178] This triad talk too is a post-New-Testament development, dating to the second century.[179] But at least such a theology doesn't, like truly trinitarian (tripersonal-god-involving) ones, clash with the clear New Testament teaching that the one god just is the Father.[180]

---

[176] "The God of Abraham and Isaac and Jacob, the God of our ancestors, has glorified his servant Jesus" (Acts 3:13). "For in this city, in fact, both Herod and Pontius Pilate, with the gentiles and the peoples of Israel, gathered together against your holy servant Jesus, whom you anointed . . . while you stretch out your hand to heal, and signs and wonders are performed through the name of your holy servant Jesus" (Acts 4:27, 30). "Now Jesus did many other signs in the presence of his disciples that are not written in this book. But these are written so that you may continue to believe that Jesus is the Messiah, the Son of God" (John 20:30–31). "[Jesus praying:] Father, if you are willing, remove this cup from me, yet not my will but yours be done" (Luke 22:42). "God sent his Son, born of a woman, born under the law" (Gal. 4:4).

[177] Buzzard, *Jesus Was Not*.

[178] On the difference between "trinity" as a plural referring term and "Trinity" as a singular referring term, see my *What is the Trinity*, ch. 3; "Flocanrib"; and sections 1.10.1, 3.7.2, and 7.4. On the status of "the Holy Spirit" in the New Testament, see p. 250, note 92.

[179] Theophilus of Antioch, writing around 180, refers in passing to some sort of triad (Greek: *trias*), although he may have held Dynamic Monarchian (biblical unitarian) views, on which see Grant, *Greek Apologists*, ch. 19; Grant, *Jesus After the Gospels*, ch. 5. Perhaps a few decades later we find Tertullia using the Latin word *trinitas* (triad); on his views see Tuggy, "Tertullian the Unitarian"; Date and Tuggy, *Is Jesus Human*, 123–26, 142–45, 153–56.

[180] Chapter 3.

CHAPTER 10

The Fulfillment Fallacy

10.1 A PARODY ARGUMENT: THE BIBLE TEACHES THAT DAVID IS GOD[1]

The Bible holds many hidden wonders. In addition to its clear and explicit teachings, by careful reasoning we can draw out many implications of what it says by comparing various parts. Aided by recent evangelical apologists and theologians, I've made some exciting scriptural discoveries that I am now privileged to share with the world.

I've made these discoveries using the same method of interpretation they use to discern how, in using Old Testament prophecies, the New Testament authors imply the divine identity of Jesus.

STEP 1: PROVE THAT JESUS IS GOD

1. When the prophet Isaiah says "prepare the way of the LORD" (Isa. 40:3) the "LORD" there is God himself (Yahweh).
2. Mark 1:1–3 applies this to Jesus; the "Lord" when he quotes Isaiah is Jesus.[2]
3. Therefore, Jesus is God himself (Yahweh). (1,2)

---

[1] This chapter developed from several blog posts at trinities.org and Date and Tuggy, *Is Jesus Human*, 29–32.

[2] Non-parody sidenote: Mark only names Isaiah, although he has pieced together language from Ex. 23:20, Mal. 3:1, and Isa. 40:3. In my view, it is possible that Mark's meaning is that *God* is coming to his people *by means of* his anointed human servant Jesus; both God and Jesus are called "Lord" in this book (Mark 2:28; 5:19; 11:3, 9; 12:11, 29–30; 12:36–37; 13:20). But most commenters understand 1:1–4 as saying that ancient Scriptures predicted that John the Baptist is the messenger who came to prepare the way *for Jesus* (Gundry, *Mark*, 36).

STEP 2: PROVE THAT JESUS IS DAVID

4. When the psalmist says, "The LORD says to my lord, 'Sit at my right hand until I make your enemies your footstool'" the words "my lord" refer to David (Ps. 110:1).[3]
5. When Peter quotes this psalm, "my lord" refers to Jesus (Acts 2:34–36).
6. Therefore, Jesus is David. (4, 5)

STEP 3: TIE IT ALL TOGETHER

7. Jesus is God. (from Step 1)
8. Jesus is David. (from Step 2)
9. Therefore, David is God. (7, 8)

Lest you have doubts about the validity of this third step of the argument, be assured that 9 follows from 7 and 8. Things that are identical to the same thing (here, Jesus) must also be identical to one another (here, God and David).[4] We have proved the deity of David, or, if you like, the Davidity of God.

The implications of this are astounding. Not only is Jesus God (Step 1), but we also know that he's not the only incarnation of God (Step 3), and that reincarnation occurs, at least sometimes. (Step 2)

I know what you're thinking: "Everyone knows that David sinned terribly! He can't be God Almighty" (2 Sam. 11). I reply: We must avoid rationalism, that lamentable habit of refusing to believe things we can't fully understand. I don't understand how God, a holy and perfect being, could commit sins of adultery and murder. But I choose to believe what the Bible says, as I've outlined above. I will not call God, the ultimate author of the Bible, a liar. I choose humility over rationalistic pride, embracing the mystery.

Perhaps you'll reject this as an unjustified innovation, as something previously absent from Christian tradition. Well, Step 3 is just simple logic. And Step 2, which you're objecting to, uses the same sort of reasoning as Step 1. Isn't Step 1 widely accepted as a sound argument?[5] Sometimes implications take a while to be noticed—even many centuries; I couldn't say why these implications (Steps 2 and 3) weren't noticed before. I suppose it

---

[3] It is unclear who, in its original setting, the human king is here, although some human king or other is being referred to. The reader should simply grant this premise for the sake of the argument; the point ultimately being made doesn't depend on the truth of this premise, as will be shown.

[4] Sections 8.3.3 and 8.4.

[5] Bowman Jr. and Komoszewski, *Incarnate Christ*, 473–74; Craig, *Reasonable Faith*, 310.

could just be due to the extraordinary intellectual humility I have been blessed with, which has enabled me to make these awesome discoveries. (It is all by God's grace, of course.) Or it could be that until now, the time was not right for these important truths to be revealed.

10.2 ANOTHER PARODY ARGUMENT: THE BIBLE ON ANOTHER PREVIOUS LIFE OF JESUS

As I have proved, the Bible teaches that King David is God, and since it also teaches that Jesus is God, it teaches that Jesus is David. In other words, David was reincarnated as Jesus—the person later called "Jesus" was earlier called "David," and this person is God himself.

But I have now discovered that there was at least one other stop for God on the way from the 10th c. BCE to the 1st c. CE. We need to reapply our method for identifying who is who using Bible prophecies.

Isaiah 7:14 predicts that a baby will be born named "Immanuel." This occurs in the prophet's lifetime, in the 8th or 7th c. BCE. Obviously, this baby is God because his name means "God with us," and it would be blasphemous to give that name to anyone other than God himself. Indeed, Matthew says that Jesus's birth is a fulfillment of this prediction (Matt. 1:20–25). Here's an additional argument:

1. The "Immanuel" in Isaiah 7:14 is a baby in Isaiah's time.
2. Matthew 1 says that Jesus is a fulfillment of Isaiah 7:14.
3. Therefore, the baby Immanuel in Isaiah's time and Jesus are one and the same. (from 1, 2)

In sum, Jesus, who is God, had at least two previous incarnations, as that baby Immanuel in Isaiah's day, and before that as King David.

Do I deviate here from "historic Christian orthodoxy"? Friend, surely you agree with 1 and 2. And you should agree that 3 follows from them if you agree with this sort of reasoning in general and with our first argument involving Mark 1: 1–3 (p. 331). Here's another example of this sort of argument, one that I have not composed.

10.3 A RECENT EVANGELICAL ARGUMENT

1. When Isaiah says that "every knee will bow," he means to Yahweh himself.[6]
2. Paul says that "every knee should bow" to the exalted Jesus, obviously referencing Isaiah (Phil 2:10).
3. Therefore, Jesus is Yahweh himself. (1,2)[7]

A Christian shouldn't disagree with premises 1 and 2; those are simply correct observations. And many evangelical apologists and theologians assure us that the conclusion 3 follows. Another advantage of this argument is that it justifies what has recently become a popular shorthand for a traditional, catholic, orthodox view of Christ, which is saying that "Jesus is Yahweh."[8]

10.4 HOW THESE ARGUMENTS GO WRONG

The main problem with these arguments (except Step 3 of the argument on p. 332) is that they are invalid; that is, even if all the premises were true, this would not imply the truth of the conclusion. They have this common form:

1. Text 1 is about Yahweh.
2. Text 2 quotes Text 1 as saying something about Jesus.
3. Therefore, Yahweh and Jesus are one and the same.

Logically speaking, there is no connection between the truth of both 1 and 2 and the truth of the conclusion 3. In sentential logic, where letters stand for propositions (assertions, claims), we would represent the structure of this argument as follows.

1. *P*
2. *Q*
3. Therefore, *R*

How is *R* related to *P* and *Q*? We don't know! Thus, we don't know that if *P* and *Q* were true, *R* would be as well—we don't know the argument to be valid.[9]

But sometimes when we informally state arguments we leave unspoken premises that are assumed to be true. Here what is assumed is the truth of

---

[6] "By myself I have sworn; from my mouth has gone forth in righteousness a word that shall not return: 'To me every knee shall bow, every tongue shall swear.'" (Isa. 45:23). This is Yahweh himself speaking (Isa. 45:18).

[7] Bowman Jr. and Komoszewski, *Incarnate Christ*, 107, 114–15, 121–22.

[8] Tuggy and White, "Debate."

[9] Contrast with this argument, which anyone can "see" to be valid: 1. *P*. 2. If *P* then *Q*. 3. Therefore, *Q*. See section 8.4.1 for other obviously valid forms of deductive arguments.

scriptural claims. We could add premises about the truth of Text 1 and Text 2 to the argument, resulting in this:

1. Text 1 is about Yahweh.
2. What Text 1 says about Yahweh is true.
3. Text 2 quotes Text 1 as saying something true about Jesus.
4. What Text 2 says about Text 1 is true.
5. Therefore, Text 1 says something true about Jesus.
6. Therefore, Yahweh and Jesus are one and the same.

This analysis better captures how the proponents of such arguments are reasoning. Premises 1 and 3 are known by simple reading comprehension, and premises 2 and 4 are founded on a doctrine of inspiration. The first conclusion 5 follows from the conjunction of premises 3 and 4. Unfortunately, this argument too is invalid—if all of steps 1–5 were true, this would not require the truth of the conclusion 6. Here is a possible scenario that will help you to see this shortcoming.[10] Let's suppose that both Text 1 and Text 2 are divinely inspired. Its human author, when writing Text 1, meant it to say something true about Yahweh. But God, while inspiring that human author, also intended that Text 1 should say something true about the future Messiah, Jesus—which is revealed by Text 2. In these circumstances, all of 1–5 will be true, yet 6 may still be false. It has not been ruled out that Text 1 had, by God's inspiration, two meanings, one saying something true about God and the other saying something true about Jesus.

10.5 WHY NOW?

I've spent about two decades reading the whole breadth of early Christian theological literature and I've never found an author employing the sorts of arguments we've been discussing. Why is that? One reason is that most ancient theologies did not posit the numerical identity of God with Jesus. The only pre-Nicene theologians who *might* have wanted to would be some among the Modalistic Monarchians. These are often characterized as collapsing together God (the Father) and the Son. It may be that some of them did that; certainly, some early New Testament readers seem to have done that.[11] However, I think a

---

[10] It is enough that we're dealing with a metaphysically possible scenario; with a valid argument, there are no possible circumstances in which all of the premises are true but the conclusion is false. Finding such a scenario proves that the argument in question is invalid.

[11] In one pseudepigraphal work from around the year 200, there are passages consistent with "Father," "Son," and "Holy Spirit" being simply various names for the one God (*Acts of Paul*, 364–65, 373–74, 378–82, 387).

more common view among the Modalists was to think of the pre-Incarnation Logos/Word as a mode of the Father—that is, a way the Father exists, such as an event involving the Father, an action of the Father, or an attribute of the Father.[12]

As for the other early mainstream wings of theology, the Logos Theology Subordinationists (such as Justin, Tertullian, Novatian, Origen, and Eusebius the church historian) and the Dynamic Monarchians (such as Theodotus of Byzantium, Artemon, and Paul of Samosata) both clearly distinguished between God and the Logos (and between God and the man Jesus) and so did not want to make any arguments that imply their numerical sameness.

On the face of it, trinitarians should not want such arguments to be sound; for them, God is tripersonal, and Jesus is not tripersonal, so they must deny the numerical sameness of God and Jesus (since it is patently impossible for one and the same thing to simultaneously differ from itself). However, some trinitarians since around the time of Augustine have interpreted "the doctrine of the Trinity" along the lines of the pseudo-Athanasian Creed, which arguably numerically identifies each Person of the Trinity with God, and, therefore, the Son of God with God. Of course, many other trinitarians deny that "the" doctrine, rightly understood, makes such identity claims.[13]

Several other factors are important for understanding the recent popularity of these "Jesus is Yahweh" arguments. One is that modern historical-critical Bible scholarship has removed nearly all the traditional proof texts for "the doctrine of the Trinity" advanced by the ancient catholic tradition.[14] Modern scholarship has revealed that no biblical text says anything about God being tripersonal, which is an idea postdating any of the biblical books by more than two hundred years.[15] This has created a felt need for new proof texts for "the Trinity"—or in the absence of those, new ways to argue that in some fashion or other "the doctrine of the Trinity" is well-founded on Scripture.

---

[12] In a long discussion the author of *Refutation of All Heresies* (writing around 222) is obviously frustrated and is having difficulty interpreting the views of contemporary Modalistic Monarchians, although it seems clear that he wants to attribute to them the numerical identification or collapse of the Father and the Son (*Refutation*, 621–59 [9.7–12]). For some discussion of how ancient modalists probably read John 1:1–18 see my opening statement in "Podcast 394" and section 1.4.1.

[13] See p. 300.

[14] See the quotation from trinitarian theologian Fred Sanders, p. 311.

[15] For discussion of primary sources for pre-trinitarian, mainstream theologies in the late 100s and the 200s, see my "Podcast 384"; "Podcast 381."

Another is the rise of what I have called "fauxthodox" language.[16] The most influential examples of this are the neologisms coined by the British Bible scholar Richard Bauckham. Seeking to replace traditional catholic language with something better,[17] he claims that throughout the New Testament we can find the view that Jesus "belongs to the identity of God."[18]

It's unclear what this means,[19] but sometimes Bauckham and others following him reason like this:

1. Only God has feature *F*.
2. Jesus has feature *F*.
3. Therefore, Jesus is God.[20]

Given the validity of the argument, the "only" in the first premise implies that the "is" in the conclusion must be an "is" of identity; the conclusion is a claim of numerical sameness, of the form $a = b$.[21] For uncritical disciples of Bauckham, who are legion among present-day evangelical scholars, it thus seems correct to say that "Jesus is Yahweh," understood as $j = y$, that is, the claim that Jesus and Yahweh are one and the same—even though the same people correctly assume Jesus and God to qualitatively differ from one another.

Third, in recent times, particularly in the more Bible-oriented wing of evangelicalism, there has been a trend to dumb down traditional catholic language to something simpler. Thus, the whole machinery of Chalcedonian and post-Chalcedonian two-natures theories about Christ becomes simply "the deity of Christ" or the claim that "Jesus is God" (meaning that Jesus is fully divine and/or that Jesus and God are one and the same—even while Jesus is human). But whatever grounds one may have for such claims, they do not include the invalid arguments we've examined so far.

Fourth, recent theological education usually fails to teach critical thinking, how to construct valid, sound, cogent arguments, and how to analyze and evaluate arguments.[22] Thus there is widespread confusion among theologians,

---

[16] Tuggy, "Podcast 393."

[17] Bauckham, "Orthodoxy in Christology."

[18] Bauckham, *Jesus*.

[19] Section 9.4.2; Tuggy, "On Bauckham's Bargain."

[20] Bauckham, *Jesus*, 6–12, 147. See section 8.3.6 for the high "cost" of such arguments.

[21] Sections 8.2 and 8.3.6.

[22] Prominent Christian philosopher Peter van Inwagen writes, "I do not contend that all, or most, theologians are unable to tell the difference between an assertion and an argument;

Bible scholars, and apologists about the concept of numerical identity and about claims and arguments employing that concept.[23]

Fifth, some recent scholars want to rebut claims that the gospel message significantly evolved between the writing of the Synoptics and the Fourth Gospel (which is widely believed to have been written later). Some ancients took in stride the fact that, on the face of it, nothing in Matthew, Mark, or Luke would lead a reader to think that Jesus is God himself, that he's fully divine, or that he's an eternal divine Person. Thus, the famous fourth-century church historian Eusebius of Caesarea writes,

> John probably omitted the genealogy of our Savior as a man since it had already been written by Matthew and Luke and began with the proclamation of his divinity, because the divine Spirit had reserved this for him as one superior to them.[24]

Eusebius and other ancients thought that the deity of Christ was taught, or clearly taught, only by John, not by Matthew, Mark, or Luke.[25] Eusebius reasons that this must have been because the apostle John was found more worthy.

I agree with evangelical scholars that it would be worrisome if John taught the deity of Christ while Matthew, Mark, and Luke did not. We would expect these books—which, according to ancient traditions, are rather closely connected to Jesus's apostles and their circles, and which were written within a fairly short span of time—not to differ so much in their central message. The "early high Christology" scholars argue, implausibly, that Matthew, Mark, and Luke teach the deity of Christ too—but only by subtle implication. There has recently been a fashion for, ridiculously, arguing that even the earliest Gospel, Mark, clearly teaches Jesus to be Yahweh. The solution is the opposite, which is to see that carefully read, John doesn't teach the deity of Christ either.[26]

---

and I do not contend that all, or most, theologians uncritically defer to the authority of Kant or Heidegger or any philosopher. I do, however, believe that these two intellectual vices . . . are not as uncommon among academic theologians as one might wish, and are no barrier to a successful academic career" (*God, Knowledge, and Mystery*, 5).

[23] Tuggy, "Apologetics Blind-Spot"; "Podcast 124." See also chapters 8 and 9.

[24] Eusebius, *Church History*, 114 [3.24]. Reader beware: this quote may mislead you into thinking that Eusebius assumes the full deity of Christ, but he was a subordinationist who held that the one true god is the Father, and that the Son is divine in a lesser way (Eusebius, *On Ecclesiastical Theology*).

[25] For Origen's view see his *Commentary on John*, 37–38 [1.22].

[26] Tuggy, "John 1"; "Podcast 70"; "Podcast 394."

The newness of these arguments in sections 10.1–4 should worry us. If there were such obviously valid arguments, and these were compatible with mainstream orthodoxy, we would have seen them often made down through the history of theology.

10.6 NEW TESTAMENT USES OF OLD TESTAMENT TEXTS

On p. 335 I used a thought experiment to show that most of the arguments of sections 10.1 and 10.2 are invalid. A key point we imagined to be true is that God, the inspirer of Scripture, had in mind an additional meaning beyond that known to the human author. This is obviously possible; it seems a small thing for an all-knowing and all-powerful being to do! Further, I will show in this section that any Christian should agree that God has actually done this with at least some of the Old Testament texts that the New Testament authors say are about Jesus.

In Matthew 2:13 an angel advises Joseph that the family should flee to Egypt to avoid the wrath of Herod. We're told in verse 15 that this sojourn in Egypt happened to fulfill Hosea 11:1, "out of Egypt I called my Son." But the first half of Hosea 11:1 reads "When Israel was a child, I loved him." The text originally focused on the nation of Israel. If Matthew 2:15 is true, then the text must also have a meaning that applies to Jesus. I don't see any grounds in the context of Hosea 11:1 for supposing that the human author had the future Messiah in mind. In Matthew 2:15 the author is assuming that *the inspirer of* this text had that in mind; it was this meaning known only to God that is fulfilled in the life of Jesus.

Earlier in this book we're told that the events of Matthew 1:18–21 were a fulfillment of ancient prophecy:

> All this took place to fulfill what had been spoken by the Lord through the prophet [in Isa. 7:14]: "Look, the virgin shall become pregnant and give birth to a son, and they shall name him Emmanuel," which means, "God is with us." (Matt. 1:22–23.)[27]

But when the reader looks in Isaiah 7, she can see that the "Emmanuel" (or "Immanuel") in question was to be a baby born not long before an ancient divine judgment against God's people (7:15–25), hundreds of years before Jesus's birth.

---

[27] Happily, this translation (unlike many English translations) inserts an "is," reminding us that this is merely a theophoric name, a name given to a human being in praise of some quality of God. It wasn't understood as implying or assuming that the baby Jesus was God or a divine Person, as per later Incarnation speculations. Of course, the name is compatible with the claim that God is visiting his people through this human Messiah.

It's implausible that the author is, by citing this text, numerically identifying Jesus with that ancient baby Immanuel, as the Jews generally did not believe in reincarnation. Nor is it plausible that the author simply didn't read beyond v. 14 of Isaiah's seventh chapter. We should instead think that he believed there was an additional meaning and so a further fulfillment of Isaiah 7:14. The argument in section 10.2 is invalid and so gives us no reason at all to agree with its conclusion. So too with Step 1 and Step 2 in the argument of section 10.1; both are invalid and so give us no reason to agree with their conclusions.

What about the argument in section 10.3 (p. 334)? I believe that the premises are true. But it's not clear that it fits the same analysis as the other arguments we've evaluated, the five-step argument analyzed in section 10.4 (p. 335). Paul doesn't explicitly say here that the post-resurrection exaltation of Jesus fulfilled that text. In a Scripture-soaked culture such as that of Second-Temple-era Pharisees or that of the earliest Christians, authors did not only quote biblical texts; often they merely (as scholars say) "echo" or "gesture" at them, and that may be true of Philippians 2:10. But let's grant for the sake of argument that Paul is assuming or implying that this exaltation of Jesus by God is, properly speaking, a fulfillment of Isaiah 45:23.

Granting that, it is still implausible that Paul, who constantly distinguishes between God and Jesus, is slyly implying their numerical identity. In this very passage Paul clearly assumes the numerical distinctness of God and Jesus, since he assumes them to have simultaneously differed.[28] Further, the identity of Jesus with God would make nonsense out of Paul's narrative. It would be nonsense for Jesus/God not to consider some sort of equality *with himself* something to be sought (or clung to, depending on the translation of *harpagmo*[29]). And Paul, like other Jews and Christians of his time, assumed that God is essentially immortal, but he says that Jesus died (Phil 2:8), something an essentially immortal being by definition can't do.[30] Finally, the idea in Philippians 2:11 is that the worship given to Jesus also flows up to one above him, to God the Father, which presupposes that God and Jesus are two objects of worship, and so two objects/beings—in other words, numerically distinct.

---

[28] Jesus humbly obeyed God, laying aside his rights, even through a terrible and painful death (Phil. 2:7–8), and was consequently raised and exalted by God (Phil. 2:9). And now worship given to Jesus flows also up to the one above him (Phil 2:11). For Paul, none of these things are true of God (a.k.a. the Father).

[29] Phil 2:6; Keown, *Philippians 1:1–2:18*, 394–401.

[30] Tuggy, "Nineteen," sec. 2.

This fact about some New Testament authors' uses of Old Testament texts presents a complication for arguments between Christians and Jews, who may deny the needed extra meanings.[31] Nonetheless, it is a fact, and it is not the only thing that may strike modern readers as odd about the ways that New Testament authors use Old Testament texts.[32]

10.7 FIXING THE ARGUMENTS?

Someone might object, "You're straw-manning our arguments! We trinitarians don't make the mistake of collapsing together the Father and the Son! Rather, our point is *only* that the Son *is fully divine*."

In reply, *some* trinitarians *do* hold that the Father is God and that the Son is God, meaning $f = g$ and $s = g$ (claims of numerical identity).[33] But yes, other trinitarians interpret "the deity of Christ" as explained in the objection, as *not* implying that Jesus = God, but only asserting that Jesus has divinity as an essential quality.[34] Further, as I mentioned, some from both groups make arguments that imply the numerical sameness of Jesus and God.[35]

But let's try to steelman the argument based on the above objection. What if we change the final conclusion, replacing that claim about numerical sameness (#6, p.335) with a claim about Jesus having the quality *divinity*? That would give us this argument:[36]

1. Text 1 is about Yahweh.
2. What Text 1 says about Yahweh is true.
3. Text 2 quotes Text 1 as saying something true about Jesus.
4. What Text 2 says about Text 1 is true.
5. Therefore, Text 1 says something true about Jesus.
6. Therefore, Jesus is fully divine.

---

[31] Singer, *Let's Get Biblical*, vol. 1 pt. 4; *Let's Get Biblical*, 2:183–88.

[32] Beale and Carson, *Commentary*.

[33] *Athanasian Creed*; Beall, *Divine Contradiction*, 13; Tuggy, "Trinity," secs. 1.4, 1.6.

[34] For example, Craig, Hasker, and Branson in McIntosh, *One God*. But then, if someone is fully divine, and if, as is plausible, full divinity entails being a god, and as all trinitarians say, the Father and Son are numerically distinct, then it seems we have implied that there are at least two gods! See my "Faith Once Delivered," 138.

[35] Section 8.3.6.

[36] Or rather, this is a general schema for constructing an argument, once we fill in actual texts for the placeholders "Text 1" and "Text 2."

Unfortunately this sort of argument too is invalid; the truth of all of 1–5 would not logically imply the final conclusion 6.[37] Text 1 may truly say something about Yahweh (so premises 1 and 2 are true), and Text 2 may truly say that Text 1 says something about Jesus (so premises 3 and 4 are true, and so also the first conclusion 5), even though Jesus is not fully divine (so 6 is false). The argument doesn't rule out that Text 1 has two meanings, and if it does have two meanings, no one has any idea why, if meaning one is about a divine being or Person, then meaning two would also have to be about a divine being or Person.

But there is a way to make the original, identity-implying argument (p. 335) valid, if we strengthen premise 1 and add a new premise 6.

1. Text 1 is *only* about Yahweh.
2. What Text 1 says about Yahweh is true.
3. Text 2 quotes Text 1 as saying something true about Jesus.
4. What Text 2 says about Text 1 is true.
5. Therefore, Text 1 says something true about Jesus.
6. Text 1 has only one meaning.
7. Therefore, Yahweh and Jesus are one and the same.

As best I can tell, this argument is valid. If Text 1 is true and has only one meaning which is about Yahweh alone (1, 2, and 6), and Text 2 truly says that Text 1 says something *about Jesus* (3–5), then that one subject-matter of Text 1 must be Yahweh/Jesus. If all of 1–6 are true, that implies the truth of the final conclusion 7—that Yahweh and Jesus are one and the same.

For many Old Testament texts premise 6 will not be true. As we've seen, it is obvious that New Testament authors assume that at least some ancient prophecies have more than one meaning and more than one fulfillment. For those cases of Text 1, our new premise 6 would be false, and so the argument, while valid, would be unsound, giving us no reason to believe 7.

Someone might push back as follows. "OK, I see that Old Testament texts such as Hosea 11:1 ('out of Egypt I called my Son') must have two meanings and two fulfillments. But the Text 1 *I* have mind *really does* have only one meaning, and so it has only one fulfillment. So when it comes to the Text 1 and Text 2 I have in mind, premises 1–4 and 6 are each true, and so the conclusions 5 and 7 must be true too, since the argument is valid. Checkmate, unitarian!"

---

[37] Of course, if you're assuming that Jesus is Yahweh himself (that Jesus and Yahweh are numerically identical), then 6 would have to be true. But remember that the point of this argument is to avoid the wrongheaded collapsing together (identification) of Jesus and God—note the objection at the start of this section.

In reply, I'm not sure how anyone could know the new premises 1 and 6 when it comes to his Text 1. That it was about Yahweh is clear to all. That God *also* had in mind an additional meaning which is *only* about Jesus the Messiah (so that in this case premises 1 and 6 are false)—how could one rule that out? I don't know; it's hard to see, then, how any case of the above argument could be known to be sound.

And there's something wrongheaded about this whole way of arguing. The final conclusion 7, if true, implies that Yahweh and Jesus could not possibly differ in any way; but every Christian, trinitarian or not, thinks that Yahweh and Jesus have qualitatively differed from one another, whether by "Yahweh" we mean the Trinity or the Father.[38] Any one such difference implies that Yahweh and Jesus are two (and so that 7 is false).[39] It seems like we'll always have more reason to think that 7 is false than we have to think that all of premises 1–4 and 6 are true. If premises 2–4 and 6 are all true, the obvious Yahweh-Jesus differences (such as the first being triune while the second is not, or the first having and the second lacking a human son) will make us think that premises 1 and/or 5 are false. The whole idea of trying to prove the numerical identity of ones we know to have qualitatively differed is a fool's errand.

Attributing these ideas to the authors of the New Testament is uncharitable. The interpreter committing a fulfillment fallacy is reading them as implying the numerical identity of Jesus and God even while believing them to have simultaneously differed (which implies that Jesus and God are *not* numerically identical). This is to read those authors as confused about the subjects they care most about: God and his Messiah. The more we are convinced that these authors are divinely inspired—or simply, in possession of common sense—the less willing we should be to attribute such confusions to them. As for those who see those New Testament authors as implying only the fully deity of Christ (as per our objector, pp. 341–42)—this too is uncharitable, since the argument one takes them to be implicitly making is invalid.

10.8 CONCLUSION: MISCONSTRUING THE GENRE OF THE GOSPELS

In conclusion, the fulfillment fallacy is a clear exegetical fallacy, specifically an over-reading that tries to derive christological implications from a New Testament text that simply are not there. Further, peddlers of the fulfillment

---

[38] Tuggy, "Podcast 124"; Tuggy, "'God' in the Challenge Argument."

[39] Section 8.3.2.

fallacy misconstrue the genre of the Gospels. If the authors of the New Testament Gospels thought that Jesus is Yahweh himself, they would have shouted this message from the rooftops. That claim—not their much less exciting claim that Jesus is God's Messiah—would have been the central thesis of these four books. There is no reason for these authors to mutter and hint at Jesus's true identity by means of prophecy fulfillments. It is true that for much of his first earthly ministry Jesus was careful about who he told that he was God's Messiah. But there is no reason why the authors of Matthew, Mark, and Luke, post-resurrection, would be reserved about sharing the fullness of their views about Jesus, merely hinting at his deity by way of fulfilled prophecies. By suggesting that the Gospel writers are doing this, purveyors of the fulfillment fallacy are interpreting the Synoptic Gospels as if they were esoteric works, compositions whose main or most important message is sneakily encoded, so that it is hidden from the unworthy masses. An esoteric work has an "outer" meaning suitable to the many and a more important "inner," hidden meaning for the few elites who are intelligent and/or holy enough to discern and benefit from it.

But the New Testament Gospels are not esoteric works. They were written to be read out loud in the earliest churches, which were a hodgepodge of the educated and uneducated, young and old, male and female, free and enslaved. This diverse audience required a certain level of clarity and simplicity, so these works often flag their main point for the benefit of the listener or reader. They were not written for scholars to decode but rather for the masses to hear and believe. Granted, John is a trickier book than Matthew, Mark, and Luke, as the author of the Fourth Gospel highlights signs, double meanings, and opponents who often miss the point because of their spiritual blindness. Yet even this author makes his main point clear (John 20:31). To the Gospel authors the big news, the good news, is that Jesus is God's Messiah, with all that entails.[40] A reader who feels the need to find some much more exciting thesis in the first three Gospels—such as that Jesus is God himself or a divine Person or a godman—has lost the plot.

---

[40] Chapter 5.

CHAPTER 11

The Bible Against Relative-Identity Trinitarianism

11.1 AN INCONSISTENT TRIAD[1]

According to many trinitarian theologians the Father and Son are numerically distinct, yet each is numerically identical with the one God. But this presents a problem, as not all three of those claims can be true. Any thinking Christian should know how to respond to the following inconsistent triad of claims:

1. The Father is not the Son. $f \neq s$[2]
2. The Father is God. $f = g$
3. The Son is God. $s = g$

Claim 1 is taught by the mainstream catholic tradition and is implied by the New Testament, which portrays the Father and Son as qualitatively differing from each other.[3] The "Athanasian" Creed seems to demand both 2 and 3 when it asserts that to be saved, you must "acknowledge each person [in the Trinity] separately [to be] both God and Lord" and yet "there are not three Gods, but there is one God."[4] This sounds like identifying each of the Father and the Son with God. Following that creed, some trinitarians argue that the Bible implicitly and/or explicitly identifies both the Father and the Son with the only god.

---

[1] An earlier version of this chapter was presented at a meeting of the Society of Christian Philosophers at Rutgers University on October 20, 2016. My thanks to Joseph Jedwab for his helpful feedback on a later draft of this chapter.

[2] For the meanings of the symbols used in this chapter, = and ≠, see pp. 255, 257–60. The lowercase letters here are for the Father (f), the Son (s), and God (g). The main text of this chapter should be intelligible on its own, but most readers will need to work through chapter 8 before they are equipped to understand the formal proofs in the footnotes.

[3] Sections 8.3.2–3.

[4] *Athanasian Creed*, 18 (19, 16).

But all is not well! If 2 and 3 are true, then 1 is false. Things numerically identical to the same thing must also be identical to each other; if the Father just is God, and the Son just is God, then it must also be true that the Father just is the Son, contrary to 1.[5] And even by itself, this further claim that the Father just is the Son goes against both reason and Scripture, as Tertullian, Novatian, and Origen pointed out in the early third century against certain Modalistic Monarchians whom they believed to have collapsed together (numerically identified) the Father and the Son.[6] A Christian should deny on scriptural grounds that the Father was crucified, for this is taught only about the Son. Also, it seems that an essentially immortal and immaterial being like the Father could not be killed by crucifixion.

Further, if both 1 and 2 are true, 3 must be false. If the Father and Son are two (1), and the Father just is God (2), then contrary to 3, the Son *isn't* God.[7] It is self-evident that numerically distinct things can't be numerically identical to the same thing.

Finally, if both 1 and 3 are true, then 2 must be false. If the Father isn't the Son (1), and the Son *is* God (3), then the Father *isn't* God, so claim 2 is false.[8]

---

[5] Here is a formal proof using standard assumptions about numerical identity:

1. $f = g$ (claim 2, p. 345)
2. $s = g$ (claim 3)
3. $g = s$ (from 2, symmetry of =)
4. $f = s$ (from 1 and 3, transitivity of =)

For the transitivity and symmetry of identity (=) see section 8.3.1.

[6] Tertullian, *Against Praxeas*; Origen, *Against Celsus*, 462 [8.14]; Novatian, *Trinity*, chs. 26–28. On ancient modalism see Heine, "Christology of Callistus."

[7] A proof using standard assumptions about numerical identity is:

1. $f \neq s$ (claim 1)
2. $f = g$ (claim 2)
3. $g \neq s$ (from 1 and 2, substituting g for f by the Indiscernibility of Identicals or IDI (p. 267). That is, if f just is g, and per premise 1 f is distinct from s, g too must be distinct from s.)
4. $s \neq g$ (from 3, symmetry of =)

To clarify the last step, $g \neq s$ is shorthand for $\neg(g = s)$—it's not the case that g just is s. Because = is symmetric, $\neg(g = s)$ is logically equivalent to $\neg(s = g)$, which means the same as $s \neq g$. That is why if 3 is true then 4 must be true too.

[8] A proof using standard assumptions about numerical identity is:

1. $f \neq s$ (claim 1)
2. $s = g$ (claim 3)
3. $f \neq g$ (from 1 and 2, substituting g for s by the Indiscernibility of Identicals or IDI, p. 267)

Given the impossibility of all three claims being true, a Christian should not believe all three. But which should be denied? My own view is that claim 1 is undeniable for anyone who accepts New Testament teachings about the Father and the Son. Claim 2 is everywhere assumed by all New Testament writers and is implicitly and clearly taught in several places.[9] In contrast, 3 is supported only by weak, unsound arguments from Scripture, and by catholic traditions that clash with the New Testament. So it should be denied by any Christian who wants to adhere to scriptural teachings about God and Jesus. Unfortunately, this last point is controversial. To many Christians, and—surprisingly—to many Protestants, it is unthinkable that there should be a clash between biblical claims and widespread and prestigious later theological traditions.

11.2 RELATIVE IDENTITY TO THE RESCUE?

But a handful of recent Christian analytic philosophers have urged that a little metaphysical and logical work can save us from such reforming agonies.[10] What they're serving is difficult to chew and has not been widely consumed. But the gist of it is easy to understand: our three statements above have been misunderstood, and when rightly understood, they are logically consistent after all, or at least they are not obviously inconsistent. A relative-identity trinitarian urges that our three claims are each ambiguous, as there are not one but many relations of numerical identity. Such relations are relative to kinds or to sortal terms.[11] The Father and the Son, on this sort of trinitarian theology, are god-identical but Person-distinct.[12] In other words, the Father and Son are numerically the same god but numerically different divine Persons. They are suggesting that the above claims (p. 345) don't correctly represent trinitarian sentences. Instead, we should write,

---

That is, if *f* and *s* are distinct, per 1, and *s* just is *g*, per 2, then *g* too must be distinct from *f*, which is what 3 says.

[9] For very strong confirmation of the thesis that the New Testament authors are committed to the identity of the one God with the Father over the thesis that they are committed to the identity of the one God with the Trinity, see my "New Testament" or my "Unfinished Business of the Reformation."

[10] This approach has only been developed in recent times, although some see precedents in some medieval philosophical theologies; for references see my "Trinity," sec. 2.1.1 and Cross, "Philosophy."

[11] Geach, "Identity"; Geach, "Ontological Relativity"; Geach, *Reference and Generality*; Martinich, "Identity and Trinity"; Martinich, "God"; Cain, "Doctrine"; Cain, "Geachian Theory." It is version of the approach we considered in section 6.5.1.

[12] Rea, "Relative Identity"; Jedwab, "Against."

1. The Father is not *the same Person as* the Son. $f \neq_P s$
2. The Father is *the same being as* God. $f =_B g$
3. The Son is *the same being* as God. $s =_B g$

This has seemed to some Christian philosophers like a neat solution to the worry that the claims of the "Athanasian" Creed are incoherent. It's far from clear that this set of claims *is* coherent—more on this below—but what is important to some of those philosophers is that it isn't *perfectly* clear that this set of claims is *in*coherent. In other words the three sentences above are not *demonstrably* incoherent.[13] This is to set the bar for correctly understanding the traditional Trinity formulas very low indeed! (Many false and wildly implausible claims are not demonstrably incoherent.) They assume that the main difficulty faced by a doctrine of the Trinity is not biblical but rather logical—namely, that, unless formulated as above, it seems to imply at least one contradiction. Their idea is that *if* we can't rule out that the doctrine is best formulated as above, *then* we can't be sure that it implies any contradiction, since (in their view) the above sentences don't imply any contradiction. This rebuts the objection that a Trinity theory is *clearly* incoherent; it's a defensive apologetic strategy.

11.3 PROBLEMS WITH RELATIVE IDENTITY

Several philosophical objections have been raised to various versions of this strategy for showing how trinitarian theology may be interpreted as coherent. These include (1) that relative-identity statements can be analyzed in terms of predications and non-relative ("absolute") identity statements (on which, see below), (2) that the defense is *ad hoc* because no one can produce any theology-independent motivation for thinking that relative-identity relations are fundamental, and (3) that it implies metaphysical antirealism.[14]

I won't rehearse all these objections here, as my main purpose is to explore a heretofore ignored biblical objection to relative-identity trinitarianism. But it's important to understand the first, widely held objection, which concerns standard logical analyses like those we explored in section 8.3.4. Any New Testament reader eventually understands this truth: "Cephas and Peter are the same apostle." For this to be true three other claims must be true; each is individually necessary for the truth of the above sentence and together they seem jointly sufficient for its truth. These are,

[13] van Inwagen, "Three Persons"; "And Yet"; *God, Knowledge, and Mystery*, 220–21.
[14] Rea, "Relative Identity," 435–36.

1. Cephas is an apostle.
2. Peter is an apostle.
3. Cephas = Peter.

Understanding the sentence "Cephas and Peter are the same apostle" is the same as understanding the conjunction of these three claims. And if any one or more of these is false, it will also be false that "Cephas and Peter and the same apostle." If (contra 1) Cephas isn't an apostle, then he can't be the same apostle as Peter. Again, if (contra 2) Peter is not an apostle, he can't be the same apostle as Cephas. And if (contra 3) it is false that Cephas just is Peter—in other words, if Cephas and Peter are not one but two—then even if (per 1 and 2) each is an apostle, at any rate they are not *the same* apostle but must be different apostles, like, for instance, John and Peter.

None of this is specific to the concept of being an apostle. The same sort of analysis holds for the statements that Cephas and Peter are the same man, brother, father, cousin, citizen, diner, fisherman, friend, Jew, etc. Nor is this specific to Cephas/Peter. It seems like a perfectly general analysis of statements of the form *a and b are the same F*, where *F* is a kind term, so that *Fa* tells us what sort of thing *a* is, namely, an *F*. That is, it seems to be true in general that, for any *a* and for any *b*, *a* and *b* are the same *F* if and only if *Fa, Fb*, and $a = b$.

What about different *F* statements, such as "Peter and John are *different* apostles"? Here too there seems to be an obvious analysis: for any *a* and any *b*, *a* and *b* are different *F's* if and only if *a* is an *F*, *b* is an *F*, and $a \neq b$. To apply this analysis, Peter and John are different apostles if and only if Peter is an apostle, John is an apostle, and Peter and John are not one and the same (that is, are numerically distinct things). This seems correct. If Peter *isn't* an apostle, he can't be a different apostle than anyone, and the same goes for John. But if both are apostles, for them to be *different* apostles, Peter and John can't be one and the same—Peter must be one, and John must be another.

Let us ask now if it is possible for some *a* and some *b* to be the same *F* while being different *G's*, where *F* and *G* express the concepts of two different kinds. Could, for instance, Cephas and Peter be the same *man* while being different *apostles*? Intuitively, the answer is: Obviously not! Our analysis explains why. Any *a* and any *b* being the same *F* implies that $a = b$. And any *a* and *b* being different *G's* implies that $a \neq b$. The claim that $a = b$ together with the claim that

$a \neq b$ constitute a contradiction,[15] and a contradiction can only be false and not true. Thus it is impossible for any *a* and any *b* to be the same *F* but different *G's*.

For any kind-concept, such as human being, god, deity, divine Person, horse, extraterrestrial object, shoe, planet, mountain, ham sandwich, etc., we can talk about things being *the same F* or *different F's*, but this language seems eliminable without remainder since as we've seen, being the same *F* amounts to each thing being an *F* and being identical, and being different *F's* amounts to each thing being an *F* while being numerically distinct (that is, not identical). This has not always been recognized in philosophy. But now that it has been recognized, to most analytic philosophers it seems undeniable. If not for the doctrine of the Trinity, probably no one would have suggested that some *a* and some *b* could be the same *F* but different *G's*.

What's the problem with the Father and Son being the same god but different divine Persons? Applying the two analyses just discussed, the Father and Son being the same god implies $f = s$, and their being different Persons implies $f \neq s$. These two implications form a logical contradiction.[16] Also, trinitarian orthodoxy seems to deny that $f = s$.[17] The suggestion, then, seems incoherent, and even apart from that, it should be a nonstarter for someone interested in creedal orthodoxy.

But never underestimate the creativity and ingenuity of a determined philosopher and logician. The brilliant Roman Catholic analytic philosopher Peter Geach initiated the modern incarnations of this idea, and to do this he, as it were, burned down a whole realm of statements and arguments like the ones we've examined here and in chapter 8 by denying that there *is* an "absolute" (non-kind-relative) relation of identity.[18]

Geach even urged that statements of the form $a = b$ are unintelligible, without any graspable meaning, since, he claimed, it is meaningless to either

---

[15] A logical contradiction is a compound claim of the form $P \wedge \neg P$ (*P and not-P*)—an assertion and a denial of a single claim. It is customary to write assertions and denials of identity as, respectively, $a = b$ and $a \neq b$, and I have followed that practice in this book. But their true logical form is of a two-place predicate, so using *I(_, _)* for the identity relation, they are *I(a,b)* and $\neg$*I(a,b)*—which is a compound statement of the form $P \wedge \neg P$, a contradiction.

The importance of contradictions is that they can only be false, never true. And any set of claims that implies a contradiction must include at least one false claim; sets of only true claims never imply any falsehood.

[16] See the previous note.

[17] Since the mid-to-late fourth century trinitarian creeds have been intended to rule out modalistic theologies on which $f = s$.

[18] See the sources in p. 347, footnote 11.

affirm or deny that *a* and *b* are numerically the same (full stop). Numerical sameness, he argued, can only be asserted or denied relative to a "sortal" or the concept of a kind of thing.[19] Thus, Geach thinks, we can ask whether some *a* and *b* are the same human, the same divine Person, the same golf ball, and so on, but it is senseless to ask whether or not $a = b$.

But it is the relative-identity trinitarian who should be worried about unintelligibility. They deny the plausible general analyses we looked at for sentences of the forms "*a* and *b* are the same *F*," and "*a* and *b* are different *G*'s." But then, it's not clear *what* they are asserting! If you say that the Father and the Son are "god-same" or "the same god" and you *deny* that therein you assert three things—the Father is a god, the Son is a god, and the Father just is the Son—then what exactly *are* you asserting?[20] It's unclear. Moreover, we're being asked to engage in some weird counting. If we're counting gods, we're supposed to count the Father and the Son as the same god. But how can one and the same god have died (Son) *and not* (Father)? (Remember: the Persons here are *not* supposed to be proper parts of a god; each is himself a god, and they're supposed to be the same one.) But what does it even mean to say they're "the same god" given that they have simultaneously differed from one another?

And philosophers have pushed back against Geach's unintelligibility claim: the question of whether some *a* and some *b* are (absolutely) identical *is* meaningful, not senseless.[21] Suppose you are thinking about some individual—say, the current president of the United States of America. Then you think about Donald J. Trump. You now ask yourself, "Did I just think of one thing, then another, or did I think of the same thing twice?" More technically, call the first thing you thought of "*a*" and the second thing you thought of "*b*." Which is true: $a = b$, or $a \neq b$? The question is both understandable and answerable. We all agree that the first would be true, if you had these thoughts in January of 2025.[22]

---

[19] A sortal concept is typically expressed by a count noun such as "cat," "woman," "oak tree," "country," "statue," or "oxygen atom." Various philosophers have held that sortals make counting possible, supply criteria for identity at a time and through times, and that at least some of them express the essences or what-it-is or defining features of things.

[20] Layman, *Philosophical Approaches*, 141–42; Merricks, "Split Brains," 301–5, 321.

[21] Alston and Bennett, "Identity and Cardinality," 558.

[22] The eagle-eyed reader may have noticed the word "thing" in the preceding. Is that not a sortal, a term expressing the concept of a kind? Isn't then identity *always* kind-relative and never absolute? In reply, the relevant concept of a thing is so thin, so devoid of content,

11.4 HOW THE NEW TESTAMENT RULES OUT RELATIVE-IDENTITY TRINITARIANISM

But an obvious and serious problem for relative-identity trinitarianism has been overlooked, a problem that lies on the face of the New Testament. In asserting the Father and Son to be the same god or god-same, relative-identity trinitarians contradict the explicit, repeated New Testament claim that the Father is the Son's god. This claim is implicit in the portrayal of Jesus in relation to God (a.k.a. the Father) throughout the New Testament; the overall picture is of a uniquely important human servant and his god. Jesus prays to, follows the lead of, and submits to the one he calls "Father." But here I'll focus on explicit claims, by at least four New Testament authors, that the Father is Jesus's god, the god over Jesus.

Let's start with the New Testament letters attributed to the apostle Paul:

> Blessed be the God and Father of our Lord Jesus Christ. (2 Cor. 1:3)
>
> The God and Father of the Lord Jesus (blessed be he forever!) knows that I do not lie. (2 Cor. 11:31)
>
> Blessed be the God and Father of our Lord Jesus Christ, who has blessed us in Christ with every spiritual blessing in the heavenly places. (Eph. 1:3)
>
> [I pray] that the God of our Lord Jesus Christ, the Father of glory, may give you a spirit of wisdom and revelation as you come to know him. (Eph. 1:17)

Similarly with Peter:

> Blessed be the God and Father of our Lord Jesus Christ! By his great mercy he has given us a new birth into a living hope through the resurrection of Jesus Christ from the dead. (1 Pet. 1:3.)
>
> For he received honor and glory from God the Father when that voice was conveyed to him by the Majestic Glory, saying, "This is my Son, my Beloved, with whom I am well pleased." (2 Pet. 1:17)

The author of the letter to the Hebrews writes,

> But of the Son he [the author of Psalm 45] says, "Your throne, O God, is forever and ever, and the righteous scepter is the scepter of your kingdom. You have loved righteousness and hated wickedness; therefore God, your God, has anointed you with the oil of gladness beyond your companions." (Heb. 1:8–9)

---

that it applies to anything that can be thought of or referred to in any way, so it is too thin of a concept to count as a kind-concept.

The author of the Gospel According to John presents Jesus as saying this to Mary Magdalene after his resurrection but before his ascension:

> "Do not touch me, because I have not yet ascended to the Father. But go to my brothers and say to them, 'I am ascending to my Father and your Father, to my God and your God.'" (John 20:17)

Finally, in the book of Revelation we read,

> To him who loves us and freed us from our sins by his blood, and made us to be a kingdom, priests serving his God and Father, to him be glory and dominion forever and ever. Amen. (Rev. 1:5–6)
>
> [Jesus speaking:] "Wake up and strengthen what remains and is on the point of death, for I have not found your works perfect in the sight of my God." (Rev. 3:2)
>
> [Jesus speaking:] "If you conquer, I will make you a pillar in the temple of my God; you will never go out of it. I will write on you the name of my God, and the name of the city of my God, the new Jerusalem that comes down from my God out of heaven, and my own new name." (Rev. 3:12)
>
> [Heavenly worshipers:] "you [Jesus] have made them to be a kingdom and priests serving our God." (Rev. 5:10)

Why is this scriptural teaching a problem for relative-identity trinitarians? Necessarily, no god is god over himself. If we're convinced that this one and that one are *the same* god, we are sure that neither is the god of the other. If the Father is *the god of* the Son, it follows that the Father and the Son are not *the same* god. It follows that any relative-identity trinitarian theology is false, for they all hold that the Father and the Son are the same god (while being different divine Persons). No trinitarian theory can stand that contradicts clear New Testament teaching.

Let's formulate the argument explicitly:

1. For any x and for any y, if either x is the god of y or y is the god of x, then x and y are not the same god.[23]
2. The Father is the Son's god.
3. Therefore, the Father and the Son are not the same god. (1, 2)
4. If there is a true relative-identity Trinity theory, then the Father and the Son are the same god.
5. Therefore, there is no true relative-identity Trinity theory. (3, 4)

[23] Or equivalently: For any x and any y, if the *god-over* relation obtains between them (in either direction), x and y are not the same god.

We've already seen why a Christian who wants to agree with clear and explicit New Testament teaching should agree with 2. But why should a Christian agree with 1? Premise 1 is self-evident, obviously true, once we understand the concept *god-over* or *being-the-god-of*. And consider the contrapositive of 1,[24] which is logically equivalent to it: For any x and for any y, if x and y *are* the same god, then neither of these is the case: x is the god of y, y is the god of x. This seems just as obviously true. Both seem to be necessary truths.[25] Premise 4 is true by definition. The conclusion 5 follows from the conjunction of 3 and 4.

Notice that the argument neither states nor assumes any claims that even the most radical, Geachian relative-identity trinitarian would deny. We can let such a relative-identity theorist have her own mysterious understanding of what it means to say that the Father and the Son are "the same god" or "god-same." *Whatever* that means, it will not be consistent with the Father and the Son being such that the Father is the Son's god. The point is purely conceptual—it's about our idea of the *god-over* relation—and it seems to apply in any theological context. If in Hindu theology Vishnu is Shiva's god, this implies that Vishnu and Shiva are not the same god, not god-same (god-identical).

Perhaps a relative-identity theorist would reply by insisting that the relation *god-over* does *not* rule out the relation *same-god*. Perhaps he would argue:

> I *agree* with the New Testament that Jesus's god is the Father. I think that when some a and some b are god-same, still a can be the god of b in cases where a and b are Person-distinct (not the same divine Person).

In reply, I have no idea what you mean when you say that the Father is "the god over" Jesus, given that you think this is compatible with their being the same god. If we are correct in thinking that *god-over* is necessarily an irreflexive relation, then if a is the god over b, they're not the same god. Adding that they're not the same some *other* sort of thing isn't relevant. Certainly, a being in authority over b is compatible with a and b being different persons, different

[24] A contrapositive of a conditional, a statement of the form *if P then Q*, is: *if not-Q then not-P*. For instance, let P be "Bob is a human" and let Q be "Bob is a mammal." This conditional is true: "If Bob is a human then Bob is a mammal." Its contrapositive is "If it is not the case that Bob is a mammal then it is not the case that Bob is a human." A conditional and its contrapositive always have the same truth-value; if one is true, so is the other, and if one is false, so is the other.

[25] That is, a statement that can only be true and that in principle can't be false, one that is, so to speak, "true in all possible worlds," such as 2+2=4, "The relation *bigger-than* is transitive," "Nothing has created itself," or "There are no married bachelors." On the concept of necessary truths see pp. 265–69.

someones or selves. But that doesn't change the fact that *god-over*, like *boss of*, is a necessarily irreflexive relation. As with *boss of*—if *a* is the boss of *b* (or *b* is the boss of *a*) then *a* and *b* are not the same boss—so with *god-over*—if *a* is the god over *b* (or *b* is the god over *a*), then *a* and *b* are not the same god.

11.5 WHY NOT DISTINGUISH JESUS FROM THE DIVINE SON?

Certain incidents in the New Testament Gospels present Jesus as under the authority of God. For instance, in a famous scene in Mark, Jesus prays in agony to God, finally deciding to submit his will to God's (Mark 14:32–42). How can this be, if Jesus is a fully divine Person who is perfect in knowledge, the owner of a (or the) divine will? There is a temptation here to posit two sons, one human and the other divine. As Roman Catholic analytic theologian Timothy Pawl points out, there is precedent in mainstream traditions for understanding each "nature" in the incarnate Christ as doing things only a someone (self, person) can do. The 451 Council of Chalcedon endorsed the "Tome" of Pope Leo, which says that it was Christ's human nature that suffered and died on the cross, but it was Christ's divine nature that called Lazarus back to life.[26] As these are things only selves can do, why not call the human nature "Jesus" and the divine nature "the Son of God"? In effect Leo says that Jesus could and did suffer, while the Son, being divine, was impassible, and so incapable of suffering. Any qualitative difference implies that Jesus and the Son are numerically distinct.[27] That's not good! As we saw, Peter Geach tried to rule out any statements of "absolute" (non-relative) identity or distinctness as unintelligible, but this fails to convince.

But not all relative-identity theorists about Incarnation and Trinity deny that we have and often use a non-relative, "absolute" concept of numerical identity, the one we explored in chapters 8 and 9. The analytic theologian Joseph Jedwab, though he doesn't *believe* relative-identity forms of the Trinity and Incarnation doctrines, nonetheless defends them at length in a recent book chapter.[28] (As to *why* he defends something he doesn't believe, see p. 214–15 above.) Sensibly, Jedwab allows that we have and reasonably employ an absolute (non-kind-

[26] Pawl, *In Defense*, 25, 39; Leo, "Letter," 80–81.

[27] See sections 8.3.3 and 8.3.5. It still remains unclear how proponents of Chalcedonian Christology can square the implications of Leo's statements with the famous assertion of that council that Christ is one person ("Definition," 86; Mullins, "Classical Theism").

[28] Jedwab, "Relative-Identity." As I write this chapter the debate book of which this chapter is a part has yet to be published, so I won't quote it or refer to page numbers. But I thank Joseph Jedwab for some helpful correspondence and for sharing his forthcoming chapter with me.

relative) concept of numerical identity, even though he also argues that it is reasonable to think that there are statements of relative identity (of the form *a* is the same *F* as *b*) that don't admit of our analysis above in section 11.3, and that there can be cases where *a* and *b* are the same *F* even though they are different *G's*. Among these cases would be the Persons of the Trinity, which would be different Persons while being the same god, and, Jedwab explains, Jesus and the Son, which would be the same Person even though they are two natures. He also admits that Jesus and the Son would, as they qualitatively differ, be non-identical in the absolute sense. This would allow him to reply in the following way to our main argument (p. 353): "Sure, *Jesus* is under a god, but *the Son* is not. I think your biblical texts are true, but they are referring to Jesus, not the Son."[29]

In reply, the New Testament doesn't allow us to distinguish between Jesus and the Son. The authors use "Jesus," "Jesus of Nazareth," "Jesus Christ," and "Christ" as co-referring with the terms "the Son" and "the Son of God," reflecting their view that these—Jesus and the Son—are one and the same.[30] That "they," Jesus and the Son, are one and the same, is part of the contents of the New Testament books, and so we're committed to those identity claims by our allegiance to them as authoritative. Dare we say that the New Testament authors are confused about this, and that they mistakenly identify what in fact are numerically distinct entities, the man Jesus and the divine Son?

Further, it's unclear what it means to say that a Jesus who is numerically distinct from the Son is "the same Person" as the Son. While we keep clearly in mind the purported differences between them, for instance that Jesus is subject to God but the Son is not, and that Jesus is not divine while the Son is, *and* that each one himself is a person (a someone, a "he"), we're going to give you the blank stare of incredulity when you tell us that they are "the same Person." What could that even mean? And if they were the same Person, and one is subject to God, wouldn't the other be as well, since he is *the same* Person? This is hardly the end of the argument, but I think we can see that Jedwab's relative-identity answer to our main argument is both costly and of doubtful intelligibility.

---

[29] Jedwab also thinks there is a crucial ambiguity in that argument, step 3, but explaining that would take us too far afield. His position is highly complex and deserves a full discussion, which unfortunately is not possible here.

[30] Mat. 16:16, 27:54; Mark 1:1 (ESV, HCSB, NIV, REV); Luke 1:31, 35; John 20:31; Rom. 1:3–4; Gal. 2:20; Heb. 4:14; 1 John 5:5, 20.

11.6 CONCLUSION: TROUBLE FOR OTHER TRINITY THEORIES

If you want a trinitarian theology that doesn't contradict any clear New Testament teachings about God and Jesus, no relative-identity Trinity theory will fit the bill. But relative-identity Trinity theories are not the only ones that clash with the New Testament teaching that the Father is the god over Jesus. Again, just conceptually, if *a* is the, or simply a god over some *b*, this implies that *a* is a god. By this self-evident truth, it follows from the New Testament teaching that the Father is the god over Jesus that the Father is a god. Since the New Testament everywhere assumes monotheism, the Father will have to be *the* god, the only god there is. But this is denied by many Trinity theories, particularly those of the "social" or three-self variety.[31]

These assume, in my view rightly, that in principle it is impossible for some *a* and some *b* to be the same *F* while being different *G's*. This being so, it can't be true that the Father and the Son are the same god while being different Persons. And the trinitarian must, following catholic traditions, deny that the Father and the Son are the same Person; no, they are different Persons and so can't be the same god. Given this, if the Father is a god and the Son is a god, there are at least two gods, and monotheism is false. Wanting to avoid this denial of monotheism, and being committed to the core trinitarian claim that the one God is one and the same with the Trinity, these theorists deny that any of the "divine Persons" is a god; it is false that the Father is a god, it is false that the Son is a god, and it is false that the Spirit is a god, for the only god is the Trinity, and each of the three aforementioned ones is distinct from the Trinity, since none is tripersonal. Some common trinitarian sentences[32] must be carefully interpreted.

1. There is only one God.
2. The Father is God.
3. The Son is God.
4. The Spirit is God.
5. The Father is not the Son.
6. The Son is not the Spirit.
7. The Spirit is not the Father.

This sort of trinitarian insists that claims 2–4 must be understood not as identity statements but only as predications—that is, each ascribes the quality divinity or deity to a Person.

[31] Tuggy, "Trinity," sec. 2.2; Moreland and Craig, *Philosophical Foundations*, 588.
[32] Section 2.3.

But as we've just seen, another problem here is that 1 doesn't say enough. Given that the Father is Jesus's god, it follows that the Father is a god, and given the truth of monotheism he must be *the* god. This trinitarian, then, is really committed to these claims:

1. There is only one God, the Father.
2. The Father is divine.
3. The Son is divine.
4. The Spirit is divine.
5. The Father is not the Son.
6. The Son is not the Spirit.
7. The Spirit is not the Father.

With 1 thus augmented, propositions 2–4 no longer clear the way for the claim that God = the Trinity. And it is problematic what "divine" means in claims 2–4. The Nicene tradition has long insisted that it is full or complete deity/divinity that the Son has, the very kind of divinity/deity enjoyed by the Father. But that, per claim 1, seems to entail being one and the same with God. If the Son has *that* sort of deity, he too will be a god, and the same god as the Father, which on the standard analysis discussed above (pp. 273–74, 348–49) implies the heretical claim that Father = Son, which contradicts claim 5. If "is divine" is used unequivocally in claims 2–4, and 2–4 are each true, then being divine must not entail being a god. One wonders then, exactly what lesser sort of divinity is at issue, and also, what extra the Father has, besides this lesser divinity, which makes him identical with the only god (per claim 1).

Most simply, any Trinity theory on which none of the Persons is identical with God clashes with the New Testament, which says that the Father is the god over Jesus, which implies that the Father *is* a god, and given the monotheistic context, it implies too that the Father is *the* god, the only god—that the Father and God are one and the same. As we've seen, if the one God and the Father are one and the same, it will not be true that the one God and the Trinity are one and the same.[33] On this point catholic traditions clash with scriptural teaching. It is the former that should give way. Until this happens, the Reformation is tragically incomplete.[34]

---

[33] Chapter 3.
[34] Tuggy, "Unfinished Business of the Reformation"; "New Testament."

The Acts of Paul. In *The Apocryphal New Testament: A Collection of Apocryphal Christian Literature in an English Translation Based on M. R. James*, edited and translated by J. K. Elliott. Clarendon Press, 1993 [c. 200 CE].

Akyol, Mustafa. *The Islamic Jesus*. St. Martin's Press, 2017.

Alcinous. *The Handbook of Platonism* [*Didaskalikos*]. Translated by John Dillon. Oxford University Press, 1993 [2nd c. CE].

Alston, William P., and Jonathan Bennett. "Identity and Cardinality: Geach and Frege." *The Philosophical Review* 93, no. 4 (1984): 553–67.

Anderson, James N. "On the Rationality of Positive Mysterianism." *International Journal for Philosophy of Religion* 83, no. 3 (2018): 291–307.

———. *Paradox in Christian Theology: An Analysis of Its Presence, Character, and Epistemic Status*. Paternoster Theological Monographs, 2007.

———. "Seeming Is Believing?: An Exploration of Doxastic Responses to the Christological Paradox." In *Paradox and Contradiction in Theology*, edited by Jonathan Rutledge. Routledge, 2023.

———. *Why Should I Believe Christianity?* Christian Focus Publications, 2016.

"The Apologists Bible Commentary: John 17." *The Apologists Bible Commentary*. https://www.forananswer.org/John/Jn17_3.htm.

"Appendix 15. [to the Revised English Version] Usages of 'Spirit.'" *Revised English Version*, 2015. https://www.revisedenglishversion.com/Appendix/15/bb.

Aquinas, Thomas. *Summa Theologica*. Translated by Fathers of the English Dominican Province and Daniel J. Sullivan. Great Books of the Western World 20. Encyclopedia Brittanica, 1952 [c. 1266–68].

Arcadi, James, and James T. Turner, eds. *T&T Clark Handbook of Analytic Theology*. T&T Clark, 2022.

Artemi, Eirini A. "The 'Logos' in the Teaching of Marcellus of Ancyra and Sabellius." *Volynskyi Blahovisnyk* 7 (October 2019): 99–121.

"The Athanasian Creed." In *The Athanasian Creed: The Paddock Lectures for 1962–63*, edited and translated by J. N. D. Kelly. Harper and Row, 1964 [5th c.].

Athanasius. *Four Discourses Against the Arians*. In *Select Writings and Letters of Athanasius, Bishop of Alexandria*, edited by Archibald Robertson, translated by John Henry Newman. Nicene and Post-Nicene Fathers, series 2, vol. 4. New York, 1892 [356–60]. Reprint: Eerdmans, 1953.

———. *Letters to Serapion on the Holy Spirit*. In *Athanasius the Great and Didymus the Blind: Works on the Spirit*. Translated by Mark DelCogliano, Andrew Radde-Gallwitz, and Lewis Ayres. St. Vladimir's Seminary Press Popular Patristics 43. St. Vladimir's Seminary Press, 2011 [359–61].

Athanassiadi, Polymnia, and Michael Frede. *Pagan Monotheism in Late Antiquity*. Oxford University Press, 2001.

Augustine. *Answer to Maximinus the Arian*. In *Arianism and Other Heresies: Heresies, Memorandum to Augustine, To Orosius in Refutation of the Priscillianists and Origenists, Arian Sermon, Answer to an Arian Sermon, Debate with Maximinus, Answer to Maximinus, Answer to an Enemy of the Law and the Prophets*, edited by John E. Rotelle, translated by Roland J. Teske. The Works of Saint Augustine: A Translation for the 21st Century, Part 1, vol. 18. New City Press, 1995 [early 5th c].

———. *[Exposition of] Psalm 45*. In *St. Augustine: Expositions on the Book of Psalms*, edited by Philip Schaff. Nicene and Post-Nicene Fathers, Series 1, vol. 8. Edinburgh, 1888 [c. 410–13]. https://ccel.org/ccel/s/schaff/npnf108/cache/npnf108.pdf.

———. *The City of God against the Pagans [De Civitate Dei]*. Translated by R.W. Dyson. Cambridge University Press, 1998 [426].

———. *The Trinity [De Trinitate]*. Translated by Edmund Hill. New City Press, 1991 [c. 420].

———. *Tractates on the Gospel of John, 55–111*. Translated by John W. Retting. Fathers of the Church 90. Catholic University of America Press, 2014 [414–20].

Baber, H. E. "The Trinity." In *Internet Encyclopedia of Philosophy*, edited by James Fieser and Bradley Dowden. n.d. https://iep.utm.edu/trinity/.

Baker, Kenneth. *Jesus Christ—True God and True Man: A Handbook on Christology for Non-Theologians*. St. Augustine's Press, 2013.

Barnett, Tim. "What Is the Trinity?" *Stand to Reason*, July 12, 2017. https://www.str.org/w/what-is-the-trinity-?.

Barrett, C. K. *A Commentary on the First Epistle to the Corinthians*. Black's New Testament Commentaries. Harper & Row, 1968.

Barrett, Matthew. *Simply Trinity: The Unmanipulated Father, Son, and Spirit*. Baker Books, 2021.

Basil of Caesarea. *Letter 8*. In *Basil: Letters and Select Works*, edited by Philip Schaff and Henry Wallace, translated by Blomfield Jackson. Nicene and Post-Nicene Fathers, second series, vol. 8. Edinburgh, 1894 [360].

Bauckham, Richard. *God Crucified: Monotheism and Christology in the New Testament*. Eerdmans, 1999.

———. *Jesus and the God of Israel*. Eerdmans, 2008.

———. "Orthodoxy in Christology." *Christian Library*, June 9, 2002. https://www.christianstudylibrary.org/article/orthodoxy-christology.

Baxter, Donald. "Self-Differing, Aspects, and Leibniz's Law." *Nous* 52, no. 4 (2018): 900–20.

Beale, G. K., and D. A. Carson, eds. *Commentary on the New Testament Use of the Old Testament*. Baker Academic, 2007.

Beall, Jc. *The Contradictory Christ*. Oxford University Press, 2021.

———. *Divine Contradiction*. Oxford University Press, 2023.

———. "*Divine Contradiction:* Replies to Critics." *Religious Studies* 60 (2024): 717–35.

———. *Spandrels of Truth*. Oxford University Press, 2009.

BeDuhn, Jason David. *Truth in Translation: Accuracy and Bias in English Translations of the New Testament.* University Press of America, 2003.

Belsham, Thomas, ed. *The New Testament, in an Improved Version, upon the Basis of Archbishop Newcome's New Translation: With a Corrected Text, and Notes Critical and Explanatory.* 5th ed. London, 1819 [1808].

Berlin, Adele, and Marc Zvi Brettler, eds. *The Jewish Study Bible.* Oxford University Press, 2004.

"Biblical Doctrine: An Overview." In *ESV Study Bible.* Crossway, 2008.

Biddle, John. *A Confession of Faith Touching the Holy Trinity; According to the Scripture.* In *The Faith of One God, Who Is Only the Father; and of One Mediator between God and Men, Who Is Only the Man Christ Jesus; and of One Holy Spirit, the Gift (and Sent) of God; Asserted and Defended, In Several Tracts Contained in This Volume; the Titles Whereof the Reader Will Find in the Following Leaf. And after That A Preface to the Whole, or an Exhortation to an Impartial and Free Inquiry into the Doctrines of Religion*, edited by Thomas Firmin. London, 1691 [1648]. Reprint: Lulu.com, 2008.

———. *The Testimonies of Irenaeus, Justin Martyr, Tertullian, Novatianus, Theophilus, Origen (Who Lived in the Two First Centuries after Christ Was Born, or Thereabouts;) As Also of Arnobius, Lactantius, Eusebius, Hillary, and Brightman; Concerning That One GOD, and the Persons of the Holy Trinity, Together with Observations on the Same.* In *The Faith of One God, Who Is Only the Father; and of One Mediator between God and Men, Who Is Only the Man Christ Jesus; and of One Holy Spirit, the Gift (and Sent) of God; Asserted and Defended, In Several Tracts Contained in This Volume; the Titles Whereof the Reader Will Find in the Following Leaf. And after That A Preface to the Whole, or an Exhortation to an Impartial and Free Inquiry into the Doctrines of Religion*, edited by Thomas Firmin. London, 1691 [1648]. Reprint: Lulu.com, 2008.

Bird, Michael F. "Did Jesus Think He Was God?" In *How God Became Jesus: The Real Origins of Belief in Jesus' Divine Nature—a Response to Bart Ehrman*, by Simon J. Gathercole, Craig A. Evans, Charles E. Hill, and Chris Tilling. Zondervan, 2014.

———. *Evangelical Theology: A Biblical and Systematic Introduction.* 2nd ed. Zondervan Academic, 2020 [2013].

———. *Jesus Among the Gods: Early Christology in the Greco-Roman World.* Baylor University Press, 2022.

———. *Jesus the Eternal Son: Answering Adoptionist Christology.* William B. Eerdmans Publishing Company, 2017.

"Birth Control." *Catholic Answers.* 2004. https://www.catholic.com/tract/birth-control.

Blomberg, Craig. "The New Testament Definition of Heresy (Or When Do Jesus and the Apostles Really Get Mad?)," *Journal of the Evangelical Theological Society* 45, no. 1 (2002): 59–72.

Boniface VIII, Pope. *Unam Sanctam*. November 18, 1302. *Papal Encyclicals Online*. https://www.papalencyclicals.net/bon08/b8unam.htm.
Bostom, Andrew G., ed. *The Legacy of Jihad: Islamic War and the Fate of Non-Muslims*. Prometheus Books, 2005.
Boteach, Shmuley. *Kosher Jesus*. Gefen, 2012.
Bowman Jr., Robert M. "The Biblical Basis of the Doctrine of the Trinity: An Outline Study." *Institute for Religious Research*, May 16, 2011, https://bib.irr.org/biblical-basis-of-doctrine-of-trinity.
———. "Dale Tuggy and the Biblical Basis of the Trinity, Part 2: Is the Doctrine of the Trinity Incoherent?" *Bowman on Target: Rob Bowman's Blog*, April 18, 2019. https://robertbowman.net/2019/04/18/dale-tuggy-and-the-biblical-basis-of-the-trinity-part-2-is-the-doctrine-of-the-trinity-incoherent/.
———. "Triadic New Testament Passages and the Doctrine of the Trinity." *The Journal for Trinitarian Studies and Apologetics* 1, no. 1 (2013): 7–55.
Bowman Jr., Robert M., and Ed Komoszewski. *The Incarnate Christ and His Critics*. Kregal Academic, 2024.
———. *Putting Jesus in His Place: The Case for the Deity of Christ*. Kregal Publications, 2007.
Boyarin, Daniel. "Logos, a Jewish Word: John's Prologue as Midrash." In *The Jewish Annotated New Testament*, 2nd ed., edited by Amy-Jill Levine and Marc Zvi Brettler. Oxford University Press, 2017.
Boyd, Gregory A. *God of the Possible: A Biblical Introduction to the Open View of God*. Baker Books, 2011.
Branson, Beau. "Ahistoricity in Analytic Theology." *American Catholic Philosophical Quarterly* 92, no. 2 (2018): 195–224.
———. "One God, the Father: The Neglected Doctrine of the Monarchy of the Father, and Its Implications for the Analytic Debate about the Trinity." *TheoLogica* 6, no. 2 (2022): 6–58.
Brent, Allen. *Ignatius of Antioch: A Martyr Bishop and the Origin of Episcopacy*. Continuum, 2009.
Brower, Jeffrey E., and Michael C. Rea. "Material Constitution and the Trinity." *Faith and Philosophy* 22, no. 1 (2005): 57–76.
———. "Understanding the Trinity." *Logos: A Journal of Catholic Thought and Culture* 8 (2005): 145–57.
Brown, Raymond Edward. *The Birth of the Messiah: A Commentary on the Infancy Narratives in the Gospels of Matthew and Luke*. Updated. Doubleday, 1999 [1977].
Bultmann, Rudolf. *The Gospel of John: A Commentary [Das Evangelium des Johannes]*. Edited by Rupert William Noel Hoare and John Kenneth Riches. Translated by George Raymond Beasley-Murray. Basil Blackwell, 1971 [1941].
Burnap, George Washington. *Expository Lectures on the Principal Passages of the Scriptures Which Relate to the Doctrine of the Trinity*. James Monroe and Company, 1845. Reprint: Lulu.com, 2008.

Buzzard, Anthony. "Anthony Buzzard Hosts Dr. Larry Hurtado: God, Jesus & the Trinity." *Focus on the Kingdom*, December 29, 2016, 01:22:59. https://www.youtube.com/watch?v=2IJ9Mz7Lnkc.

———. *Jesus Was Not a Trinitarian: A Call to Return to the Creed of Jesus.* Restoration Fellowship, 2007.

Cabrera, Frank. "Inference to the Best Explanation: An Overview." In *Handbook of Abductive Cognition*, edited by Lorenzo Magnani. Springer, 2023.

Cain, James. "The Doctrine of the Trinity and the Logic of Relative Identity." *Religious Studies* 25 (1989): 141–52.

———. "On the Geachian Theory of the Trinity and Incarnation: A Reply to Jedwab." *Faith and Philosophy* 33, no. 4 (2016): 474–86.

Caridi, Cathy. "Can a Pope Commit Heresy? ('Heresy' Defined)." *Canon Law Made Easy*, September 28, 2017, https://canonlawmadeeasy.com/2017/09/28/can-a-pope-commit-heresy-heresy-defined/.

Carter, Warren. *John: Storyteller, Interpreter, Evangelist.* Hendrickson, 2006.

Cartwright, Richard. "Identity and Substitutivity." In *Philosophical Essays.* MIT Press, 1987.

———. "On the Logical Problem of the Trinity." In *Philosophical Essays.* MIT Press, 1987.

Catechism of the Catholic Church. Paulist Press, 1994.

Celsus. *The True Teaching [Logos Alethes].* In *Celsus in His Own Words: A Translation of The True Teaching*, translated by M. David Litwa. 2024.

Chandler, Kegan. "Christological Categories and the Challenge of Messianic Agency: Dismantling 'Divine' and 'Early High' Christologies." In *A Man Who Heard from God: Human Christology from Historical, Theological, and Philosophical Perspectives*, edited by Kegan A. Chandler and Steven Nemes. Pickwick Publications, 2027.

———. *Constantine and the Divine Mind: The Imperial Quest for Primitive Monotheism.* Wipf & Stock, 2019.

———. "Cult-Rhetoric and Unitarian Christology." *Unitarian Christian Alliance*, November 9, 2024, 1:04:57, https://www.youtube.com/watch?v=EwQFRabqSqE.

———. "Early High Christology—Did Jesus Think He Was God?" *Unitarian Christian Alliance*, July 31, 2022, 54:54, https://www.youtube.com/watch?v=-L5c1nTTwoE.

Chang, Eric H. H., and Bentley C. F. Chan. *The Only Perfect Man: The Glory of God in the Face of Jesus Christ.* Ver. 2.2. CreateSpace, 2017.

Christie, William. *Dissertations on the Unity of God.* Philadelphia, 1808. Reprint: Lulu.com, 2008.

Clark, Samuel. *The Scripture-Doctrine of the Trinity, Wherein Every Text in the New Testament Relating to That Doctrine Is Distinctly Considered; and the Divinity of Our Blessed Saviour, According to the Scriptures, Proved and Explained.* In *The Works of Samuel Clarke, D.D., Late Rector of St. James's Westminster; in Four Volumes*, 4th ed., vol. 4, edited by Benjamin Hoadly. London, 1738 [1712].

"Code of Canon Law." *The Holy See.* https://www.vatican.va/archive/cod-iuris-canonici/cic_index_en.html.

Collins, Kenneth J., and Jerry L. Walls. *Roman but Not Catholic: What Remains at Stake 500 Years after the Reformation.* Baker Academic, 2017.

"Comprehensive Guide to the Names of God in the Hebrew Bible," *Biblical Hebrew,* November 24, 2024. https://biblicalhebrew.org/comprehensive-guide-to-the-names-of-god-in-the-hebrew-bible.aspx

"Constitutions of the Fourth Lateran Council—1215." In *Decrees of the Ecumenical Councils*, vol. 1, edited by Norman P. Tanner. Georgetown University Press, 1990 [1215].

"Conversation with James White." *Reformed Faith & Practice*, 2016. https://journal.rts.edu/article/conversation-with-james-white/.

Copan, Paul. "Is the Trinity a Logical Blunder? God as Three and One." In *Contending with Christianity's Critics: Answering New Atheists and Other Objectors*, edited by Paul Copan and William Lane Craig. B&H Academic, 2009.

Cowling, Sam, and Daniel Giberman. "Nominalism in Metaphysics." In *The Stanford Encyclopedia of Philosophy*, Summer 2025, edited by Edward N. Zalta and Uri Nodelman. Metaphysics Research Lab, Stanford University, 2025. https://plato.stanford.edu/archives/sum2025/entries/nominalism-metaphysics/.

Coxe, Arthur Cleveland, ed. *I. Bibliographical Synopsis, II. General Index, III. Annotated Index.* The Ante-Nicene Fathers 10. Edinburgh, 1887. Reprint: Hendrickson, 1995.

Craig, William Lane. "In Defense of Biblical Trinitarianism." In *One God, Three Persons, Four Views*, edited by Chad A. McIntosh. Cascade Books, 2024.

———. *God and Abstract Objects.* Springer International, 2017.

———. *God over All: Divine Aseity and the Challenge of Platonism.* Oxford University Press, 2016.

———. *Learning Logic.* With Marli Renee. CreateSpace, 2014.

———. *Reasonable Faith: Christian Truth and Apologetics.* 3rd ed. Crossway, 2008 [1984].

———. "Tri-Personal Monotheism." In *One God, Three Persons, Four Views*, edited by Chad A. McIntosh. Cascade Books, 2024.

Crellius, John, Jonas Schlichtingius, Martin Ruarus, Andrew Wissowatius, Benedict Wissowatius, and F. C. *The Racovian Catechism, with Notes and Illustrations, Translated from the Latin: To Which Is Prefixed a Sketch of the History of Unitarianism in Poland and the Adjacent Countries.* Translated by Thomas Rees. London, 1818 [1609].

Crescas, Ḥasdai. *The Refutation of the Christian Principles [Bittul Ikkerie ha-Nozrim]*. Translated by Daniel J. Lasker. State University of New York, 1992 [1397–98].

Crisp, Oliver. *Divinity and Humanity: The Incarnation Reconsidered*. Cambridge University Press, 2007.

———. *The Word Enfleshed: Exploring the Person and Work of Christ*. Baker, 2016.

Crisp, Oliver D., and Michael C. Rea, eds. *Analytic Theology: New Essays in the Philosophy of Theology*. Oxford University Press, 2011.

Cross, Richard. "Philosophy and the Trinity." In *The Oxford Handbook of Medieval Philosophy*, edited by John Marenbon. Oxford University Press, 2012.

Cyprian. *Cyprian to Iubaianus, His Holy Brother Bishop [Letter 73]*. In *St. Cyprian of Carthage: On the Church: Select Letters*, translated by Allen Brent. Popular Patristics Series 33. St Vladimir's Seminary Press, 2006 [256].

———. *To Demetrian*. In *St. Cyprian of Carthage: On the Church: Select Treatises*, translated by Allen Brent. Popular Patristics Series 32. St Vladimir's Seminary Press, 2006 [252].

———. *Treatise IV: On the Lord's Prayer*. In *Fathers of the Third Century*, edited by Alexander Roberts, James Donaldson, and Arthur Cleveland Coxe. Ante-Nicene Fathers 5, Buffalo, 1886 [252]. Reprint: Cosimo Classics, 2007.

———. *Treatise XII: Testimonies Against the Jews*. In *Fathers of the Third Century*, edited by Alexander Roberts, James Donaldson, and Coxe, Arthur Cleveland. Ante-Nicene Fathers 5, Buffalo, 1886 [248]. Reprint: Cosimo Classics, 2007.

———. *The Unity of the Catholic Church [De Catholicae Ecclesiae Unitate]*. In *St. Cyprian of Carthage: On the Church: Select Treatises*, translated by Allen Brent. Popular Patristics Series 32. St Vladimir's Seminary Press, 2006 [251].

Damasus of Rome. *Tome of Damasus*. In *The Christian Faith in the Doctrinal Documents of the Catholic Church*, 7th ed., edited by Jacques Dupuis, translated by J. Neuner. St. Peter's Seminary, 2001 [382].

Danker, Frederick William. *A Greek-English Lexicon of the New Testament and Other Early Christian Literature*. 4th ed. University of Chicago Press, 2021 [1928].

Date, Christopher M., and Dale Tuggy. *Is Jesus Human and Not Divine? A Debate*. Wipf & Stock, 2023 [2020].

Davis, Leo Donald. *The First Seven Ecumenical Councils (325–787): Their History and Theology*. Liturgical Press, 1983.

"[Decrees of the] First Vatican Council - 1869–1870." In *Decrees of the Ecumenical Councils*, vol. 2, edited by Norman P. Tanner. Georgetown University Press, 1990 [1869–70].

"Definition of the Faith [from the Council at Chalcedon in 451]." In *Decrees of the Ecumenical Councils*, vol. 1, edited by Norman Tanner. Georgetown University Press, 1990 [451].

DeLacy, D. R. "'One Lord' in Pauline Christology." In *Christ the Lord: Studies in Christology Presented to Donald Guthrie*, edited by Harold H. Rowdon. InterVarsity Press, 1982.

Den Dulk, Matthijs. *Between Jews and Heretics: Refiguring Justin Martyr's Dialogue with Trypho*. Routledge, 2018.

———. "Justin Martyr and the Authorship of the Earliest Anti-Heretical Treatise." *Vigiliae Christianae* 72 (October 2018): 471–83.

Dillon, John. *The Middle Platonists: 80 B.C. to A.D. 220*. rev. ed. Cornell University Press, 1996 [1977].

Dixon, Philip. *Nice and Hot Disputes: The Doctrine of the Trinity in the Seventeenth Century*. T & T Clark, 2003.

Douven, Igor. "Abduction." In *The Stanford Encyclopedia of Philosophy*, Summer 2021, edited by Edward N. Zalta and Uri Nodelman. Metaphysics Research Lab, Stanford University, 2021. https://plato.stanford.edu/archives/sum2021/entries/abduction/.

Dulles, Avery Robert. "Who Can Be Saved?" *First Things*, February 12, 2008, https://firstthings.com/who-can-be-saved/.

Dunn, James D. G. *Christology in the Making: A New Testament Inquiry into the Origins of the Doctrine of the Incarnation*. 2nd ed. Eerdmans, 1989 [1980].

———. *Did the First Christians Worship Jesus? The New Testament Evidence*. Westminster John Knox Press, 2010.

———. *Jesus According to the New Testament*. Eerdmans, 2019.

———. *The Theology of Paul the Apostle*. Eerdmans, 1998.

Edwards, Mark. *Catholicity and Heresy in the Early Church*. Routledge, 2018.

Ehrman, Bart D. *Lost Christianities: The Battles for Scripture and the Faiths We Never Knew*. Oxford University Press, 2003.

———. *The Orthodox Corruption of Scripture: The Effect of Early Christological Controversies on the Text of the New Testament*. rev. ed. Oxford University Press, 2011 [1993].

Ehrman, Bart D., and Michael F. Bird, and Robert B. Stewart. *When Did Jesus Become God? A Christological Debate*. Westminster John Knox Press, 2022.

Epiphanius of Salamis. *Panarion [Medicine Chest]*. 2nd ed. Translated by Frank Williams. 2 vols. SBL Press, 2009, 2013 [c. 376].

Esposito, Lenny. "Is the Trinity a Contradiction?" *Come Reason Ministries: Convincing Christianity*, May 20, 2014, https://apologetics-notes.comereason.org/2014/05/is-trinity-contradiction.html.

Eusebius of Caesarea. *The Church History—A New Translation with Commentary*. Translated by Paul L. Maier. Kregal Publications, 1999 [c. 324].

———. *On Ecclesiastical Theology*. In *Against Marcellus and On Ecclesiastical Theology*, translated by Kelley McCarthy Spoerl and Markus Vinzent. Fathers of the Church 135. Catholic University of America Press, 2017 [c. 336–37].

"The Exposition of the 150 Fathers [at the First Council of Constantinople, 381]." In *Decrees of the Ecumenical Councils*, vol. 1, edited by Norman P. Tanner. Georgetown University Press, 1990 [381].

Falguera, José L., Concha Martínez-Vidal, and Gideon Rosen. "Abstract Objects." In *The Stanford Encyclopedia of Philosophy*, Fall 2025, edited by Edward N. Zalta and Uri Nodelman. Metaphysics Research Lab, Stanford University, 2025. https://plato.stanford.edu/archives/fall2025/entries/abstract-objects/.

Farah, Caesar. *Islam: Beliefs and Observances*. 7th ed. Barron's, 2003 [1968].

Fee, Gordon D. *Pauline Christology: An Exegetical-Theological Study*. Baker Academic, 2007.

Ferguson, J. P. *Dr. Samuel Clarke: An Eighteenth Century Heretic*. Roundwood Press, 1976.

Finnegan, Sean. "A Unitarian View of the Holy Spirit." *Restitutio*, 2016 [2006], https://restitutio.org/2016/07/26/a-unitarian-view-of-the-holy-spirit/.

Fitzmyer, Joseph A. *First Corinthians: A New Translation with Introduction and Commentary*. Yale University Press, 2008.

Forbes, Graeme. "Frege's Problem: Referential Opacity." In *Internet Encyclopedia of Philosophy*, edited by James Fieser and Bradley Dowden. 2025. https://iep.utm.edu/referential-opacity/.

Freeman, Charles. *A.D. 381: Heretics, Pagans, and the Dawn of the Monotheistic State*. The Overlook Press, 2009.

Fulgence of Ruspe. *The Rule of Faith [De Fide Ad Petrum Seu de Regula Fide]*. In *The Faith of the Early Fathers, Volume 3, A Source-Book of Theological and Historical Passages from the Writings of St. Augustine to the End of the Patristic Age*, translated and edited by William A. Jurgens. Liturgical Press, 1979 [c. 523–26].

Galen, S. "Share of Global Population by Religion 2022." *Statista*, January 23, 2025. https://www.statista.com/statistics/374704/share-of-global-population-by-religion/.

Gaston, Thomas. *Dynamic Monarchianism: The Earliest Christology?* 2nd ed. Theophilus Press, 2023.

Geach, Peter T. "Identity." In *Logic Matters*. University of California Press, 1972.

———. "Ontological Relativity and Relative Identity." In *Logic and Ontology*, edited by Milton K. Munitz. New York University Press, 1973.

———. *Reference and Generality: An Examination of Some Medieval and Modern Theories*. 3rd ed. Cornell University Press, 1980 [1962].

Geisler, Norman L., and Abdul Saleeb. *Answering Islam: The Crescent in Light of the Cross*. 2nd ed. Baker Books, 2002 [1993].

Geisler, Norman L., and William D. Watkins. "The Incarnation and Logic: Their Compatibility Defended." *Trinity Journal* 6, no. 2 (1985): 185–97.

George, Timothy. *Is the Father of Jesus the God of Muhammad?* Zondervan, 2002.

Gilliam III, Paul. *Ignatius of Antioch and the Arian Controversy*. Brill, 2017.

Goldingay, John. *Old Testament Theology - Volume 1: Israel's Gospel*. IVP Academic, 2003.

Goodman, Nelson. "Seven Strictures on Similarity." In *Problems and Projects*. Bobbs-Merrill, 1972.

Gottlieb, Paula. "Aristotle on Non-Contradiction," *The Stanford Encyclopedia of Philosophy* Winter 2023, edited by Edward N. Zalta and Uri Nodelman. Metaphysics Research Lab, Stanford University, 2023, https://plato.stanford.edu/archives/win2023/entries/aristotle-noncontradiction/.

Grant, Robert M. *Greek Apologists of the Second Century*. Westminster John Knox Press, 1988.

———. *Jesus after the Gospels: The Christ of the Second Century*. Westminster John Knox Press, 1990.

Gregory of Nazianzus. *Oration 6 [The First Oration on Peace]*. In *St. Gregory of Nazianzus: Select Orations*, translated by Martha Vinson. The Fathers of the Church: A New Translation 107. Catholic University of America Press, 2003 [c. 364].

———. *Oration 30 [Fourth Theological Oration]*. In *On God and Christ: The Five Theological Orations and Two Letters to Cleonides*, translated by Lionel Wickham. Popular Patristics Series 23. Vladimir's Seminary Press, 2002 [380].

Gregory of Nyssa. *An Answer to Ablabius: That We Should Not Think of Saying There Are Three Gods*. Edited and translated by Cyril Richardson. In *Christology of the Later Fathers*, edited by Edward R. Hardy. Westminster Press, 1954 [late 4th c.].

Grodzins, Dean. *American Heretic: Theodore Parker and Transcendentalism*. University of North Carolina Press, 2002.

Gundry, Robert H. *Mark: A Commentary on His Apology for the Cross*. Eerdmans, 1993.

Guthrie, Kenneth Sylvan. *Numenius of Apamea: The Father of Neo-Platonism*. George Bell and Sons, 1917.

Haenchen, Ernst. *John 1. A Commentary on the Gospel of John Chapters 1–6 [Das Johannesevangelium: Ein Kommentar]*. Edited by Ulrich Busse. Translated by Robert W. Funk. Hermeneia: A Critical and Historical Commentary on the Bible. Fortress Press, 1984 [1980].

Hanson, A. T. *The Image of the Invisible God*. SCM Press, 1982.

Hanson, R. P. C. *The Search for the Christian Doctrine of God: The Arian Controversy, 318–381*. T & T Clark, 1988.

Hardegree, Gary. *Introduction to Modal Logic. Philosophy 511 - Modal Logic*, 2016, https://courses.umass.edu/phil511-gmh/text.htm.

Hardon, John A. "Heresy." In *Modern Catholic Dictionary*. Doubleday & Company, Inc., 1980.

Harris, Murray J. *Jesus as God: The New Testament Use of* Theos *in Reference to Jesus*. Baker, 1992.

Hasker, William. *God, Time, and Knowledge*. Cornell University Press, 1989.

———. "In Defense of the Trinitarian Processions." *Roczniki Filozoficzne* 71, no. 2 (2023): 59–71.

Hasker, William. "Knowing God as Trinity." In *One God, Three Persons, Four Views*, edited by Chad A. McIntosh. Cascade Books, 2024.

———. *Metaphysics and the Tri-Personal God.* Oxford Studies in Analytic Theology. Oxford University Press, 2013.

Hawthorne, John. "Identity." In *The Oxford Handbook of Metaphysics*, edited by Michael J. Loux and Dean Zimmerman. Oxford University Press, 2003.

Heer, Friedrich. *God's First Love: Christians and Jews over Two Thousand Years [Gottes erste Liebe: 2000 Jahre Judentum und Christentum. Genesis des österreichischen Katholiken Adolf Hitler].* Translated by Geoffrey Skelton. Phoenix Giant, 1970 [1967].

Heine, Ronald E. "The Christology of Callistus." *Journal of Theological Studies* 49, no. 1 (1998): 56–91.

Heiser, Michael S. "Jesus' Quotation of Psalm 82:6 in John 10:34: A Different View of John's Theological Strategy." *The Divine Council.com*, 2012. https://thedivinecouncil.com/Heiser%20Psa82inJohn10%20RegSBL2011.pdf.

———. "Should the Plural Elohim of Psalm 82 Be Understood as Men or Divine Beings." *The Divine Council.com*, 2010. https://www.thedivinecouncil.com/ETS2010Psalm82.pdf.

———. *The Unseen Realm: Recovering the Supernatural Worldview of the Bible.* Lexham Press, 2015.

Heiser, Michael S., and Trey Stricklin, hosts. "John 10, Gods or Men? [Transcript]. Episode 109." *The Naked Bible Podcast* 2.0. https://www.nakedbiblepodcast.com/wp-content/uploads/2016/07/Transcript-109-John-10-gods-or-Men.pdf.

"heresy." *Merriam-Webster.Com Dictionary*. https://www.merriam-webster.com/dictionary/heresy.

Hick, John. *The Metaphor of God Incarnate: Christology in a Pluralistic Age.* 2nd ed. Westminster John Knox Press, 2005 [1993].

Hiebert, Paul G, and R. Daniel Shaw. *Understanding Folk Religion: A Christian Response to Popular Beliefs and Practices.* Baker, 2000.

Hilary of Poitiers. *On the Trinity*. Translated by Stephen McKenna. The Fathers of the Church: A New Translation 25. Catholic University of America Press, 1954 [356–60].

Hippolytus. *On the Apostolic Tradition.* 2nd ed. Translated by Alistair C. Stewart. St. Vladimir's Seminary Press Popular Patristics Series 54. St. Vladimir's Seminary Press, 2015 [early 3rd c.].

Howard-Snyder, Daniel. "Trinity." In *Routledge Encyclopedia of Philosophy.* Routledge, 2015.

Howard-Snyder, Daniel, Frances Howard-Snyder, and Ryan Wasserman. *The Power of Logic.* 6th ed. McGraw-Hill Education, 2020 [1998].

Huffer, Alva G. *Systematic Theology*. Atlanta Bible College, 1960.

Huffman, Jr., John A. "The Holy Spirit: Know What You Believe—A Series Based on the Apostles' Creed—Part 8," *Preaching.com*, May 1, 2004, https://www.preaching.com/sermons/the-holy-spirit/.

Hurtado, Larry W. *At the Origins of Christian Worship: The Context and Character of Earliest Christian Devotion*. Eerdmans, 2000.

———. "Did Jesus Demand to Be Worshipped?" *Larry Hurtado's Blog*, October 8, 2013, https://larryhurtado.wordpress.com/2013/10/08/did-jesus-demand-to-be-worshipped/.

———. *God in New Testament Theology*. Abingdon Press, 2010.

———. *Honoring the Son: Jesus in Earliest Christian Devotional Practice*. Lexham Press, 2018.

———. *How on Earth Did Jesus Become a God? Historical Questions about Earliest Devotion to Jesus*. Eerdmans, 2005.

———. *Lord Jesus Christ: Devotion to Jesus in Earliest Christianity*. Eerdmans, 2003.

———. *One God, One Lord: Early Christian Devotion and Ancient Jewish Monotheism*. 3rd ed. T & T Clark, 2015 [1988].

Ignatius. *The Letter of Ignatius to the Smyrneans*. In *The Apostolic Fathers: Greek Texts and English Translations*, 3rd ed., translated by Michael W. Holmes. Baker Academic, 2007 [early 2nd c.].

———. *The Letter of Ignatius to the Trallians*. In *The Apostolic Fathers: Greek Texts and English Translations*, 3rd ed., translated by Michael W. Holmes. Baker Academic, 2007 [early 2nd c.].

Inan, Ilhan. "A Defense of the Indiscernibility of Identicals." *Revue Roumaine de Philosophie* 48 (2004): 61–72.

Irenaeus. *Against the Heresies: Book 1*. Translated by Dominic J. Unger and John J. Dillon. Ancient Christian Writers 55. Newman Press, 1992 [c. 180].

———. *Against the Heresies: Book 2*. Translated by Dominic J. Unger and John J. Dillon. Ancient Christian Writers 65. Newman Press, 2012 [c. 180].

———. *Against the Heresies: Book 3*. Translated by Dominic J. Unger and M. C. Steenberg. Ancient Christian Writers 64. Newman Press, 2012 [c. 180].

———. *Against the Heresies: Books 4 & 5*. Translated by Dominic J. Unger and Scott D. Moringiello. Ancient Christian Writers 72. Newman Press, 2024 [c. 180].

———. *Irenaeus on the Christian Faith: A Condensation of Against Heresies*. Edited by James R. Payton, Jr. Pickwick Publications, 2011 [c. 180].

Jedwab, Joseph. "Against the Geachian Theory of the Trinity and Incarnation." *Faith and Philosophy* 32, no. 2 (2015): 125–45.

———. "The Relative-Identity Model [of the Incarnation]." In *The Incarnation: Four Views*, edited by Andrew Hollingsworth and R. T. Mullins. Cascade Books, 2026.

Jenkins, Philip. *Jesus Wars: How Four Patriarchs, Three Queens, and Two Emperors Decided What Christians Would Believe for the Next 1,500 Years*. HarperOne, 2010.

Jenkins, Philip. *The Lost History of Christianity: The Thousand-Year Golden Age of the Church in the Middle East, Africa, and Asia—and How It Died.* HarperOne, 2008.

John of Damascus. *On Heresies.* In *St. John of Damascus: Writings*, translated by Frederic H. Chase. The Fathers of the Church: A New Translation 37. The Catholic University of America Press, 1958 [c. 730].

———. *On the Orthodox Faith: A New Translation of An Exact Exposition of the Orthodox Faith.* Translated by Norman Russell. St Vladimir's Seminary Press, 2022 [c. 730–40].

Justin Martyr. *Dialogue with Trypho.* Edited by Michael Slusser. Translated by Thomas B. Falls and Thomas P. Halton. Catholic University of America Press, 2003 [c. 160].

———. *First Apology.* In *The First and Second Apologies*, translated by Leslie William Barnard. Ancient Christian Writers 56. Paulist Press, 1997 [c. 151–55].

———. *Second Apology.* In *The First and Second Apologies*, translated by Leslie William Barnard. Ancient Christian Writers 56. Paulist Press, 1997 [c. 151–55].

Justinian. *Letter to Menam.* In *Origen: On First Principles*, vol. 2, translated by John Behr. Oxford University Press, 2017 [543].

Kalhat, Javier. "Primitive Modality and Possible Worlds." *Philosophy* 83, no. 4 (2008): 497–517.

Kapusta, Philip P. *Scripturae Contra Trinitatem: The Epistle to the Hebrews.* New Covenant Press, 2023.

Kelly, J.N.D. *The Athanasian Creed: The Paddock Lectures for 1962–63.* Harper and Row, 1964.

Keown, Mark J. *Philippians 1:1–2:18.* Evangelical Exegetical Commentary. Lexham Press, 2017.

Kerper, Michael. "What Is and Isn't a Heresy?" *Pacable*, October 2013.

Kilby, Karen. "Divine Contradiction: Fascinating but Unpersuasive." *Religious Studies* 60 (2024): 691–94.

King, Noel Quinton. *The Emperor Theodosius and the Establishment of Christianity.* SCM Press, 1961.

Kinzig, Wolfram. *A History of Early Christian Creeds.* De Gruyter, 2024.

Klinghoffer, David. *Why the Jews Rejected Jesus: The Turning Point in Western History.* New York, 2005.

Kolb, Robert. "Lutheran Theology." *The Gospel Coalition*, https://www.thegospelcoalition.org/essay/lutheran-theology/.

Küng, Hans. *Credo: The Apostle's Creed Explained for Today [Credo: Das Apostolische Glaubensbekenntnis – Zeitgenossen erklärt].* Translated by John Bowden. Doubleday, 1993 [1992].

Lampe, Peter. *From Paul to Valentinus: Christians at Rome in the First Two Centuries [Die stadtrömischen Christen in den ersten beiden Jahrhunderten: Untersuchungen zur Sozialgeschichte].* Translated by Michael Steinhauser. Edited by Marshall D. Johnson. Fortress Press, 2003 [1987, 1989].

Lamson, Alvan. *The Church of the First Three Centuries: Or, Notices of the Lives and Opinions of the Early Fathers, with Special Reference to the Doctrine of the Trinity; Illustrating Its Late Origin and Gradual Formation*. rev. ed. Edited by Ezra Abbot and Henry Ierson. London, 1875 [1860]. Reprint: Scholarly Publishing Office, University of Michigan Library, 2009.

Layman, C. Stephen. *Philosophical Approaches to the Atonement, Incarnation, and the Trinity*. Palgrave Macmillan, 2016.

Leaman, Oliver. *An Introduction to Classical Islamic Philosophy*. Cambridge University Press, 2002.

Leftow, Brian. "Anti Social Trinitarianism." In *The Trinity : An Interdisciplinary Symposium on the Trinity*, edited by Stephen T. Davis, Gerald O'Collins, and David Kendall. Oxford University Press, 1999.

———. "A Latin Trinity." *Faith and Philosophy* 21, no. 3 (2004): 304–33.

Leo I, Pope. "The Letter of Pope Leo to Flavian, Bishop of Constantinople, About Eutyches [Leo's Tome, Tome to Flavian]." In *Decrees of the Ecumenical Councils*, vol. 1, edited by Norman Tanner. Georgetown University Press, 1990 [449].

Levine, Amy-Jill, and Marc Zvi Brettler, eds. *The Jewish Annotated New Testament*. 2nd ed. Oxford University Press, 2017 [2011].

Lipton, Peter. "Inference to the Best Explanation." In *The Routledge Companion to Philosophy of Science*, edited by Stathis Psillos and Martin Curd. Routledge, 2013.

Litwa, M. David. *Found Christianities: Remaking the World of the Second Century CE*. T & T Clark, 2022.

Lloyd, Daniel. *Novatian's Theology of the Father and Son: A Study in Ontological Subordinationism*. Lexington Books/Fortress Academic, 2020.

Locke, John. *An Essay Concerning Human Understanding*. 4th ed. Edited by P. H. Nidditch. Oxford University Press, 1975 [1689, 1700].

———. *Locke on Toleration*. Edited by Richard Vernon. Cambridge Texts in the History of Philosophy. Cambridge University Press, 2010 [1685–1704].

———. *The Reasonableness of Christianity, As Delivered in the Scriptures*. Edited by George W. Ewing. Regnery Gateway, 1965 [1695].

———. *Writings on Religion*. Edited by Victor Nuovo. Oxford University Press, 2002 [1660s–1704].

Lycan, William G. "The Metaphysics of Possibilia." In *The Blackwell Guide to Metaphysics*, edited by Richard M. Gale. Blackwell Publishers, 2002.

———. "Two—No, Three—Concepts of Possible Worlds." *Proceedings of the Aristotelian Society* 91 (1991): 215–27.

Magidor, Ofra. "Arguments by Leibniz's Law in Metaphysics." *Philosophy Compass* 6, no. 3 (2011): 180–95.

Malone, Andrew S. "God the Illeist: Third-Person Self-References and Trinitarian Hints in the Old Testament." *Journal of the Evangelical Theological Society* 52, no. 3 (2009): 499–518.

Martens, Peter. "Origen's Christology in the Context of the Second and Third Centuries." In *The Oxford Handbook of Origen*, edited by Ronald E. Heine and Karen Jo Torjesen. Oxford University Press, 2022.

Martin, Walter. *The Kingdom of the Cults*. rev. ed. Edited by Ravi Zacharias. Minneapolis, 2003 [1965].

Martinich, A. P. "God, Emperor and Relative Identity." *Franciscan Studies* 39, no. 1 (1979): 180–91.

———. "Identity and Trinity." *The Journal of Religion* 58 (1978): 169–81.

The Martyrdom of the Holy Martyrs, Justin, Chariton, Charites, Paeon, and Liberianus, Who Suffered at Rome, translated by M. Dobbs. In *The Apostolic Fathers with Justin Martyr and Irenaeus*, edited by Alexander Roberts, James Donaldson, and Cleveland A. Coxe. Ante-Nicene Fathers 1. Buffalo, 1885 [late 2nd c.]. Reprint: Cosimo Classics, 2007.

Maunu, Ari. "Indiscernibility of Identicals and Substitutivity in Leibniz." *History of Philosophy Quarterly* 19, no. 4 (2002): 367–80.

Maximus of Tyre. *The Philosophical Orations*. Translated by M. B. Trapp. Oxford University Press, 1997 [second half of the 2nd c.].

Mazza, Michael J. "*Extra Ecclesiam Nulla Salus* (Outside the Church There Is No Salvation)." *Fidelity*, December 1994. https://www.ewtn.com/catholicism/library/extra-ecclesiam-nulla-salus-outside-the-church-there-is-no-salvation-1012.

McCall, Thomas H. *An Invitation to Analytic Christian Theology*. InterVarsity Press, 2015.

———. "Trinity, Simplicity, and Contradictory Theology: A Theologian's Reflections." *Religious Studies* 60 (2024): 699–705.

McClellan, Daniel. "The Gods-Complaint: Psalm 82 as a Psalm of Complaint." *Journal of Biblical Literature* 137, no. 4 (2018): 833–51.

McGrath, Alister E. *Christian Theology: An Introduction*. 4th ed. Blackwell, 2007 [1994].

———. *Heresy: A History of Defending the Truth*. Harper Collins, 2009.

McGrath, James F. "Review of Richard Bauckham, Jesus And The God of Israel." *Religion Prof: The Blog of James F. McGrath*, August 1, 2009, https://www.patheos.com/blogs/religionprof/2009/08/review-of-richard-bauckham-jesus-and-the-god-of-israel.html.

———. *The Only True God: Early Christian Monotheism in Its Jewish Context*. University of Illinois Press, 2009.

McGrath, Matthew, and Devin Frank. "Propositions." In *The Stanford Encyclopedia of Philosophy*, Fall 2024, edited by Edward N. Zalta and Uri Nodelman. Metaphysics Research Lab, Stanford University, 2024. https://plato.stanford.edu/archives/fall2024/entries/propositions/.

McIntosh, Chad A., ed. *One God, Three Persons, Four Views: A Biblical, Theological, and Philosophical Dialogue on the Doctrine of the Trinity*. With Beau Branson, William Lane Craig, William Hasker, and Dale Tuggy. Cascade Books, 2024.

Mede, Joseph. *The Works of That Reverend, Judicious, and Learned Divine, Mr. Joseph Mede, B. D.* London, 1648.

Merricks, T. "Split Brains and the Godhead." In *Knowledge and Reality: Essays in Honor of Alvin Plantinga*, edited by Thomas M. Crisp, David Vander Laan, and Matthew Davidson. Springer, 2006.

Minns, Denis. *Irenaeus: An Introduction*. T & T Clark, 2010.

Molto, Daniel. "Review of *Divine Contradiction*, by Jc Beall." *Notre Dame Philosophical Reviews*, June 4, 2024, https://ndpr.nd.edu/reviews/divine-contradiction/.

Moreland, J. P. *Love Your God with All Your Mind: The Role of Reason in the Life of the Soul.* 2nd ed. NavPress, 2012 [1997].

Moreland, J.P., and William Lane Craig. *Philosophical Foundations for a Christian Worldview*. 2nd ed. InterVarsity Press, 2017 [2003].

Morris, Thomas V. *The Logic of God Incarnate*. Cornell University Press, 1986.

———. *Understanding Identity Statements*. Humanities Press, 1984.

Mullins, R. T. "Classical Theism, Christology, and the Two Sons Worry." In *Impeccability and Temptation: Understanding Christ's Divine and Human Will*, edited by Johannes Grössl and Klaus von Stosch. Routledge, 2021.

———. "The Divine Timemaker." *Philosophia Christi* 22, no. 2 (2020): 211–37.

———. "The Doctrine of Divine Simplicity." *Theopolis Institute*, July 18, 2019, https://theopolisinstitute.com/conversations/the-doctrine-of-divine-simplicity/.

———. *The End of the Timeless God*. Oxford University Press, 2016.

———. "Hasker on the Divine Processions of the Trinitarian Persons." *European Journal for Philosophy of Religion* 9, no. 4 (2017): 181–216.

——— "Simply Impossible: A Case Against Divine Simplicity." *Journal of Reformed Theology* 7, no. 2 (2013): 181–203.

———. "The Trinitarian Processions." *Roczniki Filozoficzne* 71, no. 2 (2023): 33–57.

Mullins, R.T., and Shannon Eugene Bird. "Divine Simplicity and Modal Collapse : A Persistent Problem." *European Journal for Philosophy of Religion* 14, no. 3 (2022): 21–52.

Nemes, Steven. "Early High Christology and Contemporary Pro-Nicene Theology." *Philosophia Christi* 26, no. 1 (2024): 7–24.

NET Bible. 2nd ed. Thomas Nelson, 2019 [1996].

Newman, Paul W. *A Spirit Christology: Recovering the Biblical Paradigm of Christian Faith*. University Press of America, 1987.

Noonan, Harold, and Ben Curtis. "Identity." In *Stanford Encyclopedia of Philosophy*, edited by Edward N. Zalta and Uri Nodelman. Metaphysics Research Lab, Stanford University, 2022. https://plato.stanford.edu/entries/identity/.

Norton, Andrews. *A Statement of Reasons for Not Believing the Doctrines of Trinitarians, Concerning the Nature of God and the Person of Christ*. 3rd ed. Edited by Ezra Abbot. Boston, 1859 [1833]. Reprint: The Scholarly Publishing Office, The University of Michigan.

Novatian. *On the Trinity [The Trinity]*. In *On the Trinity, Letters to Cyprian of Carthage, Ethical Treatises*, translated by James L. Papandrea. Corpus Christianorum in Translation. Brepols, 2015 [240s].

———. *The Trinity*. In *Novatian: The Trinity; The Spectacles; Jewish Foods; In Praise of Purity; Letters*, translated by Russell DeSimone. The Fathers of the Church 67. Catholic University of America Press, 1974 [240s].

Nuovo, Victor, ed. *[John Locke's] The Reasonableness of Christianity. Extract*. In *John Locke and Christianity: Contemporary Responses to The Reasonableness of Christianity*. Thoemmes Press, 1997 [c. 1703–4].

Nye, Stephen. *A Brief History of the Unitarians, Called Also Socinians. In Four Letters, Written to a Friend*. In *The Faith of One God, Who Is Only the Father; and of One Mediator between God and Men, Who Is Only the Man Christ Jesus; and of One Holy Spirit, the Gift (and Sent) of God; Asserted and Defended, In Several Tracts Contained in This Volume; the Titles Whereof the Reader Will Find in the Following Leaf. And after That A Preface to the Whole, or an Exhortation to an Impartial and Free Inquiry into the Doctrines of Religion*, edited by Thomas Firmin. London, 1691. Reprint: Lulu.com, 2008.

———. *An Impartial Account of the Word Mystery, As It Is Taken in the Holy Scriptures*. In *The Faith of the One God*, edited by Thomas Firmin, London, 1691. Reprint: Lulu.com, 2008.

Olson, Roger E., and Christopher A. Hall. *The Trinity*. Eerdmans, 2002.

Origen. *Commentary on the Gospel According to John, Books 1–10*. Translated by Ronald E. Heine. The Fathers of the Church: A New Translation 80. The Catholic University of America Press, 2008 [c. 242].

———. *Contra Celsum [Against Celsus]*. rev. ed. Translated by Henry Chadwick. Cambridge University Press, 1986 [c. 246–48].

———. *Dialogue of Origen with Heraclides and His Fellow Bishops On the Father, the Son, and the Soul*. In *Origen: Treatise on the Passover and Dialogue with Heraclides and His Fellow Bishops on the Father, the Son, and the Soul*, translated by Robert J. Daly. Paulist Press, 1992 [c. 244–49].

———. *Exhortation to Martyrdom*. In *Alexandrian Christianity: Selected Translations of Clement and Origen with Introductions and Notes*, edited and translated by John Ernest Leonard Oulton and Henry Chadwick. Westminster Press, 1954 [235].

Origen. *On First Principles [Greek: Peri Archōn*, Latin: *De Principiis*]. 2 vols. Translated by John Behr. Oxford University Press, 2017 [c. 229–30].
———. *On First Principles: Being Koetschau's Text of the De Principiis Translated into English, Together with an Introduction and Notes by G. W. Butterworth.* Translated by G. W. Butterworth. Peter Smith, 1973 [c. 229–30].
Ortlund, Gavin. *What It Means to Be Protestant: The Case for an Always-Reforming Church*. Zondervan, 2024.
Ott, Ludwig. *Fundamentals of Catholic Dogma [Grundriss der katholischen Dogmatik]*. 4th ed. Edited by James Canon Bastible. Translated by Patrick Lynch. Tan Books and Publishers, 1960 [1952].
Ovid. *Metamorphoses*. Translated by Stanley Lombardo. Hackett, 2010 [c. 8 CE].
Pamphilus. *Apology for Origen*. In *St. Pamphilus: Apology for Origen: With the Letter of Rufinus On the Falsification of the Books of Origen*, translated by Thomas P. Scheck. The Fathers of the Church: A New Translation 120. Catholic University of America Press, 2010 [c. 310].
Parrinder, Geoffrey. *Jesus in the Qur'an*. OneWorld, 1995 [1965].
Pawl, Timothy. *In Defense of Conciliar Christology: A Philosophical Essay*. Oxford Studies in Analytic Theology. Oxford University Press, 2016.
Perriman, Andrew. *In the Form of a God: The Pre-Existence of the Exalted Christ in Paul*. Studies in Early Christology. Cascade Books, 2022.
———. "Is Jesus Included in the 'Divine Identity' in 1 Corinthians 8:6?" *P.OST*, May 21, 2014, https://www.postost.net/2015/11/jesus-included-divine-identity-1-corinthians-86.
———. "Jimmy Dunn: One God, One Lord, and the Shema." *P.OST*, September 3, 2011, https://www.postost.net/2015/11/jimmy-dunn-one-god-one-lord-shema.
Perry, Andrew. *John 1:1–18 - A Socinian Approach*. 2nd ed. revision 6. Willow Publications, 2025 [2017].
Pfizenmaier, Thomas C. *The Trinitarian Theology of Dr. Samuel Clarke (1675–1729): Context, Sources, and Controversy*. Brill, 1997.
Pharr, Clyde, trans. *The Theodosian Code. And Novels and the Sirmondian Constitutions. A Translation with Commentary, Glossary, and Bibliography*. Princeton University Press, 1952 [438].
Philo. *On Dreams, That They Are God-Sent*. In *The Works of Philo*, rev. ed., translated by C. D. Yonge. Hendrickson, 1993 [early 1st c. CE].
———. *On the Life of Moses, I*. In *The Works of Philo*, rev. ed., translated by C. D. Yonge. Hendrickson, 1993 [early 1st c. CE].
Pinnock, Clark, Richard Rice, John Sanders, William Hasker, and David Basinger. *The Openness of God: A Biblical Challenge to the Traditional Understanding of God*. InterVarsity Press, 1994.

Plantinga, Alvin. *Knowledge and Christian Belief.* Eerdmans, 2015.
———. *Warrant and Proper Function.* Oxford University Press, 1993.
———. *Warranted Christian Belief.* Oxford University Press, 2000.
Pollard, T. E. *Johannine Christology and the Early Church.* Cambridge University Press, 1970.
Popkin, Richard H. *Disputing Christianity: The 400-Year-Old Debate over Rabbi Isaac Ben Abraham of Troki's Classic Arguments.* Humanity Books, 2007.
Priest, Graham, Francesco Berto, and Zach Weber, "Dialetheism," *The Stanford Encyclopedia of Philosophy*, Winter 2025, edited by Edward N. Zalta and Uri Nodelman. Metaphysics Research Lab, Stanford University, 2025, https://plato.stanford.edu/archives/win2025/entries/dialetheism/.
Priest, Graham, Jc Beall, and Bradley Armour-Garb, eds. *The Law of Non-Contradiction: New Philosophical Essays.* Oxford University Press, 2004.
Priest, Robert J. "Wheaton and the Controversy Over Whether Muslims and Christians Worship the Same God." *Occasional Bulletin [of the Evangelical Missiological Society]*, Special Edition (2016): 1–3.
"The Profession of Faith of the 318 Fathers [at the Council of Nicaea in 325]." In *Decrees of the Ecumenical Councils*, vol. 1, edited by Norman P. Tanner. Georgetown University Press, 1990, [325].
Pruss, Alexander R. "The Actual and the Possible." In *The Blackwell Guide to Metaphysics*, edited by Richard M. Gale. Blackwell Publishers, 2002.
The Qur'an. Translated by M. A. S. Abdel Haleem. Oxford World's Classics. Oxford University Press, 2004 [610–32].
Qureshi, Nabeel. *Seeking Allah, Finding Jesus: A Devout Muslim Encounters Christianity.* 3rd ed. Zondervan, 2018 [2014].
Rahner, Karl. "*Theos* in the New Testament." In *Theological Investigations, Volume I: God, Christ, Mary and Grace [Schriften zur Theologie, Band I,]*, translated by Cornelius Ernst. Helicon Press, 1961 [1954].
Ranke-Heinemann, Uta. *Eunuchs for the Kingdom of Heaven: Women, Sexuality and the Catholic Church [Eunuchen für das Himmelreich: Katholische Kirche und Sexualität].* Translated by Peter Heinegg. Doubleday, 1990 [1988].
Ratzinger, Joseph. "Doctrinal Commentary on the Concluding Formula of the *Professio Fidei* [by Pope John Paul II]." *The Holy See*, 1998. https://www.vatican.va/roman_curia/congregations/cfaith/documents/rc_con_cfaith_doc_1998_professio-fidei_en.html.
Rea, Michael C. "Relative Identity and the Doctrine of the Trinity." *Philosophia Christi* 5, no. 2 (2003): 431–45.
Reese, Philip-Neri. "Contradictory Christology: A Conciliar Concern." *Asian Journal of Philosophy* 2, no. 14 (2023).
Refutation of All Heresies. Translated by M. David Litwa. SBL Press, 2016 [c. 222].

Ridderbos, Herman N. *The Gospel of John: A Theological Commentary [Das Evangelium nach Johannes: Ein theologischer Kommentar]*. Translated by John Vriend. W.B. Eerdmans, 1997 [1987, 1991].

Ripley, George. *The Divinity of Jesus Christ*. 3rd ed. Boston, 1855 [1830].

Robinson, John A. T. "The Fourth Gospel and the Church's Doctrine of the Trinity." In *Twelve More New Testament Studies*. SCM Press, 1984.

———. *The Priority of John*. Edited by J. F. Coakley. Meyer Stone Books, 1987.

Rufinus. *Preface to the Translations of Origen's Books Peri Archon [On First Principles]*. In *Theodoret, Jerome, Gennadius, Rufinus: Historical Writings, Etc.*, edited by Philip Schaff and Henry Wace, translated by William Henry Fremantle. Nicene and Post-Nicene Fathers, second series, vol. 3. New York, 1892 [397]. Reprint: Eerdmans, 1979.

———. *Rufinus' Apology in Defence of Himself*. In *Theodoret, Jerome, Gennadius, Rufinus: Historical Writings, Etc.*, edited by Philip Schaff and Henry Wace, translated by William Henry Fremantle. Nicene and Post-Nicene Fathers, Second Series, vol. 3. New York, 1892 [400]. Reprint: Eerdmans, 1979.

———. *Rufinus' Epilogue to Pamphilus the Martyr's Apology for Origen, Otherwise [known as]: The Book Concerning the Adulteration of the Works of Origen (Addressed to Macarius at Pinetum, A.D. 397.)*. In *Theodoret, Jerome, Gennadius, Rufinus: Historical Writings, Etc.*, edited by Philip Schaff and Henry Wace, translated by William Henry Fremantle. Nicene and Post-Nicene Fathers, second series, vol. 3. The Christian Literature Company, 1892 [397]. Reprint: Eerdmans, 1979.

Sanders, Fred. "Lose My Wits? Unhinge My Brains? Ruin My Mind? Pursue Distraction?" *The Scriptorium Daily*, September 23, 2010, https://scriptoriumdaily.com/lose-my-wits-unhinge-my-brains-ruin-my-mind-pursue-distraction/.

———. *The Deep Things of God: How the Trinity Changes Everything*. 2nd ed. Crossway, 2017 [2010].

———. *The Triune God*. Zondervan Academic, 2016.

Schäfer, Peter. *Jesus in the Talmud*. Princeton University Press, 2007.

Schlegel, Bill. "New Creation in John 1, with Dr. Andrew Perry – One God Report – Podcast Episode 66." *One God Report*, January 28, 2022, Podcast, 20:55. https://podtail.com/podcast/one-god-report/66-new-creation-in-john-1-with-dr-andrew-perry/.

Schoedel, William R. *Ignatius of Antioch: A Commentary on the Letters of Ignatius of Antioch*. Edited by Helmut Koester. Hermeneia—a Critical and Historical Commentary on the Bible. Fortress Press, 1985.

Schoenheit, John W., Mark H. Graeser, and John A. Lynn. *One God and One Lord : Reconsidering the Cornerstone of the Christian Faith*. Christian Educational Services, 2000.

"Session 7 [From the Council of Trent, 1545–63]." In *Decrees of the Ecumenical Councils*, vol. 2, edited by Norman Tanner. Georgetown University Press, 1990 [1547].

"Session 8 [of the Council of Basel]: Bull of Union with the Armenians." In *Decrees of the Ecumenical Councils*, vol. 1, edited by Norman Tanner. Georgetown University Press, 1990 [1439].

"Session 11 [of the Council of Florence]." In *Decrees of the Ecumenical Councils*, vol. 1, edited by Norman Tanner. Georgetown University Press, 1990 [1442].

Shellnutt, Kate, and Daniel Silliman. "Ravi Zacharias Hid Hundreds of Pictures of Women, Abuse During Massages, and a Rape Allegation." *Christianity Today*, February 11, 2021. https://www.christianitytoday.com/2021/02/ravi-zacharias-rzim-investigation-sexual-abuse-sexting-rape/.

"Shield of the Trinity." *Wikipedia*, https://en.wikipedia.org/wiki/Shield_of_the_Trinity.

Sijuwade, Joshua R. "Building the Monarchy of the Father." *Religious Studies* 58, no. 2 (2022): 436–55.

———. "Conciliar Trinitarianism: A Philosophical Analysis," *The Heythrop Journal* 66, no. 5 (2025): 498–518.

———. "The Logical Problem of the Trinity: A New Solution." *Religions* 13, no. 809 (2022): 1–46.

———. "Monarchical Trinitarianism: A Metaphysical Proposal." *TheoLogica* 5, no. 2 (2021): 41–80.

———. "The Nature of Monotheism: A Philosophical Explication." *Forum Philosophicum* 30, no. 2 (2025): 87–116.

———. "A Philosophical Argument for Conciliar Trinitarianism," *Journal of Analytic Theology*, forthcoming.

Silva, Moisés, ed. *New International Dictionary of New Testament Theology and Exegesis*. 4 vols. 2nd ed. Zondervan, 2014 [1975–78].

Simpson, John. *An Explanation of John 1:1–18*. In *Additional Essays on the Language of Scripture*. London, 1810.

Singer, Tovia. *Let's Get Biblical! Why Doesn't Judaism Accept the Christian Messiah?* rev. ed. 2 vols. Outreach Judaism, 2014 [1998].

Slick, Matt. "John 17:3, 'The Only True God.'" *Christian Apologetics Research Ministry*, December 5, 2018. https://carm.org/john-173-the-only-true-god.

Smith, Dustin. "The Incarnation of Wisdom in Pre-Christian Judaism." *Unitarian Christian Alliance*, December 1, 2023, 58:31, https://www.youtube.com/watch?v=VOIGLvYeE4k.

———. "An Introduction to the Theme of Misunderstanding in the Gospel of John. Episode 204." *The Biblical Unitarian Podcast*, December 23, 2021, 31:03, https://biblicalunitarianpodcast.podbean.com/e/204-an-introduction-to-the-theme-of-misunderstanding-in-the-gospel-of-john/.

Smith, Dustin. "The Plural of Majesty." *Unitarian Christian Alliance*, February 17, 2023, 53:05, https://www.youtube.com/watch?v=1SK2XHEUC9g.

———. *A Systematic Theology of the Early Church*, edited by J. Jeffery Fletcher and Scott A. Deane. Integrity Syndicate, 2025.

———. *Wisdom Christology in the Gospel of John*. Wipf and Stock, 2024.

Smith, Dustin, James White. "Dr. Dustin Smith Vs Dr. James White: Does the Bible Teach the Trinity? *The Gospel Truth*, February 16, 2026, 2:05:20, https://www.youtube.com/watch?v=xNohJq87mO8.

Sommer, Benjamin D. *The Bodies of God and the World of Ancient Israel*. Cambridge University Press, 2011.

Stark, Rodney. *One True God: Historical Consequences of Monotheism*. Princeton University Press, 2001.

Stark, Rodney. *The Triumph of Christianity: How the Jesus Movement Became the World's Largest Religion*. HarperOne, 2011.

Swinburne, Richard. *The Christian God*. Oxford University Press, 1994.

Tertullian. *Against Praxeas [Adversus Praxean]* Translated by Alexander Souter. Macmillan, 1920 [early 3rd c.].

———. *Against Praxeas [Adversus Praxean]*. Translated by Ernest Evans. SPCK, 1948 [early 3rd c.]. Reprint: Wipf & Stock, 2011.

Theophilus of Antioch. *To Autolycus [Ad Autolycum]*. In *Theophilus of Antioch: Ad Autolycum*, translated by Robert M. Grant. Oxford University Press, 1970 [c. 180].

Thompson, Keith. "Revisiting 'Where Did Jesus Say "I Am God"'—A Response to the Muhammedan Site 'Do Not Say Trinity." *Answering Islam*, https://www.answeringislam.org/authors/thompson/rebuttals/questionmark/response_where_i_am_god.html.

Thompson, Marianne Meye. *John: A Commentary*. Westminster John Knox Press, 2015.

Toulmin, Joshua. *A Review of the Life, Character and Writings of the Rev. John Biddle, M.A. Who Was Banished to Isle of Scilly, in the Protectorate of Oliver Cromwell*. London, 1791.

———. *The Meaning Which the Word Mystery, Bears in the New Testament; Considered and Applied*. London, 1791.

Trigg, Joseph Wilson. *Origen: The Bible and Philosophy in the Third-Century Church*. John Knox Press, 1983.

Troki, Isaac ben Abraham. *Ḥizuk Emunah; or, Faith Strengthened*. Translated by Moses Mocatta. Hermon Press, 1970 [1850].

Tuggy, Dale. "An Ancient, Triadic, Unitarian Theology." In *One God, Three Persons, Four Views*, edited by Chad A. McIntosh. Cascade Books, 2024.

———. "Antiunitarian Arguments from Divine Perfection." *Journal of Analytic Theology* 9 (September 2021): 262–90.

———. "The Apologetics Blind-Spot on Numerical Identity." *Trinities*, August 3, 2016, https://trinities.org/blog/apologetics-blind-spot-numerical-identity/.

Tuggy, Dale. "Changing the Subject, Cognitive Faculties, and 'God' [Reply to Craig]." In *One God, Three Persons, Four Views*, edited by Chad A. McIntosh. Cascade Books, 2024.

———. "Constitution Trinitarianism: An Appraisal." *Philosophy and Theology* 25, no. 1 (2013): 129–62.

———. "Craig's Contradictory Christ." *TheoLogica* 7, no. 2 (2023): 201–28.

———. "Christian Theologies in the Year 240." *Unitarian Christian Alliance*, August 13, 2024, 1:10:38, https://www.youtube.com/watch?v=d9W_KjktIdk.

———. "Defining the Concept of a Christian Unitarian." *Trinities*, April 24, 2012, http://trinities.org/blog/defining-the-concept-of-a-christian-unitarian/.

———. "Defining the Concept of a Unitarian." *Trinities*, April 24, 2012, http://trinities.org/blog/defining-the-concept-of-a-unitarian/.

———. "Divine Deception and Monotheism." *Journal of Analytic Theology* 2 (2014): 186–209.

———. "Exposing the Council of Nicaea [Nicaea at 1700: Myths vs. History]," *Unitarian Christian Alliance*, November 23, 2025, 1:37:38, https://www.youtube.com/watch?v=KVh8HH_ghik.

———. "Facts Are Facts." In *One God, Three Persons, Four Views*, edited by Chad A. McIntosh. Cascade Books, 2024.

———. "The 'Faith Once Delivered'?" In *One God, Three Persons, Four Views*, edited by Chad A. McIntosh. Cascade Books, 2024.

———. "Flocanrib and the Ambiguity of the Word 'Trinity.'" *Trinities*, April 25, 2013, https://trinities.org/blog/flocanrib-and-the-ambiguity-of-the-word-trinity/.

———. "God and His Son: the Logic of the New Testament." *Trinities*, June 4, 2012, Videos, https://trinities.org/blog/god-and-his-son-the-logic-of-the-new-testament/.

———. "'God' in the Challenge Argument." *Trinities*, February 2, 2016, https://trinities.org/blog/god-in-the-challenge/.

———. "Hasker's Quests for a Viable Social Theory." *Faith and Philosophy* 30, no. 2 (2013): 171–87.

———. "History of Trinity Doctrines [Supplement to 'Trinity']." In *Stanford Encyclopedia of Philosophy*, edited by Edward N. Zalta and Uri Nodelman. Metaphysics Research Lab, Stanford University, 2025 [2009] http://plato.stanford.edu/entries/trinity/trinity-history.html.

———. "Hurtado on the Early Worship of Jesus." *Trinities*, November 27, 2019, https://trinities.org/blog/hurtado-on-the-worship-of-jesus/.

———. "Jesus's Argument in John 10." *Trinities*, November 14, 2014, http://trinities.org/blog/jesuss-argument-in-john-10/.

———. "Larry Hurtado on Early Christians' Worship of Jesus." *Trinities*, June 11, 2013, http://trinities.org/blog/larry-hurtado-on-early-chrisitans-worship-of-jesus/.

Tuggy, Dale. "Metaphysics and Logic of the Trinity." *Oxford Handbooks Online*, 2016, https://doi.org/10.1093/oxfordhb/9780199935314.013.27.

———. "New Testament Theology Is Unitarian." In *One God, Three Persons, Four Views*, edited by Chad A. McIntosh. Cascade Books, 2024.

———. "Nineteen or Twenty-One Reasons Why The New Testament Jesus Is Not Fully Divine." In *A Man Who Heard from God: Human Christology from Historical, Theological, and Philosophical Perspectives*, edited by Kegan Chandler and Steven Nemes. Pickwick Publications, 2027.

———. "On Bauckham's Bargain." *Theology Today* 70, no. 2 (2013): 128–43.

———. "On Counting Gods." *TheoLogica* 1, no. 1 (2016): 188–213.

———. "On Positive Mysterianism." *International Journal for Philosophy of Religion* 69, no. 3 (2011): 205–26.

———. "Podcast 25 – Pastor Sean Finnegan on the Holy Spirit" – Part 1." *Trinities Podcast*, February 3, 2014, 35:16. https://trinities.org/blog/podcast-25-pastor-sean-finnegan-about-the-holy-spirit-part-1/.

———. "Podcast 26 – Pastor Sean Finnegan on "the Holy Spirit" – Part 2" *Trinities Podcast*. February 10, 2014, 25:54, https://trinities.org/blog/podcast-26-pastor-sean-finnegan-on-the-holy-spirit-part-2/.

———. "Podcast 70 – The One God and His Son According to John." *Trinities Podcast*, January 12, 2015, 53:43. https://trinities.org/blog/podcast-70-the-one-god-and-his-son-according-to-john/.

———. "Podcast 85 – Heretic! Four Approaches to Dropping H-Bombs." *Trinities Podcast*, May 4, 2015, 51:27, https://trinities.org/blog/podcast-85-heretic-four-approaches-to-dropping-h-bombs/.

———. "Podcast 122 – 7 Christians on 4 Questions in the "Same God" Controversy." *Trinities Podcast*, January 18, 2016, 46:56, https://trinities.org/blog/podcast-122-7-christians-on-4-questions-in-the-same-god-controversy/.

———. "Podcast 124 – a Challenge to "Jesus Is God" Apologists." *Trinities Podcast*, February 1, 2016, 41:53, http://trinities.org/blog/podcast-124-a-challenge-to-jesus-is-god-apologists/.

———. "Podcast 145 – 'Tis Mystery All: The Immortal Dies!" *Trinities Podcast*, June 27, 2016, 48:15, http://trinities.org/blog/podcast-145-tis-mystery-immortal-dies/.

———. "Podcast 168 – The Death of Unitarian Congregationalism." *Trinities Podcast*, January 16, 2017, 1:00:30. http://trinities.org/blog/podcast-168-the-death-of-unitarian-congregationalism/.

———. "Podcast 189 – *The Unfinished Business of the Reformation*." *Trinities Podcast*, July 3, 2017, 35:01, https://trinities.org/blog/podcast-189-the-unfinished-business-of-the-reformation/.

Tuggy, Dale. "Podcast 213 – Has Bauckham Clarified His "Divine Identity" Theory? – Part 1." *Trinities Podcast*, February 4, 2018, 1:04:34, https://trinities.org/blog/podcast-213-has-bauckham-clarified-his-divine-identity-theory-part-1/.

———. "Podcast 214 – Has Bauckham Clarified His "Divine Identity" Theory? – Part 2." *Trinities Podcast*. February 23, 2018, 53:18, https://trinities.org/blog/podcast-214-has-bauckham-clarified-his-divine-identity-theory-part-2/.

———. "Podcast 224 – Biblical Words for God and for His Son Part 1 – God and "God" in the Bible". *Trinities Podcast*, April 23, 2018, 42:13, https://trinities.org/blog/podcast-224-biblical-words-for-god-and-for-his-son-part-1-god-and-god-in-the-bible/.

———. "Podcast 225 – Biblical Words for God and for His Son Part 2 – Old "Lord" vs. New "Lord." " *Trinities Podcast*, April 29, 2018, 31:57, https://trinities.org/blog/podcast-225-biblical-words-for-god-and-for-his-son-part-2-old-lord-vs-new-lord/.

———. "Podcast 226 – Biblical Words for God and for His Son Part 3 – Post-Biblical Uses of Biblical Words, and New Words." *Trinities Podcast*, May 7, 2018, 45:00, https://trinities.org/blog/podcast-226-biblical-words-for-god-and-for-his-son-part-3-post-biblical-uses-of-biblical-words-and-new-words/.

———. "Podcast 227 – Who Should Christians Worship?" *Trinities Podcast*, May 14, 2018, 51:09. https://trinities.org/blog/podcast-227-who-should-christians-worship/.

———. "Podcast 232 – Trinity Club Orientation." *Trinities Podcast*, June 19, 2018, 41:48, https://trinities.org/blog/podcast-232-trinity-club-orientation/.

———. "Podcast 235 – The Case Against Preexistence." *Trinities Podcast*. June 16, 2018, 1:03:44, https://trinities.org/blog/podcast-235-the-case-against-preexistence/.

———. "Podcast 248 – How Trinity Theories Conflict with the Bible." *Trinities Podcast*, January 6, 2019, 52:03, https://trinities.org/blog/podcast-248-how-trinity-theories-conflict-with-the-bible/.

———. "Podcast 253 – The Apostle Paul a Unitarian [by Caleb Stetson (1793–1870)]" *Trinities Podcast*. February 18, 2019, 1:00:16, https://trinities.org/blog/podcast-253-the-apostle-paul-a-unitarian/.

———. "Podcast 259 – Who Is the One Creator? – Part 2." *Trinities Podcast*, April 15, 2019, 50:55, https://trinities.org/blog/podcast-259-who-is-the-one-creator-part-2/.

———. "Podcast 260 – How to Argue That the Bible Is Trinitarian." *Trinities Podcast*, May 6, 2019, 56:17, https://trinities.org/blog/podcast-260-how-to-argue-that-the-bible-is-trinitarian/.

Tuggy, Dale. "Podcast 291 – From One God to Two Gods to Three "Gods" – John 1 and Early Christian Theologies." *Trinities Podcast*, April 13, 2020, 57:40, https://trinities.org/blog/podcast-291-from-one-god-to-two-gods-to-three-gods-john-1-and-early-christian-theologies/.

———. "Podcast 333 – The Arguments of "God's Death [by Mark Cain]." *Trinities Podcast*, September 14, 2021, 48:13, https://trinities.org/blog/podcast-333-the-arguments-of-gods-death/.

———. "Podcast 334 – "Who Do You Say I Am?" " *Trinities Podcast*, September 21, 2021, 1:48:04, https://trinities.org/blog/podcast-334-who-do-you-say-i-am/.

———. "Podcast 348 – Novatian's On the Trinity – Part 2 – Two Thieves and Three Arguments." *Trinities Podcast*, May 18, 2022, 1:07:00, https://trinities.org/blog/podcast-348-novatians-on-the-trinity-part-2-two-thieves-and-three-arguments/.

———. "Podcast 372 – Book Session Identity Crisis – Part 1." *Trinities Podcast*, November 28, 2023, 1:08:27. https://trinities.org/blog/podcast-372-book-session-identity-crisis-part-1/.

———. "Podcast 373 – Book Session Identity Crisis – Part 2." *Trinities Podcast*, December 4, 2023, 1:22:01, https://trinities.org/blog/podcast-372-book-session-identity-crisis-part-2/.

———. "Podcast 381 – Mainstream Christian Theologies in the Year 240: What Trinitarian Apologists Don't Know." *Trinities Podcast*, August 15, 2024, 1:10:31, https://trinities.org/blog/podcast-381-mainstream-christian-theologies-in-the-year-240-what-trinitarian-apologists-dont-know/.

———. "Podcast 384 – Mainstream Christian Theologies in the Late 100s – Early 200s and Early Trinitarian "Fool's Gold." " *Trinities Podcast*, December 22, 2024, 1:08:17, https://trinities.org/blog/podcast-384-mainstream-christian-theologies-in-the-late-100s-early-200s-and-early-trinitarian-fools-gold/.

———. "Podcast 393 – Are You Orthodox or Fauxthodox?" *Trinities Podcast*, September 15, 2025, 59:53, https://trinities.org/blog/podcast-393-are-you-orthodox-or-fauxthodox/.

———. "Podcast 394 – Debate: Tuggy vs. White – John 1 Is Not Trinitarian – Part 1." *Trinities Podcast*, November 9, 2025, https://trinities.org/blog/podcast-394-debate-tuggy-vs-white-john-1-is-not-trinitarian-part-1/.

———. "[Review of] James Anderson, *Paradox in Christian Theology: An Analysis of Its Presence, Character, and Epistemic Status*." *Faith and Philosophy* 26, no. 1 (2009): 104–8.

———. "Some Objections to Ward's Trinitarian Theology." *Philosophia Christi* 18, no. 2 (2016): 363–73.

———. "The Standard Opening Move." *Trinities*, April 2, 2011, http://trinities.org/blog/the-standard-opening-move/.

———. "Tertullian the Unitarian." *European Journal for Philosophy of Religion* 8, no. 3 (2016): 179–99.

Tuggy, Dale. "Theories of Religious Diversity." In *Internet Encyclopedia of Philosophy*, edited by James Fieser and Bradley Dowden, 2017, https://iep.utm.edu/reli-div/.

———. "Three Roads to Open Theism." *Faith and Philosophy* 24, no. 1 (2007): 28–51.

———. "Tradition and Believability: Edward Wierenga's Social Trinitarianism." *Philosophia Christi* 5, no. 2 (2003): 447–56.

———. "Trinitarian "Fool's Gold" - Mainstream Christian Theologies - Late 100's to Early 200's." *Unitarian Christian Alliance*, December 9, 2024, 1:06:24, https://www.youtube.com/watch?v=KxYtTQDo1dA.

———. "Trinity." In *The Stanford Encyclopedia of Philosophy*, edited by Edward N. Zalta and Uri Nodelman. Metaphysics Research Lab, Stanford University, 2025 [2009]. http://plato.stanford.edu/entries/trinity/.

———. "Two Natures, Christ, and Contradictions." In *A Man Who Heard from God: Human Christology from Historical, Theological, and Philosophical Perspectives*, edited by Kegan Chandler and Steven Nemes. Pickwick Publications, 2027.

———. "The Unfinished Business of the Reformation." In *Herausforderungen Und Modifikationen Des Klassischen Theismus*, edited by Thomas Marschler and Thomas Schärtl. Aschendorff Verlag, 2019.

———. "The Unfinished Business of Trinitarian Theorizing." *Religious Studies* 39 (2003): 165–83.

———. *What Is the Trinity? Thinking about the Father, Son, and Holy Spirit*. Kindle Direct Publishing, 2017.

———. "What John 1 Meant," *Unitarian Christian Alliance*, November 12, 2021, 1:12:01, https://www.youtube.com/watch?v=nb4TogqyTrw.

———. "When and How in the History of Theology Did the Triune God Replace the Father as the Only True God?" *TheoLogica* 4, no. 2 (2020): 27–51.

———. "Who Should Christians Worship?" *Journal of Biblical Unitarianism* 1, no. 1 (2014): 5–33.

———. "Why I'm Not A Buddhist." *Khanpadawan*, April 3, 2018, 01:08:09, https://www.youtube.com/watch?v=Xgd7QNiX-ts.

Tuggy, Dale, and James White. "Dale Tuggy and James White Debate: 'Is Jesus YHWH?' ", *Unitarian Christian Alliance*, March 12, 2024, 2:04:08, https://youtu.be/ky2SaHscSIo?si=ZLvzO6Thl7hXaUbZ.

———. "Dale Tuggy vs James White: John 1 Is Not Trinitarian." *Unitarian Christian Alliance*, October 10, 2025, 2:19:03, https://www.youtube.com/watch?v=3855v9tWmVo.

"Validity and Soundness." In *Internet Encyclopedia of Philosophy*, edited by James Fieser and Bradley Dowden. n.d. https://www.iep.utm.edu/val-snd/.

Vallicella, William F. "Divine Simplicity." In *The Stanford Encyclopedia of Philosophy*, Spring 2023, edited by Edward N. Zalta and Uri Nodelman. Metaphysics Research Lab, Stanford University, 2023 [2006]. https://plato.stanford.edu/archives/spr2015/entries/divine-simplicity/

van Gorder, A. Christian. *No God but God: A Path to Muslim-Christian Dialogue on God's Nature*. Orbis Books, 2003.

van Inwagen, Peter. "And Yet They Are Not Three Gods but One God." In *God, Knowledge, and Mystery*. Cornell University Press, 1995.

———. *God, Knowledge and Mystery: Essays in Philosophical Theology*. Cornell University Press, 1995.

———. "Three Persons in One Being: On Attempts to Show That the Doctrine of the Trinity Is Self-Contradictory." In *The Holy Trinity: East/West Dialogue*, edited by Melville Stewart. Kluwer Academic Publishers, 2003.

Wallace, Daniel B. *Greek Grammar Beyond the Basics: An Exegetical Syntax of the New Testament with Scripture, Subject, and Greek Word Indexes*. Zondervan Academic, 1996.

———. "Sharp Redivivus? - A Reexamination of the Granville Sharp Rule." *Bible.Org*, June 30, 2004, https://bible.org/article/sharp-redivivus-reexamination-granville-sharp-rule.

Wallace, Robert. *A Plain Statement and Scriptural Defence of the Leading Doctrines of Unitarianism: To Which Are Added Remarks on the Canonical Authority of the Books of the New Testament, and a Candid Review of the Text of the Improved Version, in a Letter to a Friend*. Chesterfield, 1819.

Walton, John H. *Old Testament Theology for Christians: From Ancient Context to Enduring Belief*. InterVarsity Press, 2017.

Ward, Charles G., ed. *The Billy Graham Christian Worker's Handbook*. World Wide Publications, 2000 [1981].

Ward, Keith. *Christ and the Cosmos: A Reformulation of Trinitarian Doctrine*. Cambridge University Press, 2015.

———. *Christianity: A Short Introduction*. Oneworld, 2000.

———. *God: A Guide for the Perplexed*. Oneworld, 2002.

Ware Jr., Henry. *Outline of the Testimony of Scripture against the Trinity*. 2nd ed. Boston, 1834 [1827].

Warfield, Benjamin Breckinridge. "Trinity (Study Edition)." In *International Standard Bible Encyclopedia*, edited by James Orr and Fred Sanders, October 2015 [1915]. https://scriptoriumdaily.com/warfields-the-biblical-doctrine-of-the-trinity-annotated/.

Wasserman, Tommy. "Evangelical Textual Criticism: 'How on Earth Did Larry Hurtado Become a Text-Critic?'" *Evangelical Textual Criticism*, October 12, 2011, http://evangelicaltextualcriticism.blogspot.com/2011/10/how-on-earth-did-larry-hurtado-become.html.

Weatherall, Dan. "It Wasn't God on the Cross." *Unitarian Christian Alliance,* September 13, 2024, 57:00, https://www.youtube.com/watch?v=r_Tpzog7e8o.

Webster, Noah. "heresy." In *Noah Webster's 1828 Dictionary.* https://archive.org/details/noah-websters-1828-dictionary-ellen-g-white-estate.

Werther, David. "Incarnation." In *Internet Encyclopedia of Philosophy,* edited by James Fieser and Bradley Dowden. n.d. http://www.iep.utm.edu/incarnat/.

The Westminster Confession of Faith. Westminster Theological Seminary, 2023 [1646–48]. http://files1.wts.edu/uploads/pdf/about/WCF_30.pdf.

Whiston, William. *Historical Memoirs of the Life and Writings of Dr. Samuel Clarke, Including Certain Memoirs of Several of His Friends.* 3rd ed. London, 1748 [1730].

White, James R. *The Forgotten Trinity: Recovering the Heart of Christian Belief.* rev. ed. Bethany House Publishers, 2019 [1998].

Wierwille, Jerry. "Can We 'Pray' to Jesus Christ?" *BiblicalUnitarian.Com,* May 23, 2011, https://www.biblicalunitarian.com/articles/jesus-christ/can-we-pray-to-jesus-christ.

Wilbur, Earl Morse. *A History of Unitarianism.* 2 vols. Beacon Press, 1945, 1952.

Wiles, Maurice. *Archetypal Heresy: Arianism Through The Centuries.* Oxford University Press, 1996.

Wilhelm, J. "Heresy." In *The Catholic Encyclopedia.* Robert Appleton Company, 1910, http://www.newadvent.org/cathen/07256b.htm.

Willard, Dallas. *The Divine Conspiracy: Rediscovering Our Hidden Life in God.* HarperSanFrancisco, 1998.

Williams, Scott M. "Discovery of the Sixth Ecumenical Council's Trinitarian Theology: Historical, Ecclesial, and Theological Implications." *Journal of Analytic Theology* 10 (2022): 332–62.

Williams, Thomas. "The Doctrine of Univocity Is True and Salutary." *Modern Theology* 21, no. 4 (2005): 575–85.

Williamson, Timothy. "Vagueness, Identity and Leibniz's Law." In *Individuals, Essence and Identity: Themes of Analytic Metaphysics,* edited by Ermanno Bencivenga, vol. 4, edited by Andrea Bottani, Massimiliano Carrara, and Pierdaniele Giaretta. Springer Netherlands, 2002.

Wilson, John. *Scripture Proofs and Scriptural Illustrations of Unitarianism.* 3rd ed. Chapman Brothers, 1846 [1833].

———. *Unitarian Principles Confirmed by Trinitarian Testimonies: Being Selections from the Works of Eminent Theologians Belonging to Orthodox Churches.* 13th ed. American Unitarian Association, 1890 [1855].

Wilson, Marlon, host. "Dustin Smith/William Barlow vs Samuel Nesan/Kyle Essary: Jesus Is Yahweh? EP 263". *The Gospel Truth,* April 2, 2023, 02:48:21, https://www.youtube.com/watch?v=iSPU45IWErA.

Winter, Timothy. "The Trinity Is Incoherent." In *Debating Christian Theism,* edited by J. P. Moreland and Chad Meister. Oxford University Press, 2013.

Witherington, Ben. *The Living Word of God: Rethinking the Theology of the Bible.* Baylor University Press, 2007.

Worcester, Noah. *Bible News: Or, Sacred Truths Relating to the Living God, His Only Son, and Holy Spirit.* Boston, 1854. 5th ed. Reprint: Lulu.com, 2008 [1810].

Wright, Brian J. "Jesus as *Theos*: A Textual Examination." In *Revisiting the Corruption of the New Testament: Manuscript, Patristic, and Apocryphal Evidence*, edited by Daniel B. Wallace. Kregel Publications, 2011.

Wright, N. T. *The Challenge of Jesus: Rediscovering Who Jesus Was and Is.* InterVarsity Press, 1999.

———. *The Climax of the Covenant: Christ and the Law in Pauline Theology.* Fortress Press, 1993.

———. *How God Became King: The Forgotten Story of the Gospels.* HarperOne, 2016.

———. *Jesus and the Victory of God.* Fortress Press, 1996.

———, trans. *The Kingdom New Testament: A Contemporary Translation.* HarperOne, 2011.

Yandell, Keith. *Philosophy of Religion: A Contemporary Introduction.* Routledge, 1999.

Yates, James. *A Vindication of Unitarianism: In Reply to the Rev. Ralph Wardlaw.* 4th ed. London, 1850 [1815].

Zarley, Kermit. *The Restitution of Jesus Christ: Biblical Proof Jesus Is Not God.* 2023 [2008].

A

INDEX

B

D

E

F

G

H

I

J

M

P

T

U

V

W

Y

Z

www.ingramcontent.com/pod-product-compliance
Lightning Source LLC
LaVergne TN
LVHW010555100826
845148LV00014B/2723

9781737578321